NTOA 14

van der Horst · Essays on the Jewish World
of Early Christianity

NOVUM TESTAMENTUM ET ORBIS ANTIQUUS (NTOA)

Im Auftrag des Biblischen Instituts
der Universität Freiburg Schweiz
herausgegeben von Max Küchler
in Zusammenarbeit mit Gerd Theissen

Zum Autor:

Pieter Willem van der Horst, born in 1946, studied classical philology and theology at the University of Utrecht, where he received his doctor's degree in 1978. From 1971 onwards he has been a lecturer in New Testament literature and the cultural milieu of early Christianity at the Faculty of Theology in Utrecht.

His most important books are: The Sentences of Pseudo-Phocylides (1978), Aelius Aristides and the New Testament (1980), Chaeremon, Egyptian Priest and Stoic Philosopher (1984, 2nd ed. 1987), Joods-hellenistische poëzie (1987), De onbekende god: essays over de joodse en hellenistische achtergrond van het vroege christendom (1988), Studies on the Hellenistic Background of the New Testament (together with G. Mussies, 1990).

NOVUM TESTAMENTUM ET ORBIS ANTIQUUS   14

Pieter W. van der Horst

Essays on the Jewish World of Early Christianity

UNIVERSITÄTSVERLAG FREIBURG SCHWEIZ
VANDENHOECK & RUPRECHT GÖTTINGEN
1990

CIP-Titelaufnahme der Deutschen Bibliothek

Horst, Pieter W. van der:
Essays on the Jewish World of Early Christianity / Pieter W. van der Horst. – Freiburg
[Schweiz]: Univ.-Verl.; Göttingen: Vandenhoeck u. Ruprecht, 1990
  (Novum testamentum et orbis antiquus; 14)
  ISBN 3-7278-0683-4 (Univ.-Verl.)
  ISBN 3-525-53915-0 (Vandenhoeck u. Ruprecht)
NE: Horst, Pieter W. van der: [Sammlung]; GT

Veröffentlicht mit Unterstützung des Hochschulrates
der Universität Freiburg Schweiz

© 1990 by Universitätsverlag Freiburg Schweiz
Paulusdruckerei Freiburg Schweiz
ISBN 3-7278-0683-4 (Universitätsverlag)
ISBN 3-525-53915-0 (Vandenhoeck und Ruprecht)

For

Mechtild

TABLE OF CONTENTS

Erstveröffentlichungen

1. Pseudo-Phocylides and the New Testament: *ZNW* 69 (1978) 187-202.

2. Pseudo-Phocylides Revisited: *Journal for the Study of the Pseudepigrapha* 3 (1988) 3-30.

3. Moses' Throne Vision in Ezekiel the Dramatist: *Journal of Jewish Studies* 34 (1983) 21-29)

4. Some Notes on the *Exagoge* of Ezekiel: *Mnemosyne* 37 (1984) 354-375.

5. The Role of Women in the Testament of Job : *Nederlands Theologisch Tijdschrift* 40 (1986) 273-289.

7. The Measurement of the Body. A Chapter in the History of Ancient Jewish Mysticism: D. van der Plas (ed.), *Effigies Dei*, Leiden 1987, 56-68.

8. The Samaritan Diaspora in Antiquity: Revised version of an originally Dutch article in *Nederlands Theologisch Tijdschrift* 42 (1988) 134-144.

9. The Jews of Ancient Crete: *Journal of Jewish Studies* 39 (1988) 183-200.

10. Jews and Christians in Aphrodisias in the Light of Their Relations in Other Cities of Asia Minor: Revised version of an English original in *Nederlands Theologisch Tijdschrift* 43 (1989) 106-121.

11. "Lord, Help the Rabbi". The Interpretation of SEG XXXI 1578b: *Journal of Jewish Studies* 38 (1987) 102-106.

12. The Interpretation of the Bible by the Minor Hellenistic Jewish Authors: M. J. Mulder (ed.), *Mikra* [CRINT II 1], Assen-Philadelphia 1988, 519-546.

14. Seven Months' Children in Jewish and Christian Literature from Antiquity: *Ephemerides Theologicae Lovanienses* 54 (1978) 346-360.

INTRODUCTION

The present volume contains 14 essays written over the past dozen years. Their purpose is to shed some light on less well known aspects of Judaism in the Hellenistic and Roman periods (ca. 300 BCE to 500 CE)[1]. The title of the volume indicates that these studies have been written with an eye on the relevance their subjects might have for the study of early Christianity. In this short introductory chapter I will sketch the main areas in which I believe the topics discussed in this book have that relevance. These areas can be indicated by the following catchwords: ethics, women's studies, mysticism, diaspora, use of Scripture, anthropology.

The volume opens with two essays which together represent the oldest and the youngest in the volume. My dissertation, The Sentences of Pseudo-Phocylides (Leiden 1978), dealt with a long neglected Jewish writing from probably the first century CE. When writing a commentary on this Wisdom poem, I was struck by the many similarities between the ethical admonitions in this document on the one hand and the New Testament parenesis on the other. Half a century earlier the great Martin Dibelius had already tried to draw the attention of NT scholars to this document, convinced as he was of the relevance of this Jewish pseudepigraphon for the study of the NT. In the first article of this volume I have collected the material from this poem which shows most points of contact with the NT writings and which demonstrates that much of NT parenesis has its roots in the ethical teachings of first century Greek-speaking Judaism. Of course, taken by itself this can hardly be called a startling conclusion, but the surprises often lie in the details, in this case for example in the striking observation that Pseudo-Phocylides uses the traditional scheme of the Haustafel for an extensive exposition of his sexual ethics (largely based on Leviticus 18). Another instance is the verse (228) that served Klaus Berger as the chief witness for his theory of the existence of a Jewish-Hellenistic conception of the Torah which emphasizes the social commandments but neglects the cultic ones, and which Berger sees at the background of Mark 7:15.[2] Moreover, a discussion of two lines which reflect the originally pagan Hellenistic charis anti charitos principle (vv. 80 and 152) clarifies what may lie behind the critical remarks in Luke 6:32-35.

---

1 For a similar volume with 'pagan' essays see P. W. van der Horst and G. Mussies, *Studies on the Hellenistic Background of the New Testament*, Utrecht: Rijksuniversiteit, 1990.

2 *Die Gesetzesauslegung Jesu* I, Neukirchen 1972, 260 and 467.

Both my dissertation and the one by the distinguished editor of this series, Max Küchler[3], have done much to rehabilitate Ps-Phoc., as a result of which a resurgence of research on this poem has taken place during the last decade. In the second contribution in this volume, I discuss no less than twelve publications which deal with our author and date from the period 1978-1987. In these years a demonstrable progress has been made in the research on this writing. This is also the case with regard to its relevance for NT studies as has been demonstrated, for instance, by K. W. Niebuhr's fine dissertation on 'katechismusartige Weisungsreihen' in early Jewish literature[4] and by the continuing debate over the exact meaning of v. 228 in relation to Jesus's and Paul's attitudes to the Torah (especially in the publications by R. P. Booth and H. Räisänen). Further research on the poem has induced me to include in this contribution some retractationes, i.e. addenda et corrigenda to my commentary (ch. 2).

Another author which in my opinion has not yet been sufficiently exploited for his relevance to NT studies is the second century BCE dramatist Ezekiel. After having written a more general article on this fascinating author in Dutch[5], I tried to discover the meaning of the most curious scene in his play, the Exagoge, namely the dream-vision of Moses in which God leaves His own throne and actually places Moses upon it. Although my interpretation remains somewhat speculative, I assume this scene must have a connection with the later attested idea that an originally human being is exalted to divine status and becomes God's highest angel and plenipotentiary. Henoch-Metatron (in 3 Enoch = Sefer Hekhalot) is of course the most well-known example, but there is a gap of at least 5 or 6 centuries between the Exagoge and this mystical writing. Judaism must have known traditions - suppressed because heretical[6] - about these and other figures being transformed from a human being into God's deputy. Witness to this is inter alia the fact that in Matt. 28:18 the evangelist has Jesus say: "All authority in heaven and on earth has been given to me" (RSV), i.e. "God has committed His authority to me". There can be little doubt that Matthew here refers to traditions about Moses (and other OT figures) who were believed to have become God's vice-regent. In a short contribution (ch. 3) I try to find traces

---

3   *Frühjüdische Weisheitstraditionen*, Freiburg CH - Göttingen 1979.

4   *Gesetz und Paränese*, Tübingen 1987.

5   De joodse toneelschrijver Ezechiël, *Nederlands Theologisch Tijdschrift* 33 (1982) 97-112, now also in my *De onbekende god. Essays over de joodse en hellenistische achtergrond van het vroege christendom*, Utrecht 1988, 85-103.

6   The reason for this suppression was inter alia the threatening conception of 'two powers in heaven', on which see A. F. Segal, *Two Powers in Heaven*, Leiden 1977. It is telling that the figure of Metatron, which can be met on almost every page of the Hekhalot-literature, is mentioned only three times in Talmudic literature, two of which are negative. On "Ausschaltung der Henoch-Spekulationen" in rabbinic Judaism see H. Odeberg in *TWNT* 2 (1935) 555.

of such traditions in Jewish literature and to demonstrate that Ezekiel proves the antiquity of these ideas, which have turned out to be so fruitful for the development of early christology.

Shortly after the publication of that article the magnificent commentary on the Exagoge by Howard Jacobson was published.[7] He advocates an explanation of Moses' throne vision which is completely different from mine. The editor of Mnemosyne was so kind as to allow me to take up as much space as I wanted in writing a review article on Jacobson's work. In that article (ch. 4) I cross swords with Jacobson on this passage[8], and add some other observations on particular points of translation and interpretation of this, the only Jewish play from antiquity we still have. In the end I leave the reader in no doubt that Jacobson's work is an excellent example of what a combination of Classical and Judaic learning in one scholar can achieve, a combination, I might add, that unfortunately is only too rare in our field of study.

Part of the discussion between Jacobson and myself revolved around the question of whether or not the passage on Moses' dream-vision should be seen in the light of the Jewish mystical tradition. Mysticism and ecstatic phenomena in general continued to exert a great fascination on me ever since as an 18 year old boy I saw people entering into a trance and speaking in tongues in a meeting of the Pentecostal community in my home village. This longstanding interest was one of the reasons to turn to the Testament of Job, where these phenomena play such a significant role. In this first century CE Jewish writing ecstaticism and especially glossolalia play a prominent role especially in chapters 46-53, that is, in that part of the work which other researchers had already surmised - for different reasons than mine - must be derived from another source than the rest of the book. The sheer fact of the occurrence of glossolalia in this part of the book's story has led several scholars to assume that these chapters cannot but derive from Christian circles. I came to the conclusion, however, that nothing whatsoever justifies this assumption. On the contrary, it can be proved with relative certainty that this ecstatic form of religious experience has its roots in early Judaism and that in this respect, too, Christianity is in debt to its mother-religion (ch. 5).

The other striking fact in these final chapters of the Testament of Job is that it is only women, Job's three daughters, that have these enriching spiritual experiences.Indeed the author (or authoress?) cannot resist emphasizing that they are far superior to all men in the story from a spiritual point of view. The complete reversal of roles of men and women as compared to the previous chapters of the book is one of the most remarkable characteristics of

---

[7] H. Jacobson, *The Exagoge of Ezekiel*, Cambridge 1983

[8] The Dutch scholar D. T. Runia reacted upon this debate in his article 'God and Man in Philo of Alexandria', *Journal of Theological Studies* 39 (1988), esp. 49-53 (with useful critical observations).

this writing as a whole, and it can hardly be explained in another way than by assuming that the person who wrote these final chapters - whether he/she was a man or a woman we will never be able to determine - had a strong feminist 'Anliegen' and was convinced that women have the capacities required to play a leading role in Jewish religious communities. This is, to say the least, a rare point of view in ancient Judaism.[9] The synagogue inscriptions to which Bernadette Brooten had so aptly and rightly drawn our attention[10], prove that there must have been some communities, especially in the diaspora, where female leadership in the synagogue was accepted. But these were most probably exceptions, and no literary confirmation of this epigraphical evidence is adduced by Brooten. Testament of Job 46-53 may now confirm her findings, but it does not stand alone.

When we turn our attention to Pseudo-Philo's Liber Antiquitatum Biblicarum, which also dates from the first century CE, we again find women portrayed in a striking manner. In his rewriting the stories of Tamar, Debora, Jael, and Seila (LAB's name for Jephtha's daughter), the author of LAB makes conspicuous and remarkable changes in the Biblical stories to the effect that the roles of these women is consistently put on a par with those of the patriarchs or Moses. One cannot avoid the conclusion that here again a very specific 'Anliegen' plays a part which does not differ from that in the final chapters of the Testament of Job, even if the means by which this is brought to the fore are quite dissimilar (ch. 6). So in two contemporary but completely different Jewish writings from the NT period we find, to our surprise, strongly emancipatory tendencies which we can now no longer deny must have been present in first century Judaism alongside and in opposition to the current 'frauenfeindliche' atmosphere and sentiments. This opens unexpected vistas which demand further exploration.

Another relatively unknown aspect of early Judaism, which has already been touched upon, is its mystical side. In the merkavah speculations of Ezekiel the dramatist and in the ecstaticism of Job's daughters we see only the first ingredients of what was to become a powerful movement in the Judaism of Talmudic and post-Talmudic times. Gershom Scholem's classic study of 1941, Major Trends in Jewish Mysticism[11], has brought this aspect of Judaism to the attention of the scholarly community in an impressive way. But in the last 50 years, and especially in the last decade, the study of

---

[9] The best way to get a feeling of the 'frauenfeindliche' atmosphere in much of early Jewish literature is to read the first volume in this series (NTOA), Max Küchler's *Schweigen, Schmuck und Schleier* (1986).

[10] *Women Leaders in the Ancient Synagogue*, Chico 1982.

[11] New York 1941, third ed. 1954. See also his small but brilliant *Jewish Gnosticism, Merkabah Mysticism, and Talmudic Tradition*, New York 1960, 2nd ed. 1965.

ancient Jewish mysticism witnessed revolutionary developments.[12] In this area no contribution has been greater than that of the Berlin Judaic scholar Peter Schäfer, who in the eighties has published not only his tremendously important Synopse zur Hekhalot-Literatur, but also a concordance to that corpus, a translation of it, and a whole series of studies, which with impressive methodological strictness and clarity have opened our eyes for a range of problems that were played down or neglected by Scholem.[13] The most important element in this new approach is the fact that Schäfer denies that there is any possibility to constitute the original text of Hekhalot-treatises, because something like an 'Urtext' never existed. The divergence between the manuscripts is so great that one cannot speak of a text with variant readings which could be printed in a critical apparatus. We obviously have to do with fluctuating traditions which were never organized in antiquity into treatises with titles and definite contents. Hence we should no longer write about Hekhalot Rabbati and Hekhalot Zutarti etc. as if these ever existed as treatises. Hence in his Synopse, Schäfer has decided not to provide a critical edition of treatises but to print the text of 7 manuscripts in parallel columns[14.]

Another important point in which Schäfer entirely disagrees with Scholem (and for that matter with Gruenwald and Chernus)[15] is the antiquity of merkavah mysticism. Scholem and his followers posited that there existed a continuous mystical undercurrent in Judaism from the beginning of the Hellenistic era till the end of Antiquity. Crown-witnesses for this essential continuity were inter alia the throne vision described in 1 Enoch 14 and various other apocalypses[16], the fragments of the Songs of the Sabbath Sacrifice from Qumran (4Q Shirot 'olat ha-shabbath), and 2 Cor. 12:2-4. In the latter passage, Paul writes about his own experience of being caught up into Paradise and hearing unutterable things. Scholem regarded this passage as

---

12 For a survey of these develoments see my article "De studie van de joodse mystiek sinds Scholem: de 'major trends' na *Major Trends"*, *Nederlands Theologisch Tijdschrift* 44 (1990).

13 *Synopse zur Hekhalot-Literatur*, Tübingen 1981. *Genizah-Fragmente zur Hekhalot-Literatur*, Tübingen 1984. *Konkordanz zur Hekhalot-Literatur*, 2 vols,. Tübingen 1986-88. *Übersetzung der Hekhalot-Literatur,* 4 vols, Tübingen 1987- ... *Hekhalot-Studien*, Tübingen 1988.

14 For two important reactions to Schäfer's enterprise I refer to P. S. Alexander, *Journal of Jewish Studies* 34 (1983) 102-106, and D. J. Halperin, *Journal of the American Oriental Society* 104 (1984) 543-552.

15 See I. Gruenwald, *Apocalyptic and Merkavah Mysticism*, Leiden 1980; idem, *From Apocalypticism to Gnosticism*, Bern - Frankfurt 1988. I. Chernus, *Mysticism in Rabbinic Judaism,* Berlin 1982.

16 "The apocalypses occupy a special place in Scholem's view because they represent the earliest stage of *merkavah* mysticism and are thus the ancestors of the *hekhalot* literature", thus M. Himmelfarb, Heavenly Ascent and the Relationship of the Apocalypses and the Hekhalot Literature, *Hebrew Union College Annual* 59 (1988) 75 (73-100).

the closest parallel to the rabbinic stories of the four who entered pardes, which he took to be a description of a mystical heavenly ascent. But Schäfer, and in his wake Halperin[17], propose a very different interpretation of these and related passages, to the effect that this continuum of mysticism has never existed, but that the relevant Jewish material should be explained as exegetical midrash or speculation about Ezekiel's vision in Ez. 1 (the so-called ma'aseh merkavah) and that only in a late stage, i.e. in the 4th - 6th century CE or even in post-Talmudic times, mystical practice can be assumed to have existed with certainty. Halperin explains the opposition of the rabbis to ma'aseh merkavah in the light of exegetical traditions about the appearance of the merkavah at Sinai which had the disastrous consequence that Israel began to worship one of the four chayyot of the merkavah (Ez. 1:5 ff.), namely the calf (Ex. 32), so that it was actually God's own theophany which led his people to apostasy. The much later Hekhalot-literature, says Halperin, is a curious offshoot of this ma'aseh merkavah in that it reflects the striving of 'amme ha'aretz to procure a complete knowledge of Torah by magical means without any effort to attain the same status and power in society as the rabbis had. So in spite of the rabbinic aim (knowledge of Torah) that is set as the goal, this literature is essentially inimical to the rabbis. The validity of these and other new theories about early Jewish mysticism[18] has still to be tested, but it is more than clear that a simple repetition of Scholem's position definitely belongs to the past (although it should not be denied that many 'ingredients' of later Hekhalot traditions appear already in much older sources).

This is also apparent from recent studies on one of the most bizarre segments of Hekhalot-literature, the so-called Shi'ur Qomah, literally 'the measurement of the body'. In Shi'ur Qomah texts the visionary describes God's body as seated upon the merkavah, and he gives details of all God's limbs, that is, especially their secret names and their astronomical measures. Martin Cohen's edition of and studies on these traditions[19] have made clear that we probably have to do here with magical-theurgical traditions from the end of the Talmudic or the early Gaonic period. To give a first impression of what Shi'ur Qomah is all about, I have translated and briefly annotated one of the shorter manuscripts edited by Cohen (ch. 7). One correction to what I have written in that article is necessary. The manuscript translated by me is presented by Cohen as probably the oldest we have (10th cent.) and I have followed him without checking that dating. Last year, however, Schäfer published an important article in which he criticized Cohen's dating of the manuscript concerned: on closer inspection it turns out to date from the

---

17 *The Merkabah in Rabbinic Literature*, New Haven 1980, and esp. *The Faces of the Chariot. Early Jewish Responses to Ezekiel's Vision*, Tübingen 1988.

18 See e.g. also J. Dan, *Three Types of Ancient Jewish Mysticism*, Cincinnati 1984.

19 *The Shi'ur Qomah: Liturgy and Theurgy in Pre-Kabbalistic Jewish Mysticism*, Lanham-London 1983. *The Shi'ur Qomah: Texts and Recensions*, Tübingen 1985.

18th (!) century, not the 10th[20]. So the reader should know that what my article offers is in fact a translation of one of the youngest crystallizations of Shi'ur Qomah traditions we have. This, I presume, will not detract from its value as a first introduction to this kind of material, for the text is typical enough of its genre.

Quite another area on which I hope four of the essays in this volume will shed some new light is that of the Jewish diaspora. To begin with its least well-known aspect, the existence of a large Samaritan diaspora is becoming more and more evident as recent excavations bring to light at a regular pace inscriptions of Samaritan communities all over the ancient world. This in turn has led to a renewed search for literary evidence for a Samaritan diaspora, yielding a considerable body of material, of which I have presented the most relevant items. Since the Samaritans should be regarded as a Jewish religious community from a religio-historical point of view, and since the revival of Samaritan studies in recent years[21] has rightly drawn our attention again to the important role this community has played throughout antiquity, it seemed reasonable to include a short study on the Samaritan diaspora in the ancient world (ch. 8). The documents and monuments discussed reveal an amazingly widespread and vital Samaritan diaspora which must have been of considerable size, although its exact numbers must remain a matter of guesswork.

Guesses at the numbers of Jews living in the diaspora in the ancient world vary widely. Salo Baron estimates the total Jewish population around the turn of the era to have been some 8.000.000, of which some 3.000.000 lived in Palestine and some 5.000.000 in the diaspora.[22] These numbers may be on the high side, but there can be little doubt that a majority of at least several million Jews lived outside Palestine. As is well-known, that fact has been of tremendous importance for the history and expansion of early Christianity. Therefore it is of great value to get as precise a picture as possible of the position of these Jews in their respective societies or countries. For many countries or cities such investigations have already been carried out. Not as yet, however, for the important island of Crete; while for Asia Minor the existing surveys, have by now become more or less outdated by a spectacular recent find in one of the major cultural centres of Western Asia Minor, Aphrodisias. The report on the data concerning Crete (ch. 9) is by no means sensational, but it does show us a steadily growing community which held aloof from anything that might damage their position in the Cretan cities, as far as we can judge from the scanty testimonies of course. But even

---

20   *Shi'ur Qoma*: Rezensionen und Urtext, in his *Hekhalot-Studien* 75-83.

21   By way of example I point only to the important recent multi-author volume *The Samaritans*, ed. A. D. Crown, Tübingen 1989, and to the fact that recently an international *Society of Samaritan Studies* has been founded.

22   S. W. Baron, *A Social and Religious History of the Jews* I, Philadelphia - New York 1952², 170 (with the extensive discussion of other estimates in note 7).

this quiet community came in the grip of a messianic fever in the first half of the fifth century CE, probably due to the growing pressure of the Christian Emperors which led to such a dramatical deterioration of their living conditions.[23] The results of this messianic revolt were probably disastrous, although the legendary nature of the source hides the details from our view.

The new evidence from Aphrodisias sheds an unexpected light on the phenomenon of the Godfearers, exactly at the moment that they were declared never to have existed but to have been a figment of Luke's theological imagination.[24] The surprisingly high numbers of Godfearers in an inscription recording the names of Jews and non-Jews who had given donations in order to found a Jewish soup-kitchen for the local poor, requires us to rethink the whole matter of Jewish influence in the diaspora.[25] The question I want to ask in my essay (ch. 10) is whether there might be any relation between the very strong position Judaism had built up in co-operation with the gentiles in Aphrodisias and other cities in ancient Caria on the one hand and the very late breakthrough of Christianity in that area on the other. Tentative though the answer may be, in the light of the situation in other cities in Western Asia Minor, it is difficult to avoid the conclusion that Judaism was an enormously strong and influential force in that area and that till far in the post-Constantinian era Christianity had to engage in a heavy competition with Judaism in order to win the gentile soul.

The Aphrodisias inscription was published in an exemplary way by competent scholars who had their eyes open for all possibilities of interpretation and possible pitfalls. When, however, new Jewish inscriptions are discovered by archaeologists that have little or no acquaintance with ancient Judaism, things may go wrong. A small but not insignificant example thereof can be found in the contribution on the inscription from ancient Libya (ch. 11) published by an Italian archaeologist as a Christian inscription in spite of the occurrence of the word rabbi (in Greek) in it. According to this scholar, the rabbi was the bishop of the local Christian community. To make things worse, this conclusion was even adopted by the editors of the authoritative Supplementum Epigraphicum Graecum. After having corrected this obvious misinterpretation of the inscription, I found to my surprise that this very small graffito of only four words appeared to shed light on the question of whether or not any continuity in the Jewish presence in ancient Cyrenaica after the disastrous revolt of 115-117 could be assumed (no. 11). The text of the inscription, "Lord, help the rabbi!", evokes gloomy thoughts about the situation of this diaspora community in a predominantly Christian town of the middle of the fourth century CE.

---

[23] See now for the imperial legislation on Jews in the post-Constantinian era A. Linder, *The Jews in Roman Imperial Legislation*, Detroit - Jerusalem 1987.

[24] See A. T. Kraabel, The Disappearance of the God-fearers, *Numen* 28 (1981) 113 ff.

[25] The inscription was published by J. Reynold and R. Tannenbaum, *Jews and Godfearers at Aphrodisias*, Cambridge 1987.

The final three contributions deal with aspects of the use of Scripture in ancient Jewish literature, varying from the earliest Hellenistic Jewish historians in the third century BCE to late rabbinic writings from the early
Middle Ages. The essay on the minor Jewish Hellenistic authors focuses on
the fragments from these pioneers in the confrontation of Judaism and Hellenism that have been handed down in the excerpts made by Eusebius of
Caesarea from the voluminous output of the first century BCE pagan histo-
riographer Alexander Polyhistor. The authors dealt with are a very mixed
bag, and what they display is a fascinating variety of ways in which they
appropriated the biblical traditions and tried to reshape them in Greek literary modes. The variety of religious outlooks is as great as that of literary
forms and can hardly be reduced to a common denominator. In spite of that,
they do have in common an emphatic concern to strengthen Jewish self-
consciuousness, for instance by repeated assertions that all cultural achievements in history ultimately derive from the Torah. Conspicuously
enough, we nowhere find in these fragments any emphasis on the Torah as a
book of commandments. The focus is completely on the non-halakhic parts
of the Bible: the Torah is regarded as a book about great inventors, cultural
benefactors, kings, etc. Here we are in a world quite different from that of
rabbinic literature. What these Greek writings do have in common with later
rabbinic texts, however, is haggadic techniques, albeit in a more rudimentary form. It is very instructive to see the free and creative ways in which
these Jewish pioneers rewrote their Bible in an attempt to respond to the
changed political, social, and religious situation of their times (ch. 12).

The haggadic procedures of both early and later Jewish writers are exemplified by two studies on individual themes. The enigmatic figure of Nimrod
has appealed to the imagination of the readers since early times. The first
traces of Nimrod haggada date from the second century BCE and the haggadic potential of the few biblical lines about this hunter is brought to full
fruition in the first five or six centuries CE. The growth of the Nimrod traditions sheds light on the ways the Bible was read and used by Jewish interpreters in the early Christian period (ch. 13). Although Nimrod does not occur in the NT, the way in which the haggada about this figure grew helps to
clarify the 'techniques' behind several Jewish haggadic elements in the
NT.[26]

The final example of haggada dealt with in this volume is especially interesting in that it shows how elements from Greek lore and science were adduced by Jews to clarify problems of Scriptural interpretation. In this case
that procedure resulted in Isaac, Moses, and Samuel being declared to have
been seven months' children. This haggadic model of explanation continued
to make itself felt in early Christianity, for from the second century onwards

---

[26] For examples see e.g. M. McNamara, *The New Testament and the Palestinian Targum
to the Pentateuch*, Rome 1978 (2nd ed.), and R. Le Déaut, *The Message of the New Testament and the Aramaic Bible (Targum)*, Rome 1982

Mary and Jesus too are regarded as belonging to this category (ch. 14). As early as 1937 R. Meyer had published a study on Hellenistisches in der rabbinischen Anthropologie. In the past half century a good deal of research on the hellenization of early Judaism has been done (Lieberman, Bickerman, Hengel, Fischel, etc.), but much more still remains to be done, also in the area of anthropology, of which embryology is only a part. For instance, not only hellenistic theories on seven months' pregnancies but also Greek ideas on the female contribution to the origin of the embryo (the theory of the 'female semen') have contributed to a very own variety of rabbinic embryology.[27] That traces of these and similar theories are found in sources of the first century CE is one of the gauges for the hellenization of Judaism in the NT period. But what we have here is still largely unexplored territory.

The author hopes that these essays will contribute to a better understanding of ancient Judaism. To be true, they do not focus on 'mainstream Judaism', but that is done on purpose. It is especially in the often somewhat neglected corners of this field that one may find treasures. The small tesserae that make up this volume are intended to contribute to the great mosaic of ancient Judaism being put together by modern scholars. If in the process we are able to draw attention to the remarkable variety of colour and shape that characterized the matrix from which Christianity developed, then our aims will have been amply fulfilled.

I owe thanks to the following publishers and institutions for granting me permission to reprint some of my articles: W. de Gruyter (Berlin) for no. 1; Sheffield Academic Press for no. 2; Oxford University Press and The Oxford Centre for Postgraduate Hebrew Studies for nos. 3, 9, and 11; E. J. Brill (Leiden) for nos. 4 and 7; Boekencentrum (Den Haag) for no. 5; the foundation Compendia Rerum Iudaicarum ad Novum Testamentum (Amsterdam) for no. 12; Peeters (Louvain) for no. 14. The other articles either have not been previously published or have been translated from earlier Dutch versions.

I also wish to express my gratitude to the editors of the series NTOA, Max Küchler and Gerd Theissen, for accepting this collection of essays for publication.

Utrecht, December 1989   P. W. van der Horst

---

[27] See my "Sarah's Seminal Emission. Hebrews 11:11 in the Light of Ancient Embryology", in: *Greeks, Romans, and Christians*, Minneapolis 1990 (forthcoming).

1. PSEUDO-PHOCYLIDES AND THE NEW TESTAMENT

Dedicated to the Memory of W. C. van Unnik

It was Martin Dibelius who drew the attention of N.T. scholars to the relevance of Ps-Phoc. for the study of N.T. parenesis. In several of his writings he demonstrates that much of the parenetic material in early Christian writings, esp. the "Tugend- und Lasterkataloge", the socalled "Haustafeln" and the "Two Ways", are not Christian creations, but only christianizations of either Jewish materials or of pagan materials that reached the Christian authors either directly or by way of Hellenistic Judaism. In this connection he often mentions Ps-Phoc. as a striking example of a Jewish parenetic writing that had taken over all kinds of pagan Greek ethical materials and woven them into what is actually a very Jewish ethical poem. In his commentaries on N.T. books Dibelius often quotes lines from Ps-Phoc. as parallels to N.T. passages in order to show that this author presents the kind of parenetic material that several authors of the N.T. drew upon for their own writings.[1] Although Dibelius wrote these things in the first quarter of this century, in the fifty years since then not much attention has been paid to Ps-Phoc. by N.T. scholars. An exception is James Crouch who, in his dissertation on the Colossian *Haustafel*[2] extensively discusses the relevance of this poem to the subject of his study. But in general one can say that Ps-Phoc. is a rather neglected author in our field. There are two commentaries on his poem, both written by classical scholars, one in 1910 by M. Rossbroich[3], a pupil of W. Kroll, the other in 1962 by A. Farina[4]. The latter is of little value, for the author has very far-fetched theories about the origin of the poem and, as he has no knowledge of Jewish literature, his commentary

---

* Paper read at the 32nd meeting of the SNTS in Tübingen, August 1977.

[1] See M. Dibelius, Geschichte der urchristlichen Literatur, Berlin 1926 (repr. München 1975), 141; Die Formgeschichte des Evangeliums, Tübingen ²1933 (= ⁶1971), 239; Der Brief des Jakobus, KEK XV, hrsg. von H. Greeven, Göttingen 1964, 17 f.; An die Kolosser, Epheser, Philemon, HNT 12, hrsg. von H. Greeven, Tübingen 1953, 49; Die Pastoralbriefe, HNT 13, hrsg. von H. Conzelmann, Tübingen ⁴1966. For instances of quotations from Ps-Phoc. see e.g. his commentary on 2 Thess 3₆ 1 Tim 6₁₀ Jak 3₆.

[2] J. E. Crouch, The Origin and Intention of the Colossian Haustafel, Göttingen 1972.

[3] M. Rossbroich, De Pseudo-Phocylideis, Münster 1910.

[4] A. Farina, Silloge Pseudofocilidea, Naples 1962.

is extremely one-sided. Rossbroich's book is better, but he, too, seriously underestimates the Jewishness of the poem, being in this respect a real pupil of Wilhelm Kroll who (in 1941) published the Pauly-Wissowa article on Ps-Phoc. in the *RE*[5], an article about which M. Hengel rightly remarked: "Kroll unterschätzt den überwiegend jüdischen Gesamt-charakter der Schrift"[6]. A new commentary is needed and I hope that the one I have tried to write will to a certain extent meet this need[7].

In this paper I can do no more than make some general remarks about the character of the poem[8] and single out for discussion some verses which are more or less of interest to N.T. studies. As to the origin of the poem, since Jacob Bernays' study of 1856[9], most scholars assume — rightly, in my view — that Ps-Phoc. was a Hellenistic Jewish author[10]. He most probably wrote his poem during the reign of Augustus or Tiberius, possibly in Alexandria (though other places of origin cannot be excluded).

He assumed the pseudonym Phocylides, after an Ionian poet who wrote short wisdom-maxims in verse, who lived in the middle of the sixth century B.C. in Miletus and whose poetry was regarded in antiquity as a source of wise and useful advice for daily life[11]. Phocylides was held in high esteem throughout antiquity.

The most perplexing problem that the poem puts before us is the question of the author's purpose. But before discussing that we must first glance at the content of the poem.

The most conspicuous feature appears to be that, though the author renders much O.T. ethical material, he consistently avoids all the really

---

[5] PW(RE) XX,1, 1941, 505–510.

[6] M. Hengel, "Anonymität, Pseudepigraphie und 'literarische Fälschung' in der jüdisch-hellenistischen Literatur", in: Pseudepigrapha I (Entretiens sur l'antiquité classique XVIII), Vandœuvres-Geneva 1972, 296, n. 3.

[7] P. W. van der Horst, The Sentences of Pseudo-Phocylides, Leiden 1978.

[8] For details the reader must be referred to the Introduction of my Commentary.

[9] Über das phokylideische Gedicht, Berlin 1856 (reprinted in his Gesammelte Abhand-lungen I, Berlin 1885, 192–261).

[10] Scholars who, after Bernays, assumed a non-Jewish origin include: A. von Harnack (ThLZ 10, 1885, 159 ff.), who asserted that the author was a Christian; M. Rossbroich (De Pseudo-Phocylideis, Münster 1910), who sees the author as a "Godfearer"; K. F. A. Lincke (Samaria und seine Propheten, Tübingen-Leipzig 1903), A. Ludwich (Programm Königsberg 1904) and F. Dornseiff (Echtheitsfragen antik-griechischer Literatur, Berlin 1939) assume a pagan origin. W. Kroll (PW XX,1, 1941, 505–510) is hesitant; see also his remark in his review of Ludwich's Programm in: Berliner Philologische Wochen-schrift 25, 1905, 243: "einen hellenisierten Juden von einem judaisierenden Hellenen zu scheiden, ist in solchen Fällen kaum möglich."

[11] See the collection of ancient texts testifying Phocylides' fame in the Introduction to my Commentary.

characteristically Israelite commandments; thus there is not a word about the Sabbath, circumcision, idolatry and the host of cultic purity rules of the O.T. What remains is a set of rules that *are* Israelite but nevertheless of such a nature that they could be expected to find a sympathetic hearing with non-Jews, too. And all this is mixed up with maxims of pagan Greek wisdom poetry. Hence in the case of the majority of the verses parallels both of the O.T. or Jewish literature and of Greek (or Latin) literature can be adduced. It looks as if the author did his utmost to conceal the Jewish origin of many of his rules of conduct[12]. The name Israel does not pass his lips, as with the O.T. Wisdom teachers, and he omits anything specifically Jewish. What could he mean by this? What or whom did he aim at? Since one cannot assume that the author wrote this poem for sheer pleasure, as an exercise in versification, one must consider what kind of public he had in view. Most often it has been asserted that the author wrote for a pagan public. This thesis[13] runs as follows: in antiquity there was a widespread, universalistic, Jewish propaganda movement that was not intent on making proselytes but only on inculcating in pagans a number of universally valid ethical precepts. One simply tried to humanize pagan society. But unambiguous evidence of this widespread movement has never been brought to the fore, and parallel passages to which one refers (Noachian commandments, and two sections in Philo's *Hypothetica* and Josephus *Contra Apionem*)[14] appear in recognizably Jewish contexts, whereas Ps-Phoc. is not recognizably Jewish or at least not meant to be. This theory has more weaknesses upon which I cannot expatiate now.

Another theory is that Ps-Phoc. wrote for his fellow Jews. The defenders of this thesis believe that all Jewish-Hellenistic literature was meant not for the Gentiles but for the Jews, either to satisfy the literary

---

[12] He succeeded so well in doing this that throughout antiquity and the Middle Ages the authenticity of his poem was taken for granted, in spite of the many Biblical allusions. It was only the great J. Scaliger who discovered the falsification; see his Animadversiones in Chronologica Eusebii, printed in his Thesaurus Temporum, Leiden 1606, 88–89. The great popularity of Ps-Phoc. as a schoolbook in the Byzantine period and also in the sixteenth century was due to the fact that people rejoiced that the "natural reason" of a pagan author could agree to such a great extent with the Bible; see Bernays, op. cit., 193.

[13] Originated by the Stockholm rabbi G. Klein, Der älteste christliche Katechismus und die jüdische Propagandaliteratur, Berlin 1909, and modified and developed by M. Guttmann, Das Judentum und seine Umwelt, Berlin 1927, and J. E. Crouch, op. cit. (see above).

[14] Philo, Hyp. in Eusebius, Praep. Ev. VIII 7; Josephus, C. Ap. II 188–219. P. Wendland ("Die Therapeuten und die philonische Schrift vom beschaulichen Leben", Jahrb. für class. Philol., Suppl. 22, 1896, 709–712) was the first to point out the striking similarities between these two passages and Ps-Phoc.

needs of the Greek-speaking Jews or to hold out to hellenized Jews a more or less current presentation of the ethical principles of the Torah in order to check further decline into a non-Jewish way of life[15]. But this theory has met with serious criticisms[16] and it must be admitted that it cannot be strictly proved. However, it cannot be disproved either.

A third possibility is to assume that the poem was written by a "God-fearer", a heathen that moved on the fringe of the Jewish community[17]. He is then supposed to direct himself to pagans. That would explain well both the Jewish and the Greek elements in the poem. But we do not have any other evidence for the existence of literature from this category of people on the borderline between paganism and Judaism[18].

So, whatever theory one proposes about the author's purpose, serious objections can always be raised against it and no theory can be proved, so elusive is the nature of our poem. Much more should be said about these problems but for the moment these brief remarks may suffice to indicate what kind of questions are put before us by this poem, which, after all, undoubtedly is a writing of a Jew who is well-versed in Greek literature.

After these preliminary remarks let us turn to the text itself. Only a few lines can be briefly dealt with here. To begin with the Prologue: vv. 1–2 are the "sphragis"[19] of the poem: ταῦτα δίκησ᾿ ὁσίησι θεοῦ βουλεύματα φαίνει | Φωκυλίδης ἀνδρῶν ὁ σοφώτατος ὄλβια δῶρα, "These counsels of God by his holy judgements Phocylides the wisest of men sets forth, gifts of blessing." Although the authenticity of these lines (that is, whether they belong to the original poem) is disputed, I believe they are part of the original poem. The text is somewhat obscure (e. g.

---

[15] V. Tcherikover, "Jewish Apologetic Literature Reconsidered", in: Symbolae Raphaeli Taubenschlag dedicatae III, Wratislawa 1957, 169–193, esp. 178f. M. Hengel, Judentum und Hellenismus, Tübingen ²1973, 129f.; also in Pseudepigrapha I,306f. N. Walter will defend this stance (which he had already adopted in some of his earlier writings) in respect of Ps-Phoc. in his forthcoming German translation of Ps-Phoc. (in the series Jüdische Schriften aus hellenistisch-römischer Zeit). Such a view was also taken by G. Alon, "The Halakah in the Teaching of the Twelve Apostles", in his Studies in Jewish History in the Times of the Second Temple, the Mishnah and the Talmud I (in Hebrew), Hakibbutz Hame'uchad ²1967, 274ff.

[16] See for example W. Speyer, Die literarische Fälschung im heidnischen und christlichen Altertum, München 1971, 158ff.

[17] This stance was taken by M. Rossbroich, op. cit., 16–23.

[18] Although J. P. Audet ("La sagesse de Ménandre l'Égyptien", RB 59, 1952, 55–81) maintains that the Syriac sentences of Menander are the work of a Godfearer.

[19] On this see W. Kranz, "Sphragis. Ichform und Namensiegel als Eingangs- und Schluß-motiv antiker Dichtung", RheinMus 104, 1961, 3–46 and 97–124 (repr. in his Kleine Schriften, 1967, 27–78).

the function of the dative δίκησ' ὁσίῃσι is unclear), but the important point is that the author claims great authority for the rules of conduct he is going to give by means of the words θεοῦ βουλεύματα: his poem consists of "counsels of God"! Note also the word σοφώτατος, which is a traditional epithet of Solomon.

In vv. 3−8 follows a kind of summary of the Decalogue. A significant feature here is that the author puts the prohibition of adultery (v. 3) before that of murder (v. 4), in contrast to the order of the Masoretic text. That had already been done in the Septuagint and this sequence of these commandments is also found in the New Tetament, e.g. Luke 18 20 Romans 13 9, James 2 11.[20] Note also that nearly all the vices enumerated in vv. 3−6 recur in the catalogue of Mark 7 21−22: ... πορνεῖαι, κλοπαί, φόνοι, μοιχεῖαι, πλεονεξίαι, πονηρίαι, δόλος, ἀσέλγεια.

In vv. 9−41 follows a very remarkable section, since in these lines a great part of the commandments of Leviticus 19 is rendered in a more or less hidden way.[21] Leviticus 19 was probably considered by the Jews in antiquity as a kind of summary of the Torah, although the texts which testify this are of a later date.[22] I single out for discussion vv. 32−34, 3 lines that accidentally do not have parallels in Lev. 19: τὸ ξίφος ἀμφιβαλοῦ μὴ πρὸς φόνον, ἀλλ' ἐς ἄμυναν. εἴθε δὲ μὴ χρήζοις μήτ' ἔκνομα μήτε δικαίως. ἢν γὰρ ἀποκτείνῃς ἐχθρόν, σέο χεῖρα μιαίνεις. "If you gird on a sword, let it be not to murder but to protect. But may you not need it at all, neither without the law nor justly. For if you kill an enemy, you stain your hand." The exceptional quality of these lines is the pacifistic ring about them. The author says: even justified self-defence stains your hands when somebody is killed as a result. The rule not to stain your hands with blood in v. 4 (μήθ' αἵματι χεῖρα μιαίνειν) is very strictly applied here.

In vv. 42−47 we find the very common theme of the disastrous consequences of love of money, and v. 42 (ἡ φιλοχρημοσύνη μήτηρ κακότητος ἁπάσης) is closely paralleled by 1 Tim 6 10 ῥίζα γὰρ πάντων τῶν κακῶν ἡ φιλαργυρία, a text which has numerous parallels in Greek literature.[23] The short catalogue of calamities in vv. 46−47 ("For your sake [i.e. for money] there are battles and plunderings and

---

20 On this problem of sequence see B. Reicke, Die Zehn Worte in Geschichte und Gegenwart, Tübingen 1973, 21 ff.

21 The first to note this was J. Bernays, op. cit., 228−233.

22 See Sifra Qedoshim, Parasha I (on 19 1); Lev. Rabbah XXIV 5; cf. W. Bacher, Die Agada der palästinischen Amoräer II, Strasbourg 1896, 369.

23 See C. Spicq, Les épitres pastorales, Paris ⁴1969, 564 and R. Renehan, "Classical Greek Quotations in the New Testament", in: The Heritage of the Early Church (Festschrift for G. V. Florovsky), Rome 1973, 18f.

murders, and children become the enemies of their parents and brothers the enemies of their kinsmen") is traditional. It is found in many texts in Greek and Latin literature in connection with φιλαργυρία. The last part of it (on the enmity between kinsmen) also occurs outside this context to indicate the utter depravity of the human race in a late stage of history[24], in the N.T. for example in Mark 13 12 parr. in an eschatological context.

Vv. 48–69 treat the virtues honesty, modesty, self-control and moderation. We skip over them, mentioning only the εἷς θεός formula in v. 54 and the fact that vv. 63–67 clearly betray Stoic influence: the distinction between different kinds of anger[25], of zeal and of love are demonstrably Stoic. In vv. 70–75 the author warns against envy (φθόνος) and mentions the ἀφθονία of the heavenly bodies as an example worth imitating. The fact that he calls the heavenly bodies οὐρανίδαι (71) and μάκαρες (75) has led several scholars[26] to the conviction that the author cannot have been a Jew, for οὐρανίδαι and μάκαρες nearly always are terms for the gods, whereas Judaism has always denied the divinity of the stars. However, the terms need imply nothing more than the ascription of personality to the heavenly bodies, which is common in Judaism. And in view of the fact that Philo (Opif. 27) calls heaven θεῶν ... αἰσθητῶν ... οἶκος (the house of the visible gods) this seemingly pagan terminology in Ps-Phoc. should not lead us astray. The same applies to v. 163 where μάκαρες is again used for the sun and moon.

We move to v. 80, which is of importance for N.T. ethics. It runs: νικᾶν εὖ ἔρδοντας ἐπὶ πλεόνεσσι καθήκει, "it is proper to surpass your benefactors with still more benefactions." This verse should be read together with v. 152: μὴ κακὸν εὖ ἔρξῃς· σπείρειν ἴσον ἔστ᾽ ἐνὶ πόντῳ, "do no good to a bad man, it is like sowing in the sea." Behind both lines is the so-called χάρις ἀντὶ χάριτος principle, the utilitarian principle of reciprocity that was, in Bolkestein's words, "eine der Grundlagen des sozialen Verkehrs der Griechen"[27] (one of the fundamentals of social intercourse of the Greeks). It meant that one could not accept a benefaction, not even from a friend, without repaying it

---

[24] See e.g. W. Kroll on Catullus LXIV 397ff. (Catull, Stuttgart ³1959, 194f.).

[25] This theory of *irarum differentiae* (on which see M. Giusta, I dossografi di etica II, Turin 1967, 257ff.) is also reflected in Hermas, Mand. V 2,4.

[26] E. g. Ludwich and Dornseiff (see above p. 188, n. 10).

[27] H. Bolkestein, Wohltätigkeit und Armenpflege im vorchristlichen Altertum, Utrecht 1939, 158. See on this matter also S. C. Mott, "The Power of Giving and Receiving: Reciprocity in Hellenistic Benevolence", in: Current Issues in Biblical and Patristic Interpretation (Festschrift for M. C. Tenney), Grand Rapids 1975, 60–72.

or even, if possible, surpassing it[28] (note the verb νικᾶν in v. 80 and in many other texts on this theme). Sometimes this principle is even called one of the "unwritten laws" (ἄγραφοι νόμοι)[29]. Its consequences are well illustrated by v. 152 where it is said that it is of no use (!) to do good to a bad man (for σπείρειν ἐνὶ πόντῳ is equivalent to vain effort and useless activity[30]); because from a bad man one cannot expect a gift in return, and one must only benefit someone if one can reasonably expect to benefit by it oneself. This originally pagan Greek principle had penetrated into early Judaism. This is proved not only by this text (which would be begging the question), but by some texts in Sirach, in Josephus and in the N.T. Sirach 12 1-7 runs: "If you do a good deed, know for whom you are doing it, then you will have credit for your kindness. Do good to a devout man, and you will receive a reward, if not from him, then from the Most High. No good will come to a man who persists in evil, or who refuses to give alms. Do good to a humble man, give nothing to a godless one. Refuse him bread, do not give him any, it might make him stronger than you are; then you would be repaid evil twice over for all the good you had done him . . . . Give to the good man, but never help a sinner." In Josephus the same motive is found again[31]: *Antiquities* V 30, VIII 111, XIX 184 ("It is a most noble deed, and such as becomes free men, to requite a benefactor"). In all these passages, the catchwords χάρις, ἀγαθοποιεῖν or εὖ ποιεῖν, ἀποδοῦναι or ἀνταπόδομα and ἀμοιβή occur. This leads us to a passage in the N.T., Luke 6 32-35: ἐὰν ἀγαθοποιῆτε τοὺς ἀγαθοποιοῦντας ὑμᾶς, ποία ὑμῖν χάρις ἐστίν; καὶ οἱ ἁμαρτωλοὶ τὸ αὐτὸ ποιοῦσιν. καὶ ἐὰν δανείσητε παρ' ὧν ἐλπίζετε λαβεῖν, ποία ὑμῖν χάρις ἐστίν; καὶ ἁμαρτωλοὶ ἁμαρτωλοῖς δανείζουσιν ἵνα ἀπολάβωσιν τὰ ἴσα. πλὴν ἀγαπᾶτε τοὺς ἐχθροὺς ὑμῶν καὶ ἀγαθοποιεῖτε καὶ δανείζετε μηδὲν ἀπελπίζοντες· καὶ ἔσται ὁ μισθὸς ὑμῶν πολύς, καὶ ἔσεσθε υἱοὶ ὑψίστου, ὅτι αὐτὸς χρηστός ἐστιν ἐπὶ τοὺς ἀχαρίστους καὶ πονηρούς. As W. C. van Unnik remarked, these words had "für die Griechen einen direkten Anschluß an eine weitverbreitete ethische Lehre"[32], and he thinks that

---

[28] Cf. L. Schmidt, Die Ethik der alten Griechen II, Berlin 1882, 370 who calls it "jene krankhafte Sucht der Griechen . . . selbst von den Freunden keine Wohltaten anzunehmen, ohne sie zu erwidern und womöglich zu überbieten."

[29] Ps-Aristotle, Rhet. ad Alex. I,1421 b 37 ff.; cf. Xenophon, Memorabilia IV 4,24.

[30] See Epigrammata Graeca 1038,8 f. (ed. G. Kaibel, Berlin 1878):
εἰς πέλαγος σπέρμα βαλεῖν καὶ γράμματα γράψαι,
ἀμφότερος μόχθος τε κενὸς καὶ πρᾶξις ἄδηλος.

[31] See W. C. van Unnik, "Eine merkwürdige liturgische Aussage bei Josephus", in: Josephus-Studien O. Michel zum 70. Geburtstag gewidmet, Göttingen 1974, 364 f.

[32] "Die Motivierung der Feindesliebe in Lukas 6 32-35", in his Sparsa Collecta I, Leiden 1973, 122 (see the whole article, 111-126).

Luke (or Jesus) here sharply criticizes this part of Greek, and also Jewish-Hellenistic ethics. The two unambiguous lines of Ps-Phoc. help us to see this matter more clearly.

As to vv. 84–85 (μηδέ τις ὄρνιθας καλιῆς ἅμα πάντας ἑλέσθω, μητέρα δ᾽ ἐκπρολίποις, ἵν᾽ ἔχῃς πάλι τῆσδε νεοσσούς), it should be remarked that these lines do not have any parallels in Greek literature[33], and they are patently a rendering of Dtn 22 6–7. Philo and Josephus, too, have it in their summaries of Jewish laws.[34] "That all three authors, drawing material directly from the O.T. and working independently of one another, would include this relatively insignificant commandment in a selective survey of 'Jewish' laws, is highly improbable. More probable is the suggestion that they drew from a common sources."[35] And this suggestion is confirmed by several other similarities in these three authors. The question of what kind of document was at their disposal still awaits closer scrutiny.

Vv. 100–102:"Do not dig up the grave of the deceased, neither expose to the sun what may not be seen, lest you stir up the wrath of heaven. It is not good to dissolve the human frame."[36] In these lines the author forbids the opening of graves in order to dissect the corpses of deceased (something that was only practised in Alexandria, as far as we know)[37], and his reason for this is found in the two following lines (vv. 103–104), where he preaches the bodily resurrection of the dead, who were sometimes believed to be raised in the same form as they were in the tomb.[38] Vv. 103–104 run: "For in fact we hope that the remains of the departed will soon come to the light again out of the earth. And afterwards they become gods."[39] These are the most typically and

---

[33] Porphyry, De Abstinentia IV 14 explicitly mentions it as a Mosaic commandment.

[34] Philo, Hyp. in Eus., PE VIII 7,9 and Jos., C. Ap. II 213.

[35] Crouch, Origin 86. Crouch takes over an old suggestion of Wendland, "Therapeuten", 709 ff.

[36] μὴ τύμβον φθιμένων ἀνορύξῃς μηδ᾽ ἀθέατα
δείξῃς ἠελίῳ καὶ δαιμόνιον χόλον ὄρσῃς.
οὐ καλὸν ἁρμονίην ἀναλυέμεν ἀνθρώποιο.
F. Christ, "Das Leben nach dem Tode bei Pseudo-Phokylides", Theologische Zeitschrift 31, 1975, 140 wrongly translates ἀθέατα by "unsichtbar". His interpretation of these lines is wrong in some other respects as well.

[37] See L. Edelstein, "History of Anatomy in Antiquity", in his Ancient Medicine, Baltimore 1967, 247–301; F. Kudlien, "Anatomie", PW Suppl. XI, 1968, 38–48. The verse might also mean: do not dismember a corpse by digging it up.

[38] See e.g. Apoc. Bar. syr. 50,2; H. C. C. Cavallin, Life After Death. Paul's Argument for the Resurrection of the Dead in I Cor. 15, Part I: An Inquiry into the Jewish Background, Lund 1974, 88 ff. D. Daube, The New Testament and Rabbinic Judaism, London 1956, 307 f.

[39] καὶ τάχα δ᾽ ἐκ γαίης ἐλπίζομεν ἐς φάος ἐλθεῖν
λείψαν᾽ ἀποιχομένων· ὀπίσω δὲ θεοὶ τελέθονται.

exclusively Jewish (i. e. un-Greek)[40] lines in the whole poem. It is very remarkable that this author, who otherwise conceals his Jewishness to the utmost, presents this tenet of the bodily resurrection in his poem. The second half of v. 104 (ὀπίσω δὲ θεοὶ τελέθονται) has evoked more discussion than any other passage in the poem. Some scholars assert that these words prove that the author was not a Jew but a pagan, others emend the text, others again say it proves the author to be a Christian.[41] But one should bear in mind that in Judaism the deceased were often believed to become stars or angels, and angels were often called gods.[42] One is reminded in this connection of Matthew 13 43 "The righteous will shine as brightly as the sun in the kingdom of their Father", and of Matthew 22 30 about the men and women who in the resurrection will be like angels in heaven, ὡς ἄγγελοι, which is clarified by Luke (20 36) into ἰσάγγελοι γάρ εἰσιν, καὶ υἱοί εἰσιν θεοῦ.

Now in vv. 105 ff. it looks as if the author drops his opinion of the bodily resurrection, for he speaks about the immortal soul and about the spirit that goes up into the air, and still more "inconsistencies" could be pointed to, but, as Nock said, "to press this point would be to ignore the widespread tendency of language about the after life to admit inconsistencies."[43] The same phenomenon also occurs in other Jewish writings of the intertestamental period.[44]

Quite illustrative of the mixture of Greek and O.T. ideas in this poem is v. 106 πνεῦμα γάρ ἐστι θεοῦ χρῆσις θνητοῖσι καὶ εἰκών, "the spirit is a loan from God to mortals, and his image." Here we find the Hellenistic motif of the spirit (or soul or life) as a loan from God[45], immediately followed by the O.T. motif of God's image, but that in a hellenized form, namely not man but his spirit or soul as God's image, as we find it so often in Philo.[46] The motif of the spirit as loan from God is found also in other Jewish-Hellenistic texts and lies behind Luke 12 20 τὴν ψυχήν σου ἀπαιτοῦσιν ἀπὸ σοῦ, "they are demanding your soul back from you".[47]

---

[40] How un-Greek they were can be seen from Aeschylus, Eumenides 647f.; Acts XVII 32; Celsus ap. Orig., C. Cels. V 14. See W. Pötscher, "Die Auferstehung in der klassischen Antike", Kairos 7, 1965, 208–215.

[41] For instance Harnack, ThLZ 10, 1885, 160 on the basis of Theophilus, Ad Autol. II 27.

[42] Christ, ThZ 31, 1975, 143: Seelen = Engel = Gestirne = Götter. See also Hengel's remarks in Pseudepigrapha I 297 and cf. Judentum und Hellenismus, 424, n. 727.

[43] A. D. Nock, Essays on Religion and the Ancient World I, Oxford 1972, 507, n. 19.

[44] See on this esp. Cavallin, op. cit., 197, 202, n. 1 et passim.

[45] See for example E. Rohde, Psyche II, Leipzig-Tübingen ²1898, 394, n. 2.

[46] E. g. R. A. Baer, Philo's Use of the Categories Male and Female, Leiden 1970, 21 ff.

[47] Cf. W. Bauer, WB⁵, s.v. ἀπαιτέω.

The common wisdom expressed in v. 110 ("It is impossible to take riches and money with you into Hades")[48] is reflected in the N.T. in 1 Tim 6 7: "We brought nothing into the world; for that matter we cannot take anything with us when we leave."

About v. 140 ("If a beast of your enemy falls on the way, help it to rise")[49] we only mention the curious fact that the great Scaliger assumed that Ps-Phoc. must have been a Christian because of the word ἐχθροῖο[50], simply overlooking the fact that this line is a faithful rendering of Ex 23 5. And as to v. 149 b (μαγικῶν βίβλων ἀπέχεσθαι), we need only recall the magical books in Acts 19 19 in the story of the sons of the Jewish priest Sceva.

We now pass to vv. 153–174, one of the very few larger coherent blocks in this poem. It deals with the usefulness of labour[51], a theme which is not prominent in the N.T. (but see 2 Thess 3 10: "The man who will not work shall not eat", a tone which is also struck in vv. 153–174)[52]. But is is noteworthy that the whole of vv. 164–174 derives demonstrably from the LXX of Prov 6 6-8c. In spite of the Homeric diction[53] and in spite of the fact that ants and bees are sometimes mentioned together in Hellenistic literature[54], it is only in the LXX of Prov 6 6-8c (not in the Hebrew text, where only the ant is mentioned!) that ant and bee are mentioned in combination as examples worth imitating for man.[55] Bienert sees here a "Synthese von jüdischem und griechischem Ethos"[56], in which the ant is of Jewish and the bee of Greek origin.

Another coherent section in the poem is vv. 175–227. This section is of great importance for N.T. studies, since it appears to be a close parallel to the *Haustafeln* in Col 3 18–4 1 and Eph 5 22–6 9. It was again Dibelius who pointed this out.[57] Both Ps-Phoc. and the N.T. *Haustafeln* deal successively with marriage, the education of children and the treatment of slaves. That cannot be pure coincidence. Crouch (in his book on *The Origin and Intention of the Colossian Haustafel*) sees it

---

[48] οὐκ ἔνι εἰς Ἄιδην ὄλβον καὶ χρήματ' ἄγεσθαι.

[49] κτῆνος δ' ἢν ἐχθροῖο πέσῃ καθ' ὁδόν, συνέγειρε.

[50] Animadversiones 89.

[51] See W. Bienert, Die Arbeit nach der Lehre der Bibel, Stuttgart ²1956, 159–164 on this passage; he exaggerates the un-Greek character of these lines.

[52] Note also v. 158 εἰ δέ τις οὐ δεδάηκε τέχνης, σκάπτοιτο δικέλλῃ in connection with Luke 16 3 σκάπτειν οὐκ ἰσχύω.

[53] See esp. v. 172, which echoes Iliad XXI 495.

[54] E.g. Ovid, Ars amatoria I 93 ff.

[55] However, the thing to be imitated is in Prov wisdom, in Ps-Phoc. toil.

[56] Die Arbeit, 162.

[57] An die Kolosser, Epheser, Philemon, 49 (first ed. 1913).

as a traditional, fixed code, deriving from Jewish propaganda-literature.[58] Dibelius and his pupil Weidinger[59] had asserted that the *Haustafeln* were a slightly christianized version of a non-Christian code, that was essentially Stoic in nature. But, as Crouch says[60], they too easily overlooked the differences between the Christian and Hellenistic codes. One must assume an intermediate stage between the Stoic καθήκοντα-scheme and the N.T. *Haustafeln*. This stage, the Jewish-Hellenistic stage, is reflected in parts of Philo's *Hypothetica* and of Josephus' *Contra Apionem* and in Ps-Phoc. 175–227. Though seemingly presented as a summary of Jewish laws, the material offered goes in so many instances beyond the injunctions of the Torah that one must explain the similarities between these three authors by assuming that they drew upon a common source in which the universally valid principles of the Torah were amalgamated with a Stoic καθήκοντα-scheme into which, in turn, several Greek so-called ἄγραφοι νόμοι, unwritten laws, had been incorporated. The composers of this source borrowed freely from the Hellenistic tradition. To quote Crouch: "They felt free to make use of anything which was morally superior and could be counted on to win a sympathetic hearing for the message of ethical monotheism."[61] Thus we find a considerable amount of material in these Hellenistic-Jewish writings that is of Greek origin, but that, nevertheless, is labelled "Jewish" by Philo and Josephus; not by Ps-Phoc. "who identifies neither himself nor his material".[62] Crouch asserts that all these materials were intended to serve the propagandistic or missionary purposes of Hellenistic Judaism. As already said, one can seriously doubt such a theory. The context of this material in Philo and Josephus is apologetic, not missionary. And, as we saw, the purpose of Ps-Phoc. is obscure. But it is an established fact that Ps-Phoc. drew upon a source which was also used by Philo and Josephus, and that writings like those of these three authors were, in turn, sources for some N.T. authors.

As regards the passage under consideration in Ps-Phoc., it should be remarked that the *Haustafel*-scheme (women – children – slaves)[63] is used by the author as a framework for his material. For within the section on the relationship between husband and wife he deals with all kinds of sexual offences, esp. incest, largely basing himself upon Leviticus 18 (see vv. 179–192).

---

[58] Comparable to Josephus, C. Ap. II 198–210.
[59] Die Haustafeln. Ein Stück urchristlicher Paränese, Leipzig 1928.
[60] Op. cit., 21.
[61] Op. cit., 97.
[62] *ibid.*
[63] This strongly reminds us of the rabbinic trias "women, slaves and minors", on which see S. Zucrow, Women, Slaves and the Ignorant in Rabbinic Literature, Boston 1932.

Let us turn now to a few lines of this section. Though not of direct relevance to the N.T., but rather to other early Christian writings, vv. 184–185 deserve some observation: μηδὲ γυνὴ φθείρῃ βρέφος ἔμβρυον ἔνδοθι γαστρός, μηδὲ τεκοῦσα κυσὶν ῥίψῃ καὶ γυψὶν ἕλωρα, "Let not a woman destroy the unborn babe in her belly, nor after its birth throw it before the dogs and the vultures as a prey." Abortion and the exposure if children were the current methods of family-planning in antiquity.[64] Though now and then protests were raised against these practices in the Hellenistic world, it was only in Judaism and Christianity that they are firmly condemned.[65] It was the LXX text of Exodus 21 22-23 (which differs from the M.T.)[66] that gave rise to this. The interesting point is that, although that text speaks only of abortion, Philo[67] derives from it not only the prohibition against abortion but also against exposure, which remained ever since as a set combination in both Jewish-Hellenistic[68] and in Christian literature.[69]

In vv. 190–191 ("Transgress not for unlawful sex the limits set by nature; for even animals are not pleased by intercourse of male with male")[70] one should note that the background of the somewhat odd expression παραβαίνειν εὐνὰς φύσεως is the concept of νόμος φύσεως, the law of nature, a concept that was (and is) often used as an argument against homosexuality[71], which is then considered as being παρὰ φύσιν. This motive we meet also in Paul's Epistle to the Romans 1 27 where he speaks of people who give up natural intercourse with persons of the other sex, exchanging it for unnatural intercourse. It is somewhat amusing to see that Ps-Phoc. tries to support his stance by a reference to the "natural" animal world in v. 191, which is in fact a zoological error,

---

[64] See J. H. Waszink, "Abtreibung", RAC I, 1950, 55–60; A. Cameron, "The Exposure of Children and Greek Ethics", Classical Review 46, 1932, 105–114.

[65] See F. J. Dölger, "Das Lebensrecht des ungeborenen Kindes und die Fruchtabtreibung in der Bewertung der heidnischen und christlichen Antike", in his Antike und Christentum IV, Münster 1934 (²1975), 1–61. Also R. Crahay, "Les moralistes anciens et l'avortement", Antiquité Classique 10, 1941, 9–23.

[66] See on this divergence D. M. Feldmann, Birth Control in Jewish Law, New York-London ³1973, 257f.

[67] Spec. leg. III 108–119. See I. Heinemann, Philons griechische und jüdische Bildung, Breslau 1932 (repr. Hildesheim 1962), 390–398.

[68] E.g. Sap. Sal. XII 4 f.(?); Josephus, CAp. II 202; Orac. Sib. II 281 f.

[69] E.g. Didache 2 2; Ep. Barn. 19 5; Athenagoras, Legatio XXXV 6; Minucius Felix, Octavius XXX 20; Tertullian, Apol. IX 8; see J. Geffcken, Zwei griechische Apologeten, Leipzig 1907 (repr. Hildesheim 1970), 235.

[70] μὴ παραβῇς εὐνὰς φύσεως ἐς Κύπριν ἄθεσμον.
οὐδ᾽ αὐτοῖς θήρεσσι συνεύαδον ἄρσενες εὐναί.

[71] E.g. by Philo, Abr. 135, Spec. leg. II 150, III 37 ff.; but see already Plato, Leges 636 c.

as Dornseiff already pointed out[72], an error, however, that was a current opinion in antiquity.[73]

The theme of reciprocal love between spouses, as we know it from the N.T. *Haustafeln*, is actually only found in vv. 195–197: "Love your own wife, for what is sweeter and better than that a wife is kindly disposed towards her husband and a husband towards his wife till old age, without strife divisively interfering?"[74]. The diction of these lines was inspired by a passage from Homer, which was much quoted in antiquity to illustrate the joy of harmony in marriage.[75] It must be remarked that, when Wolfgang Schrage (in his article "Zur Ethik der neutestamentlichen Haustafeln")[76] says that in Ps-Phoc. "der Mann auf sein Verhältnis zur Ehefrau gar nicht angesprochen (wird)", "die Frau wird dagegen in 195f. zur Liebe (...) aufgerufen", this is a misrepresentation.

The attitude towards children, also treated in the N.T. *Haustafeln*, is discussed in vv. 207–209: "Be not harsh with your children, but be gentle. And if a child sins against you, let the mother check her son or else the elders of the family or the chiefs of the people."[77] Note in 207 the characteristic word ἤπιος, also used in this connection in 1 Thess 2 7[78]. The similarities with Col. 3 21 and Eph 6 4 are obvious, though there is a different emphasis: the N.T. authors use παροργίζειν and ἐρεθίζειν which means approximately "to make angry", whereas Ps-Phoc. uses χαλεπαίνειν which is "to be angry with". The interesting thing in these lines is that the principle expressed in v. 207 is illustrated in vv. 208–209 by a very toned down reformulation of the commandment of Dtn 21 18ff. In Deuteronomy it is said that if a son is even disobedient to his father or his mother after punishment, they shall bring him to the elders of the town and these shall stone him to death. Philo, in his rendering of this law[79], omits only the mothers's right of chastise-

---

[72] Echtheitsfragen, 47.

[73] See e.g. Plato, Leges 836c; Plutarch, Bruta animalia etc. 7,990D; Ps-Lucian, Amores 22; cf. Athenagoras, Legatio III 1.

[74] στέργε τεὴν ἄλοχον· τί γὰρ ἡδύτερον καὶ ἄρειον
ἢ ὅταν ἀνδρὶ γυνὴ φρονέῃ φίλα γήραος ἄχρις
καὶ πόσις ᾖ ἀλόχῳ, μηδ᾽ ἐμπέσῃ ἄνδιχα νεῖκος.

[75] Homer, Od. VI 182–184, quoted, for example, by Ps-Dionysius Halic., Ars rhet. IV 3; Plutarch, Amat. 24,770A; Hierocles Stoicus p. 54,25–7 Arn. (= Stobaeus IV 22,24). See further G. Delling, "Eheleben", RAC IV, 1959, 691.

[76] NTS 21, 1974/5, 13 with n. 3.

[77] παισὶν μὴ χαλέπαινε τεοῖσ᾽, ἀλλ᾽ ἤπιος εἴης.
ἢν δέ τι παῖς ἀλίτῃ σε, κολουέτω υἱέα μήτηρ
ἢ καὶ πρεσβύτατοι γενεῆς ἢ δημογέροντες.

[78] See the discussion by A.J. Malherbe, "Gentle as a Nurse. The Cynic Background to 1 Thess. 2", NovTest 12, 1970, 203–217.

[79] Spec. leg. II 232.

ment, but retains the possibility of the death-penalty. Ps-Phoc. omits both the father's right of chastisement and the death-penalty. This is characteristic of the humaneness of Ps-Phoc., which will also be seen in his attitude towards slaves.

It can only be remarked in passing that in vv. 210–212 the first half of v. 212a (ἄρσεσιν οὐκ ἐπέοικε κομᾶν, "the wearing of long hair is not fit for men") is reminiscent of 1 Cor 11 14. But now we come to the section on the slaves, vv. 223–227: "Provide your slave with the tribute he owes to his stomach. Apportion to a slave what is appointed, so that he will be according to your desire. Insult not your slave by branding him. Do not hurt a slave by slandering him to his master. Accept advice also from a kindly disposed slave."[80] It is typical of the great humanity of Ps-Phoc. that he only mentions duties of masters toward slaves and not the reverse. This emphasis, probably inspired by the Stoa[81], was necessary in antiquity. Both in Judaism and in pagan culture slaves were mostly very despised people and were treated accordingly. It is especially in Stoic, Hellenistic-Jewish and early Christian writings that there is an insistence on a more humane attitude toward slaves. Ps-Phoc. is a good instance of this. One can even wonder whether he goes beyond the N.T. *Haustafeln* in this respect.[81a]

We now come to the verse that has, perhaps, the most relevance to N.T. studies, *scil.* v. 228: ἁγνείη ψυχῆς, οὐ σώματός εἰσι καθαρμοί. The translation is uncertain, since the text is uncertain. The text as it stands could be translated as: "purity concerns the soul, not concerning the body are purifications" (thus Berger).[82] Personally, I am inclined to read ἁγνείῃ (dative), a negligibly small change proposed by Ludwich[83], and to translate: "Purifications are for the purity of the soul, not (for the purity) of the body." Be that as it may, it is very probable that, in Greek cultic terminology[84], Ps-Phoc. wants to say that the O.T. cultic purity rules (which have no place in his poem) are "auf die Reinheit der

---

[80] γαστρὸς ὀφειλόμενον δασμὸν παρέχειν θεράποντι.
     δούλῳ τακτὰ νέμοις, ἵνα τοι καταθύμιος εἴη.
     στίγματα μὴ γράψῃς ἐπονειδίζων θεράποντα.
     δοῦλον μὴ βλάψῃς τι κακηγορέων παρ' ἄνακτι.
     λάμβανε καὶ βουλὴν παρὰ οἰκέτου εὖ φρονέοντος.

[81] See e.g. Seneca, Epist. 47.

[81a] Prof. Morton Smith remarked in the discussion in Tübingen that it should be borne in mind that Ps-Phoc. did not expect slaves as readers, whereas the N.T. authors did. This may explain the difference.

[82] K. Berger, Die Gesetzesauslegung Jesu I, Neukirchen 1972, 467: "die Reinheit betrifft die Seele, nicht auf den Körper beziehen sich die Reinigungen."

[83] Programm, 23.

[84] Th. Wächter, Reinheitsvorschriften im griechischen Kult, Gießen 1910, 1 f. Cf. also F. Sokolovski, Lois sacrées des cités grecques, Paris 1962, *passim*.

Seele hin umzudeuten."[85] In his book *Die Gesetzesauslegung Jesu* Klaus Berger discusses this line[86] and accords it a very important place in the explanation of the crucial text Mark 7 15. There we read: "Nothing that goes into a man from outside can defile him; no, it is the things that come out of him that defile a man." Berger, who denies that this logion was spoken by Jesus, says it reflects a Jewish-Hellenistic conception of the Torah which emphasizes the social commandments, but neglects the cultic ones. This conception was taken over by the Christian community in its controversy with Pharisaic Judaism. Now Berger's proof that there was such an anti-cultic "Gesetzesverständnis" in Hellenistic Judaism is actually based on only two texts, sc. Philo, *Spec. leg.* III 208–9 and Ps-Phoc. 228. Philo says there: "Everything else, too, Moses says [in Numbers 19 22], that the unclean person touches must be unclean, being defiled by its participation in the uncleanness. This pronouncement may be thought to include a more far-reaching veto, not merely stopping short with the body (οὐκ ἐπὶ σώματος . . . μόνον ἱστάμενος) but extending its inquiry to matters of temperament and characteristics of soul. For the unjust and impious man is in the truest sense unclean." In a criticism of Berger's thesis Hans Hübner has rightly objected "daß Philo (. . .) *noch nicht* den Gedanken einer antithetischen Ausschließung formuliert hat: *nicht* körperliche, *sondern* seelische Reinheit."[87] Note the essential difference between Philo's οὐκ ἐπὶ σώματος μόνον and Ps-Phoc.' οὐ σώματος. Hübner rightly rejects Berger's appeal to Philo (as he also rightly rejects Berger's verdict of unauthenticity of Mark 7 15). However, Hübner also rejects Berger's appeal to Ps.-Phoc. with only a short remark in a footnote: "Der Hinweis auf Ps-Phokylides (. . .) sagt solange nichts, wie es nicht möglich ist, diese Schrift hinsichtlich ihrer Abfassungszeit und ihrer Herkunft zu fixieren."[88] One cannot dismiss our author that easily. If Ps-Phoc. is a Jewish-Hellenistic author from the time of Jesus — which is very probable — he must be allowed to play a part in this discussion. But does that mean that Berger is right after all? One should say that, if the passage from Philo is dropped, this single line from Ps-Phoc. of which the text is uncertain, is a very small basis for his theory. But a text like *Ep. Arist.* 234 "Honouring God is done not with gifts or sacrifices, but with purity of soul, etc.", comes very close to it and is a good parallel. But things are complicated by the fact that Jesus' statement in Mark 7 15 is perhaps not as "torah-kritisch" as

---

[85] Berger, *op. cit.*, 260.

[86] Esp. *op. cit.*, 467.

[87] H. Hübner, "Markus VII 1–23 und das 'jüdisch-hellenistische' Gesetzesverständnis", NTS 22, 1975/6, 337.

[88] *ibid.*, 338, n. 4.

it looks at face value.[89] And as long as we are not sure of the purpose of Ps-Phoc. in his selective rendering of the O.T. rules, it has hard to decide what value this verse has. Perhaps it has less conclusive value than Berger thinks and more than Hübner wants it to have. The problem cannot be solved here and now. It is enough to point out here that our author may even have a great relevance for the solving of a central problem in N.T. theology like Jesus' attitude to the Torah.

The last two lines of the poem (vv. 229−230)[90] are very interesting both because of the mystery-terminology and because of the structural resemblance of these verses to other, Jewish and Christian, closing passages. But reasons of time and space forbid it to expatiate upon them.

Finally, it should be emphasized that it is the Epistle of James to which our poem as a whole has most spiritual affinity. To a great extent both writings show a lack of theological foundation in their ethics. They contain many imperatives without revealing their underlying indicatives.

As I hope, the materials presented, however sketchily, in this paper (and it was only a selection) sufficed to demonstrate that a much neglected author like Pseudo-Phocylides does not only have numerous points of contact with the New Testament, but even has in some cases a special relevance for the study of some important N.T. problems.[91]

---

[89] See e.g. R. Pesch, Das Markusevangelium I (HThK II), Freiburg-Basel-Wien 1976, 384 and esp. the discussion in H. Hübner, Das Gesetz in der synoptischen Tradition, Witten 1973, 158−175. In the discussion in Tübingen Dr. A. Nissen rightly remarked that spiritualization of commandments of the Torah need not be the same as Torah-criticism.

[90] ταῦτα δικαιοσύνης μυστήρια, τοῖα βιεῦντες
ζωὴν ἐκτελέοιτ᾽ ἀγαθὴν μέχρι γήραος οὐδοῦ.

[91] Some "minor agreements" (often only on the level of terminology) between Ps-Phoc. and the N.T. are: Mt 7 2 − Ps-Phoc. 11; Mt 15 14 (and 23 16) − Ps-Phoc. 24; Mt 19 11 − Ps-Phoc. 89; Lk 3 11 − Ps-Phoc. 28; Lk 6 38 − Ps-Phoc. 14; Lk 16 21 − Ps-Phoc. 156; Joh 7 24 − Ps-Phoc. 9; Joh 17 12 − Ps-Phoc. 13; Act 28 4 − Ps-Phoc. 77; Rom 1 26 − Ps-Phoc. 192; Rom 1 29 − Ps-Phoc. 70+75 (ἔρις − φθόνος); Rom 8 39 − Ps-Phoc. 73; Rom 12 13 − Ps-Phoc. 24 a; Rom 12 17+19 − Ps-Phoc. 77; Rom 12 21 − Ps-Phoc. 80 (νικᾶν); Rom 13 13 − Ps-Phoc. 69; Rom 16 17 − Ps-Phoc. 151; Rom 16 27 − Ps-Phoc. 54; 1 Cor 5 1 ff. − Ps-Phoc. 179; Gal 5 20 − Ps-Phoc. 151; Eph 4 19 and 5 3+5 − Ps-Phoc. 3−6; Eph 4 25 − Ps-Phoc. 7; Eph 6 2 − Ps-Phoc. 8 b; Phil 1 15 − Ps-Phoc. 70+75; Phil 3 19 − Ps-Phoc. 69; 1 Thess 4 6 − Ps-Phoc. 35 (absolute use of ὑπερβαίνειν?); 1 Thess 5 15 − Ps-Phoc. 77; 1 Tim 2 9 − Ps-Phoc. 212 b; 1 Tim 3 2+12 and 5 9 − Ps-Phoc. 205(?); 1 Tim 6 4 − Ps-Phoc. 70+75; 1 Tim 6 8 − Ps-Phoc. 6; 1 Tim 6 17 − Ps-Phoc. 62; Hebr 4 12 − Ps-Phoc. 124; Hebr 13 2 − Ps-Phoc. 24; Hebr 13 5 − Ps-Phoc. 6; Jas 1 9 and 3 1 ff. − Ps-Phoc. 20; Jas 3 6 − Ps-Phoc. 27 (τροχός); Jas 5 4 − Ps-Phoc. 19; Jas 5 12 − Ps-Phoc. 16; 2 Petr 2 7 and 3 17 − Ps-Phoc. 190; 2 Petr 2 13 − Ps-Phoc. 61; 3 Joh 11 − Ps-Phoc. 77. On these and other parallels see my Commentary.

2. PSEUDO-PHOCYLIDES REVISITED

Ten years ago I published *The Sentences of Pseudo-Phocylides* (Leiden, 1978), containing an introduction, the Greek text of the poem with an English translation, and an extensive commentary. The past decade has seen considerable important research on this Jewish Wisdom poem. The purpose of this article is to present a survey of this research in order to indicate which problems have come closer to a solution. Also, I intend to point out the areas in which I have changed or adjusted my opinion. In this presentation I will follow, for the convenience of the reader, the outlines of my book so that there will be paragraphs on: (A) research in the decade 1978-1987; (B) authenticity, pseudonymity, teaching, purpose, genre, date, and provenance; (C) matters of interpretation of individual verses.

A. *Research 1978-1987*

The first publication dealing with Pseudo-Phocylides (hereafter Ps-Phoc) after the appearance of my commentary was Ulrich Fischer's *Eschatologie und Jenseitserwartung im hellenistischen Diasporajudentum* (BZNW 44; Berlin, New York, 1978), pp. 125-43. Since this book was finished before my commentary appeared, there is no 'Auseinandersetzung' with my view of Ps-Phoc's ideas on afterlife.[1] Fischer takes Ps-Phoc to be a Jewish poet from the first or second century CE. After having translated vv. 97-117, Fischer points out that vv. 103-17 contain almost only verbs in the indicative, in contrast to the rest of the poem where imperatives predominate. Of these indicatives four are in the first person plural (vv. 103, 107, 108, 114), whereas the other 215 lines contain only three such verbal forms (vv. 40, 201, 203). That implies that what the author wants to convey to his readers is of the highest personal interest to him. He wants to convince his readers of the truth of his statements and clarifies this intention by the accumulative use of the argumentative γάρ in vv. 105-107.[2] He wants to argue that the incorruptible soul will become divine after death. So there is no juxtaposition of contradictory ideas here, as has been asserted so often; the λείψαν' ἀποιχομένων (v. 104) are not the bodies that will be resurrected (ἐς φάος ἐλθεῖν, v. 103), but the immortal souls (ψυχαί. . .ἀκήριοι, v. 105). Only these θεοὶ τελέθονται (v. 104). Ps-Phoc does not teach bodily resurrection, but only the divinization of the soul after death, based upon the 'Gottebenbildlichkeit' of the human soul (v. 106). Only in the formulation of the way in which the souls leave their 'intermediate state' in order to reach eternal bliss, is some influence from Jewish beliefs in resurrection discernable. Fischer concludes that 'das jüdische Traditionsgut bei Ps-Phok. entschieden unter die Dominanz hellenistischen Denkens gerät' (p. 143), but he does not explain why an author who wanted to emphasize the immortality of the human soul would obscure his meaning by using traditional terminology for the resurrection of the body. There are no parallels for λείψαν' ἀποιχομένων in the sense of 'souls', whereas its use for the bodily remains of the dead is common. When the author says that he hopes (ἐλπίζομεν) that these remains 'will soon come to the light out of the earth' (v. 103)—immediately after an injunction not to dissolve the human body when it is dead (v. 102, cf. vv. 100-102)—one cannot escape the conclusion that Ps-Phoc is referring to the resurrection. Fischer's ingenious construction is not convincing.

In 1979 Max Küchler published his magisterial *Frühjüdische Weisheitstraditionen. Zum Fortgang weisheitlichen Denkens im Bereich des frühjüdischen Jahweglaubens* (OBO 26; Freiburg, Göttingen, 1979). In this book Küchler gives a comprehensive survey of post-biblical Wisdom literature. Chapter 3 ('Logoi Sophōn in frühjüdischer Zeit') contains *inter alia* a discussion of *Avoth*, and *Avoth de R. Nathan*, Pseudo-Menander, the 'Gesetzesepitome' in Philo and Josephus (i.e., those passages that have so much in common with Ps-Phoc), and Ps-Phoc ('Die "Gnomen des Phokylides" im Rahmen der griechischen Gnomologien', pp. 236-302). The introductory survey of Greek gnomologies from the archaic period until late antiquity is one of the most complete and useful treatments I know.[3] Küchler concludes that 'die mehr oder weniger lose Aneinanderreihung kurzer, möglichst prägnanter Worte ist die einzige sich durchhaltende formale Gemeinsamkeit' (p. 258) and that 'eine Gesamtstruktur ist *nirgends* zu finden, sodass mit völligem Recht die Strukturlosigkeit solcher Sammlungen als Wesensmerkmal der Gattung selbst behauptet werden kann' (p. 261). Ps-Phoc is then shown to share these characteristics to a certain extent, but also to have tried to impose a minimal structure upon his diversified material, e.g. by means of the 'Rahmung' (cf. vv. 1-2 with the closing lines 229-230) and the distribution of the modi (a preponderance of imperatives in the first and last parts and of indicatives in the middle parts). For the rest 'scheint *assoziative Sprunghaftigkeit* das einzige kompositorische Prinzip zu sein, welches PseuPhok durchhält' (p. 273).[4]

Küchler then characterizes my compilation of material comparable to Ps-Phoc as follows: 'Sein Kommentar (...) besteht aus 230 Materialschlachten, aus denen manchmal kein Sieger hervorgeht, einige Male zwar das griechische Element stärker ist, meist jedoch biblisch-jüdisches Gedankengut die Oberhand bekommt' (p. 279). He then systematically orders my comparative material according to an 'abgestufte Beweiskräftigkeit der Vergleichspunkte' (p. 280). This ordering demonstrates that in at least 40 lines Ps-Phoc is directly dependent upon the LXX; that in hardly fewer lines Ps-Phoc draws upon the same source as Philo (*Hypothetica* 7, 1-9) and Josephus (*Contra Apionem* 2, 190-219) in their 'summaries' of the Torah. Moreover there are a number of other lines with a clear 'Präsenz typisch jüdischer Anliegen' (pp. 283f.). Some cases of allusion to Jewish doctrine I had noticed in my commentary (vv. 54, 102-104, 129, 131, 228) are discarded as unproven. Küchler judges that, in spite of the impressive presence of non-biblical material of Greek origin, 'in PseuPhok *biblische Anweisungen und frühjüdische, apologetische Weisheitsmaterialen* vorhanden sind, und dass darin ein echt *jüdisches Anliegen* zum Ausdruck kommt' (p. 285), even though Ps-Phoc never betrays 'eine explizite apologetische Tendenz' (p. 287).

Finally, Küchler deals with the relation between Jewish and Greek elements in Ps-Phoc's ethics, exemplified by the passage on labour (vv. 153-174), and concludes: 'PseuPhok erreicht in seinen Inhalten ein so gutes Gleichgewicht von biblisch-frühjüdischen und griechischen Weisheitstraditionen, dass sich die einzelnen Gewichte nicht mehr gegeneinander ausspielen lassen. Die Konkurrenz der beiden Bereiche ist verschwunden—und mit ihr auch jegliche propagandistische

Tendenz' (p. 298). Küchler is of the opinion that Ps-Phoc, in contradistinction to the Pharisees and Rabbis (cf. *Avoth!*), is a Jew who no longer lives 'aus den tragenden Kräften einer auftragsbewussten Gruppe' (p. 301). This conclusion gave rise to some criticism (see below).

In 1980 Pascale Derron published her important article 'Inventaire des manuscrits du Pseudo-Phocylide' (*Revue d'histoire des textes* 10 [1980], pp. 237-47), in which she catalogues and describes no less than 157 MSS of our poem. This represents the most extensive collection of MSS ever gathered by a student of Ps-Phoc, and its import will be discussed below when Derron's new critical edition will be dealt with.[5]

In 1983 there appeared almost simultaneously two books that do not deal with Ps-Phoc, but that are mentioned here because they have added a new dimension to the study of Jewish Wisdom poetry in general. The first is J.T. Sanders, *Ben Sira and Demotic Wisdom* (Chico, CA, 1983); and the second is Miriam Lichtheim, *Late Egyptian Wisdom Literature in the International Context. A Study of Demotic Instructions* (OBO 52; Freiburg, Göttingen, 1983).[6] Sanders first sketches Ben Sira's relation to the Jewish proverbial tradition, then his relation to the Hellenic gnomic (or gnomological) tradition, and finally his relation to Egyptian, especially Demotic or late Egyptian, Wisdom literature. He shows that, besides Ben Sira's dependence upon OT Wisdom Literature (which was to be expected), this author is also entirely open to Hellenic thought (especially Theognis' gnomic wisdom) 'as long as it can be Judaized' (p. 58). Sanders also argues that Ben Sira is demonstrably more comfortable with and more apt to use Egyptian Wisdom material than he is Hellenic (see e.g. p. 69). The Egyptian material he draws on is especially to be found in the work of the early Hellenistic Egyptian scribe Phibis, the author of the instructions of Papyrus Insinger. There is, says Sanders, very strong evidence for Ben Sira's borrowing from Phibis. Over 15% of the instructions of Papyrus Insinger have close parallels in Ben Sira's work: 'Phibis is *more* like Ben Sira, in both style and content, than is *any other collection of proverbs, Theognis included, save only the Book of Proverbs itself*' (p. 105, Sanders's italics). Ben Sira must have read Phibis.

Lichtheim's work has a different scope. She begins by observing that the strictly monostichic form of the Demotic Instructions (of which the prime examples are the Instruction of Ankhsheshonqy, the Papyrus Insinger, and the Louvre Demotic Papyrus 2414) is an innovation as compared to older Egyptian instructional works: 'The Demotic instructional monostich has no known precursor in earlier Egyptian wisdom' (p. 12). She then analyzes the Instruction of Ankhsheshonqy and finds that this writing shows a number of striking parallels to the Ahiqar traditions (i.e., Aramaic, Syriac, Greek, Armenian, and Slavonic collections of sayings of the sage Ahiqar). The author must have known (an) early version(s) of this sapiential monostichic collection. The author also certainly had knowledge of Greek gnomic collections that circulated so widely in Graeco-Roman Egypt and these collections could have served as models for his own manner of composition: 'single sentence sayings; the culling of sayings from different sources; the simple devices for obtaining a minimum of order; and the freedom in the use or non-use of organizational devices' (pp. 27f.). There are also parallels with biblical and rabbinic proverbs. In general, the Instruction of Ankhsheshonqy contains 'a significant number of pithy sayings that were popular international adages' (p. 37). Lichtheim argues that 'its formulations arouse such numerous and precise echoes from Aramaic, Hebrew, and Hellenistic Greek sources as to make it evident that the Demotic writer had drawn on widely shared international sapiential topics, treated in the prevailing modes of aphoristic gnomologia' (p. 65). The same applies to the Louvre Demotic Papyrus 2414 and some other minor Wisdom texts (pp. 93-106).

The greatest part of Lichtheim's book (pp. 107-234) is devoted to Papyrus Insinger. Again one is struck, even more than in the case of Ankhsheshonqy, by the large measure of congruity between the main themes of Hellenistic moral treatises and gnomic collections and those of Papyrus Insinger.[7] In a detailed investigation of its themes Lichtheim demonstrates this close convergence of topics, e.g. self-control (especially in matters of sex), shame, patience, gentleness, generosity, fear of God or piety, right measure, the paradoxes of fate and fortune, behaviour towards strangers, women, children and slaves, etc. At the end of the book she presents a new translation of this papyrus (see n. 6). Although she does not pay a great deal of attention to Ps-Phoc (he is mentioned in passing on p. 158), almost everything Lichtheim says about Papyrus Insinger reminds the reader of Ps-Phoc. (In section C of this article a considerable selection of parallels to Ps-Phoc from Papyrus Insinger will be quoted or referred to in order to enable the reader to get some idea of the close convergence of ideas.) There is a difference between Sanders and Lichtheim as to the question of whether the author of Papyrus Insinger is dependent upon Jewish and Greek gnomic literature or if it is the other way round. This of course depends partly upon its dating. While Sanders dates it to the early Hellenistic period (making Ben Sira the dependent one), Lichtheim places it in late Hellenistic or early Roman times. I am not able to judge in this matter myself, but since Lichtheim is one of the greatest experts in this field at the moment, I feel inclined to follow her dating. That would make Phibis a contemporary of Ps-Phoc. This makes it impossible to tell whether either of the two knew the other's work. But it is worthwhile and important to notice that these two Wisdom writers, working in the same country and in the same period, shared a great many ethical ideas although they were adherents of widely differing religions. This demonstrates once again Wisdom's 'international context', as Lichtheim calls it.[8]

The next major contribution is Nikolaus Walter's translation (with rich annotations) of Ps-Phoc in the series *Jüdische Schriften aus hellenistisch-römischer Zeit* (vol. IV. 3; Gütersloh, 1983, pp. 182-216). Though concise, this is an excellent piece of work. In the introduction (pp. 182-96), Walter emphasizes the Jewish character of the poem, and deals with its textual history, its sources (both Jewish and pagan Hellenistic), its provenance (Alexandria in the first century BCE or CE), and its purpose:

> M.E. legt die vom Autor bewusst vollzogene gegenseitige Integrierung von biblisch-weisheitlicher und hellenistisch-popularethischer Tradition die Annahme nahe, dass er seinen Glaubensgenossen unter vorgeblichem Bezug auf einem griechischen Autor, der als "Weiser" galt [V.2], zeigen wollte, wie eng gut-griechische und gut-biblische Moral beieinanderliegen. Er wollte wohl auf dieser Weise einer unangebrachten Faszination mancher hellenistischer Juden durch die Welt hellenistischer Bildung und einem Abschwenken vom jüdischen "Weg der Gerechtigkeit" [vgl. V.229f.] zu einem ewta als höherstehend empfundenen griechischen Lebensstil entgegenwirken (p. 192).

Walter's translation is solid and presents at some places a justified correction to mine as will be shown below *ad locos* (section C).

A year later M. Gilbert devoted a three page paragraph to Pseudo-Phocylides in his chapter on Wisdom literature in M.E. Stone (ed.), *Jewish Writings of the Second Temple Period* (Compendia Rerum Iudaicarum ad Novum Testamentum II. 2; Assen, Philadelphia, 1984), pp. 313-16. In a brief, but informative, *status quaestionis*, Gilbert agrees in almost every respect with the points of view I chose in 1978. He gives a survey of the poem's contents and discusses its pseudonymity, date and place of origin, and major themes. Gilbert speaks of the 'meagre doctrinal contents' of the poem and states that its interest 'lies in the fact that the ethics and wisdom of Israel here encounter those of pagan Hellenism' (p. 316).

In 1985 the second volume of J.H. Charlesworth's *The Old Testament Pseudepigrapha* (New York) was published. My contribution on Ps-Phoc (II, pp. 565-82) does not contain anything new as compared to my book of 1978, since both manuscripts were completed in the same year (1976/77).[9]

A short contribution also may be found in Eckart Reinmuth's dissertation, *Geist und Gesetz. Studien zu Voraussetzungen und Inhalt der paulinischen Paränese* (Berlin, 1985), pp. 29-31. In the important chapter, 'Die Enthaltung von Unzucht und Habgier als zentrale Forderung des Gesetzes' (pp. 12-47), Reinmuth demonstrates that the central position in the Pauline corpus of the admonitions to abstain from fornication and greed or avarice has its background in early Jewish parenesis. In several Jewish writings abstention from these two vices is presented as the 'Zusammenfassung eines dem Willen Gottes entsprechenden, gesetzestreuen Verhaltens' (p. 28). Ps-Phoc is one of these writings. Sins of a sexual nature and sins with regard to money and possessions are singled out by our author for a more detailed treatment than are other vices (see e.g. vv. 42ff. and 177ff.). As Reinmuth notes, already in the introductory lines (vv. 3-6) they receive the heaviest emphasis:

> Denn die Umschreibung des Ehebruch- und Diebstahlverbotes durch mehrere Wendungen im Gegensatz zur eher knappen Formulierung des Tötungsverbotes (V.4b) macht deutlich, dass mit der vom Verfasser gegebenen Paraphrase des Dekalogs eine Akzentuierung der Warnung vor Unzucht und Habgier beabsichtigt ist. (. . .) Durch die theologische Rahmung [sc. vv. 1-2 and 229-230] ist die Absicht des Autors, seine Weisungen als Wiedergabe des Gesetzes in der Autorität Gottes ergehen zu lassen, klar

erkennbar. Den beiden Lastern Unzucht und Habgier gilt dabei
eine betonte gedankliche Bemühung; sie werden als dem Willen
Gottes in besonderem Masse zuwiderlaufend aufgefasst (p. 31).

These are valuable observations which were supplemented by
Niebuhr (see below).

Martin Goodman gives a short but excellent survey of research
and a discussion of all relevant issues in the revised version of E.
Schürer, *The History of the Jewish People in the Age of Jesus Christ*
(III, 1, ed. G. Vermes, F. Millar, and M. Goodman; Edinburgh,
1986), pp. 687-92. He regards the poem as written by a Jew for Jews
in order to reinforce their attachment to Judaism and their belief in
the possibility of reconciling their religion with the Greek culture
they had already adopted. It was written between 100 BCE and 100
CE, probably in Alexandria, but possibly elsewhere. The survey
concludes with a good bibliography which covers the period from
1856 through 1980.

In 1986 the Italian scholar G.C. Bottini published an article
('Sentenze di Pseudo-Focilide alla luce della Lettera di Giacomo',
Studii Biblici Franciscani Liber Annuus 38 [1986], pp. 171-81) in
which he discusses the motifs that Ps-Phoc shares with the Epistle of
James (Ps-Phoc 3-4/Jas 2.11; Ps-Phoc 16-17/Jas 5.12; Ps-Phoc 19/Jas
5.4; Ps-Phoc 20/Jas 1.19, 26; Ps-Phoc 27/Jas 3.6; Ps-Phoc 57/Jas
1.19). He concludes that there is a great affinity between the two
writings on the basis of data drawn from my commentary. Although
his conclusion is correct, the article does not advance our knowledge
of Pseudo-Phocylides very much.

The most recent contribution is Karl-Wilhelm Niebuhr's dissertation *Gesetz und Paränese. Katechismusartige Weisungsreihen in der
frühjüdischen Literatur* (Tübingen, 1987), esp. pp. 5-31.[10] Niebuhr
investigates catechism-like summaries of the Torah such as can be
found in Ps-Phoc, Philo, Josephus, the Testaments of the Twelve
Patriarchs, Sibylline Oracles, 2 Enoch, Testament of Abraham,
Jubilees, Tobit, etc. His hypothesis is 'dass die Vergegenwärtigung
der Gesetzesforderungen in der frühjüdischen Paränese traditionell
geprägt ist und einer unterweisenden Intention dient' (p. 1). He
observes that Ps-Phoc's dependence upon the Torah is limited to
three 'Überlieferungskomplexe', *sc.* Exodus 20-23 (esp. the Decalogue
in Exod. 20), Leviticus 17-26 (esp. Lev. 18-20), and Deuteronomy
27. This is not an arbitrary choice by Ps-Phoc since 'diese

Überlieferungskomplexe haben bereits innerhalb des Pentateuchs eine herausgehobene und selbständige Bedeutung' (p. 13). For the Decalogue and Leviticus 19 that is a generally recognized fact; Leviticus 18 and 20 are the only two 'sich überschneidenden Reihen von Gesetzen aus dem sexualethischen Bereich' (p. 14); Deut. 27.15-26 is a 'formal straff gestaltete Fluchreihe (...), deren Einzelsätze bis auf den ersten ausschliesslich 'sittliche' Vergehen betreffen' (p. 14). That is to say, Ps-Phoc's use of the Pentateuch is limited to portions of which it can be said: 'Die in ihnen enthaltenen materialen ethischen Aussagen sind frei von nationalen und kultischen Spezifika. Im Vordergrund stehen sexuelle Vergehen, Mord, Körperverletzung, Besitzrecht, Gerichtswesen, Schutz der "Geringen"' (pp. 14-15). However, it should be added that Ps-Phoc draws upon these chapters as they have been explained and actualized in the early Jewish exegetical tradition, in which, for example, the commandments of the Decalogue have been combined with those in chapters like Leviticus 19 and some other pericopae: 'das Toragut ist in bereits interpretierter und umgestalteter Form von Pseu-Phok als geprägte Tradition aufgenommen worden' (p. 31). The same situation is found in Philo (*Hypothetica* VII 1-9) and Josephus (*Contra Apionem* II 190-219), who draw upon the same tradition as Ps-Phoc. Both these authors also heavily emphasize sexual ethics and care for the weak and minimize ritual commandments. Like Ps-Phoc, both Philo and Josephus present non-biblical precepts as God's commandments. Niebuhr argues that this does not mean, as Küchler thinks, that biblical and non-biblical injunctions are indiscriminately mixed up, but rather that 'durch solche Ergänzungen sollen offensichtlich die Toragebote aktualisiert und konkretisiert werden. Es handelt sich bei den aufgenommenen Weisungen häufig um Gut, das zwar nicht direkt in der Tora vorkommt, aber doch ihren Intentionen entspricht und aus ihr abgeleitet worden sein kann' (p. 51). Both Philo and Josephus (and implicitly Ps-Phoc) designate as Torah both early Jewish commandments and originally non-Jewish ethical rules. These non-Jewish rules stand in relation to similar injunctions of the Torah and can be seen as their actualizing interpretations (pp. 56-57). This 'Fonds frühjüdischer Weisungen (...) enthielt sentenzartige Gebotsreihen' which contained 'ethisches Material aus der Tora, nicht-mosaisches frühjüdisches Gut und dem Ursprung nach griechische Weisungen', but they did not contain 'exklusiv jüdische Gebote wie das Verbot des Götzendienstes, die Beschneidung, das Bilderverbot und der Sabbat'. 'Inhaltlich ist der Fonds geprägt durch Weisungen, die das alltägliche Leben des Einzelnen betreffen. Dabei spielt die Sexualethik eine hervorgehobene Rolle' (pp. 58-59). 'Wir können deshalb von einer geprägten katechismusartigen Vergegenwärtigung der Tora, von katechismusartigen Gesetzeszusammenfassungen des Frühjudentums sprechen' (p. 65). For Ps-Phoc this implies that his work is 'nur als ein an jüdische Adressaten gerichtetes Werk verständlich' (p. 67). His work is neither missionary nor propagandistic or apologetic. The purpose of his poem is 'eine erbauende und unterweisende' (p. 69); his intended audience is Jewish: 'Gerade wenn man eine jüdische Adressatenschaft voraussetzt, ist es denkbar, dass sich eine erbaulich-unterweisende Mahnschrift zunächst auf die ethischen Konkretionen im Leben des Alltags konzentriert, da ja vorauszusetzen ist, dass solche "Einseitigkeit" durch andere Lebensäusserungen derselben angesprochenen Gruppe ausgeglichen wird. Die religiösen Motivierungen der Gebote, die sich ja bei PseuPhok auch finden, sind demnach nicht mit leichter Hand beiseite zu schieben' (p. 72, contra Küchler). I have quoted extensively from Niebuhr since his study is an important contribution to a solution of one of the most puzzling aspects of our poem, the author's purpose (see below section B).

Although Pascale Derron's new edition of Ps-Phoc appeared earlier than Niebuhr's dissertation, I will deal with her book as the last item of our 'Forschungsbericht' since it is probably the most important publication in the last decade of research on Ps-Phoc. As has already been said, Derron has collected 157 MSS of Ps-Phoc (see above). These form the basis of her Budé edition, *Pseudo-Phocylide, Sentences* (Paris, 1986 [CXVI+54 (17 double) pp.]). Her lengthy introduction has five parts: Chapter 1 ('L'œuvre et sa place dans la littérature gnomologique') is a short history of Greek gnomological literature in which she emphasizes that its constant elements are: its use for educational purposes, the recurrence of traditional moral themes, the attribution to a great name in the past, the disconnected juxtaposition of phrases, the elevated diction, and the use of antithesis. All these elements are also characteristics of Ps-Phoc, even though he must be regarded as a Jewish Wisdom poet (this is not contradictory, 'car la littérature gnomologique constitue l'équivalent grec de la littérature sapientiale du Proche-Orient, et juive en particulier' [p. XXVII]). Both biblical and post-biblical Jewish Wisdom literature share these same characteristics (pp. XXVIII-XXIX). In Chapter 2 ('L'auteur et la littérature pseudépigraphique') Derron presents a short but competent discussion of the phenomenon of both Greek and Jewish pseudepigraphy, emphasizing that the non-authenticity of our poem is an established fact. She also raises the question of the purpose of the author's assuming this pseudonym ('le genre littéraire et la langue déterminent donc le choix du pseudonym, plus que le public à atteindre', p. XLIX; 'en prenant pour modèle un poète ancien et reconnu, l'auteur aurait obéi à la mode du classicisme, caractéristique de la période gréco-romaine et en particulier d'auteurs non-grecs', p. L). Chapter 3 ('Morale et date des Sentences') discusses the main themes of the poem (justice, philanthropy, moderation, love of money, labour, sex, etc.) and tries to establish the poem's spiritual climate, which she calls 'un courant syncrétiste de morale populaire' (p. LIX) with strong Pythagorean influence (this is the least convincing part of the introduction). She dates Ps-Phoc to the first century CE and sees Alexandria as a possible, but certainly not the only possible place of origin. Chapter 4 ('Forme et style du poème') is an important and extensive treatment of the poem's metre (which turns out to prove that the poem must have originated much later than the sixth century BCE!) and grammar, esp. phonetics and morphology, its vocabulary, syntax and style (all of which point to a period around the turn of the era for its composition). This is the only competent treatment of Ps-Phoc's language in existence. The final chapter ('La tradition manuscrite') is a thirty-page discussion of the intricate textual tradition, represented by 157 MSS (in many, significantly enough, Ps-Phoc is accompanied by [other] schoolbooks, grammatical and ethical works). As far as the present writer can judge it, this is a dependable piece of research; it is followed by a *stemma codicum* (p. CXIII).

In spite of the great number of new MSS found by Derron, her own new edition is based upon the same five early MSS (10th–13th cent.) as were used by Diehl and Young for their Teubner editions, with information from ten more recent MSS occasionally added in the apparatus. The result is that, although the critical apparatus is more informative than in any of the existing editions, Derron's text is rather conservative and differs from Young's in only a handful of places (discussed below, section C). The volume contains brief, but useful explanatory notes in which intractable textual problems are discussed in a well-balanced way and with sound judgment. There is also a highly valuable eighteen-page appendix in which Derron has ordered in two columns all the parallel passages I quote in my commentary from pagan Greek and Latin literature (col. I) and from Jewish and Christian literature (col. II), with some material of her own added. This appendix enables the reader to see at a single glance which verses have only Jewish or only Graeco-Roman parallels, or which have both. I am extremely grateful to Dr Derron for taking on the tiresome task of making these lists of 'passages parallèles', which enhance the value of her edition and at the same time make my work more accessible.

To summarize the results of ten years of research: more light has been thrown on the problems of Ps-Phoc's sources, his literary affinities, his place in early Judaism, his purpose, his language and style, and the textual history of the poem. There is clearly also a growing consensus on the main issues; the extreme positions of the first half of this century are no longer defended. That is a happy development.[11]

B. *Authenticity, Pseudonymity, Teaching, Purpose, Genre, Date and Provenance*

Part of this happy development is that no recent attempts have been made to maintain the untenable position that our poem was written by the real Phocylides in the sixth century BCE (as Lincke and Dornseiff did in the first half of our century). In my book I tried to demonstrate that the vocabulary of the poem points to a late Hellenistic or early Imperial origin (*Sentences*, pp. 55-58, 81-83). Derron's analysis of Ps-Phoc's metre, language, and style (Derron 1986, pp. LXVI-LXXXII) should now dissipate all doubts, for she has proved definitively that our poet must have written in that period and not in the sixth century BCE. New Linckes and Dornseiffs are unlikely to return.

Regarding the pseudonym, my survey of ancient testimonies concerning Phocylides has convinced reviewers and investigators that the name Phocylides was a guarantee for wise counsels for daily conduct, and that there was no other pagan pseudonym more suitable for the purposes of a Wisdom poet than this one. I now also surmise that the name Phocylides was especially attractive for a Jewish Wisdom poet since he was the only Greek Wisdom poet to mention Nineveh in one of his sentences (see his frag. 4(5) Diehl).

My analysis of Ps-Phoc's teaching may now be compared to Goodman's summary in the revised Schürer (III, pp. 687ff.) and to Derron's appraisal (pp. LI-LXI). Derron denies my assertion (p. 65) that concern for the poor and the needy, concern for strangers, the idea of the resurrection of the body, the warning against eating meat of torn animals, etc., are typically Jewish, but I have already indicated that I have not been convinced by her thesis that these ideas may also be explained from a Pythagorean background. On the other hand, my thesis that Leviticus 19 (which was so basic to Ps-Phoc) was regarded in early Judaism as a central chapter of the Torah since it formed a sort of summary of its essentials, has now been confirmed in the investigations by L.T. Johnson ('The Use of Leviticus 19 in the Letter of James', *JBL* 101 [1982], pp. 391-401) and Niebuhr.

Genre, date, and provenance are no longer controversial matters. All scholars agree that Ps-Phoc is both a (Greek) gnomology and a (Jewish) Wisdom poem and that the poem is a typical example of cross-cultural didactic poetry. As to date and place of origin, some scholars favor the first century BCE, others the first century CE, some both centuries, but hardly any go beyond these limits. Ten years ago I fixed the poem's date to the period between 30 BCE and 40 CE. Now I am less sure and am inclined to extend this period so as to include the whole first century BCE, although I admit that I have no proofs to justify the extension. Alexandria remains the favourite among scholars with regard to provenance, but Derron and others have rightly stressed that our ignorance of Jewish communities in other cultural centres should not make us blind to other possibilities.

The purpose of the poem has occupied the attention of students of Ps-Phoc more than any other issue, and my chapter on this topic has received the most critical response. Critics have blamed me for wavering between three different opinions: the author was a Jew who wrote for his fellow Jews; he was a Jew who wrote for a pagan public in order to make 'sympathizers'; he was not a Jew but a 'Godfearer' who wanted to win over people to his way of life. If there is anything that the research of the last decade has made clear, it is that the second and third alternatives are no longer viable theses. Apart from the fact that the alternative 'either a Jewish or a pagan audience' is false since an author could have had in mind both audiences (like Philo?), it has to be said that the studies by Walter, Reinmuth, Niebuhr, Derron and others have made abundantly clear that the characteristics of our poem, such as its pseudonimity, the omission of anything exclusively Jewish (circumcision, shabbath, kashrut, etc.), and the incorporation of originally non-biblical commandments, can all be explained on the assumption that the author wrote a kind of compendium of *miṣvot* for daily life which could help Jews in a thoroughly Hellenistic environment to live as Jews without having to abandon their interest in Greek culture. If our author intended to write a schoolbook (and we have seen how often gnomologies served educational purposes), one could imagine that, as a Jewish writer, he tried to provide a 'pagan' text that could be used safely in Jewish schools to satisfy Jewish parents who wanted their children to be trained in the classical pagan authors. However that may be, the hypothesis that Ps-Phoc addressed himself to a pagan audience in order to win them over to a kind of 'ethical monotheism' (and that this was the function of his pseudonym) is a theory that has now definitively to be laid *ad acta*.

C. *Notes on Individual Passages of Ps-Phoc*

By way of a preliminary remark I want to say that some reviewers of my commentary have justly criticized my division of the poem into fifteen units as rather arbitrary. I agree with that and concede that a division into smaller units makes more sense. In the two most recent editions one finds divisions into eighteen units (Derron) and into forty units (Walter). For instance, I dealt with the whole section of vv. 175-227 as one 'Haustafel' under the heading 'marriage, chastity, and family life', whereas Derron subdivides the passage into three sections, 'on marriage' (vv. 175-206), 'on children and parents' (vv. 207-222), and 'on masters and slaves' (vv. 223-227); Walter has a still more refined and sensible subdivision into nine small units.

V. 2: Ps-Phoc describes himself with the Solomonic epithet 'the wisest of men'. A good parallel exists in 4QEn⁸1.11.23 where Enoch calls himself 'the wisest of men' (J.T. Milik, *The Books of Enoch* [Oxford, 1976], p. 260; but see the different reading by K. Beyer, *Die*

aramäischen Texte vom Toten Meer [Göttingen, 1984], pp. 246f.).
The authenticity of vv. 1-2 is now strongly defended by Derron
(pp. XLV-XLVII).
Vv. 3-8: Derron (p. 19 n. 15) remarks that these lines, besides being a
summary of the Decalogue, also have each of them parallels in
Delphic precepts as formulated by Sosiades *ap.* Stobaeus III 1, 173
(III, pp. 125-28 W-H). Reinmuth, *Geist und Gesetz* (pp. 29-31),
rightly points out that the two vices most frequently condemned in
early Jewish literature, lasciviousness and greed, take pride of place
in vv. 3-6. More parallels are offered by Niebuhr (*Gesetz*, pp. 16f.,
20). Niebuhr (p. 16 n. 36) gives more evidence for the reversed order
of the Decalogue's prohibitions of adultery and murder. On the
theme of homosexuality (3b) K.J. Dover's *Greek Homosexuality*
(London, 1978) should now be consulted. *Ad* 5a (μὴ πλουτεῖν
ἀδίκως) cf. also 1En 97.8: 'Woe unto you who gain silver and gold by
unjust means'.
V. 8: The phrase πρῶτα θεὸν τιμᾶν, μετέπειτα δὲ σεῖο γονῆας is
paralleled also in Sosiades *ap.* Stobaeus III 1, 173 (θεοὺς σέβου,
γονεῖς αἰδοῦ; III p. 125 W-H). On πρῶτα to indicate teaching that is
of the highest importance see Berger, 'Hellenistische Gattungen im
NT', *ANRW* II.25.2 (Berling—New York 1984), p. 1206; on the verse
as a whole also Niebuhr, *Gesetz*, pp. 18f.
Vv. 9-41: Niebuhr (*Gesetz*, pp. 20-26) sees in these verses Jewish
traditions in which Leviticus 19 and the Decalogue have been
intertwined. He demonstrates that this combination also existed
elsewhere in summaries of the Torah.
V. 10 (μὴ ρίψῃς πενίην ἀδίκως): ρίπτειν may also mean 'to abandon,
to leave someone to fend for himself'; see C. Spicq, *Notes de
lexicographie néotestamentaire* I-II (Fribourg, Göttingen, 1978),
pp. 780-83.
V. 13: On παρθεσίη = παραθήκη see now also Spicq, *Notes*, pp. 651-
55. On πίστις in this line see O. Wischmeyer in *Zeitschrift für die
neutestamentliche Wissenschaft* 69 (1978), p. 214 n. 4.
V. 14 (καλὸν δ' ἐπίμετρον ἀπάντων): M.L. West (*Classical Review* 30
[1980], p. 137) proposes to read καλὸν δ' ἐπὶ μέτρον ἄπασι ('it is
good to have measure in all circumstances') with some MSS, referring
to Hesiod, *Op.* 694.
V. 17 (ψεύδορκον στυγέει θεὸς ἄμβροτος ὅστις ὁμόσσῃ): M.L. West
takes ψεύδορκον to be an internal accusative governed by ὅστις

ὀμόσσῃ: 'the eternal God hates anyone who swears falsely', an attractive proposal (letter of 25.viii.80).

V. 18 (σπέρματα μὴ κλέπτειν): Morton Smith suggests: 'It was hardly necessary to prohibit Alexandrian Jews from stealing seed. Can this refer to fellatio?' (letter of 2.x.78). But my suggestion that it may refer to stealing crops by means of magic seems to be confirmed by Vergil, *Eclogae* VIII 80ff., esp. 100: *atque satas alio vidi traducere messes*. Walter (*ad loc.*) takes the words to mean 'dass dem abhängigen Armen wenigstens das Saatgut für die nächste Aussaat belassen werden soll' (p. 199). This is an alternative view to be considered seriously.

V. 20: Walter takes κρυπτὸν λόγον ἐν φρεσὶν ἴσχειν to mean: 'ein Wort im Vertrauen behalte fest für dich', which seems better than my 'keep your word hidden in your heart'. To the verse as a whole, cf. Papyrus Insinger XXVI 22.

V. 21: μήτ' οὖν is not 'nor therefore', but οὖν here 'emphasizes the duality (...) of the ideas negatived' (J.D. Denniston, *The Greek Particles*, 2nd edn, Oxford, 1954, p. 419).

V. 22 (πτωχῷ δ' εὐθὺ δίδου μηδ' αὔριον ἐλθέμεν εἴπῃς): on 22a see Niebuhr, *Gesetz*, p. 24. Walter (*ad loc.*) aptly quotes Publilius Syrus, *Sent.* 274: *inopi beneficium bis dat qui dat celeriter*.

V. 23: As to the text-critical problem of πληρώσει σέο χεῖρ' ('you should fill your hand)'), Derron opts for the *varia lectio* πληρώσεις ἕο χεῖρ' ('tu remplira sa main'), but Morton Smith conjectures πληρώσει σέο χεῖρ' ἔλεον χρῄζοντι παρασχεῖν (MSS -σχου; 'you should fill your hand in order to give alms to the needy'), assuming that an original infinitive was substituted by a copyist with an imperative, which could easily happen in view of the frequency of imperatives in the immediate context. For the content (and also that of v. 28) cf. Papyrus Insinger XVI 12-15.

V. 25: Instead of Young's ναυηγοὺς οἴκτιρον Derron reads ναυηγοὺς οἴκτειρον, which is only a spelling variation (see Moulton-Howard, *Grammar*, II, p. 402; and Blass-Debrunner-Rehkopf, *Grammatik*, par. 23). That 'shipwrecked' is a metaphor here (so Derron, p. 21 n. 4) is improbable in view of the parallels adduced in my commentary, to which may be added Secundus Taciturnus 14-15 (pp. 86-88 Perry) where seafaring is also called ἄδηλος.

V. 27: For ἄστατος ὄλβος, cf. also Philo, *Vita Mosis* I 31, 41.

V. 29: The duty to give to the needy some of that which God has given to you is also formulated in Tob. 4.7-9 and Papyrus Insinger XVI 4-5.

V. 30: Derron rightly compares *SVF* III 625: τήν τε ὁμόνοιαν ἐπιστήμην εἶναι κοινῶν ἀγαθῶν, δι' ὃ καὶ τοὺς σπουδαίους πάντας ὁμονοεῖν ἀλλήλοις διὰ τό συμφωνεῖν ἐν τοῖς κατὰ τὸν βίον.

V. 32: τὸ ξίφος ἀμφιβαλοῦ μὴ πρὸς φόνον ἀλλ' ἐς ἄμυναν = 'if you gird on a sword, let it be not to murder, but to protect'. For the construction (imperative to be translated by 'if+verb. fin.'), cf. Eph. 4.26: ὀργίζεσθε καὶ μὴ ἁμαρτάνετε = 'if you are angry, do not sin'. For the sentiment, cf. JosAs 29.3; Crates *ap.* Diog Laert. VI 85; P. Oxy. 1795 (referred to by Derron).

Vv. 42-47: On the theme of φιλοχρημοσύνη (= φιλαργυρία) in general see now Spicq (*Notes*, pp. 928ff.) and K.S. Frank (Habsucht, *RAC* XIII, pp. 226ff.). Cf. the striking parallel to these lines in Papyrus Insinger XV 12-19:

> (12) Greed puts strife and combat in a house. (13) Greed removes shame, mercy, and trust from the heart. (14) Greed causes disturbances in a family. (15) He who is greedy does not like to give to him who gave to him. (16) He does not think of the morrow because he lives for the moment. (17) He does not eat of a thing to satiety because of stupidity. (18) Money with greed, its wrong does not end. (19) Money is the snare the god has placed on the earth for the impious man so that he should worry daily (trans. Lichtheim).

On the oxymoron in 45 (πῆμα ποθεινόν), cf. Secundus Taciturnus 16 (p. 88 Perry) where riches are called a φιλούμενον ἀτύχημα and a πολυπόθητον ταλαιπώρημα. See also the Jewish parallels to v. 47 (ἐχθρὰ δὲ τέκνα γονεῦσιν κτλ.) in Jub. 23.19; 1En 100.2; m.*Sotah* IX 15; cf. Lk. 12.53.

V. 48 (μὴ δ' ἕτερον κεύθῃς κραδίῃ νόον ἀλλ' ἀγορεύων): Again a striking parallel in Papyrus Insinger XXV 21: 'Do not let your tongue differ from your heart in counsel when you are asked' (trans. Lichtheim).

V. 49: For the proverbial polyp, cf. also Julian, *Contra Galilaeos* 106B; *Misopogon* 349D; on the adaptability (πολύτροπος) theme see W.B. Stanford, *The Ulysses Theme* (2nd edn, Ann Arbor, 1976).

V. 50: On ἁπλότης, cf. Spicq, *Notes*, pp. 125ff.

Vv. 51-52: Behind v. 51 (ὅστις ἑκὼν ἀδικεῖ, κτλ.) may also be the discussion of sinning unwittingly (or wittingly) in Leviticus 4 and 5, where LXX has ἀκουσίως; cf. also Exod. 21.12-13, where LXX has ἐκών. West (letter of 25.viii.80) thinks that Young's translation of 52a (οὐκ ἐρέω τὸ τέλος), 'I shall not state the result/consequence', is better than my 'I shall not pass sentence'. Compare also Walter's 'so will ich kein Urteil fällen' with Derron's 'je ne me prononcerai pas définitivement'. For 52b Derron rightly refers to Philo, *Quaest. in Gen.* IV 204-206, 228, 426.

V. 54 (εἷς θεός ἐστι σοφὸς δυνατός θ'): For God as δυνατός see the Hellenistic and Jewish passages in Bauer's *Wörterbuch, s.v.*; in the NT, cf. Lk. 1.49; 1 Tim. 6.15 (there in combination with μόνος, cf. εἷς in v. 54).

V. 57a (μή προπετὴς ἐς χεῖρα): Walter's 'werde nicht übereilt tätlich' and Derron's 'pas de geste prompt' are more adequate renderings than my 'be not rash with your hands'. On προπετής see now Spicq, *Notes*, pp. 756f.

Vv. 59-69: This whole section on moderation (Derron: 'la juste mesure') again has striking parallels in Papyrus Insinger IV 16-21:

> (16) All things that are good through right measure, their owner does not offend. (17) The great god Thoth has set a balance in order to make right measure on earth by it. (18) He placed the heart hidden in the flesh for the right measure of its owner. (19) If a wise man is not balanced, his wisdom does not avail. (20) A fool who does not know balance is not far from trouble. (21) If a fool is not balanced, he cannot live off another (trans. Lichtheim).

V. 61: ἔρωτες need not be limited to sexual desires but can have a wider sense, as in Sophocles, *Ant.* 617 (*pace* Walter).

V. 62 (ὑψαυχεῖ δ' ὁ πολὺς πλοῦτος καὶ ἐς ὕβριν ἀέξει): Walter may be right in taking the verbs to be transitive: 'Viel Reichtum lässt den Kopf hoch tragen und bläht auf zum Hochmut'. Derron takes a middle position by translating: 'trop de richesse est présomption et nourrit la démesure'.

V. 65: Walter takes ὑπέρογκος to mean here 'unbearable', which makes good sense (though this meaning is not given by LSJ). Derron's 'exagérée' comes close to my 'excessive'.

V. 67 (σεμνὸς ἔρως ἀρετῆς, ὁ δὲ Κύπριδος αἶσχος ὀφέλλει): On σεμνός see Spicq, *Notes*, pp. 791ff. Morton Smith writes that he sees no warning against sexual excesses in this line, for Ps-Phoc 'says flatly that sexual affection is shameful. Stoic?' (letter of 2.x.78).

V. 68: The translation of ἡδὺς ἄγαν remains problematic. My 'a man who is too simple' is criticized by Derron because it 'rendrait alors ἄγαν inutile'; she translates by 'l'homme trop conciliant'. Walter tries: '(Wer sich jedermann) allzu angenehm (macht)'. Both renditions seem preferable to mine. Of this ἡδὺς ἄγαν, this person who always wants to please everyone, it is said that he 'is called a fool among the citizens'; cf. Papyrus Insinger III 4: 'Do not let yourself be called a fool because of your thoughtless gluttony' (one of a long series of maxims all of which begin with 'do not let yourself be called a. . . ').

Vv. 69-69b: Both lines have parallels in Demotic and in Sassanian (and other) Wisdom literature, e.g. Papyrus Insinger IV 16, VI 8. 12-13; *Denkart* VI 38-40 (in S. Shaked, *The Wisdom of the Sasanian Sages* [Jerusalem, 1979], p. 17).

V. 70: μὴ φθονέοις ἀγαθῶν ἑτάροις was translated by me as 'do not envy others their goods', which should be 'do not envy (your) friends their goods'; ἕταρος = ἑταῖρος, not ἕτερος. But it should be added that in papyri of the early Imperial period one often finds the change ε→α in accented syllables (see F.T. Gignac, *A Grammar of the Greek Papyri of the Roman and Byzantine Periods I: Phonology* [Milano, 1977], p. 284, who quotes as an instance P. Grenf. II 41 [from 46 CE] where ἑτάρις = ἑτέροις). On φθόνος see now also Spicq, *Notes*, pp. 919ff.; and P. Walcot, *Envy and the Greeks* (London, 1979).

V. 71: ἄφθονοι Οὐρανίδαι καὶ ἐν ἀλλήλοις τελέθουσιν should be translated as 'the heavenly ones are without envy even among themselves', since καί emphasizes what follows. On my remark that 'Judaism has always consistently denied the divinity of the stars', Morton Smith aptly comments: 'We do not know enough about ancient Judaism to support such statements about what "it" has "always" or "never" done' (letter of 2.x.78).

Vv. 72-74: On the theme of concord (ὁμόνοια) or rivalry between sun and moon there are Jewish parallels, e.g. b.Ḥullin 60b, *Ber. Rabbah* VI 3, *PRE* 6 (see the discussion by J. Bowker, *The Targums and Rabbinic Literature* [Cambridge, 1969], p. 105). For more literature on ὁμόνοια see now H.J. Sieben, *Voces* (Berlin, 1980), pp. 153f.

V. 76: More literature on σωφροσύνη can be found in Sieben, *Voces*, p. 193.

V. 77 (μὴ μιμοῦ κακότητα, δίκῃ δ' ἀπόλειψον ἄμυναν): Papyrus Insinger III 20: 'Do not be concerned about vengeance, do what is before you'; XXXIII 20: 'He who does harm for harm, his old age will be harmed' (trans. Lichtheim). About the Philonic passages on *Dike* I quote, M.L. West remarks that Philo's source is surely Orph. fr. 23 (*Classical Review* 30 [1980], p. 137 n. 3).

V. 79: I should have noted also the earlier parallels in Hesiod, *Op.* 372 and Theognis 75ff. (West *ibid.*). Cf. also Papyrus Insinger XI 23: 'Do not trust one whom you do not know in your heart'; XII 6: 'Do not trust another on the way if there are no people near you' (trans. Lichtheim). On the curious construction of πρίν+future indicative see now the remarks by Derron, p. LXXVII (with note 3).

V. 80: To the χάρις ἀντὶ χάριτος principle expressed here there is a fine parallel in Josephus, *Ant.* II 262, where he has Raguel say to Moses 'that he had not bestowed this service upon those who had no sense of gratitude, but on persons well able to requite a favour, indeed to outdo(!) by the amplitude of the reward the measure of the benefit'.

Vv. 81-82: Papyrus Insinger III 21: 'Better the small deed of the quick than the large one of him who delays' (trans. Lichtheim).

V. 88 (τὴν σοφίην σοφὸς εὐθύνει, τέχνας δ' ὁμότεχνος): The translation of this verse remains problematic. I now think that εὐθύνειν = κρίνειν (see W.J. Verdenius's commentary on Hesiod, *Op.* 25f.); cf. Walter's translation: 'Ein Weiser kann Weisheit recht würdigen, (so wie) ein Berufskollege die handwerksgerechte Ausführung'.

V. 91: On κόλαξ see now Spicq, *Notes*, pp. 436ff.

Vv. 92-94: Papyrus Insinger VI 19, VII 10, XXVI 5.

V. 95: On the πολύτροπος theme see, beside Stanford's *Ulysses Theme* (see *ad* v. 49), also F.D. Caizzi, *Antisthenis Fragmenta* (Milano, 1966), frag. 51 with comments (pp. 105-107); and A. Rostagni, *Scritti minori* I (Turin, 1955), pp. 3ff.

V. 96 (λαὸς γὰρ καὶ ὕδωρ καὶ πῦρ ἀκατάσχετα πάντα): Diehl had inserted γάρ for metrical reasons; Derron has now found it in some fourteenth century MSS and adopted it in her text edition. On the sea as image of instability, cf. also Jas 1.6.

Vv. 97-115: On this whole section, see Fischer, *Eschatologie*, discussed above at the beginning of our Forschungsbericht.

V. 98: Printed by Derron as follows: μέτρα δὲ † τεῦχε θεοῖσι † (see her discussion of this crux on pp. 25f.). The problem of the MSS reading remains unsolved. Walter opts for Young's ingenious τεῦχ' ἔθ ἑοῖσι ('rate auch den Deinen zur Mässigung'), but Derron correctly remarks: 'comment comprendre alors ἔτι?' H.J. de Jonge adds to the long list of conjectures the following one: τεῦχ' ἐθέεσσι, 'keep measure in your (mourning) customs', which is palaeographically defensible (*Nederlands Theologisch Tijdschrift* 33 [1979], p. 246). My colleague Gerard Mussies drew my attention to the fact that the final note in my commentary, on the unusual position of γάρ, is incorrect.

V. 99: On the duty to bury the dead, see also M. Hengel, *Nachfolge und Charisma* (Berlin, 1968), pp. 9ff., who gives many parallels, to which may be added Papyrus Insinger II 9.

Vv. 100-101: Curses on tomb-violators are dealt with by J.H.M. Strubbe, 'Vervloekingen tegen grafschenners', *Lampas* 18 (1983), pp. 248-74; also G. Klingenberg, 'Grabrecht', *RAC* XII (1983), pp. 590ff., esp. 617ff.

V. 102: This verse was explained by me as prohibiting the dissection of deceased persons since the body was sometimes believed to be raised in the same shape as it had in the tomb. E. Norden quotes in his classic commentary on Vergil's *Aeneid* VI (*ad* v. 446) pagan parallels to 'die Vorstellung, wonach die Spuren der Gewalt am εἴδωλον haften' (p. 251)', which is a comparable conception.

V. 104b: For the belief that the deceased become (divine) stars reference should have been made to F. Cumont, *Lux perpetua* (Paris, 1949), pp. 144ff.

Vv. 105-107: For the repetition of γάρ see n. 2 above. On the idea of the spirit (or soul) as a loan from God, see also the many passages collected in D. Winston's *The Wisdom of Solomon* (Garden City, NY), pp. 286f. Cf. also Job 27.8. To v. 107 (ἐκ γῆς. . .κἄπειτα πρὸς αὖ γῆν), cf. Papyrus Insinger XXX 6: 'What comes from the earth returns to it again'.

V. 110 (οὐκ ἔνι εἰς Ἅιδην ὄλβον καὶ χρήματ' ἄγεσθαι): Parallels now also in Lichtheim, *Ancient Egyptian Wisdom Literature*, pp. 157f.

V. 111: Cf. *WisSol* 3.8.

Vv. 112-113: Τὸ μέλαθρα αἰώνια (and *beth 'ālemā*), cf. also the evidence in F. Cumont, *Les religions orientales dans le paganisme romain* (4th edn, Paris, 1929), pp. 247f.; and the two texts from Murabba'at (Mur. 20ar and 21ar) in J.A. Fitzmyer and D.J. Harrington, *A Manual of Palestinian Aramaic Texts* (Rome, 1978), nos. 41 and 42; R. Lattimore, *Themes in Greek and Latin Epitaphs* (Urbana, 1942), pp. 165ff. Τὸ ξυνὸς χῶρος ἅπασι, cf. *Orph. Hymn.* 87, 6.

[V. 116]: Cf. the *Instruction of Amenemope* 18: 'Man ignores how tomorrow will be' (trans. Lichtheim, *Ancient Egyptian Literature* II [Berkeley, 1976], p. 157).

V. 118 (μήτε κακοῖς ἄχθου μήτ' οὖν ἐπαγάλλεο χάρμῃ): Derron and West refer to Archilochus, fr. 128, 4-5 West...καὶ μήτε νικέων ἀμφάδην ἀγάλλεο, μηδὲ νικηθεὶς ἐν οἴκῳ καταπεσὼν ὀδύρεο. Cf. also Porphyry, *Vita Pyth.* 35. Οὖν in this line should not be translated 'therefore', since it only 'emphasizes the duality of the ideas negatived' (Denniston, *Gr. Part.* 419); cf. *ad* v. 21.

Vv. 119-120: ἄπιστον πῆμα perhaps not 'incredible calamity' but 'a calamity that makes them lose their trust' (enallage, suggested by H.J. de Jonge, *Nederlands Theologisch Tijdschrift* 33 [1979], p. 247). On the theme of 'Schicksalswechsel' see Solon, frag. 13(1), 67-70; Philos, *Vita Mosis* I 31, 41.

V. 121: Τὸ καιρῷ λατρεύειν, cf. the *varia lectio* τῷ καιρῷ δουλεύειν in Rom. 12.11 (reference by Walter *ad loc.*).

V. 122: 'τρυφῶν is probably a corruption of τυφῶν', M.L. West in *Class. Rev.* 30 (1980), p. 137.

V. 123: To the theme of speaking the right word in the right situation, cf. the precepts in Papyrus Insinger III 10-11.

V. 127: Derron now restores ταύροις δ' αὐτοχύτως κέρα ἐστίν ('chez les taureaux, les cornes viennent d'elles-mêmes'), but see her own hesitations expressed on p. 27 n. 3: 'le présent ἐστίν surprend entre les aoristes...αὐτοχύτως est difficile à traduire, et on serait tenté de corriger, comme Bernays, en αὐτοφύτως'.

[V. 129]: Τὸ θεόπνευστος, cf. Spicq, *Notes*, pp. 372ff.

V. 130 (βέλτερος ἀλκήεντος ἔφυ σεσοφισμένος ἀνήρ): Euripides, *Antiope* fr. 18,2-3 Kambitsis εἰ γὰρ εὖ φρονεῖν ἔχω, κρεῖσσον τόδ' ἐστὶ καρτεροῦ βραχίονος. Cf. Prov. 16.32.

V. 137 (μοίρας πᾶσι νέμειν, ἰσότης δ' ἐν πᾶσιν ἄριστον): Walter prefers to read παῖσι with MS M and translates: 'Teile den Kindern ihre (Erb-) Anteile (gleichmässig) zu—Gleichheit unter allen ist am besten'. The first πᾶσι may be a morphological anticipation of the second.

V. 139 (μὴ κτήνους ᾿νητοῖο βορὴν κατὰ μέτρον ἕληαι): The translation of this line remains controversial. Compare Walter's 'Nimm dem sterblichen Vieh nicht gegen (alles) Mass sein Futter weg' to Derron's 'Du bétail d'un mortel ne t'arroge pas la ration de nourriture'. Although 'mortal' seems to be the only possible meaning of θνητός ('dead' being unattested as a meaning), M.L. West writes: 'I find the expression "a mortal beast" too strange to believe, and despite the lack of a parallel I am inclined to think that "dead" was the meaning intended' (letter of 25.viii.80). I would now rather suggest to adopt Young's proposal by taking κτήνους θνητοῖο βορήν to mean 'the fodder of a man's domestic animal'; cf. v. 141 where βροτός = man. As Derron (p. 28 n. 3) remarks, the expression is paralleled in the next line by κτῆνος ἐχθροῖο.

V. 140: Water returns to Diehl's text which followed three MSS in reading κτῆνος κἢν (Young and Derron δ' ἢν) ἐχθροῖο πέσῃ καθ' ὁδόν, συνέγειρε: 'Wenn das Vieh selbst eines Feindes auf dem Wege niedergestürzt ist, so hilf mit, es aufzurichten'.

V. 141: Both Walter and Derron have good discussions of the very corrupt state of the text of this line, but neither of them proposes new readings. Perhaps better 'never accuse/reproach' than 'never expose' for οὔποτ' ἐλέγξεις.

V. 142: Cf. *Denkart* VI 322 (p. 129 Shaked). On φίλος/φιλία see now also J.C. Fraisse, *Philia. La notion d'amitié dans la philosophie antique* (Paris, 1974); and Spicq, *Notes*, pp. 936ff.

V. 143 (ἀρχόμενον τὸ κακὸν κόπτειν ἕλκος τ' ἀκέσασθαι): Walter correctly takes ἀρχόμενον to belong not only to κακόν but also to ἕλκος.

V. 145: On ἐγκράτεια, cf. Spicq, *Notes*, pp. 61ff. Cf. also Papyrus Insinger V 17: 'The great praise of a wise man is self-control in his manner of life' (trans. Lichtheim).

[V. 146]: On avoiding a bad reputation see Hesiod, *Op.* 760 (and M.L. West *ad loc.*).

V. 149: On ancient Jewish magic see now the excellent survey by P.S. Alexander, 'Incantations and Books of Magic', in E. Schürer, *The History of the Jewish People in the Age of Jesus Christ* III 1, pp. 342-79. On pp. 348f. he dates *Sepher ha-Razim* to the second half of the fourth century CE or even later, so my remark 'written in the Tannaitic period' has to be corrected. For the collocation of φάρμακοι and μάγοι, cf. also Euripides, *Or.* 1497.

V. 154: On ἀεργός now Spicq, *Notes*, pp. 142ff.

Vv. 156-157: See the parallel in Hesiod, *Op.* 397-400. Küchler (*Weisheitstraditionen*, pp. 295f.) suggests that the whole section vv. 153-174 has more Hesiodic flavor than my commentary suggests.

V. 162 (οὐδὲν ἄνευ καμάτου πέλει ἀνδράσιν εὐπετὲς ἔργον): This sentence of the oracle of the Branchidae has parallels both in Hesiod, *Op.* 42-44, and in Gen. 3.19.

V. 163a: The labouring of the heavenly bodies is also referred to by Ps-Phoc's contemporary, compatriot and coreligionist Philo in *Cher.* 88-89; cf. also Mimnermus 12(10).

V. 173 (δρυὸς ὠγυγίης): Cf. Josephus, *Ant.* I 186: τὴν ᾿Ωγύγην καλουμένην δρῦν (= the terebinths of Mamre!).

Vv. 175-227: See the discussion of this whole 'Haustafel' by K. Berger, 'Hellenistische Gattungen im NT', *ANRW.*II 25, 2, pp. 1079ff.

Vv. 177-183: Cf. the several parallels in Papyrus Insinger VII 20-VIII 20, where a similar sexual ethic is to be found.

V. 178 (οὐ γὰρ τίκτει παῖδας ὁμοίους μοιχικὰ λέκτρα): This theme is discussed, with many parallels, by D. Winston in his commentary on WisSol 4.6 (pp. 134f.).

V. 181: To this prohibition of intercourse with one's father's concubines S.P. Brock compares 2 Sam. 3.7; 16.21 (*JJS* 30 [1979], p. 247).

V. 183: All editors after Bernays followed him in placing this line here although all MSS have it between 194 and 195. Derron has now shown that Bernay's replacement is confirmed by a thirteenth-century MS. E. des Places compares Mk 6.18: οὐκ ἔξεστίν σοι ἔχειν τὴν γυναῖκα τοῦ ἀδελφοῦ σου (*Biblica* 60 [1979], p. 271).

Vv. 184-185: On the theme of abortion in Graeco-Roman and Jewish antiquity see also E. Nardi, *Procurato aborto nel mondo greco-romano* (Milano, 1971), esp. pp. 291f. on Ps-Phoc; E. Eyben, 'Family Planning in Graeco-Roman Antiquity', *Ancient Society* 11-12 (1980), pp. 5-82; R. Freund, 'The Ethics of Abortion in Hellenistic Judaism', *Helios* n.s. 10 (1983), pp. 125-37.

V. 189: On ὑβρίζειν now Dover, *Greek Homosexuality*, pp. 34ff.

V. 190: For this verse see, beside Dover, also R. Scroggs, *The New Testament and Homosexuality* (Philadelphia, 1983), esp. pp. 60, 96f., 131ff.

V. 191: The motif that homosexual behaviour does not occur among animals is also found in Philo, *De animalibus* 49 (p. 89 Therian); cf. Seneca, *Phaedra* 911ff. Discussions in U. Dierauer, *Tier und Mensch im Denken der Antike. Studien zur Tierpsychologie, Anthropologie und Ethik* (Amsterdam, 1977), pp. 63 and 272; F. Buffière, *Eros adolescent* (Paris, 1980), pp. 518-21.

V. 193: M.L. West remarks on my translation that γυναικός without further specification is not sufficient to convey the meaning 'your wife' (letter of 25.viii.80). I agree, so the correct translation is : Do not deliver yourself wholly unto unbridled lust for a woman' (*pace* Walter, *contra* Derron); see also the note to my translation in *OTP*, II, p. 581.

Vv. 195-197: A good parallel in the Demotic *Instruction of Ankhshe-shonqy* XXV 14: 'May the heart of the wife be the heart of her husband, that they may be far from strife' (trans. Lichtheim).

V. 207: On ἤπιος see now Spicq, *Notes*, pp. 355ff.; and J. de Romilly, *La douceur dans la pensée grecque* (Paris, 1979).

V. 212 (ἄρσεσιν οὐκ ἐπέοικε κομᾶν): See Dover, *Greek Homosexuality*, pp. 78f. on the (accidental) association of long hair and homosexuality in antiquity.

Vv. 223-227: On the theme of slavery in general see now also N. Brockmeyer, *Antike Sklaverei* (Darmstadt, 1979); Th. Wiedemann, *Greek and Roman Slavery* (London, 1981); on humane treatment of slaves, A. Dihle, 'Ethik', *RAC* 6 (1966), pp. 667f. On the variegated terminology for slaves, partly reflected in Ps-Phoc 223-227, see C. Spicq, 'Le vocabulaire de l'esclavage dans le Nouveau Testament', *RB* 85 (1978), pp. 201-26; idem, *Notes*, pp. 211-27. *Ad* 223: on the duty to feed one's slaves see E. Bickerman, 'The Maxim of Antigonos of Socho', in his *Studies in Jewish and Christian History*, II (Leiden, 1980), pp. 270-89, esp. 276ff. *Ad* 224: on καταθύμιος see L. Robert, *Hellenica* XIII (Paris, 1965), Index *s.v. Ad* 226: S.P. Brock (in his review in *JJS* 30 [1979], p. 247), remarks on the intriguing problem that the only real parallel is the *Hebrew* text of Prov. 30.10 (*not* the LXX), that one might tentatively ask whether the author knew of an early hebraizing recension of the LXX such as that found in the Antinoopolis papyrus of Proverbs (928), itself unfortunately not available for ch. 30.

V. 228 (ἁγνείη ψυχῆς, οὐ σώματός εἰσι καθαρμοί): This remains the most debated line of Ps-Phoc. M.L. West (*Classical Review* 30 [1980], p. 137) proposes to read ἄγν' εἴη ψυχῆς οὐ σώματός εἰσι καθαρμοί, 'let there be purity of soul where there are (taking place) (ritual) purifications of the body'. This would fit in well with the suggestion by H.J. de Jonge (*Nederlands Theologisch Tijdschrift* 33 [1979], p. 247) to regard this line as an example of criticism of lustrations which were thought to be effective *ex opere operato*, for which he adduces as parallels Ovid, *Fasti* II 45-46: *ah nimium faciles, qui tristia crimina caedis fluminea tolli posse putatis aqua*; and Josephus, *Ant.* XVIII 117, where he mentions John the Baptist as an ἀγαθὸν ἄνδρα καὶ τοῖς Ἰουδαίοις κελεύοντα ἀρετὴν ἐπασκοῦσιν καὶ τὰ πρὸς ἀλλήλους δικαιοσύνῃ καὶ πρὸς τὸν θεὸν εὐσεβείᾳ χρωμένοις βαπτισμῷ συνιέναι. Another possibility would perhaps be to take ἁγνεία as meaning 'fasting', a meaning of ἁγνεία not registered by LSJ but well attested (see my *Chaeremon. Egyptian Priest and Stoic Philosopher* [2nd edn, Leiden, 1987], p. 57 n. 10, where references are given). Then the line would have to be rendered as follows: 'Fasting means: purifications of the soul, not of the body', implying a spiritualization of Jewish fasting precepts. For the grammatical peculiarity that εἰσιν is written instead of ἐστιν, Derron (p. 18 n. 2) refers to Herodotus I 93: ἡ μὲν δὴ περίοδος (. . .) εἰσι στάδιοι ἕξ (for further evidence she refers to Gildersleeve's *Syntax of Classical Greek*, par. 124f.). Walter translates: '(Rituelle) Reinigungen bedeuten die Heiligung der Seele, nicht des Körpers'. The debate continues as to whether or not this line can be regarded as a testimony to a radical anti-cultic attitude in some Hellenistic Jewish circles, thought to be reflected also in LetAris 234 and in the position taken by Philo's opponents in *De migr.* 89. Berger regarded v. 228 as crown witness for his thesis of an absolute denial of the validity of cultic purity rules in Hellenistic Judaism and as an important antecedent of the logion in Mk 7.15 (see his *Gesetzesauslegung Jesu*, I, p. 467). R.P. Booth (*Jesus and the Laws of Purity* [Sheffield, 1986], pp. 85-87) agrees with Berger in that he, too, interprets v. 228 as denying the validity of cultic purity rules, but he does not detect the same point of view in Jesus' words (which he regards as stating *priority* of inner purity, not as abolishing cultic purity). However, the discussion of our line in H. Räisänen, *Paul and the Law* (Tübingen, 1983), pp. 36-38, comes to different conclusions. He does not agree with Berger either, but on grounds different from those of Booth. He rightly remarks that, whichever of the proposed readings of v. 228 is adopted, the verse always takes the existence of purification rites for granted. So one cannot conclude that rites of purity are rejected by Ps-Phoc. The verse 'would seem to be intended to point out the real *meaning* of external rites, a meaning that is spiritual and internalized. (. . .) There is, to be sure, a heavy *concentration* on the moral side of the Law (. . .) but *no* demonstrable *reduction* of it to a moral law' (p. 38, his italics). I agree with this explanation. It also accords well with Niebuhr's investigation (see above in the Forschungsbericht), but absolute certainty is unattainable.

V. 230 (ζωὴν ἐκτελέοιτ' ἀγαθήν μέχρι γήραος οὐδοῦ): On the history of the Homeric tag γήραος οὐδός see now L.H. Feldman, 'Josephus' Version of the Binding of Isaac', *SBL Seminar Papers 1982* (Chicago, CA, 1982), pp. 114-15 n. 10; and idem, 'Josephus as a Biblical Interpreter', *JQR* 75 (1985), pp. 216-17 n. 13. For the motif of v. 230, cf. *Orph. Hymn.* 87, 12.

NOTES

1. My review of Fischer's book was published in *Nederlands Theologisch Tijdschrift* 33 (1979), pp. 244f.

2. It should be said here that an almost meaningless use of γάρ occurs more often in Wisdom literature, e.g. WisSol 7.22-30; 17.1-11.

3. Cf. also D. Gutas, *Greek Wisdom Literature in Arabic Translation. A Study of the Graeco-Arabic Gnomologia* (New Haven, 1975), pp. 9-35 (see also below on Derron).

4. In this connection Küchler rightly criticizes some of my rather vague 'chapter headings' which suggest more thematic unity in the various sections than there actually is (p. 273 n. 18).

5. The MSS are to be found in libraries in Aachen, Alexandria, Ankara, Arezzo, Athens, Athos, Basel, Berlin, Bucharest, Cambridge, Copenhagen, Escurial, Florence, Geneva, Heidelberg, Jerusalem, Karlsruhe, Leiden, London, Milan, Modena, Moscow, Munich, Naples, Oxford, Padua, Paris, Parma, Perugia, Rome, Salamanca, Turin, Uppsala, Venice, Vienna. The great number and ubiquity of MSS testify to the enormous popularity of Ps-Phoc's poem in the Middle Ages.

6. In both works Ps-Phoc is mentioned only once or twice in passing. It is striking that Sanders and I had a similar experience of discovery. As he wrties in his Forward, when in 1977 he obtained a copy of F. Lexa's translation of Papyrus Insinger, he 'was struck, even startled, by the degree to which the author of *Insinger* seemed to have had many of the same ideas that Ben Sira also expressed'. It was in 1980, three years before Sanders's book came out, that I was struck in exactly the same way when I happened to be reading in vol. III of Miriam Lichtheim's *Ancient Egyptian Literature* (Berkeley, Los Angeles, London, 1980), and came across the text of Papyrus Insinger (pp. 184-217) in which I found a great number of striking parallels to Ps-Phoc.

7. As an example Lichtheim quotes the catalogue of basic principles of moral behaviour as given by Plutarch in *De liberis educandis* 10 (7D-E), also quoted in my *Sentences of Pseudo-Phocylides*, p. 64 n. 1.

8. See for an enterprise similar to that of Sanders and Lichtheim now also J.-P. Mahé, *Hermès en Haut-Egypte*, II (Quebec, 1982), esp. pp. 278-305: 'Gnomologies grecques et sagesses égyptiennes'.

9. Cf. also my Dutch translation of Ps-Phoc, published together with T. Baarda's translation of Ps-Menander in 1982: *De spreuken van Pseudo-Phocylides. De spreuken van Pseudo-Menander* (De Pseudepigrafen 3; Kampen).

10. Both Reinmuth's and Niebuhr's studies were dissertations written under the direction of Traugott Holtz in Halle/Saale (DDR).

11. Some minor *addenda et corrigenda* to my Forschungsbericht of 1978: *Ad* p. 4: on Scaliger see now esp. A. Grafton, *Joseph Scaliger* (2 vols., Oxford 1983–?). *Ad* p. 5 n. 9: the second edition of Scaliger's *Thesaurus Temporum* was not in 1608 but in 1658. *Ad* pp. 26f.: I now think I have been too mild in saying that G. Klein's book presents an important new theory; it was influential but based on sheer apologetics. *Ad* pp. 35f.: the same applies to my kind verdict on J. Guttmann's theories. *Ad* p. 41 n. 156: Morton Smith writes me: 'Gordon and Astour should be pitied, not cited'. *Ad* p. 51: Crouch, too, should have been more critically dealt with.

3. MOSES' THRONE VISION IN EZEKIEL THE DRAMATIST

Somewhere between the end of the third and the beginning of the first century BCE,[1] a Jewish poet, probably in Alexandria but possibly elsewhere,[2] wrote a drama about the exodus of the Jewish people from Egypt. The poet's name was Ezekiel,[3] the play was called *Exagôgê*,[4] and only about 20 to 25% of it has been preserved in bishop Eusebius' excerpts from Alexander Polyhistor's work, *Peri Ioudaiôn*, in the ninth book of his *Praeparatio Evangelica* (IX 28, 2-4; 29, 5-16).[5] It is a drama of great importance in more than one respect. First, almost all of the extensive Greek dramatic literature of the Hellenistic period has been lost; Ezekiel's *Exagôgê* is the only play with considerable portions still extant (altogether 269 iambic trimeters). It is thus an important source for the study of the

---

* Paper read at the first Congress of the European Association for Jewish Studies in Oxford, 18-21 July, 1982.

[1] There is a *communis opinio* about a second century BCE dating of Ezekiel. He must have written after the completion of the LXX version of Exodus and before Alexander Polyhistor, who made his excerpts from Ezekiel most probably in the first half of the first century BCE.

[2] See P. M. Fraser, *Ptolemaic Alexandria* I, Oxford 1972, 707. For contrary opinions see e.g. K. Kuiper, "Le poète juif Ezéchiel", *Revue des études juives* 46 (1903), 174ff. Y. Gutman, *Ha-sifrut ha-yehudit ha-hellenistit* II, Jerusalem 1963, 66ff. M. Hadas, *Hellenistic Culture*, New York 1959, 100. A. M. Denis, *Introduction aux pseudépigraphes grecs d'Ancien Testament*, Leiden 1970, 276.

[3] Very probably this was the man's real name, not a pseudonym. It was admittedly used as a pseudonym by the author of the so-called "Apocryphon of Ezekiel" (see Denis, *Introduction* 187ff. and the text in Denis, *Fragmenta pseudepigraphorum quae supersunt graeca . . .*, Leiden 1970, 121ff.), but the name was in use, albeit seldom, among Jews (and Christians), as were other great biblical names (like Abraham, Isaac, Jacob, Isaiah, Daniel, etc.; see the prosopographies and name-lists in *Corpus Papyrorum Judaicarum* vol. III and *Corpus Inscriptionum Judaicarum* vol. I): *Epistula Aristeae* 50 mentions an Ezekiel as one of the LXX translators; there was an early Amoraic Babylonian rabbi with that name; *CIJ* I 630 has an instance (*CPJ* has not). A Christian named Ezekiel is mentioned in an Egyptian inscription in F. Preisigke, *Sammelbuch griechischer Urkunden aus Aegypten* I, Strassburg 1915 (repr. Berlin-New York 1974), nr. 643,6.

[4] Philo also sometimes calls the book of Exodus *Exagôgê* (e.g. *Migr. Abr.* 14, *Quis heres* 251); see further J. Daniélou, "Exodus", *Reallexikon für Antike und Christentum* VII (1969), 22.

[5] On Alexander Polyhistor see J. Freudenthal, *Alexander Polyhistor* (*Hellenistische Studien* 1 + 2), Breslau 1875; A Lesky, *Geschichte der griechischen Literatur*, Bern 1971[3], 873. The extant fragments of Ezekiel's drama can be found in Denis' *Fragmenta* 207-216 (Denis prints the text from Mras' edition of Eusebius' *PE* in the GCS series), but have been better edited by B. Snell in his *Tragicorum graecorum fragmenta* I, Göttingen 1971, 288-301. The only commentary is by M. Wiencke, *Ezechielis Judaei poetae Alexandrini fabulae quae inscribitur EXAGOGE fragmenta*, diss. Münster 1931 (a very one-sided treatment by a classicist). A new commentary has been announced by Prof. Howard Jacobson of the University of Urbana-Champaign, Illinois. It is to appear at the Cambridge University Press.

history of post-classical drama.[6] Second, it is the earliest Jewish play in history, and as such a fascinating example of what can happen when a hellenized Jew tries to mould biblical material into Greek dramatic forms by means of techniques developed by Greek tragedians. (I leave aside here the debate concerning whether or not the play was ever produced, but I think it was).[7] Third, in the curious passage on which I wish to focus in this paper, we find one of the earliest post-biblical merkavah-visions.[8] Fourth, in the same passage, the earliest instance occurs of the idea of a viceregent or plenipotentiary of God, a concept which was to occupy a more important role in later Jewish and Christian circles.[9]

Before translating and discussing the text in question, let me give a brief outline of the play in order to clarify the position of this passage within the work as a whole. The play probably consisted of five acts, in Hellenistic fashion.[10] In the first (vv. 1-65), Moses summarizes in a long monologue the events recorded in Exodus 1 and 2, and this is followed by the encounter with Jethro's seven daughters.[11] The second act (vv. 66-69) contains a scene that is non-biblical, a dialogue between Moses and Jethro (here called Raguel = Reuel),[12] in which Moses relates a strange dream or vision. His father-in-law tries to interpret the vision. The third act (vv. 90-192) describes how, from the burning bush, God commands Moses to lead his people out of Egypt (Exod. 3) and how he removes Moses' doubts by performing the miracles with the rod and the leprous hand (Exod. 4). Subsequently, God enumerates and describes in a long monologue the ten plagues that he will bring down upon Egypt (Exod. 7-11),[13] and the institution of Pesach (Exod. 12).[14] In act four (vv. 193-242), an Egyptian messenger gives an eye-witness

---

[6] See K. Ziegler, "Tragoedia", Pauly-Wissowa's *Realenzyklopädie der classischen Altertumswissenschaft* VI 2A (1937), 1967ff., esp. 1971-81. A. Lesky, "Review of Wieneke's dissertation" (see n. 5), *Deutsche Literaturzeitung* 3. Folge 3 (1932), .217ff. A Lesky "Das-hellenistische Gyges-Drama", *Hermes* 81 (1953), 1-10. B. Snell, "Ezechiels Moses-Drama", in his *Szenen aus griechischen Dramen*, Berlin 1971, 170-193.

[7] On this question see especially the discussion (and bibliography!) in H. Jacobson, "Two Studies on Ezekiel the Tragedian", *Greek, Roman, and Byzantine Studies* 22 (1981), 167ff.

[8] See I. Gruenwald, *Apocalyptic and Merkavah Mysticism*, Leiden 1980, 127-129. Gruenwald was the first scholar to draw attention to this text as an early example of merkavah-literature. See my article "De Joodse toneelschrijver Ezechiel", *Nederlands Theologisch Tijdschrift* 36 (1982), 97ff., esp. 112 n. 75.

[9] See J. E. Fossum, *The Name of God and the Angel of the Lord. The Origins of the Idea of Intermediation in Gnosticism*, diss. Utrecht 1982, *passim*. Unfortunately, Fossum nowhere draws Ezekiel into his discussion.

[10] See Ziegler, *PW* VI 2A (1937), 1973 (see n. 6); Snell, *Szenen* 172ff. (see n. 6).

[11] Ezekiel follows faithfully, with some notable exceptions (see below), the LXX text of Exodus 1-15.

[12] For the different traditions about the name of Moses' father-in-law see W. F. Albright, "Jethro, Hobab, and Reuel in Early Hebrew Tradition", *Catholic Biblical Quarterly* 25 (1963), 1-11; H. W. Schmidt, *Exodus*, Bibl. Komm. Lieferung II 2, Neukirchen 1977, 85f.

[13] In a slightly different order than the biblical text. To make God predict the ten plagues is, of course, a dramatic technique to avoid playing them on stage, which would be impossible.

[14] It is notable that in the elaborate rendering of the institution of Pesach, the obligatory circumcision of the participants (Exod. 12:44 and 48) is omitted by Ezekiel; see P. Dalbert, *Die Theologie der hellenistisch-jüdischen Missionsliteratur*, Hamburg 1954, 54.

account of the complete destruction of the Egyptian army in the sea (Exod. 14).[15] In act five (vv. 243-269), scouts report to Moses that they have found a suitable and excellent place for the encampment, viz. Elim (Exod. 15:27),[16] and describe at length a marvellous bird they have seen there, a phoenix: the second major non-biblical scene.[17]

Turning now to the most puzzling passage of all, Moses' vision and its explanation by Raguel, the lines translated run:

(68)   I dreamed that on the summit of mount Sinai
(69)   was a great throne which reached to the corners of heaven.[18]
(70)   On it was seated a noble man,
(71)   who had a diadem (on his head) and a great sceptre
(72)   in his left hand. And with his right hand
(73)   he beckoned me, and I took my stand before the throne.
(74)   He handed me the sceptre and he summoned me
(75)   to sit upon the great throne. And he also gave me
(76)   the royal diadem, and he himself descended from the throne.
(77)   And I saw the full circle of the earth
(78)   and what was below the earth and above heaven.
(79)   And a multitude of heavenly bodies fell on their knees
(80)   before me and I counted all of them.
(81)   And they moved past me like a host of mortals.
(82)   Thereafter I awoke from my sleep in a frightened state.

Moses' father-in-law then interprets the dream:

(83)   Stranger, it is a good thing that God has shown to you.
(84)   I hope to be still alive when these things happen to you.
(85)   For behold you will raise a great throne
(86)   and you will sit in judgment and be a leader of mortals.
(87)   And that you saw the earth and the whole inhabited world
(88)   and the things below it and the things above God's heaven,
(89)   (this means that) you will see what is, and what was before,
         and what will be hereafter.[19]

[15]   Most probably, his message is delivered to the Egyptian queen. This is a striking parallel to Aeschylus' *Persae*, where the crushing defeat of the Persian army is reported to the Persian queen, another well-known device for realizing dramatic scenes impossible to stage.
[16]   On Elim see L. Ginzberg, *The Legends of the Jews* III, Philadelphia 1911, 40-41, and VI, 1928, 15-16 nn. 86-88.
[17]   On this scene see my article mentioned in n. 8, where special reference is made to R. van den Broek, *The Myth of the Phoenix in Classical and Early Christian Traditions*, Leiden 1972.
[18]   Lit. "folds of heaven", but see R. Kannicht, *Euripides: Helena* II, Heidelberg 1969, 31 (on *Hel.* 44).
[19]   The Greek text translated here is that constituted by Bruno Snell (see n. 5), with the exception of v. 85, where Snell prints *megan tin' exanasteseis thronou* (instead of *thronon* in the mss.), "you will drive away a great one (*sc.* Pharaoh) from his throne"; but this conjecture implies that the *phôs gennaios* in v. 70 should be taken to refer to the Pharoah, which is impossible (see my article, n. 8, p. 108).

The first feature to be noted is that the introduction of a dream into a play is a classical dramatic device. Dreams predicting future events occur, for instance, in Aeschylus' *Persae* (a drama having much in common with the present work), in Sophocles' *Electra*, and in Euripides' *Hecuba*. These dreams foretell disaster, however, and are interpreted by the dreamer himself (or herself).[20] But in the play *Brutus,* by Ezekiel's contemporary, the Latin dramatist Accius, one of the main actors, has a dream that is interpreted by someone else.[21] The *contents* of Moses' dream-vision, nevertheless do not have classical antecedents. No doubt, the vision of God in human shape seated on the throne is based on the first chapter of the biblical Ezekiel. Furthermore, our author has been influenced by Exodus 24, with its anthropomorphic representation of God on Sinai. The same holds true for the scene in Daniel 7, where God bestows eternal kingship and most probably a throne on someone of human appearance. Finally, Joseph's dream in Genesis 37 also has the motif of heavenly bodies falling on their knees before a mortal, and in Psalm 147 we read that God counts all the heavenly bodies.

These biblical reminiscences can, however, only be assessed when our passage is compared to later merkavah-treatises or hekhalot-literature, especially the *Hebrew Book of Enoch* (called *3 Enoch* by H. Odeberg).[22] Although this book was probably composed after the fourth century CE, much of its traditional material (especially in chapters 3-15 from which we draw the parallels)[23] is considerably older. The story told there of Enoch, who is identified with the highest angel Metatron, bears a striking resemblance to what is said of Moses in the dream-vision.[24] For instance, God makes a throne for Enoch which is similar to the throne of Glory, God's own throne (10:1); God gives him a garment of Glory and a royal crown (12:1-3); God makes him ruler over all kingdoms and all heavenly beings (10:3); all the angels of every rank, and the angels of sun, moon, stars, and planets, fall prostrate when Enoch sits on his throne (14:1-5); he knows the names of all the stars (46:1-2; here is an explicit reference to

[20] A. Kappelmacher, "Zur Tragoedie der hellenistischen Zeit", *Wiener Studien* 44 (1924-25), 78-80. E. Starobinski-Safran, "Un poète judéo-hellénistique: Ezéchiel le tragique", *Museum Helveticum* 31 (1974), 220.

[21] This fragment of Accius is quoted by Cicero in *De Divinatione* I 22, 44-5.

[22] On this literature see G. Scholem, *Major Trends in Jewish Mysticism*, New York 1946; *Jewish Gnosticism, Merkabah Mysticism, and Talmudic Tradition*, New York 1965[2]; I. Gruenwald, *Apocalyptic and Merkavah Mysticism*, Leiden 1980. The publication by H. Odeberg referred to in the text is his edition and translation of 3 Enoch: *3 Enoch or the Hebrew Book of Enoch*, Cambridge 1928, repr. New York 1973 with Prolegomenon by J. C. Greenfield. This is the only critical (?) edition of a merkavah-treatise. The accessibility of this literature has very recently reached a new stage with P. Schäfer's *Synopse zur Hekhalot-Literatur*, Tübingen 1981.

[23] See P. S. Alexander, "The Historical Setting of the Hebrew Book of Enoch," *JJS* 28 (1977), 156-180.

[24] This was already seen by W. A. Meeks, "Moses as God and King", in *Religions in Antiquity. Essays in Memory of E. R. Goodenough*, Leiden 1968, 354ff., esp. 367f.

Psalm 147:4 "He [sc. God!] counts the number of stars"); God reveals to him all the secrets and mysteries of heaven and earth so that Enoch knows past, present and future (10:5; 11:1; cf. 45:1; 48(D):7); God calls him "YHWH ha-qaton", the lesser Adonai, with reference to Exod. 23:21, where it is said of the angel of the Lord: "My name is in him" (12:5).[25] It should be noted that some of these elements already occur in the earlier *I Enoch* (Eth.) and and *2 Enoch* (Slav.). Like Moses, Enoch is assigned a cosmic and divine function that involves the wearing of regalia.

The similarities are clearly striking. But there is also a striking difference. In Moses' vision, there is only one throne, God's. And Moses is requested to be seated on it, not at God's side, but all alone. God leaves his throne. This scene is unique in early Jewish literature and certainly implies a deification of Moses.[26] In effect, since the publication of Wayne Meeks' important article, "Moses as God and King",[27] we know that in some Jewish circles Moses was indeed regarded as a divine being. Alan Segal has in addition demonstrated that Jewish traditions existed concerning divine rule in which "a principal angel was seen as God's primary or sole helper and allowed to share in God's divinity. That a human being, as the hero or exemplar of a particular group, could ascend to become one with this figure — as Enoch, Moses or Elijah — seems also to have been part of this tradition".[28] The theme of Moses' divine kingship over the universe can also be found in Philo of Alexandria. "Philo came to connect Moses' installation as ideal king with (1) a mystic ascent read into the Sinai episode, and (2) the scriptural report that Moses was called *theos*".[29] In *Quaestiones in Exodum* I 29, Philo writes that on Sinai Moses was changed into a truly divine person (cf. *ibid.* 40); and in *De Vita Mosis* I 155-158 he says that God placed the entire universe into Moses' hands and that all the elements obeyed him as their master. Philo calls Moses god and king, probably alluding to God's words in Exodus 4:16 that Moses will be as a god to Aaron, or in Exodus 7:1, that he makes him a god over Pharaoh (cf. *Sacrif.* 9). Meeks remarks that "the analogy between Moses and God . . .

[25] The name "the little YHWH" also occurs in the Gnostic writing *Pistis Sophia*, see Odeberg (n. 22) 188ff. In later Hekhalot-literature Metatron is simply called YHWH, Elohim, Shaddai; see Odeberg 111ff. Sometimes Metatron is just one of God's names; see P. S. Alexander (n. 23) 166f. The seminal function of Exod. 23:21 is rightly stressed by Fossum in his diss. (n. 9).

[26] Contra I. Gruenwald, *op. cit.* (n. 8) 129.

[27] See note 24. Cf. also his important book *The Prophet-King. Moses Traditions and the Johannine Christology*, Leiden 1967, esp. 147ff.

[28] A. F. Segal, *Two Powers in Heaven*, Leiden 1977, 180; idem, "Ruler of this World": Attitudes about Mediator Figures and the Importance of Sociology for Self-Definition", in: E. P. Sanders (ed.), *Jewish and Christian Self-Definition* II, London 1981, 245ff. Segal nowhere discusses Ezekiel.

[29] Meeks, *The Prophet-King* 111. Meeks has collected the relevant passages from Philo.

approaches consubstantiality".[30]

The same or similar traditions can also be found in rabbinic literature, again most often in the context of Moses' meeting with God on Sinai, which was widely regarded as an ascent to heaven.[31] One example may suffice. In *Pesiqta de Rav Kahana* (Supplement I 9),[32] the expression "Moses, the man of God" (*Mosheh 'ish ha'elohim*) in Deuteronomy 33:1 is explained as, Moses, a man (*'ish*), a god (*'elohim*); *sc.* he was a man when he ascended Mount Sinai, he was a god when he descended from Mount Sinai. Elsewhere, it is indicated that Moses in a sense shared God's kingship.[33] Nowhere in rabbinic literature, however, is Moses represented as a hypostasis of God or as a second god reigning in heaven. That traditions of this kind were opposed by the rabbis is clear, e.g., from Bavli *Hagiga* 15a, where Metatron is punished and humiliated as soon as Aher (Elisha ben Abuya) thinks that there are "two powers in heaven" (*shte reshuyot bashamayim*), or from *Sanhedrin* 38b, where R. Idi says, "Do not put Metatron in God's place".[34] Segal has demonstrated that in some Jewish circles such traditions did circulate, and in his recent dissertation, the Norwegian scholar Jarl Fossum has pointed out with ample evidence that certain Jewish groups came to identify the figure of the angel of the Lord in different ways: as Adam, Moses, Enoch (-Metatron), Melchizedek, Michael or Jesus.[35] This plenipotentiary of God, who possessed God's name (Exod. 23:21!), was really the "Little Adonai" of *3 Enoch*. Many Jews speculated about a principal angelic mediator hypostasis of God with charge over the world. And, as Segal says, these intermediaries "are not just angels, but become dangerously close to being anthropomorphic hypostases of God himself". Often these intermediaries "began as humans and later achieved a kind of divine status in some communities".[36]

In a recent publication, Saul Liebermann argues convincingly that "Metatron" is not a name but a title, to be identified as the Greek word *metathronos*, which has the same meaning as the more common *synthronos*.[37] Liebermann also says that a *synthronos theou* need not

[30] Meeks, *op. cit.* 104f. In *De Somn.* I 164 there is a prayer to Moses (see Meeks, *ibid.* 125 n. 3). It should be noted here that Artapanus (2nd cent. BCE) regarded Moses as a divine being (Hermes); see Eusebius, *PE* IX 27.

[31] Meeks, "Moses as God and King", 354-371. On the link between Sinai and merkavah see now also D. J. Halperin, *The Merkabah in Rabbinic Literature*, New Haven 1980, 128-133.

[32] See the translation by W. G. Braude and I. J. Kapstein, *Pesiqta deRav Kahana*, London 1975, 451.

[33] Meeks, *The Prophet-King* 192ff.

[34] Segal, *Two Powers in Heaven* (n. 28) 60-73.

[35] J. E. Fossum, *The Name of God and the Angel of the Lord* (n. 9).

[36] Segal, "Ruler of this World", (n. 28) 248, 255-6. In Josephus' description of the end of Moses' life (*Ant.* IV 326), there are traces both of a tradition that Moses *was* translated to heaven, and of one expressing the fear that this notion leads to idolatry! (see Meeks, *The Prophet-King*, 140f.). The same holds true for a passage in *Petirat Mosheh* (Jellinek, *BM* I p. 118; see Meeks, *ibid.* 211).

[37] S. Liebermann, "Metatron, the meaning of his name and his functions", Appendix in Gruenwald's *Apocalyptic and Merkavah Mysticism* 235-241, esp. 237-9.

necessarily be one with whom God shares his throne; it can also refer to one who has a throne beside the throne of God, like Metatron. This may be right, but my hypothesis is that the idea of a *synthronos theou* in the sense of one who sits on God's own throne, either alone or together with him, is the origin of the notion of a Metatron, a viceregent of God. In 1 Chronicles 28:5 and 2 Chronicles 9:8, we already come across the idea that God has set Solomon "on the throne of the Lord".[38] In Wisdom of Solomon 9:4 and 10, Wisdom herself is presented as sharing God's throne with Him. In the Similitudes of *1 Enoch*, we find Enoch a co-occupant of God's throne, albeit only for the eschatological judgment.[39] In our Ezekiel, Moses is the sole occupant of God's throne. I surmise (for reasons that I have advanced elsewhere)[40] that in pre-Christian times there were (probably rival) traditions about Enoch and Moses as *synthronoi theou*; and I think that these ideas were suppressed (for obvious reasons) by the rabbis and replaced by the less unacceptable notion of a *metathronos* in the sense of one whose throne comes only second, after (*meta*), God's throne.[41] True, the original idea of the *synthronia* of Moses and God has been drastically modified by Ezekiel the dramatist in that he causes God to leave the throne. With this bold and almost shocking symbolic scene, he probably meant to convey that it is only in and through Moses that we can know God. To quote John 14:6 with a slight variation: "No one can come to the Father except through Moses".[41a] It is only in and through Moses that God is active in this world, Moses' kingship expresses God's kingship. For Ezekiel, Moses is "an active and present power",[42] which is also divine. It is clear that all this has implications for the development of christology.[43]

Some scholars have pointed out that a certain discrepancy exists between Moses' vision and Raguel's interpretation of it.[44] Whereas in the vision the emphasis is on the divine kingship, in the interpretation more emphasis is

---

[38] G. Widengren, "Psalm 110 und das sakrale Königtum in Israel", in P.H.A. Neumann (ed.), *Zur neueren Psalmenforschung*, Darmstadt 1976, 187ff.

[39] 1 Enoch 45:3; 51:3 (v.1.); 55:4; 61:8, 69: 27-9. It is not necessary to enter here into the thorny question of the dating of the Similitudes (*1 Enoch* 37-71), but a date before the second century CE seems to be defensible.

[40] See my article mentioned in note 8.

[41] For this explanation of the term *metathronos* see Odeberg, *3 Enoch* (n. 22) 138ff. On "rabbinische Ausschaltung der Henoch-Spekulationen" see Odeberg, "Henoch", *TLWNT* II (1935), 555 (*TDNT* II, 1964, 558-559) and P. S. Alexander, *art. cit.* (n. 23) 176.

[41a] In this connection, it may be useful to remark that according to some scholars the background of John 12:41 is a tradition that the Lord on the throne in Isaiah 6:1 is not God but Jesus; see Segal, *Two Powers* 214.

[42] The expression is E. R. Goodenough's, who uses it for Philo's view of Moses in *By Light, Light. The Mystic Gospel of Hellenistic Judaism*, New Haven 1935 (repr. Amsterdam 1969), 233. Goodenough's interpretation of Ezekiel (*ibid.* 289-291) is to be rejected. See in general on this book, A. D. Nock, "The Question of Jewish Mysteries", in his *Essays on Religion and the Ancient World* I, Oxford 1972, 459-468.

[43] See esp. Meeks, *The Prophet King*, Leiden 1967, *passim*.

[44] E.g. Kuiper (n. 2) 59.

given to Moses' prophetic function. The final line of the interpretation runs as follows: "You will see what is, and what was before, and what will be hereafter" (v. 89). The late W. C. van Unnik demonstrated convincingly that throughout antiquity — pagan, Jewish and Christian — this was a "formula describing prophecy".[45] Already Homer, in the first book of the *Iliad* (A 70), describes the prophet (*mantis*) Calchas as one who "knew what is, what will be, and what was before", and from Homer onwards it becomes a standard formula, as the wealth of material collected by van Unnik clearly shows. This observation led the American scholar Carl Holladay to believe that Ezekiel wished to depict Moses as a *mantis*, a prophet or seer, and that it is only in this way that the discrepancy between the throne-vision and its interpretation can be solved. He argues that the enthronement should be seen in the light of what Aeschylus says about Apollo's being enthroned by Zeus: he is to be Zeus' prophet (*mantis*) (*Eumenides* 18, 29, 616). Here Moses is modelled on Apollo, Zeus' spokesman sitting on a mantic throne, and Ezekiel "is consciously placing Moses in direct competition with Apollo". The point of the dream-scene, according to Holladay is that "Sinai replaces Delphi as the place where the divine oracles are issued; Moses replaces Apollo as the spokesman for God; accordingly, the whole of mankind is to seek the divine will not from the oracle of Apollo at Delphi, but from the law of God given to Moses at Sinai".[46]

Fascinating as this interpretation may be, it fails to do justice to several elements in the dream-vision, which as I have tried to show can only be explained against the background of merkavah-speculation or -mysticism, and of theories relating to a human, yet divine, plenipotentiary of God. Moreover, Apollo never sits on Zeus' own throne. The seeming discrepancy between vision and interpretation is probably due to Ezekiel's making use of two different traditions about Moses, that of king of the universe on the one hand, and of great prophet on the other, traditions which were already merging in this period.[47]

Compared to later merkavah-literature, Moses' vision is very

---

[45] This is the title of his article of 1961, now to be found in his *Sparsa Collecta* II, Leiden 1980, 183-193. Lines 88 and 89 of Ezekiel are strongly reminiscent of *mHag.* 2:1 and *Sifre Zutta* 84, quoted by Meeks, *The Prophet-King* 208.

[46] C. R. Holladay, "The Portrait of Moses in Ezekiel the Tragedian", in G. MacRae (ed.), *SBL Seminar Papers 1976*, Missoula 1976, 447-452 (the quotations on 452).

[47] See Meeks, *The Prophet-King* 100ff. Already 80 years ago, Kuiper (see n. 2) defended, albeit on very weak grounds, the thesis that Ezekiel was a Samaritan. This theory won little acceptance, but has now become attractive once more, not only in view of conspicuous parallels between Ezekiel and the Samaritan Pentateuch, as well as the *Memar Marqa*, but also because Samaritan Moses traditions show many striking similarities to Ezekiel's dream-vision in our play, including the merging of Moses' prophetic and royal functions. The similarities can easily be found by reading J. MacDonald's chapter "Moses, Lord of the World", in his *The Theology of the Samaritans*, London 1964, 147-222, and in Meeks, *The Prophet-King* 216-257. Nevertheless, this does not yet constitute sufficient evidence of what Samaritans believed in the second century BCE.

rudimentary. It contains no elaborate descriptions of the hosts of angels and their leaders, or of heavenly palaces, or of the throne itself. Furthermore, the human shape of God receives no elaborate treatment, and no attention is paid to the fabulous dimensions of his limbs, so often discussed in detail in the Shi'ur Qomah speculations of later hekhalot-treatises.[48] Even when compared with the earliest post-bibilical merkavah-vision, *I Enoch* 14, Ezekiel's description is much more sober. He was not interested in merkavah-mysticism in itself. But he did see that the literary form of a merkavah-vision[49] was quite suitable as a medium for expressing a notion of more importance to him: namely that Moses is God's viceregent, that the man who liberated the people of Israel from the Egyptians is not merely a personage from the distant past but still present and ruling over the universe, and that through his heavenly enthronement the nation of the Jews is validated as divinely established.[50]

[*Postscript*. In the meantime, Howard Jacobson's commentary, *The Exagoge of Ezekiel*, has appeared (January, 1983). His interpretation of the dream-vision is very different from mine. My review-article, "Some Notes on the Exagoge of Ezekiel", will be published in *Mnemosyne*].

---

[48] See G. Scholem, *Von der mystischen Gestalt der Gottheit*, Zürich 1962, 7-47.
[49] This merkavah-vision has here the function of a "Deute-Vision", as it has been described by F. Lentzen-Deis, *Die Taufe Jesu nach den Synoptikern*, Frankfurt 1970, 195-248.
[50] See F. T. Fallon, *The Enthronement of Sabaoth. Jewish Elements in Gnostic Creation Myths*, Leiden 1978, 48.

I am very grateful to Dr. W. L. Petersen for the correction of my English.

4. SOME NOTES ON THE *EXAGOGE* OF EZEKIEL

Dedicated to Maarten J. Vermaseren
on his 65th birthday (7-4-1983)

The *Exagoge* is a drama on the exodus of the people of Israel from Egypt, written by a Jew called Ezekiel at some time during the second century B.C. It is of great interest not only for being the only surviving specimen of Jewish drama from antiquity but also because it is the only Greek tragedy from the Hellenistic period of which extensive portions have been preserved[1]). This piece, consisting of several continuous passages totalling 269 iambic trimeters, has been neglected. When surveying the scholarly work on Ezekiel of the last century, one finds only three major publications. First, the edition with some explanatory notes by K. Kuiper in Mnemosyne n.s. 28 (1900) 237-280[2]). Second, the edition with commentary by J. Wieneke, *Ezechielis Iudaei poetae Alexandrini fabulae quae inscribitur ΕΞΑΓΩΓΗ fragmenta*, Münster 1931, for more than half a century the only commentary on our play[3]). Third, the critical edition of the text by Bruno Snell in *Tragicorum Graecorum fragmenta* I, Göttingen 1971, 288-301[4]). Now, however, the situation has been changed by the appearance of Howard Jacobson's

---

1) Only the quotations by Eusebius of Caesarea from Alexander Polyhistor's excerpts from the *Exagoge* in *Praeparatio Evangelica* IX 28-29 have been preserved. Vv. 7-40 are also quoted by Clemens Alexandrinus, *Stromateis* I 23, 155-156.

2) A French version of this article appeared in the *Revue des études juives* 46 (1903), 48-73 and 161-177.

3) See A. Lesky's review in *Deutsche Literaturzeitung* 3. Folge 3 (1932), 2217-2221, and O. Stählin's in *Gnomon* 9 (1933), 56-58.

4) See also Snell's *Die Jamben in Ezechiels Moses-Drama*, Glotta 44 (1967), 25-32, and especially his *Ezechiels Moses-Drama* in his *Szenen aus griechischen Dramen*, Berlin 1971, 170-193. Of course K. Mras' edition of Eusebius' *Praeparatio Evangelica* in the series *Die griechischen christlichen Schriftsteller* (2 vols., Berlin 1954-1956) was also an important event, but Mras tried to reconstruct Eusebius' text of Ezekiel, Snell Ezekiel's text.

The Exagoge of Ezekiel, Cambridge 1983 [5]). The distinctive feature of
this edition with commentary is that for the first time the *Exagoge*
is explained against the background of post-biblical Jewish exegesis
of the Exodus-story. To be sure, Jacobson is a classical scholar but,
unlike his predecessors, he is acquainted with all the sources of ancient Judaism, and the result is that all kinds of details in the play,
especially deviations from the biblical narrative, are only now put
into the proper light. Jacobson remarks: ''Snell fails to place
Ezekiel adequately within his Jewish context'' (2), but the same
could be said of Kuiper, Wieneke, and many other (even Judaic)
scholars. Jacobson's commentary is an original, well documented,
and capable work with many stimulating insights, and my notes
will be no more than comparatively minor additions to his, with
one exception (see below) [6]).

In the long introduction (1-47 with notes on 175-193), Jacobson
briefly discusses the name Ezekiel (5 with n. 4 on 176) without raising the question of whether it might be a pseudonym. That this
name was indeed used for pseudepigraphic purposes is well-
known [7]). The fact that vv. 68-89 are so evidently based upon the
first chapter of the biblical Ezekiel (see below) might raise the suspicion that the author has assumed this name as a pseudonym. But
although this possibility cannot entirely be ruled out, I think it is
more probable that it was his own name. The name did occur

---

5) Cambridge University Press 1983; 252 pages; £25. See also the series of recent articles by Jacobson: *Two Studies on Ezekiel the Tragedian*, GRBS 22 (1981),
167-178; *Mysticism and Apocalyptic in Ezekiel's Exagoge*, ICS 6 (1981), 272-293;
Ezekiel the Tragedian and the Primeval Serpent, AJPh 102 (1981), 316-320; *The Identity
and Role of Chum in Ezekiel's Exagoge*, The Hebrew University Studies in Literature
9 (1981), 139-146.

6) My first critical remark is that, although his book is to be read not only by
theologians but also by classicists, Jacobson takes for granted too much knowledge
of things Jewish, e.g. abbreviations of the names of Talmudic treatises, terms like
'midrashic' (introduced without any explanation on p. 20), and even untranslated
Hebrew and Aramaic quotations. He never gives any indication of the probable
date of composition of Jewish sources either although he quotes from writings
varying from the third century B.C. to the thirteenth century A.D. For classical
scholars, this will make the book much less easy to read and to assess than would
have been necessary.

7) See A. M. Denis, *Introduction aux pseudépigraphes grecs d'Ancien Testament*,
Leiden 1970, 187 ff.; J. H. Charlesworth, *The Pseudepigrapha and Modern Research*,
Missoula 1976, 109 f.

among ancient Jews, not often[8]), but there are more instances than Jacobson adduces. He mentions the 'Αζαχιελ in *Corpus Papyrorum Judaicarum* III no. 464, 24 and the 'Εζεχῆλος in *Epist. Aristeae* 50. But he could also have mentioned the Ezekiels occurring in a Hebrew-Latin inscription in *Corpus Inscriptionum Judaicarum* I no. 630 and in the ostracon inscription from Medinet-Habu in F. Preisigke, *Sammelbuch griechischer Urkunden aus Ägypten* I, Berlin 1915, no. 643, 6 (though the latter may be Christian). There was also a third century A.D. Babylonian rabbi called Ezekiel (*Berakhot* 11a). Some early Byzantine instances can be found in F. Preisigke's *Namenbuch*, Heidelberg 1922, 146, and in D. Foraboschi's *Onomasticon alterum papyrologicum*, Milano 1971, 143[9]).

When discussing the date of Ezekiel, Jacobson states that most of the proposed datings are not supported by "cogent argument"[10]). He himself opts for the late second century B.C., mainly for the following reasons: "there is nothing in the fragments to suggest hostility toward Greeks or any other pagans aside from the Egyptians", but "there was probably some deterioration taking place ... in the Jews' situation vis-à-vis the Greeks, such as to motivate Ezekiel's engaging in this kind of propaganda/public relations endeavor" (9). Moreover, Ezekiel "eliminated from his version of the Exodus all references to the land of Israel ... because Judaea was at the time of his writing not under Ptolemaic rule" (10). All this favours a date in the second century. Pre-Christian references to the phoenix (the miraculous bird that is described by Ezekiel in vv. 254-269) suggest that there was a "heightened interest in the phoenix at the beginning of the first century" (12). This favours a late second century dating, according to Jacobson.

I do not find this a "cogent argument". The many affinities with chapter 7 of the book of *Daniel*, commonly dated about 165 B.C.,

---

8) E.g., the name does not occur in A. Schalit's *Namenwörterbuch zu Flavius Josephus*, Leiden 1968.

9) A quick glance at the indexes of proper names in *Corp. Pap. Jud.* III 167-196 and *Corp. Inscr. Jud.* I 603-626 shows that names of other biblical prophets were also current among Jews in the Hellenistic-Roman period.

10) See his survey of some twenty proposals on p. 6, varying from the middle of the third to the middle of the first century B.C. The *termini post* and *ante quem* are, of course, the composition of the LXX translation of Exodus and Alexander Polyhistor's work on Jewish history.

and with chapters 47-49 of the book of *Jubilees*, commonly dated about the middle of the second century B.C., rather suggest a dating in the second quarter of that century[11]). But that is not a "cogent argument" either. The matter is best left open, as Jacobson himself admits (13). His suggestion that possibly *Sapientia Salomonis* and Pseudo-Phocylides were also written in the second century B.C. (11) is curious; there is a growing consensus that these writings were both composed around the turn of our era or in the first half of the first century A.D.[12]).

When discussing "The Provenance of the *Exagoge*" (13-17), Jacobson opts for Alexandria ("It would be surprising if Ezekiel wrote anywhere else but in Alexandria", 17). Hence he combats Kuiper's thesis for a Samaritan origin of the play. I agree with him when he says that Kuiper's arguments are weak, but I do not agree when he states that "the portrait of Moses in the *Exagoge* does not appear to tally with the grandiose view of Moses held by the Samaritans (at least as evident in late sources)" (15). John Mac-Donald's chapter on "Moses, Lord of the World" in his *The Theology of the Samaritans* (London 1964, 147-222) presents a view of Moses strikingly similar to the presentation of Moses in *Exagoge* 68-89. It is Jacobson's faulty interpretation of this passage which makes him take this position. I shall return to this below, but it should be added here that there are quite a number of noticeable parallels (apart from vv. 68-89) between the *Exagoge* and the *Memar Marqah* (Teaching of Marqah, a fourth century A.D. Samaritan treatise)[13]). Of course, we scarcely know what Samaritans of the second century B.C. believed, but I want to stress that this whole question deserves to be studied anew. Maybe Kuiper was more right than he could imagine. And a Samaritan author might have lived in Alexandria.

11) For these datings see O. Eissfeldt, *Einleitung in das Alte Testament*, Tübingen 1964³, 705-708; G. W. E. Nickelsburg, *Jewish Literature Between the Bible and the Mishnah*, London 1981, 78-79; J. C. VanderKam, *Textual and Historical Studies in the Book of Jubilees*, Missoula 1977, 207-285.

12) See e.g. D. Winston, *The Wisdom of Solomon*, New York 1979, 20-25. P. W. van der Horst, *The Sentences of Pseudo-Phocylides*, Leiden 1978, 81-83.

13) See John MacDonald, *Memar Marqah. The Teaching of Marqah*, 2 vols., Berlin 1963. See for instance I 1 (4), I 2 (5, 7, 10, 12), I 4 (18), I 9 (35-36), I 11 (42), II 6 (56), II 8 (58-59, 60), II 12 (80), IV 6 (156). The page references between brackets are to MacDonald's English translation.

In this chapter on "The *Exagoge* and Fifth Century Tragedy" (23-28), Jacobson emphasizes that, although it is undeniable that Ezekiel's style is heavily influenced by Euripides[14]), Aeschylus' influence on him is much underrated. Wieneke had already surmised that the *Persae* was an important model for Ezekiel. Jacobson confirms this: "In the story told in Aeschylus' *Persae* he saw the Hellenic counterpart to the Jews' victory over the Egyptians. In each case the small, seemingly helpless people overcomes the awesome and hybristic enemy with divine aid" (24). But a new element is that Jacobson points out a number of striking parallels between Aeschylus' Danaid trilogy (in so far as this is extant) and the *Exagoge*: Ezekiel "saw in the myth of the Danaids the story of the primeval Greeks' escape from Egypt and return to their ancestral homeland. ... Ezekiel would have perceived himself as recreating Aeschylus' *Danaides*, as well as *Persae*, in its Jewish guise, quite likely to elicit sympathy and respect for the Jews from his Greek audience, showing that both Greeks and Jews have similar ancestral stories of persecution, escape and return to a homeland" (25). In an article in *GRBS* of 1981 (see note 5), Jacobson had already pointed out the parallellism between the figure of Oedipus in Sophocles' *Oedipus Coloneus* and Moses in the *Exagoge*. "Ezekiel may have seen the *OC* as a Greek dramatic exemplar for Moses' exile from his native land, his encounter with divinity on sacred ground, and his future role as benefactor of the nation" (*ibid.* 178). These points of view are a useful corrective to the opinion (repeated time and again since Wieneke) that it was mainly Euripides who influenced Ezekiel. One may say now: Euripides' influence mainly concerned Ezekiel's style and diction (and metre)[15]), but it was themes of Aeschylus and Sophocles that helped him to mould the biblical story into the form of a Greek drama.

　　In his chapter on the dramatic structure of the play (28-36), Jacobson shows that there is an excessive neglect of the ideal of the unities of time and place in Ezekiel, much more than has often been assumed. No ancient tragedy, he says, covers so long a period of

---

14) This is the main emphasis in Wieneke's commentary.
15) But see Jacobson's excursus, "The metre and prosody of the *Exagoge*", 167-173.

time as the *Exagoge* and there is also no evidence for so bold a shift-
ing of scenes in Greek tragedy. There were at least three different
locations, but more probably five, and possibly ten different scenes.
In a reconstruction of the play that goes beyond the extant
fragments, Jacobson assumes that there must also have been
presented a meeting of Aaron with Moses (*Exodus* 4:27-28), a talk
of Moses with the elders of the people (*Exod.* 4:29-31), and also a
scene in which Moses directly confronted Pharaoh (repeatedly in
Exod. 5-12). This is very probable as to the first two of these scenes,
the more so since Jacobson convincingly argues that vv. 175-192
are not part of God's words to Moses but part of a speech by Moses
to the elders of the Jewish people in which he reviewed for them
God's commands concerning the Exodus and the celebration of
Pesach (see 121 ff.). This is a splendid solution for the problem of
the repetition of so many items from vv. 152-174 in vv. 175-192,
and it also explains why in vv. 109f. God says to Moses σήμαινε τοῖς
ἐμοῖς λόγοις ... πᾶσιν Ἑβραίοις. But as to the assumption that there
was a single scene in which Ezekiel may have compressed all the
meetings of Moses with Pharaoh, I have doubts. The description
of the ten plagues that God will bring upon Egypt in vv. 132-151
has no biblical basis.
Nowhere in *Exodus* these plagues are enumerated by God in advance. There is little doubt that this was a dramatic device
employed by Ezekiel in order to avoid the insurmountable problems of putting these ten plagues on the stage. The biblical account of the plagues is inextricably interwoven with that of the
meetings of Moses with Pharaoh. If Ezekiel decided to adopt the
dramatic technique of having the plagues described beforehand by
God, he should also do without these meetings of Moses and
Pharaoh. And to reproduce the ten plagues again in one compressed scene of such a meeting would have amounted to a tedious
repetition which I can hardly imagine Ezekiel would have committed. So I am more skeptic about this part of his reconstruction than
about his other suggestions[16]).

---

16) The repetition of the rules for Pesach (vv. 175-192) in a sense did have a
biblical basis in that *Exod.* 12 has a first set of rules in vv. 1-28 and, after an in-
termezzo in vv. 29-42, a second set in vv. 43-51.

After the text (Snell's text slightly modified) with facing translation of the fragments (50-67) follows the commentary (69-166 with
notes on 193-221). A general remark must precede my notes on
Jacobson's interpretation of the individual verses. It is not a line by
line commentary, but rather a discussion of whole passages. Jacobson focuses upon Ezekiel's train of thought, whereas discussion of
problems of textual criticism, the meaning of rare words, syntac-
tical peculiarities and the like is relegated to the footnotes.
Knowledge of Wieneke's commentary (especially Wieneke's
diachronic treatment of words and phrases) is taken for granted as
is acquaintance with Jacobson's articles (see note 5). The contents
of those publications are not repeated, often not even summarized.
Unfortunately, this gives the commentary a somewhat unbalanced
character. It does not give a full account of modern scholarship,
neither on this drama as a whole nor on the individual verses. In
order to get a full survey of the relevant material one must consult
not only Jacobson's commentary (with the notes) but also his articles, Wieneke's commentary, some articles of other scholars
Jacobson does not mention (see below), and my articles[17]). In view
of the fact that Wieneke's commentary is sometimes hard to obtain
(as are some of Jacobson's articles) it would have been better if the
relevant materials from those publications were repeated or summarized in this commentary, not just supplemented.

The first fragment starts with: ἀφ' οὗ δ' 'Ιακὼβ γῆν λιπὼν
Χαναναίαν | κατῆλθε κτλ. This inevitably raises the question
whether a book could start with δέ (cf. the same problem in e.g.
Heraclitus' first fragment). Wieneke and Kraus[18]) assumed,
because of this δέ, that the original opening lines were lost, but
Jacobson rightly refers to Verdenius' convincing studies of inceptive δέ[18a]). However, Verdenius discusses only this usage in the
classical period. Examples of inceptive δέ from the post-classical

17) My article *De joodse toneelschrijver Ezechiël*, Nederlands Theologisch
Tijdschrift 36 (1982), 97-112, is mentioned in Jacobson's bibliography but I know
it appeared too late to be used by him in his commentary. My article *Moses'
Throne-Vision in Ezekiel the Dramatist* was published in the Journal of Jewish Studies
34 (1983), 21-29.

18) C. Kraus, *Ezechiele poeta tragico*, RFIC 96 (1968), 166 n. 1 (164-175).

18a) Mnemosyne (ser. 3) 13 (1947), 274 f.; (ser. 4) 8 (1955), 17; (ser. 4) 27
(1974), 173 f.

period are given in my article *Some Late Instances of Inceptive ΔE*, Mnemosyne (ser. 4) 32 (1979), 377-379.

Vv. 2-3 κατῆλθ' ἔχων Αἴγυπτον ἑπτάκις δέκα | ψυχὰς σὺν αὐτῷ. Jacobson examines in detail the problem that the Hebrew Bible has here the number 70 (as Ezekiel) whereas the LXX has 75[19]). I fully agree with his conclusion that "there are several ways in which Ezekiel could have known the figure 70 without any direct knowledge of the Hebrew Bible" (84). A reference to D. Barthélemy, *Études d'histoire du texte de l'Ancien Testament*, Göttingen 1978, 104 ff. and 333 n. 29, would have been in order here.

Vv. 4-6 κακῶς πράσσοντα .. | ... κακούμεθα | κακῶν ὑπ' ἀνδρῶν καὶ δυναστείας χερός yield, apart from a good example of paronomasia (see E. Schwyzer, *Griech. Gramm.* II, 1950, 700), examples of *abstractum pro concreto* (δυναστεία = δυνάστης or rather δυνάσται) and of καί explicativum. So δυναστεία = κακοὶ ἄνδρες.

In vv. 1-6 the whole period of Israel's sojourn in Egypt is described as a period of sheer oppression. The initially favourable situation, e.g. Joseph's viceroyalty over Egypt, is suppressed by Ezekiel, as Jacobson acutely remarks, because it would have reminded his audience or readers of the (since Manetho current) anti-Semitic accounts of a Jewish reign of terror over Egypt in Moses' days. In this respect it is significant that Moses and Joseph are sometimes very closely connected and made contemporaries by Alexandrian anti-Semitic authors, e.g. in fragment 1 of Chaeremon the Stoic[20]).

Jacobson does not discuss the problem of v. 10 where Pharaoh is said to be οἰκοδομίαις τε βαρέσιν αἰκίζων βροτούς. One expects βαρείαις, not the masculine form. Wieneke accepts the emendation (by Sylburg and Gaisford) οἰκοδομίας βάρεσιν, rendering this by "molestias quae aedificatione efficiuntur" (42). Früchtel suggests: "βαρέσιν liegt etwa eine Reminiszenz an das ägyptische Wort βᾶρι vor (also βάρισί τ')? Allerdings ist diesem Dichter βαρέσι für βαρείαις

---

19) It is inconvenient that it is only at the very end of his discussion of the Prologue (vv. 1-59) that Jacobson raises this problem (on pp. 81-84), instead of at its proper place. This occurs more often in this commentary.

20) See the notes to fragment 1 in my *Chaeremon, Egyptian Priest and Stoic Philosopher. The Fragments Collected and Translated with Explanatory Notes*, Leiden 1984, 49-51.

zuzutrauen''[21]). If one takes βᾶρις to mean 'big house' or 'tower' (see LSJ *s.v.* 2), a meaning it occasionally has in the LXX, βάρισι would fit perfectly with πόλεις τ' ἐπύργου in the next line, but then οἰκοδομίαις should indeed be changed into οἰκοδομίας. Yet I prefer to take βαρέσιν as a slip for βαρείαις (*pace* Früchtel).

V. 11 πόλεις τ' ἐπύργου is Sylburg's plausible emendation of the manuscripts' πόλεις τε πύργους. The biblical basis, *Exod.* 1:11, has just ᾠκοδόμησαν πόλεις, but *Jubilees* 46:14 says, ''they built all the walls and all the fortifications which had fallen in the cities of Egypt''.

In vv. 14-15 Moses says: ἐνταῦθα μήτηρ ἡ τεκοῦσ' ἔκρυπτέ με | τρεῖς μῆνας. This datum from *Exod.* 2:2 was the basis for the later theory that Moses was a six or seven months' child, as Jacobson remarks in another context (81 with n. 49). This motif is treated in my article *Seven Months' Children in Jewish and Christian Literature from Antiquity*, Ephemerides Theologicae Lovanienses 54 (1978), 346-360.

The construction λάσιον εἰς ἕλος δασύ in v. 17, which has one adjective before the noun and a second one asyndetic after it, occurs more often in Ezekiel (as Wieneke 46 already noted): 221 μέγας στῦλος νεφώδης, 249 δαψιλὴς χῶρος βαθύς (cf. Euripides, *Phoen.* 653). See on this usage H. Zilliacus, *Zur Abundanz der spätgriechischen Gebrauchssprache*, Helsinki 1967, 37 ff., especially 48 ff.

V. 22 says of the Egyptian princess who finds Moses: ἔγνω δ' Ἑβραῖον ὄντα. *Exod.* 2:6 has ὁρᾷ, but Philo, *Vita Mosis* I 15, has γνοῦσαν here, so this may be added to Jacobson's list of possible instances of Ezekiel's influence on Philo on 38 f.

V. 37 has the well-known theme that Moses was educated τροφαῖσι βασιλικαῖσι καὶ παιδεύμασιν (cf. *Acts* 7:22). On this terminology see W. C. van Unnik's article *Tarsus of Jerusalem: the City of Paul's Youth*, in his *Sparsa Collecta* I, Leiden 1973, 259-320, especially 274 ff.

Ad v. 40 ἐξῆλθον οἴκων βασιλικῶν (said by Moses) it should have been noticed that this non-biblical remark has its exact parallel in *Jubilees* 47:10 ''you went forth from the royal palace''.

Vv. 48-50 ... ἰδὼν ἄνδρας δύο, | μάλιστα δ' αὐτοὺς συγγενεῖς, πατουμένους | λέγω· κτλ. The mss. have παρουμένους. Wieneke

---

21) In Stählin and Früchtel's edition of Clement's *Stromateis*, vol. I, p. 97.

adopts Stephanus' conj. κακουμένους, Snell and Jacobson adopt
Dübner's πατουμένους. Jacobson translates this by 'fighting', but,
according to LSJ, πατέω has the meaning of "to tread upon, to
trample upon". Could it be that the manuscripts' παρουμένους is the
Doric form of πηρόω, 'to mutilate, to maim'? This fits the context,
and Doric forms do still occur in Hellenistic times[22]).

In vv. 60-62 the country of Moses' future wife, Sepphora, is
called Λιβύη, where οἰκοῦσιν ... Αἰθίοπες ἄνδρες μέλανες, whereas the
Bible calls it Midian, in NW-Arabia. This is rightly explained by
Jacobson against the background of the Jewish identification of
Sepphora with Moses' Ethiopian wife mentioned in *Numbers* 12:1
(γυναῖκα Αἰθιόπισσαν ἔλαβε). See on this theme the important article
by I. Lévi, *Moïse en Éthiopie*, Revue des études juives 53 (1907),
201-211, who discusses this passage of Ezekiel, and also T. Rajak,
Moses in Ethiopia: Legend and Literature, Journal of Jewish Studies 29
(1978), 111-122; cf. S. P. Brock, *Some Syriac Legends Concerning
Moses*, ibid. 33 (1982), 237-255[23]).

In vv. 68-89 we read:

> ἔ⟨δο⟩ξ’ ὄρους κατ’ ἄκρα Σιν⟨αί⟩ου θρόνον
> μέγαν τιν’ εἶναι μέχρι ’ς οὐρανοῦ πτύχας,
> 70 ἐν τῷ καθῆσθαι φῶτα γενναῖόν τινα
> διάδημ’ ἔχοντα καὶ μέγα σκῆπτρον χερί
> εὐωνύμῳ μάλιστα. δεξιᾷ δέ μοι
> ἔνευσε, κἀγὼ πρόσθεν ἐστάθην θρόνου.
> σκῆπτρον δέ μοι πάρδωκε καὶ εἰς θρόνον μέγαν
> 75 εἶπεν καθῆσθαι. βασιλικὸν δ’ ἔδωκέ μοι
> διάδημα καὶ αὐτὸς ἐκ θρόνων χωρίζεται.
> ἐγὼ δ’ ἐσεῖδον γῆν ἅπασαν ἔγκυκλον
> καὶ ἔνερθε γαίας καὶ ἐξύπερθεν οὐρανοῦ,
> καί μοί τι πλῆθος ἀστέρων πρὸς γούνατα
> 80 ἔπιπτ’, ἐγὼ δὲ πάντας ἠριθμησάμην,
> κἀμοῦ παρῆγεν ὡς παρεμβολὴ βροτῶν.
> εἶτ’ ἐμφοβηθεὶς ἐξανίσταμ’ ἐξ ὕπνου.

---

22) See J. H. Moulton-W. F. Howard, *A Grammar of New Testament Greek* II,
Edinburgh 1929, Register *s.v.* Doric.

23) There is also no reference to F. M. Snowden, *Blacks in Antiquity. Ethiopians
in the Greco-Roman Experience*, Cambridge (Mass.) 1971.

Moses' father-in-law, Raguel, reacts with the words:

ὦ ξένε, καλόν σοι τοῦτ' ἐσήμηνεν θεός·
ζώην δ', ὅταν σοι ταῦτα συμβαί⟨ν⟩η ποτέ.
85 ἀρά γε μέγαν τιν' ἐξαναστήσεις θρόνον
καὶ αὐτὸς βραβεύσει καὶ καθηγήση βροτῶν.
τὸ δ' εἰσθεᾶσθαι γῆν ὅλην τ' οἰκουμένην
καὶ τὰ ὑπένερθε καὶ ὑπὲρ οὐρανὸν θεοῦ·
ὄψει τά τ' ὄντα τά τε πρὸ τοῦ τά θ' ὕστερον.

My own interpretation of this fascinating non-biblical passage has been elaborated elsewhere (see note 17) and can be summarized as follows. This is one of the earliest post-biblical throne-visions of which there are so many in the later so-called *merkavah*-literature (*merkavah* = throne)[24]. All this literature is based upon the biblical Ezekiel chapter one, in which the prophet has a vision of a mighty throne and of God in human shape upon that throne. Speculations about the throne and the heavenly abodes and the outward appearance of God gave rise to a strong mystical current in late antique and early medieval Judaism[25]. But that is not the only component in this scene. In early post-biblical Judaism there was, in some circles, a tradition in which the highest angel, called 'the angel of the Lord' in the Old Testament, was seen as God's primary or sole helper and allowed to share in God's divinity. It was part of this tradition that a human being, as the hero or exemplar of a particular group, could ascend to become one with this figure, as Enoch or Moses. So these angelic mediators often began as humans and later achieved a kind of divine status in some communities. They had charge over the world and became close to being anthropomorphic hypostases of God himself[26]. That Moses

24) Now most of these treatises have been conveniently edited by P. Schäfer, *Synopse zur Hekhalot-Literatur*, Tübingen 1982.

25) See G. Scholem, *Major Trends in Jewish Mysticism*, New York 1941; the same, *Jewish Gnosticism, Merkabah Mysticism and Talmudic Tradition*, New York 1965²; I. Gruenwald, *Apocalyptic and Merkavah Mysticism*, Leiden 1980.

26) See A. F. Segal, *Two Powers in Heaven*, Leiden 1977; the same, *Ruler of This World: Attitudes About Mediator Figures and the Importance of Sociology for Self-Definition*, in E. P. Sanders (ed.), *Jewish and Christian Self-Definition* II, London 1981, 245-268. See now also J. E. Fossum, *The Name of God and the Angel of the Lord*, diss. Utrecht 1982, *passim* (to be published Tübingen 1985).

was qualified for such a position is comprehensible in itself and was further suggested by the fact that twice he is called 'god' in the book of *Exodus* (4:16 "you will be a god to Aaron", and 7:1 "I make you a god to Pharaoh"; these are words spoken by God). That Moses was indeed deified in some Jewish circles is beyond any doubt. In his important article *Moses as God and King*, Wayne Meeks has proved this with a wealth of material[27]). Another serious candidate was Enoch (see *Genesis* 5:24 "Enoch walked with God. Then he vanished because God took him away"). Hence it is no great surprise that the most striking parallels, even in details, to this dream-vision of Moses can be found in the Enochic literature, especially in the Hebrew Book of Enoch (or 3 Enoch), where Enoch is identified with Metatron (= μετάθρονος or σύνθρονος, sc. θεοῦ)[27a]), the highest angel. Metatron is called the 'little Yahweh' which is exactly what Moses is in Ezekiel. It is probable that there was a certain rivalry between Moses and Enoch/Metatron in this function[28]). Be that as it may, Moses is here clearly envisaged as God's viceregent and plenipotentiary who rules over the world from God's throne.

Jacobson's interpretation must be gathered from both his commentary (89-97) and his long article *Mysticism and Apocalyptic in Ezekiel the Tragedian* in ICS 6 (1981), 272-293. It is diametrically opposed to my interpretation. He repeatedly emphasizes the *anti*-mystical character of our Ezekiel's description of Moses and stresses the playing down of anything supernatural or divine in Moses as a characteristic of the play as a whole, and especially of this scene. The many other stories of heavenly ascension by Moses, Jacobson says, "speak of a real ascension, not a visionary one. None reports his ascension as a dream. (...) In other words, Ezekiel deliberately chose to portray the 'ascension' as an imaginary event" (*art. cit.* 277). In Ezekiel we find a conscious rejection of the

---

27) In J. Neusner (ed.), *Religions in Antiquity. Essays in Memory of E. R. Goodenough*, Leiden 1968, 354-371. See now also G. Mussies, *The Interpretatio Iudaica of Thot-Hermes*, in M. Heerma van Voss e.a. (edd.), *Studies in Egyptian Religion Dedicated to Professor Jan Zandee*, Leiden 1982, 89-120. The publications of Scholem, Gruenwald, Segal and Meeks mentioned in nn. 25-27 are nowhere mentioned by Jacobson.

27a) See S. Lieberman, *Metatron, the meaning of his name and his functions*, Appendix in I. Gruenwald, *Apocalyptic and Merkavah Mysticism* 235-241.

28) See my *De joodse toneelschrijver Ezechiël* (n. 17) 105 f.

legend that Moses actually ascended to heaven, beheld God, etc. The reason for this rejection is to be found in the Bible itself. In *Numbers* 12:6-8 God says: "If any man among you is a prophet I make myself known to him in a vision, I speak to him in a dream. Not so with my servant Moses: he is at home in my house; I speak with him face to face, plainly and not in riddles, and he sees the form of the Lord". The downright fact that in Ezekiel God *does* make himself known to Moses in a vision and speaks to him in a dream makes all this "no more than the substance of a dream" (*ibid.* 278). So actually Ezekiel's account should be read as polemic against the notion of Moses' divinization and cosmic kingship and against throne-mysticism.

I take exception to this interpretation, ingenious though it is, for the following reasons. In the play itself, so far as we have it, there is not the slightest indication that this scene should be interpreted in this way. Only the Jewish part of Ezekiel's audience (or of his reading public), if well acquainted with the book of Numbers, might have caught the subtle hint. For his non-Jewish, Greek public, which— as Jacobson himself says—must have been the most important part of his addressees, this dream could have been nothing else than a vision of Moses' future exaltation to cosmic rulership, to be exercised from God's throne. Since the play draws its biblical material only from the first fifteen chapters of *Exodus*, it is unthinkable that *Numbers* 12:6-8 could have been brought in somewhere. But without that, none of his Greek audience could be expected to see this supposed point. Moreover, would not Ezekiel completely overshoot his mark by representing his hero as a kind of megalomaniac, dreaming about his exaltation to divine status? If that was the point Ezekiel wanted to make, he could have made it by having Raguel say in his interpretation that Moses was completely mistaken. But Raguel says nothing of the sort. He emphasizes that Moses will establish a great throne and also become a great prophet. Raguel's interpretation seems to give more weight to the prophetic element, because, as Jacobson himself notes, "the royal aspect of the dream is straightforward and simple and requires no elaborate interpretation. The mantic aspect is not so clearcut and demands more detailed attention" (*ibid.* 288). So once more we find that the play itself does not offer us a clue to an anti-mystical interpretation, or rather an explanation directed against notions of Moses' heavenly status. As to *Numbers* 12:6-8, this text would no more have inhibited Ezekiel from presenting his view in the form of a dream-vision than the prohibition of animal worship in *Exod.* 20:4-5 inhibited his contemporary Artapanus from depicting Moses as the founder of the Egyptian animal cults (Eusebius, *Praep. Ev.* IX 27). In the light of the studies by Segal and Fossum (although they do not mention Ezekiel), one can only say that Jacobson is mistaken when he states: "all the mysticism of the Philonic accounts is lacking in the *Exagoge*" (*ibid.* 273), or: "the 'non-mystical character of Ezekiel's description may be appreciated by contrasting it to Philo's observation that Moses' ascent at Exod. 24 is his divinization" (*ibid.* 290 n. 13)[29]). I think the contrary is true.

Let us now look at some minor details of this passage. In v. 68 the manuscripts' reading ἐξ ὄρους κατ' ἄκρας ἵνου was brilliantly emended by Dübner to ἔ⟨δο⟩ξ' ὄρους κατ' ἄκρα Σιν⟨αί⟩ου. Jacobson still has doubts about Σιναίου, since a medieval (?) Hebrew translation of this verse only has 'a high mountain'[30]), and he tentatively proposes ὄρους κατ' ἄκρον αἰπεινοῦ (200 n. 2). That might be correct, but it should be said that there is a traditional link between Sinai and throne-visions in early Jewish literature[31]). Moreover, Ginzberg quotes rabbinic traditions about a pre-Exodus Sinai-ascent by Moses including a throne-vision[32]). In the ancient Near East God's throne was often envisaged as occupying the top of a high mountain[33]). For the imagery of the passage as a whole a reference

29) The reference is to *Quaestiones in Exodum* II 40. For a contrary interpretation of this and similar passages in Philo see my *Moses' Throne-Vision in Ezekiel the Dramatist* (n. 17).

30) A. Jellinek, *Beth ha-Midrasch* V, Jerusalem 1967 (repr. of the 1872 ed.), 159. Interestingly enough, the Hebrew manuscript translates only vv. 68-89! It is astonishing that, although this Hebrew translation was published already 110 years ago, Jacobson is the first to notice its existence.

31) See e.g. D. J. Halperin, *The Merkabah in Rabbinic Literature*, New Haven 1980, 128-133.

32) L. Ginzberg, *The Legends of the Jews*, 7 vols., Philadelphia 1909-1938, II (1920) 304-309 and V (1925) 416-418 n. 117.

33) See G. Widengren, *Psalm 110 und das sakrale Königtum in Israel*, in P. A. H. Neumann (ed.), *Zur neueren Psalmenforschung*, Darmstadt 1976, 191.

to H. P. l'Orange, *Studies on the Iconography of Cosmic Kingship in the Ancient World*, Oslo 1953, would have been in order[34]).

The use of μάλιστα in v. 72 is curious. As in v. 49 (ἄνδρας δύο, | μάλιστα δ' αὐτοὺς συγγενεῖς, πατουμένους), it must have here the sense of 'nota bene' which is not attested elsewhere, although μάλιστα tends to become a particle giving emphasis to the words immediately preceding or following it; see W. Bauer-W. F. Arndt-F. W. Gingrich-F. W. Danker, *A Greek-English Lexicon of the New Testament and Other Early Christian Literature*, Chicago 1979, s.v. (H. Thesleff's discussion of μάλιστα in his *Studies on the Greek Superlative*, Helsingfors 1955, 79-92, deals only with the classical usage and sheds no light on these passages). Here, however, this emphasis is not called for, since the holding of the sceptre in the left hand was quite normal; see l'Orange, *op. cit.* 154 *et al*[35]). On 139 ff. l'Orange discusses the symbolism of the raising of the right hand, the σύμβολον σωτηρίας, which is relevant to vv. 172-173 δεξιᾷ δέ μοι ἔνευσε.

In v. 174 θρόνος is used in the singular, in v. 176 in the plural without any obvious change in meaning. This is parallelled in *Sapientia Salomonis* 9:4 and 10 (and compare the plural θρόνοι in Aeschylus' *Eumenides* 18 and 29 with the singular in exactly the same context in Euripides' *Iphigeneia Taur.* 1254 f.). For the poetic use of the plural instead of the singular, the so-called *amplificatio*, see Kühner-Gerth (n. 44) I 18-9 and Schwyzer, *Gramm.* II 42-4.

Ad vv. 79-80 Jacobson rightly refers to Psalm 147:4 (LXX 146:4 ὁ ἀριθμῶν πλήθη ἄστρων) but fails to mention that this counting of the multitudes of the stars is *God*'s activity and that this divine activity is ascribed to Enoch/Metatron in *3 Enoch* 46:1-2 with an explicit reference to Psalm 147. His remark, "Ezekiel distinctly limits the obeisance to a τι πλῆθος ἀστέρων, which does not seem equivalent to 'all the stars', nor does he mention the sun and moon", is quibbling. The χἀμοῦ παρῆγεν of the mss. was emended to χἀμοὶ παρῆγεν by Stephanus (adopted by Kuiper and Wieneke), but Mras, Snell, and Jacobson retain it. Mras translates: "und von

---

34) I owe this reference to my colleague Prof. Maarten J. Vermaseren. For the diadem see also H. W. Ritter, *Diadem und Königsherrschaft*, München 1965.

35) See also J. W. Salomonson, *Chair, Sceptre and Wreath. Historical Aspects of Their Representation on Some Roman Sepulchral Monuments*, Amsterdam 1956.

mir [meinem Sitz] aus zog die Sternenschar vorüber'', but that is forced, and Jacobson's "they paraded past me" ignores the problem. Renehan's καὶ ἰδού is unnecessary[36]). κἀμοί gives the least problems from a palaeographical point of view and yields good sense.

As to vv. 85-86, Jacobson discusses the problem whether one should read θρόνον or θρόνου, and what the meaning of ἐξαναστήσεις is, but he does not discuss the related matter of whether the sentence is a question and what is the meaning of the initial ἆρά γε. The context (sc. the interpretation of a dream) makes it clear that it is not a question—here Jacobson rightly sides (in his translation, not in the printed Greek text!) with Kuiper and Wieneke against Mras and Snell. Therefore, ἆρά γε must be here equivalent to ἄρα γε, expressing a lively feeling of interest; see J. D. Denniston, *The Greek Particles*, Oxford 1954², 43.

The formula τά τ' ὄντα τά τε πρὸ τοῦ τά θ' ὕστερον (v. 89) and its variations are discussed by W. C. van Unnik, *A Formula Describing Prophecy*, in his *Sparsa Collecta* II, Leiden 1980, 183-193[37]).

Jacobson offers a brilliant emendation for the difficult δωρημάτων in v. 106 μνησθεὶς δ' ἐκείνων καὶ ἔτ' ἐμῶν δωρημάτων, sc. θεός (one expects 'promises', not 'gifts'). He suggests ἐμῶν δὴ ῥημάτων, which to my mind is much more feasible than his attempt to prove that τὰ ἐμὰ δωρήματα means here "the gifts that I have received" (109-112). Nevertheless, I think that Jacobson too easily dismisses the probability that passages like Josephus' *Ant.* II 212 καὶ τοῖς προγόνοις αὐτῶν[38]) δωρησάμενος(sc. θεός) τὸ γενέσθαι τοσοῦτον πλῆθος αὐτοὺς ἐξ ὀλίγων may be a support for δώρημα = 'promise' here (205 n. 49).

Vv. 113-114 οὐχ εὔλογος πέφυκα, γλῶσσα δ' ἐστί μοι | δύσφραστος, ἰσχνόφωνος. Jacobson rightly says that this is based upon *Exod.* 4:10 οὐχ ἱκανός εἰμι (...). ἰσχνόφωνος καὶ βραδύγλωσσος ἐγώ εἰμι, but wrongly thinks (204 n. 32) that Ezekiel's οὐκ εὔλογος is his version of *Exod.* 6:12 ἐγὼ δὲ ἄλογός εἰμι, for mss. F and M and some minuscles of the LXX read in *Exod.* 4:10 οὐκ εὔλογος instead of οὐχ

---

36) R. Renehan, *Studies in Greek Texts*, Göttingen 1976, 68 f.

37) In his criticisms of C. Holladay, I happen to fully agree with Jacobson; see my articles in n. 17.

38) *Sc.* Abraham, Isaac and Jacob, who are the ἐκεῖνοι in v. 106 of Ezekiel.

ἱκανός. This variant reading may have been Ezekiel's text, the more so since Philo (*Vita Mosis* I 83), too, has it[39]).

Ad v. 134 πηγαί τε πᾶσαι καὶ ὑδάτων συστήματα, it should be noted that it is either a quotation from or quoted by Ps-Aeschylus 8 (*ap.* Ps-Justin, *De monarchia* 2, and Clemens Alexandrinus, *Strom.* V 14, 131, 1) καὶ πᾶσα πηγὴ χῦδατος συστήματα.

Vv. 133-151 enumerate the ten plagues in a different order from the account in *Exodus* itself. Jacobson refers to parallels for this different order in *Jubilees*, Artapanus and Philo, but the same phenomenon can be found already in Psalms 78:43 ff. and 105: 28 ff.[40]). Jacobson's discussion of the reasons for this deviation from the Exodus account (114-115) is excellent.

The meaning of σκνίψ (or κνίψ) in v. 135 is not certain. In the LXX of *Exod.* 8:16 (= LXX 8:12) it is the translation of a Hebrew word for a kind of mosquito. But the *Suda s.v.* σκνίψ says it is a ζῷον μικρὸν ξυλοφάγον (LSJ *s.v.*: an insect found under the bark of trees, eaten by the woodpecker). This uncertainty is reflected in Jacobson's book in that he translates it by 'lice' in his translation, but by 'fleas' in his commentary (115). Jacobson criticizes Sutton by stating: "When D. F. Sutton writes, 'LSJ incorrectly reports the accusative ... as σκνῖπας' (at *Exagoge* 135), 'σκνῖπας is guaranteed by the meter', he himself is wrong (*Glotta* 55 (1977) 212). As the verse stands in our manuscripts σκνῖπας is guaranteed by the meter. It is for this reason that Snell posits the lacuna" (206 n. 5). Snell (*Glotta* 44 (1967) 29) assumes a lacuna because σκνῖπας, not σκνίπας, is correct and would be metrically impossible. Hence he proposes

βατράχων τε πλῆθος ⟨–∪–×–∪–
×–∪–⟩ καὶ σκνῖπας ἐμβαλῶ χθονί.

I agree with Jacobson that these metrical problems should not lead us to assume a lacuna but I would prefer J. Strugnell's βατράχων τε πλῆθος σκνῖπά τ' ἐμβαλῶ χθονί[41]).

---

39) Thus E. Bickerman, *Some Notes on the Transmission of the Septuagint*, in his *Studies in Jewish and Christian History* I, Leiden 1976, 145.

40) See J. L. Mihelic-G. E. Wright in the *Interpreters Dictionary of the Bible* III (1962), 823.

41) J. Strugnell, Notes on the Text and Metre of Ezekiel the Tragedian's *Exagoge*, HThR 60 (1967), 451 n. 6 (449-457).

In vv. 149 f. God says to Moses: Φαραὼ δὲ βασιλεὺς πείσετ' οὐδὲν ὧν λέγω, | πλὴν τέκνον αὐτοῦ πρωτόγονον ἕξει νεκρόν. This raises the question whether πείσεται comes from πάσχω or from πείθω. Although rejected by Kuiper and Wieneke, Jacobson defends the thesis that the sentence means, ''Pharaoh will not suffer any of the plagues I have mentioned'', which has some slight support from Jewish midrashim. But (a) this contradicts the biblical tale (*Exod.* 11:9 has: οὐκ εἰσακούσεται ὑμῶν Φαραώ), as Jacobson himself is aware (119), and (b) the following v. 151 καὶ τότε φοβηθεὶς λαὸν ἐκπέμψει ταχύ makes it more probable that what is meant here is, ''Pharaoh will not pay heed to anything said to him''.

V. 156 says that the people should mark the doorposts with blood ὅπως παρέλθῃ σῆμα δεινὸς ἄγγελος and in v. 186 in the same context ὅπως παρέλθῃ θάνατος Ἑβραίων ἄπο, whereas in *Exodus* 12 it is the Lord himself, not an angel or death that is the actor. Jacobson (209 n. 8) rightly refers to rabbinic debates over the issue. The same is also found in a variant reading in *Targum Neofiti I* of *Exod.* 12:13 ''and the destroying angel who is appointed over death will not have power to injure you'', and in the Samaritan *Memar Marqah* I 9 (see J. E. Fossum, *The Name of God and the Angel of the Lord*, diss. Utrecht 1982, 244).

The non-biblical notion that the objects taken from the Egyptians by the Jews at the exodus are in fact a payment for all the work done by the Jews in Egypt (v. 165-166 ἵνα | ⟨ἀνθ'⟩ ὧν ἔπραξαν μισθὸν ἀποδῶσιν βροτοῖς) is amply discussed by Jacobson (126 f.), but he has no reference to the article by the Dutch Jewish scholar E. Stein, *Ein jüdisch-hellenistischer Midrasch über den Auszug aus Ägypten*, Monatsschrift für Geschichte und Wissenschaft des Judentums 78 (1934), 570 ff.[42]. This is actually one of the very few publications on Ezekiel missed by Jacobson. In general, his coverage of the secondary literature is very complete.

The construction of the verbs in vv. 180-183 is remarkable:

οὕτως φάγεσθε ταῦτα· περιεζωσμένοι
καὶ κοῖλα ποσσὶν ὑποδέδεσθε καὶ χερί
βακτήριον ἔχοντες. ἐν σπουδῇ τε γάρ
βασιλεὺς κελεύσει πάντας ἐκβαλεῖν χθονός.

42) See also R. Le Déaut, *Targum du Pentateuque* II, Paris 1979, 30 n. 92.

Jacobson suggests (211 n. 44) that ὑποδέδεσθε "might govern, in a kind of zeugma, both κοῖλα ποσσίν and χερὶ βακτήριον with ἔχοντες merely tacked on". When discussing Hebraisms in Ezekiel (in the introduction, 43), however, he suggests this might be a case of the use of the participle as a finite verb (which is common in post-biblical Hebrew). If this is a case of Semitism at all, it is the participle as an imperative: the future form φάγεσθε has an imperative function (as so often in the LXX) and ὑποδέδεσθε is an imperative. The use of the participle as an imperative is a common phenomenon in Mishnaic Hebrew and in Hebraizing Greek[43]. But I would rather take this as an instance of ellipsis of the imperative of εἶναι, which occurs also, for instance, in another Jewish-Hellenistic poem, Ps-Phocylides 57 μὴ προπετὴς ἐς χεῖρα[44]).

In the following line, v. 184, the manuscripts continue: κεχλήσεται δὲ πᾶς, καὶ ὅταν θύσητε δέ, | δέσμην λαβόντες κτλ. In view of the context, κεχλήσεται δὲ πᾶς should mean "and each shall be summoned", but Strugnell (see n. 41) has argued that κεχλήσεται can only be translated by 'will be named'; only κληθήσεται could mean 'will be summoned". Hence he suggests that an original κεχλήσεται δὲ πάσχ'· ὅταν θύσητε δέ was wrongly divided up into πᾶς χόταν → πᾶς καὶ ὅταν. His conjecture κεχλήσεται δὲ πάσχ' (= πάσχα) has been adopted by Snell, but Jacobson once again, like Mras, defends the mss. He points out the fact that "virtually every detailed Jewish account of the Passover from antiquity lays stress on its universal application, i.e. that *all* are solicited to perform the sacrificial rite" (133). Moreover, it is odd to say in v. 184 'it will be called Pascha', when the name Pascha has already been mentioned in v. 157. This seems to be convincing, but the καὶ ... δέ in καὶ ὅταν θύσητε δέ remains problematic[44a]). Jacobson does not

43) D. Daube, *Participle as Imperative in 1 Peter*, in E. G. Selwyn, *The First Epistle of Peter*, London 1946 (repr. 1964), 467-488. M. H. Segal, *Grammar of Mishnaic Hebrew*, Oxford 1927, 159 (par. 330). N. Turner, *A. Grammar of New Testament Greek III: Syntax*, Edinburgh 1963, 343 (with lit. in n. 1).

44) See my *The Sentences of Pseudo-Phocylides*, Leiden 1978, 152 and the discussion of this phenomenon in R. Kühner-B. Gerth, *Ausführliche Grammatik der griechischen Sprache* II 2, Hannover-Leipzig 1904 (repr. Darmstadt 1966) 42, and in Turner, *op. cit.* (n. 43) 303, 308, 310.

44a) The examples of καὶ ... δέ mentioned by Denniston, *Greek Particles* 200-202, are all of a different category.

discuss this problem. It might be solved either by deleting καί, as Dindorf proposed, or by changing δέ into δεῖ and the following λαβόντες into λαβόντας, with Stephanus: κεκλήσεται δὲ πᾶς· καὶ ὅταν θύσητε, δεῖ | δέσμην λαβόντας χερσὶν ὑσσώπου κόμης | εἰς αἷμα βάψαι καὶ θιγεῖν σταθμῶν δυοῖν. Nevertheless, the fact that the corresponding biblical text, *Exod.* 12:11, has πάσχα ἐστὶν κυρίῳ makes Strugnell's emendation extremely attractive. After all, κεκλήσεται δὲ πάσχα may just mean: 'then it will be Pesach'. For this weakened use of καλεῖσθαι as an equivalent of εἶναι see LSJ *s.v.* II 2.

V. 190 κακῶν γὰρ τῶνδ' ἀπαλλαγήσεται is hard to translate. Jacobson does not discuss the problem but translates: "for you shall receive release from these evils". Mras and Snell retain the manuscripts' reading and Mras *ad locum* remarks: "unpersönlich: Befreiung wird stattfinden", but there is little support for this. Kuiper changed the whole sentence into κακῶν γάρ ἐστι τῶνδ' ἀπαλλαγή. Wieneke reads ἀπαλλαγήν τέ σοι, with ἀπαλλαγήν depending upon the verb διδοῖ in the next line. The best thing is to read ἀπαλλαγήσετε (with the inferior manuscripts): "you will be released". Jacobson does translate it this way, but he prints ἀπαλλαγήσεται. The ending -ήσεται has originated from the ending of the previous line: βρωθήσεται[45]). This assimilation was of course furthered by the fact that from the third or second cent. B.C. onwards there was no longer a difference in pronunciation between αι and ε; see F. Blass-A. Debrunner-F. Rehkopf, *Grammatik des neutestamentlichen Griechisch*, Göttingen 1975[14], par. 25.

In vv. 193-4 ἀφώρμησεν δόμων | βασιλεὺς Φαραὼ μυρίων ὅπλων μέτα, we have a good instance of the use of ὅπλα for ὁπλῖται; see LSJ *s.v.* III 4.

Ad v. 203 μυριάδες⟨ἦσαν⟩ ἑκατὸν εὐάνδρου λέω, Jacobson rightly refers to the striking parallel in *Jubilees* 48:14, where the number of Egyptians destroyed in the sea is given as one million[46]). It should be noted that also elsewhere in Jewish literature there is speculation about the number of drowned Egyptians: Josephus, *Antiquitates* II 324 and *Mekhilta, Beshallach* 2 (I p. 202 Lauterbach).

---

45) Another solution is to read, as Stephanus proposed, ἀπαλλαγὴ ἔσσεται, with synizesis.
46) See my *De joodse toneelschrijver Ezechiël* (n. 17) 99.

V. 210 says the Israelites were ἄνοπλοι when they left Egypt, whereas the Hebrew Bible says they were well armed (*Exod.* 13:18 ḥamushim). Although most ancient translations have a word meaning 'armed' here, the LXX has πέμπτη δὲ γενεά, deriving the Hebrew word from ḥamesh, 'five'. Possibly this induced Ezekiel, Josephus (*Ant.* II 321) and others to deny the Jews weapons, as Jacobson rightly remarks (216 n. 53). The uncertainty about the exact meaning of the Hebrew at *Exod.* 13:18, the discussion of it in early Jewish literature (e.g. *Mekhilta, Beshallach* 1, I p. 174 f. Laut.) and the divergent consequences thereof have recently been masterfully examined by R. Le Déaut, *A propos du Targum d'Exode 13, 18: La Tôrah, arme secrète d'Israël*, in M. Carrez-J. Dorez-P. Grelot (edd.), *De la Tôrah au Messie (Mélanges Henri Cazelles)*, Paris 1981, 525-533 (531 n. 7 on Ezekiel).

V. 214 ἡμᾶς δὲ χάρμα πάντας εἶχεν ἐν μέρει is translated by Jacobson as "We in contrast were delighted". But χάρμα here is 'malicious pleasure', 'Schadenfreude', as it is in Aeschylus' *Persae* 1034. This instance could be added to Jacobson's impressive list (136-138) of echoes of the *Persae* in this messenger's report by a member of the defeated nation in the *Exagoge*.

There is a crux in vv. 221-222 καί τις ἐξαίφνης μέγας | στῦλος νεφώδης ἐστάθη πρὸ γῆς, μέγας, | παρεμβολῆς ἡμῶν τε καὶ Ἑβραίων μέσος. Jacobson only says, "πρὸ γῆς μέγας makes no sense. We should probably adopt some adjective like Kuiper's πυριφλεγής or a shorter one which would allow us to keep μέγας" (214 n. 27). Kuiper's conjecture is based upon *Sapientia Salomonis* 18:3 πυριφλεγῆ στῦλον. I do not see why the second μέγας, again belonging to the same στῦλος, should be retained; it is too awkward. And Snell's μέλας (in *app. crit.*) does not get rid of the impossible πρὸ γῆς. Jacobson does not know the brilliant emendation proposed by E. Stein (*Een merkwaardige Griekse tragedie*, Hermeneus 9, 1936/37, 20), who reads πρὸ ἡμέρας instead of πρὸ γῆς μέγας. This is much closer to the original than Kuiper's πυριφλεγής, and it is in perfect agreement with the biblical account; note the mention of the φυλακὴ ἑωθινή in *Exod.* 14:24 in this context.

Ad vv. 225-226 Αἰγύπτῳ κακά | σημεῖα καὶ τερ⟨ά⟩ατ' ἐξεμήσατο it should be noted that ἐκμήδομαι does not occur in any of the lexicons. It is a *hapax* meaning 'to contrive, to devise', as was noted by D. F. Sutton, *Notes on the Vocabulary of Minor Tragic Poets*, Glotta 55 (1977), 209 (208-212; Sutton gives more instances of new words, new forms or new meanings in Ezekiel)[47]). Μήδομαι occurs frequently in classical poetry, and often composita with ἐκ were nothing more than strengthened forms of the simplex, especially in later Greek. Ἐκμήδομαι can also have been modelled upon a verb like ἐξευρίσκω which was current since Homer.

It could have been noted (against Wieneke) that in v. 239 φεύγωμεν οἴκοι πρόσθεν Ὑψίστου χέρας we either have a unique instance of πρόσθεν *cum accusativo* or else we have to change χέρας into χερός, as Stephanus did[48]).

In vv. 252-253 the mss. have καὶ ἐπίρρυτος | πέφυκε χλοίη θρέμμασιν χορτάσματα. Since there is a hiatus after καί, Wieneke proposed περίρρυτος, followed by Snell and Jacobson ("Wieneke's convincing emendation", 217 n. 1). But ἐπίρρυτος in the sense of 'overflowing, abundant' is much more fitting here than περίρρυτος which is mostly said of islands washed by the sea. Cf. the use of καρπὸς ἐπίρρυτος in Aeschylus' *Eumenides* 907. And there are other instances of un-classical hiatus in Ezekiel[49]), vv. 158, 235, 255. So we can retain the manuscripts' reading.

In v. 261 it is said of the phoenix: χάρα δὲ κοττοῖς ἡμέροις παρεμφερές. This is a good instance of *comparatio compendiaria* (against Wieneke 113): "His head was like that of domesticated cocks"; see Kühner-Gerth II 2, 310 f.[50]).

These notes do not detract anything from the great value of Prof. Jacobson's book. They are no more than minor supplements to a major commentary which is to be regarded as an important step forward in our study of this play.

---

47) Because the word is nowhere attested, Wieneke 102 changed it into τέρατ' ἐξεμηχανήσατο, unnecessarily.

48) *Ad* v. 250 see now also R. Le Déaut, *Targum du Pentateuque* I (1978), 56; II (1979), 130 n. 23; III (1979), 199 n. 36.

49) See also V. Schmidt, *Sprachliche Untersuchungen zu Herondas*, Berlin 1968, 75 n. 6.

50) There are two recent Italian publications on Ezekiel that I have been unable to obtain. Neither does Jacobson mention them. These are R. Anastasi, *Note di filologia greca 2: Ezechiele, Exagoghe*, SicGymn n.s. 26 (1973), 102-109, and C. K. Reggiani, *Per una revisione di Ezechiele tragico in chiave aristotelica*, Vichiana n.s. 4 (1975), 3-21.

5. THE ROLE OF WOMEN IN THE TESTAMENT OF JOB

The *Testament of Job (TJ)* is a writing that has the characteristics which we can also find in other Jewish 'testaments' of the Hellenistic-Roman period: a deathbed-scene, a retrospective view of his life by the dying protagonist, followed by ethical admonitions that derive from this life-story and finally death, burial, and lamentation[1]. This retrospect with admonitions occupies the greater part of the treatise and amply makes use of biblical material. So, as might be expected, *TJ* is based on the biblical book of Job, but it should be added immediately that this Testament adopts from the biblical story scarcely more than the framework; and much material of this story is not used at all. Especially of the many long speeches, little is taken over, notably even of God's speech in chapters 38-41, whereas motifs that play only a minor role in the biblical story are heavily emphasized or are strongly expanded in a haggadic way[2]. For instance, it is striking that the theme of the rebellious Job who protests against his sorry fate recedes completely to the background (and with it the question of the theodicy) and gives way to that of Job as a paragon of ὑπομονή, of patience and long-suffering, an image of Job that we know also from the New Testament, which is roughly contemporaneous with *TJ*, when in James 5:11 Job's ὑπομονή is held up as an example to be imitated by the readers.

Now it should not be forgotten that the great differences between *TJ* and the biblical story of Job are partly due to the fact that the author does not use the MT but the LXX[3], and the LXX version of Job is no less than 15 to 20 percent shorter than MT. Yet the changes made in the Job story by the LXX translator are mostly of quite another kind than those in *TJ*[4]. The LXX abbreviates often and expands only in some places (2:9 and 42:17), whereas the author of *TJ* not only abbreviates but also completely rewrites the whole story and does not shrink from drastic changes. Of this procedure of drastic rewriting, several examples could be given (a very striking example would be, e.g., the much expanded role of Satan, especially

1 See E. van Nordheim, *Die Lehre der Alten I: Das Testament als Literaturgattung im Judentum der hellenistisch-römischen Zeit*, Leiden 1980, 119-135. J. J. Collins, Structure and Meaning in the Testament of Job, *SBL Seminar Papers 1974*, Missoula 1974, I 37-39.
2 A survey of the deviations of *TJ* from the biblical story of Job can be found in D. Rahnenführer, Das Testament des Hiob und das Neue Testament, *ZNW* 62 (1971) 68-93, on p. 70. A discussion of some of these motifs in I. Jacobs, Literary Motifs in the Testament of Job, *JJS* 21 (1970) 1-10.
3 B. Schaller, Das Testament Hiobs und die Septuaginta-Übersetzung des Buches Hiob, *Biblica* 61 (1980) 377-406.
4 For the LXX see G. Gerleman, *Studies in the Septuagint I: The Book of Job*, Lund 1946; D. H. Gard, *The Exegetical Method of the Greek Translator of the Book of Job*. Philadelphia 1952; H. M. Orlinsky, Studies in the Septuagint of the Book of Job, *HUCA* 28 (1957) 53-74; 29 (1958) 229-271; 30 (1959) 153-167; 32 (1961) 239-268; 33 (1962) 119-151; 35 (1964) 57-78; 36 (1965) 37-47; H. Heater, *A Septuagint Translation Technique in the Book of Job*, Washington 1982.

in chapters 2-27). In this paper, however, we want to focus on one specimen of this haggadic procedure, *sc.* the role of women.

As is well-known, in the biblical book of Job women definitely do not play a prominent role. In 1:2.4.13.18 only the mere existence of Job's daughters is mentioned; in 2:9 his wife summons him to speak a word against God (lit. to bless God = to curse God) and die, and in 19:17 she is only mentioned in passing; in 31:9-10 Job says that, if another man's wife should succeed in seducing him, his own wife would have to perform a slave's labour for others; in 42:13-15 his three daughters are mentioned by name (Jemima, Keṣiʿa and Keren happukh) and they are said to be the most beautiful girls in the country and, remarkably enough, to share with their brothers in the inheritance. Apart from a couple of traditional phrases like 'widows and orphans' or 'who is born from a woman', not even one percent of the verses of the book of Job speak of women, his wives and his daughters. In the LXX this percentage is somewhat higher of course, but in essence the situation is the same. As a contrast to this, no less than 107 out of 388 verses in *TJ* deal with women, *i.e.* almost 30 times as much space as in the biblical book. What could be the reason for this and what image of women arises out of this conspicuous material? Let us first make an inventory of the data.

In 1:3 we read, besides the names of the seven sons (which do not figure in either MT or LXX)[5], those of the three daughters from his second wife, in conformity with the LXX: Hemera, as a translation of Jemima[6], Kasia as a transliteration of Keṣiʿa[7], and Amaltheias Keras, as a very free rendering of Keren happukh[8]; Keren happukh means 'horn (*i.e.* box) of mascara', Amaltheias Keras means 'horn of Amaltheia', who was the goat that nurtured Zeus on Crete when he was a little child and whose horn become a symbol of abundance: *cornucopia*[9]. In 1:6 the mother of these children is mentioned, Job's second wife, Dinah, the only daughter of the patriarch Jacob, a tradition that was already adumbrated in 1:1 where it is said that Job is also called Jobab, the second king of Edom (Gen. 36:33; cf. LXX Job 42:17d), which immediately gives the whole story a setting in the time of the patriarchs and makes Job, as a descendant of Esau, a descendant of Abraham as well. The tradition that Dinah was Job's wife is also

---

5 On the tendency to give names to nameless persons in the Bible see B. Heller, Die Scheu vor Unbekanntem, Unbenanntem in Agada und Apokryphen, *MGWJ* 83 (1939) 170-184; cf. B. M. Metzger, Names for the Nameless in the New Testament, in his *New Testament Studies, Philological, Versional and Patristic*, Leiden 1980, 23-45.
6 W. Pape - G. Benseler, *Wörterbuch der griechischen Eigennamen* I, Braunschweig 1933³ (=repr. Graz 1959), 459 mentions Hemera as a feminine proper name.
7 Pape - Benseler (n. 6) I 631 does mention Kasia as a topographical name (of a mountain and an island), not as a feminine proper name (although Kasios as a masculine proper name is common). But there is a ninth century Byzantine poetess called Kasia; see I. Rochow, *Studien zu der Person, den Werken und dem Nachleben der Dichterin Kasia*, Berlin 1967.
8 Further only attested as a toponym according to Pape - Benseler (n. 6) I 69.
9 On the names of the daughters see also K. Kohler, The Testament of Job, in *Semitic Studies in Memory of A. Kohut*, Berlin 1897, 288 ff.

known from Ps-Philo, *LAB* 8:7-8, *Gen. Rabba* 57:4, 76:9, Targ. Job 2:9, *et. al.*[10]. The name of Job's first wife we will discuss presently. In 7:5-11, in the franework of the story of Satan's repeated attempts to bring Job to apostasy, it is a significant feature that Job's true-hearted slave-girl does not recongnize Satan in the beggar at the gate. In her kindness she gives Satan *not* the burnt loaf that Job had ordered her to give him – of course, Job had seen through his disguise –, but she gives him a good loaf of her own. The Satan then criticizes her for her disobedience, she declares that he is right and gives him the charred loaf (a salient feature we will come back to). Striking too is that, where the LXX in 31:13 makes Job's slave-*girls* complain, 'who will provide for us from his meats that we may be filled?', the *TJ* puts these words in the mouth of his *slaves*, and adds a curse (13:4-5); at first sight this seems to be a change that is kindly towards women, but it is neutralized in the next chapter (14:4-5) that speaks about the (δια)γογγύζειν, the murmuring, of his female slaves, to which Job reacts by singing songs about the payment of recompense, accompanying himself on the harp.

These passages, however, are only trifles when compared to the extensive chapters devoted to Job's first wife, Sitidos. Let us begin with here name. Some translators call her Sitis, following their feeling for the Greek language that Sitidos must be the genitive of Sitis[11]. But in the mss. there is considerable confusion about the correct spelling of her name. Some read Sigidos, others Sitodos, or Sitida, or Sites, or Site, or Sitis, whilst some omit the name altogether. The reading Sitidos is more self-evident as the *lectio difficilior*, for copyists would have been more inclined to change this apparent genitive into the required nominative (Sitis) than the other way round. All the other forms are only variations upon these two alternatives. The reading Sitis is probably based upon the thought that this name must have been derived from Ausitis, the name of the country that Job came from (mentioned in LXX Job 1:1; 42:17b, as a translation of Uz). Even some modern scholars support this derivation[12], but it is unnecessary and improbable. Although the name Sitidos (or Sitis) does not occur elsewhere, the *Wörterbuch der griechischen Eigennamen* by Pape-Benseler (see n.6) mentions quite a number of (male) proper names and toponyms beginning with Σιτ- or Σιτι-, all of them deriving from σῖτος, 'bread', or σιτίζω, 'to give bread, to feed'. In view of the fact that in the story about Job's wife it is a dominant theme that she does every

---

10   This and other Job-haggada has been collected by L. Ginzberg in *The Legends of the Jews* II, Philadelphia 1920, 225-242, and V, Philadelphia 1925, 381-390. Much of it can be found in a long passage in Talmud Bavli, *Bava Bathra* 15a-16b, where *inter alia* there is much discussion of the question in which period Job had lived, the answers varying from patriarchal to postexilic times. Quite interesting is the remark by an anonymous rabbi (*BB* 15a) that in his view Job had never existed (*lo haya welo nibra*) but was only a *mashal*, a parabolic type, an acute remark which his colleagues do not appreciate.
11   So e.g. R. P. Spittler in J. H. Charlesworth (ed.), *The Old Testament Pseudepigrapha* I, New York 1983, 848 ff.
12   Spittler *ad* 25:1 (see n. 11), and B. Schaller *ad* 25:1 in *JSHRZ* III 3, Gütersloh 1979.

possible thing in order to be able to give bread to Job daily, I presume that this unusual name has some connection with this motif[13].

In ch. 21-25, the author states that Sitidos, since Job is sitting on the dung-heap, has been working as the slave of a rich man (cf. Job 31:9-10) in order to earn bread for Job and herself. When after some time her boss withholds Job's part of the bread, she shares her own meagre portion with her husband and, moreover, goes to the market in order to beg for the bread she wants to give to Job. When Satan disguises himself as a breadseller, Sitidos does not recognize him and begs him for bread. He first asks her for money, which she does not possess; then he asks for her hair in exchange for the bread. She thinks: 'What value to me is the hair of my head as compared to my hungry husband?' (23:9), so she has her coiffure removed by him[14]. When she has delivered the loaves to Job, she bursts into a bitter and desperate lamentation about herself. What is conspicuous in this lament (ch. 25) is that there is a sudden transition from the first to the third person in 25:1 and again a sudden transition from the third to the first person in 25:9. Vv. 25:1-8 are thought by some scholars to be a later interpolated lament *about* Job's wife. It has a poetic structure in which 6 times, after descriptions of her former wealth and happiness, there is the refrain, 'but now she sells her hair for loaves' (with minor variations). The fact that this 'hymn' is thematically related to the immediately preceding chapters and structurally related to a similar hymn on Job's fate by one of his friends (ch. 32, with the refrain, 'Where is now the glory of your throne?') seems to me to plead against this interpolation-hypothesis. Sitidos'lamentation ends with the words, 'Speak a word against the Lord and die', the only thing we hear her saying in the biblical book of Job (2:9), directly followed (and somewhat mitigated) by the remark, 'Then I too shall at last be freed from the despair about your bodily sufferings' (25:10). This remark emphasizes that even her call to speak a word against God arises from good intentions and from sheer despair about Job's misery. Then Job reveals to her that these words had been delivered to her by Satan, who at that very moment stood behind her in disguise (and about whom the author had said in 23:11 that he led her heart astray). It is he, says Job, who confuses her thoughts and who wishes that she behaves like a foolish woman who deceives her husband's integrity. So Job's wife is rather a victim than an agent in this first long passage devoted to her.

She returns in chs. 39-40, after Job's confrontation with his friends who are called kings here (ch. LXX Job 42:17e; in *TJ* 28:7 Job himself is called king of Egypt). There we read that Sitidos has run away from slavery because one even impeded her to go out of the house. She prostrates herself before the kings and

---

13   My colleague, Prof. T. Baarda, suggests that Sitidos might be a corruption of the Hebrew '*ishto*, 'his wife'.
14   Several texts show clearly that being shorn was the utmost disgrace to a woman: e.g. Aristophanes, *Thesm.* 830f.; Paul, 1 *Cor.* 11:6; Tacitus, *Germ.* 19; Apuleius, *Met*, 7.6.3.; Lucian, *Dial. meretr.* 5:3. See also S. Lieberman, Shaving of the Hair and Uncovering of the Face among Jewish Women, in his *Texts and Studies*, New York 1974, 52-56.

crying she points out to them her bitter poverty, whereupon one of them drapes his purple robe around her shoulders. She asks them to have their soldiers remove the ruins of the house that had collapsed on top of her children, so that she can bury their bones. Then Job intervenes by saying that such an action would be in vain since they would not find his children, for they had been taken up into the heavens by their creator (ἀνελήφθησαν, 39:12), an idea of bodily assumption into heaven which contrasts with that of Job's own death when only his soul is taken up into heaven (ch. 52). The kings declare him to be mad, but Job rises and prays to 'the Father' and says thereafter, 'Look toward the east and see my children crowned alongside the *doxa* of the Heavenly One' (40:3). Sitidos sees it, falls to the ground, and says, 'Now I know that I have a memorial with the Lord' (40:4). Then she goes to the stall of the cows that her masters had stolen from Job, lies down in one of the mangers, and dies cheerfully. When she is found dead, all the animals start weeping so loudly over her that the entire town comes to see what has happened. She is buried near the delapidated house, and the poor of the city sing a lamentation over her of which the author says that it has been written down in the *Paralipomena*[15], certainly a fictitious writing.

What is the picture that the author wishes to draw of this woman? There is little doubt that at first sight she is a sympathetic woman. With never-failing loyalty and sincere love she exerts herself to the utmost on behalf of her husband. Even the greatest possible humiliation, *i.e.* having her head shorn, she undergoes rather than letting him go hungry. Also her great care to have the bones of her children buried is a testimony that she lives up to the standards of Israel's piety. It is therefore, not without reason that both men and animals burst into lament when this noble woman is found dead. But there is also another side of the picture, *sc.* her 'lack of perception'[16]. The whole *TJ* is imbued with the contrast between the supramundane reality and this world where Satan is active. Job has insight into this distinction and he is contrasted with those who do not have this insight. This starts already in ch. 7 where his female slave does not recognize Satan in the beggar at the gate, wheras Job knew beforehand that it was Satan who hid behind that disguise. A second contrast that is much elaborated is that between Job and the kings. Time and again they wonder whether Job has gone insane. When Job says that his own throne is in heaven, and that his kingdom will last forever, Eliphas and the other ones think that his mental faculties are no longer intact (ch. 33). And when he says that his children have been taken up into heaven, they are convinced that he has gone mad. Their spiritual blindness and lack of insight, by which they become an easy prey for Satan, is a recurring theme in the episode of Job and the kings[17]. Although Job's wife is presented as a more sympathetic

15 Probably the *Paralipomena of Eliphaz*, which are mentioned in 41:6. The name of Eliphaz has probably dropped out by haplography since the first word of the next sentence is Eliphaz.
16 G. W. E. Nickelsburg, *Jewish Literature Between the Bible and the Mishnah*, London 1981, 245.
17 See J. J. Collins, Structure (n. 1) 42: 'The real issue between Job and his friends is awareness of heavenly reality'.

personality than the kings, in the final analysis for her, too, the verdict is valid that, in spite of her good intentions, she does not have awareness of and insight into the invisible background of the things that happen. She has no spiritual intelligence and in spite of her virtues she errs repeatedly. She does not perceive that she is led astray by Satan. It is Job who has to reveal that to her. She does not know that her children need not be buried. It is Job who has to disclose that to her. It is therefore not without reason that she is not, like Job, reinstated into her former splendor; unlike Job's wife in the biblical story, she dies before the deliverance out of the misery has arrived and so she makes way for no less a person than Dinah, Jacob's only daughter.

But, one could ask: why, then, is she assigned such a significant role when compared to the biblical story? That is because only in that way can she serve as a foil to show off Job's superior handling of the situation[18]. Athalya Brenner makes the following pertinent comments: 'She is used in order to create a symmetry in the plot, so that two mirror images complement eachother. Job and God are on the one side. Job is aware of the significance of the proceedings, because God has alerted him beforehand. The Satan and the wife are on the other side. The wife, however (like the servant girl earlier, a nice anticipatory touch), joins the side she is on unwittingly. A nice comment on religious awareness of males and females respectively, of the 'wise' and 'foolish' of wisdom literature in general. Again this is hardly complimentary towards women'[19]. However well and properly Sitidos fulfills her role as spouse of Job and as mother of her children, finally she belongs to the category of the ignorants and the fools whom the Satan can easily get into his grip. This is an image of women that is well-know to us from many other Jewish writings of the Hellenistic and Roman periods. Not only Philo and Josephus, who are notorious in this respect[20], but also Ecclesiastes, Ecclesiasticus, the Testament of Ruben, the Mishnah, and a great number of other sources present women as creatures who can easily be misled and seduced (and are easily seducing), who need to be protected against themselves and can best be kept inside the home as much as possible[21]. So we see that, although, on the one hand, the author of *TJ* has an open eye for the excellent qualities women can have as spouse and mother

---

18   See Collins, Structure (n. 1) 40.
19   Dr. Brenner wrote me this in a letter of April 20, 1986. I am very grateful to her for several valuable insights.
20   On Philo see e.g. I. Heinemann, *Philons griechische und jüdische Bildung*, Breslau 1932 (repr. Hildesheim 1962), 231-241; on Josephus e.g. A. Schlatter, *Die Theologie des Judentums nach dem Bericht des Josephus*, Gütersloh 1932, 148-149, 163-169.
21   See *inter alia* L. Swidler, *Women in Judaism. The Status of Women in Formative Judaism*, Metuchen 1976, L. J. Archer, The Role of Jewish Women in the Religion, Ritual and Cult of Graeco-Roman Palestine, in A. Cameron-A. Kuhrt (edd.), *Images of Women in Antiquity*, Kent 1983, 273-287; J. Leipoldt, *Die Frau in der antiken Welt und im Urchristentum*, Gütersloh 1962, 49-79. It is striking to see that in the Greek and Roman world there was a gradual movement from an inferior position of women towards a position of equality, whereas in Judaism the development was the other way round. See K. Thraede, Frau, *RAC* 8 (1972) 197-269; C. Schneider, *Kulturgeschichte des Hellenismus* I, München 1967, 78-117; L. Bringmann, *Die Frau im ptolemäisch-kaiserlichen Aegypten*, Bonn 1939, now superseded in many respects by S. B. Pomeroy, *Women in Hellenistic Egypt*, New York 1984.

(cf. Prov. 31), on the other hand he combines that with a low opinion of women as far as their spiritual abilities are concerned. She does not see where evil powers lie in wait, neither does she see what God is doing; she is spiritually blind. Kind though she may be, she is dull, and it is only fitting that it is the cows that are the first to bewail her death.

Sitidos, however, is not the only woman who plays a prominent role in *TJ*. There are also Job's daughters, not his daughters by Sitidos, but those by his second wife, Dinah. In ch. 46-53 they are the protagonists. There we read that Job divides his inheritance among his 7 sons, whereas his daughters receive nothing (in conformity with Num. 27; cf. m*BB* 9:1). When the girls raise a sad protest by saying, 'Are we not also your children? Why then did you not give us some of your goods?' (46:2), Job answers: 'I have not forgotten you, I have designated for you an inheritance that is better than that of your brothers' (46:3-4). It is clear that the conspicuous fact that in the biblical book of Job 42:15 his daughters are explicitly said to be the coheiresses of their brothers, is the starting-point of this passage. Job then asks his first daughter, Hemera, to get three golden boxes (or goldboxes, *i.e.* boxes with gold, see below p. 279) out of the treasury or crypt. Out of these boxes Job takes three girdles or sashes which the three daughters have to wear about their breasts. (It is very difficult to get a clear image of these girdles since the author uses a different word every time for them, except the word one would expect, *sc.* ζώνη. In 46:6 he uses χορδή = string, cord; in 48:1 σπάρτη = rope, cord; in 52:1 περίζωσις = belt, girdle; in 47:11 φυλακτήριον = amulet. In view of the fact that the objects designated are placed over the breast, what is rendered elsewhere by ζώνη, see e.g. Apoc. 1:13 and 15:6, I translate with 'girdle')[22]. These girdles are so radiant that no one can describe them, because they are not from the earth but from heaven, and sparks shoot from them like rays from the sun. Job tells his daughters to wear them over their breasts so that it may go well with them all the days of their life (46:9). Then his second daughter, Kasia, remarks that although Job had said, to be sure, that this inheritance is better than that of their brothers, yet to her mind they cannot possibly make a living from those strange girdles. Job answers: These girdles will enable you not only to live, but they will also lead you into 'the greater world', *i.e.* to live in the heavens. For these are the girdles that God himself had given to Job when he said to him: 'Arise, gird your loins like a man' (Job 38:3, 40:7)[23]. Job put them on and immediately he was healed in body and soul and God revealed to him the past and the future (a

---

22 On girdles in antiquity in general see W. Speyer, *Gürtel*, *RAC* 12 (1983) 1232-1266; for different types of girdles used by Jews see esp. S. Krauss, *Talmudische Archäologie* I, Leipzig 1910, 172-175. 613-618.
23 In the biblical text, the quotation continues, 'I shall question you, and you should answer me'. This second part of the quotation is in all the mss. of *TJ*, but does not make any sense in the context. It may be a later addition. See Schaller *ad* 47:5 in *JSHRZ* III 3, 368. On Job 38:3 in post-biblical literature see H. Kosmala, *Hebräer-Essener-Christen*, Leiden 1959, 217 f.

formula describing prophecy)[24]. These girdles, Job now says, will make you immune to the enemy (Satan) for it is a φυλακτήριον τοῦ πατρός (47:11), probably not 'an amulet of your father', but 'an amulet given by your Heavenly Father'[25]. 'Gird yourselves with them in order that you may be able to see those who are coming to take my soul to heaven' (47:11). When Hemera puts on her girdle, she receives another heart[26], so that she is no longer mindful of earthly things, and she sings a hymn to God in the language of the angels and in accord with the way the angels sing hyms (τῇ ἀγγελικῇ διαλέκτῳ and κατὰ τὴν τῶν ἀγγέλων ὑμνολογίαν). The Spirit lets her songs be inscribed on her garment (or on her *stele*, if one reads στήλη instead of στολή)[27]. When Kasia binds on her girdle, her heart changes as well, so that she no longer regards worldly things. She too becomes ecstatic and sings of the work of the exalted τόπος (= *maqom*, a well-known periphrasis for 'God') in the language of the ἀρχαί, a class of angels (cf. Rom. 8:38; 1 Cor. 15:24; Eph. 1:21,etc.; Col. 1:16,etc). If anyone wishes to know the work of the οὐρανοί (= *shamayim*, another periphrasis for 'God'), it can be found in the Hymns of Kasia, obviously another fictitious writing. When Amaltheias Keras binds on her girdle, her heart is changed as well, so that she keeps aloof from worldly matters, and she sings of the δεσπότης τῶν ἀρετῶν, 'Master of virtues' or 'Master of mighty deeds', in the language of the cherubim. The author concludes this scene by saying that whoever wants to see a trace of the *doxa* of the Father[28], will find it written down in the Prayers of Amaltheias Keras[29].

Quite unexpectedly, in the final three chapters (ch. 51-53) the 'I' is no longer Job but his brother, Nereus. He describes Job's final hours and burial. He says that together with God and the Holy Spirit he has been present at the angelic vocal performance of the daughters and that he has written down all hymns on the basis of the notes, *i.e.* probably the translations, that the sisters made for one another (cf. 1 Cor. 14:27-28). These are the great acts of God, he says, τὰ μεγαλεῖα τοῦ θεοῦ = *magnalia dei*. Three days later Job falls ill and he sees the angels who come for his soul. He gives a lyre to Hemera, a censer to Kasia, and a kettledrum to Amaltheias Keras, so that they may praise the angels who are coming to bring Job's soul to heaven. The three ladies see the gleaming chariots with the angels and they glorify them each one in her own heavenly tongue. Only the daughters,

---

24   See W. C. Unnik, A Formula Describing Prophecy, in his *Sparsa Collecta* II, Leiden 1980, 183-193.
25   For the apotropaic powers of magic girdles in many cultures see I. Scheftelowitz, *Die altpersische Religion und das Judentum*, Giessen 1920, 77 ff; also W. Speyer, Gürtel, *RAC*, XII (1983) 1234 ff.
26   The expression 'another heart' derives from 1 Sam. 10:9 where it is said of Saul at the moment he becomes ecstatic.
27   See the discussion of this problem in Schaller and Spittler *ad loc.* R. Reitzenstein, *Poimandres, Studien zur griechisch-ägyptischen und frühchristlichen Literatur*, Leipzig 1904, 57 n. 9 mentions a late Graeco-Egyptian parallel to the motif of a holy text being inscribed upon a garment.
28   The mss. read λοιπὸν ἴχνος ἡμέρας καταλαβεῖν τῆς πατρικῆς δόξης. The meaning of this, esp. of ἡμέρας (*om.* ms. V), is far from clear.
29   The references to fictitious writings are modelled upon OT passages like 1 Kings 14:29; 2 Chron. 35:25 *et al.*

no one else, see how Job's soul is taken up and ascends to the east by chariot. Job's body is buried, and at the burial the daughters lead the way, girded with their heavenly sashes and singing hymns to God. Job's brother and his sons raise a lament.

In my opinion we have here an image of women that is markedly different from that of Sitidos in the preceding chapters. Now John Collins remarks that what holds good for Job's wife and his servant, also applies to his daughters, sc. that they, in contrast to Job himself, only receive insight into the heavenly reality after Job has pointed out this reality to them or, in the case of the daughters, has given them the means to gain that insight. Collins says: 'Womankind in *Test. Job* symbolizes (. . .) the human state of ignorance'[30]. But this is too generalizing a statement in my opinion. The agreement or similarity between both groups of women does not go further than just the motif that Job's intervention is needed in order to help the women to gain insight. But Job's servant and his wife are enlightened only incidentally and momentarily, it is not a lasting insight which they obtain. Their heart is not changed, to put it in the terms of ch. 48-50. For that is what it turns on with the daughters: they undergo a radical and lasting change; in fact they become virtually heavenly beings. A number of elements in the story are indicative of that. Firstly there are the girdles. In my opinion these are golden girdles. For, in 46:5 it is stated that these three girdles are kept in τρία σκευάρια τοῦ χρυσοῦ, which, it is true, one might translate as 'the three golden boxes', but, since one rather expects then τρία σκευάρια χρυσᾶ, one may equally well translate 'the three boxes with gold', *i.e.* the three receptacles of golden objects. This perfectly fits in with the fact that in 46:6-7 it is said that sparks shoot from the girdles like rays from the sun and that no one could describe their beauty. This detail, combined with the fact that the girls have to wear these girdles around their breasts, makes one immediately think of two passages in the Apocalypse of John, *sc.* 1:13, where it is said of the heavenly Christ that he wears a golden girdle round his breast, and 15:6, where it is said of the seven angels that they had girdles of gold round their breasts. These two texts do not stand isolated; there are several other Jewish and Christian texts that speak of the golden girdles of heavenly beings[31]. This would seem to me, therefore, to be an indication that the 'changed heart' here means that their whole being has been transmuted from an earthly into a heavenly one, and that it is for that reason that it is said so explicitly three times that τὰ τῆς γῆς or τὰ κοσμικά are no longer live options for them[32].

Their heavenly status becomes still more evident by their newly acquired ability to speak in the languages of the angels. We meet here a Jewish notion, known also

---

30 J. J. Collins, Testaments, in M. E. Stone (ed.) *Jewish Writings of the Second Temple Period* (CRINT II 2), Assen - Philadelphia 1984, 352-3, idem, *Between Athens and Jerusalem*, New York 1983, 223.
31 See Speyer, *RAC* 12 (1982) 1251. 1253; add *Visio Dorothei* (Pap. Bodmer 29) 334.
32 Interesting in this connection is the interpolation of ms. V. at 48:1 where it is said of Hemera: καὶ παράχρημα ἔξω γέγονε τῆς ἑαυτῆς σαρκός.

from 1 Cor. 13:1, that the angels speak their own language and that the diverse classes of angels speak each of them their own dialect or tongue[33]. Almost superfluously it is added that the 3 sisters sing in accordance with the *hymnologia* of the angels[34]. Their ability to praise God in the language and in the way of the angels[35] actually indicates that they have already ascended from the earth and that they have their *politeuma* in heaven, to put it in a Pauline way (Phil. 3:20). The fact that in the final chapter (53) it is said that after Job's death his brother and his sons do nothing else than raising a lament together with the widows and orphans, whereas the 3 daughters cheerfully lead the burial singing hymns to God, indicates a radical reversal of the usual roles. For, whereas usually the giving utterance to laments was the role of women[36], here it is the men who play this role. In fact by doing so they betray a 'feminine' 'lack of perception', since they do not share in the joyful insight of their sisters into the glorious fate of their father's soul. And, it should be stressed, besides Job it is only the daughters who are able to see how their father's soul is brought to heaven by heavenly figures in gleaming chariots. Emphatically it is stated that no one else could see that (52:9), Nereus and Job's sons included. Nothing of this applies to Sitidos. And this essential difference makes it impossible, in my opinion, to speak in a generalizing way of women as symbols of ignorance in the *TJ*. In ch. 46-53 women play an extraordinarily positive role, in fact they play the leading part instead of Job, who is in these chapters no more than a supernumerary actor. It is not the sons but the daughters who rise to an almost superhuman spiritual level by means of the God-given magic belts, and it is they and not the men who gain insight therefore, and a permanent one at that, into the heavenly reality that is the background of the earthly one. One must say that this is an image of women that is rather unique in early Jewish literature.

It is for precisely that reason that some scholars have contested both the authenticity and the Jewish character of these chapters. Various arguments have been put forward against their authenticity[37]. These chapters could not have been written by the original authot of *TJ* for the following reasons: 1. In 1:2 Job wants to address his children because he has fallen ill, whereas in 52:1 he falls ill only three days *after* his address. 2. In 1:4-6 the author presents a concise summary of the chapters that will follow, approximately in these words: I will tell you all that the Lord has done to me and everything that has happened to me; this is out of tune with chs. 46-53 in which Job plays only a very insignificant role. 3. In ch. 51, where Nereus represents himself as the author of the book, he reports as the

---

33   See 1 *Hen.* 40; *Asc. Is.* 7:15; *Apoc. Abr.* 15:7; 17:1ff; *et al.* P. Billerbeck, *Kommentar zum Neuen Testament aus Talmud und Midrasch* III, München 1926, 449: J. Michl. Engel. *RAC* 5 (1962) 69; S. D. Currie, Speaking in Tongues. Early Evidence Outside the New Testament Bearing on 'Glossais Lalein', *Interpretation* 19 (1965) 274-294, esp. 281 ff.
34   I. Gruenwald, Angelic Song, *Enc. Jud.* 15 (1971) 144.
35   That it is praise of God that all is about is clear from the use of δοξολογεῖν in 49:2 and 30:2 and of τὰ μεγαλεῖα τοῦ θεοῦ in 51:4.
36   M. Alexiou, *The Ritual Lament in Greek Tradition*, Cambridge 1974, 10-18.
37   See most recently E. von Nordheim, *Die Lehre der Alten. I* (see n. 1), 131 f.

book's contents especially the translation of the hymns of the three daughters, in which they sang of the *magnalia dei*; this does not fit in with the contents of chs. 1-45. 4. In 45:1-3 Job draws the most important conclusions from the story of his life in the form of ethical admonitions: to do well to the poor, not to neglect the helpless, not to take foreign wives. These conclusions do not suit the contents of chs. 46-53. As a matter of fact one does not expect these chapters at all; one does expect a short report of Job's death, not a long report of his daughters' ecstasy. 5. The *ego* in chs. 1-45 is Job himself, the *ego* in chs. 46-53 is his brother, a quite unexpected turn. This cannot come from the same writer.

Not all these arguments are equally convincing. But it is clear that in 46:1 there occurs a *metabasis*, especially in view of the other *ego* in ch. 51-53. The differences, however, can also be explained from the fact that the author has joined different sources in a rather maladroit way[38]. In the same way the fact that a summary of one part of the book does not agree with the contents of the other part can be explained as well. There certainly is a clear tension between chs. 1-45 on the one hand and 46-53 on the other, and especially in view of the very different images of women in both parts it seems to be indubitable that both parts cannot have come from the same source. But one may assume that the Jewish redactor has used various haggadic traditions about Job and his family and has not ironed out the discrepancies everywhere. The fact that in Job 42:15 there is such an explicit mention of the exceptional fact that the daughters were fellow-heirs with their brothers could not fail to evoke haggadic elaboration of this motif. And the author/redactor did not let the opportunity slip to adopt such a piece of haggada into his *Testament*.

But, as has already been said, there are scholars who do not regard chs. 46-53 as Jewish at all, but as Christian[39]. The one who has defended this position most recently is Russell Spittler[40]. His line of argument is as follows: The phenemenon of Jewish or Christian ecstatic women has its closest parallel in Montanism in the second half of the second century. The only allusion to *TJ* in the first five centuries of our era is to be found in the *De patientia* (14:5) of Tertullian, an author who went over to Montanism, though only after he had written that treatise. Josephine M. Ford's thesis that Montanism was originally a Jewish-Christian sect makes it very probable that Montanists were interested in the possibility of inserting Montanist interpolations into Jewish writings[41]. In his *Hist. Eccl.* V 17, 1-4 Eusebius gives a quotation from an anti-Montanist writing in which the author asks where in the Bible prophets behave ecstatically; according to him nowhere.

---

38 That the author used diverse sources is also clear from a comparison of chs. 2-27 on the hand and 28-45 on the other; see Collins, Structure and Meaning (n. 1) 46-7, and especially the discussion of *TJ*'s 4 sources in P. Nicholl's Jerusalem 1982 diss. mentioned in note 54.

39 Names of scholars who see these chapters or the whole *TJ* as a christian document can be found in Challer, JSHRZ III 3, 308 n. 43 and Rahnenführer, *ZNW* 62 (1971) 70-72.

40 R. P. Spittler, *The Testament of Job. Introduction, Translation, and Notes,* unpublished dissertation Harvard University 1971. A summary by himself in *OTP* I 834.

41 J. M. Ford, Was Montanism a Jewish-Christian Heresy?, *JEH* 17, (1966) 145-158.

In this situation of polemics in the last decade of the second century a Montanist author would have reacted to this by adding to *TJ* a passage that gave the required biblical model for ecstatic prophecy. All these data taken together add up to the thesis that chs. 46-53 are a piece of Montanist propaganda.

This theory seems to me to be untenable for the following reasons; 1. The fact that in his pre-Montanist period Tertullian perhaps gives evidence of a knowledge of *TJ* is obviously no proof whatsoever that chs. 46-53 are Montanist. 2. Ecstatic prophecy, also by women, did not only occur in Montanism. 3. Ford's theory of the Jewish-Christian character of Montanism has found little positive response[42]. 4. The biblical precedent for ecstatic prophecy required by the anti-Montanist author could, of course, not be created by interpolating ecstatic women into a non-biblical writing. At the end of the second century almost everyone, anti-Montanists too, knew how to distinguish between the Bible and post-biblical stories as far as the Old Testament was concerned. If a Montanist had wanted to react adequately to this challenge, he would have done better, e.g., to put upon the stage in a pseudepigraphon the four daughters of Philip, who in Acts 21:9 are explicitly called prophetesses. That would have had much more cogency than such a procedure with Job's daughters, for whom the biblical tradition did not yield such a starting-point. 5. Apart from the daughters'ecstacy there is not the slightest reason to think of a Montanist origin of chs. 46-53, for nothing that was characteristic of Montanism is to be found there: no prohibition of a second marriage, no emphasis on strict fasting-rules, no warning against fleeing in times of persecution, no descent of the heavenly Jerusalem in Pepuza in Phrygia, etc. We have to conclude that that this original and bold hypothesis cannot be maintained.

It has to be added that a number of striking points of agreement with the New Testament should not tempt us to assume a Christian origin of these chapters. Of course, the glossolalia of the daughters reminds one of 1 Cor. 12 and 14, the languages of the angels of 1 Cor. 13:1, the μεγαλεῖα τοῦ θεοῦ of Acts 2:11 (there, too, used in a context of ecstatic speech; note also the use of ἀποφθέγγεσθαι and διάλεκτος in Acts 2:4.6 and *TJ* 48:3), the renouncing of τὰ κοσμικά of Titus 2:12 (ἀρνήσασθαι ... τὰς κοσμικὰς ἐπιθυμίας), and the μηκέτι τὰ τῆς γῆς φρονεῖν (48:2) of Col. 3:2. One should not misjudge these similarities in terminology and motives for to the majority of them Jewish parallels can be adduced. To the renouncing of wordly affairs there are, of course, Jewish analogies, for even if one can probably find only Christian parallels to this pejorative use of κοσμικός, the idea is to be found in Jewish writings, certainly in an apocalyptic context (cf. in *TJ* itself also 36:3!). The same applies to the idea of keeping one's thoughts no longer fixed on earthly things: the most litteral parallels are Christian, the idea is definitely not exclusively Christian. As to the *magnalia dei*, there is a parallel in *TJ*

---

42   See e.g. W. H. C. Frend, Montanism: Research and Problems, *Rivista di storia e letteratura religiosa* 20 (1984) 521-537, esp. 533.

itself when Job says in 38:1, 'why should I not speak of the μεγαλεῖα τοῦ κυρίου?' But especially in the book of Ben Sira the author/translator often mentions the *megaleia* of God (17:9, 18:4, 33:8, etc.), a term that, incidentally, was already used by the LXX translators of Deut. 11:2 for God's great deeds (cf. Ps. 104:1 *v.l.* 105:21 *v.l.*, and 3 Macc. 7:22). As to the languages of the angels, it has already been said above that this is a Jewish conception (see p. 281 with n. 33). What remains, however, is the glossolalia.

In his *Religion des Judentums*, Bousset remarked on our passage: 'Stände der jüdische Charakter des betreffenden Abschnittes fest, so wäre damit bewiesen, dass die eigentümliche Erscheinung des Zungenredens im Judentum ihre Heimat habe'[43]. That is the problem we have to deal with now. We have no other indisputable testimonies to the existence of glossolalia in early Judaism. Do we have to conclude, therefore, that a text in which this ecstatic phenomenon is described cannot be Jewish? Gerhard Dautzenberg denies that in his article 'Glossolalie' in the *Reallexikon für Antike und Christentum*[44]. He points out that the earliest reports on Christian glossolalia, 1 Cor. 12-14 and Acts 2, contain several Jewish elements and that one may assume, therefore, that it is a phenomenon that has its roots in Jewish religiosity: there is the motif of the language of the angels (1 Cor. 13:1), the speaking about God's great acts (Acts 2:11), the fact that the earliest manifestations of this phenomenon occur in Jerusalem; all this is indicative of Jewish roots. Obviously this is not compelling proof. But Dautzenberg adds the following considerations. From the beginning there have been ecstatic components in ancient Israelite prophecy. Especially in the early period of biblical prophecy the ecstatic element is prominent (1 Sam. 10:5-11; 19:18-24; 1 Kings 18:22-29; Num. 11:25-27; 24:3-9.15-19). But also in the classical and later periods this element is not absent (e.g. Ez. 1:28; 3:15.23.26; 24:27; 29:21; 33:22; Jerem. 23:9; 29:26; Zech. 13:2-6; Dan. 10:9-11). And some texts seem to indicate that in ecstasy sometimes unintelligible language was spoken (see esp. Is. 28:10)[45]. Also in post-biblical times unintelligible, ecstatic speech by charismatics was not unknown[46]. This is indicated for instance by the fact that Philo and Josephus extensively deal with prophetic ecstasy, especially with immediate speech by God or his Spirit through a person in ecstasy, also in their own time[47]. And even if the

---

43 W. Bousset - H. Gressmann, *Die Religion des Judentums im späthellenistischen Zeitalter*, Tübingen 1926³, 296.
44 *RAC* XI (1981) 226-246.
45 See W. Jacobi, *Die Ekstase der alttestamentlichen Propheten*, München - Wiesbaden, 1920; J. Lindblom, *Prophecy in Ancient Israel*, Oxford 1962, 47-65, 122-137; C. G. Williams, Ecstaticism in Hebrew Prophecy and Christian Glossolalia, *Studies in Religion* 3 (1973/1974) 320-338; D. E. Aune, *Prophecy in Early Christianity and the Ancient Mediterranean World*, Grand Rapids 1983, 86-87 with notes on 370.
46 See e.g. P. Volz, *Der Geist Gottes und die verwandten Erscheinungen im Alten Testament und im anschliessenden Judentum*, Tübingen 1910, 78 ff.; E. Mosiman, *Das Zungenreden geschichtlich und psychologisch untersucht*, Tübingen 1911, 39 f.; Dautzenberg (n. 44) 232 f.; S. D. Currie, Speaking in Tongues. Early Evidence Outside the New Testament Bearing om 'Glossais Lalein', *Interpretation* 19 (1965) 274-294.
47 See Dautzenberg (n. 44) 232 for references.

expression 'speaking in tongues' is used nowhere, in this line of development (or 'trajectory') *TJ* 48-50 gets its natural place. This impression is confirmed when one sees that in the probably first century C.E. Jewish *Apocalypse of Zephaniah* the visionary author reports an experience that comes very close to what we read in *TJ* 48-50. In a vision he has been taken up into heaven and he sees myriads of angels in prayer. He puts on an angelic dress and joins them in their prayers, in there own language which he says he knew because they spoke to him in that language (*Apoc. Zeph.* 8:1-5)[48]. Praying in the language of the angels is, as appears from 1 Cor. 14:14-17 and probably Rom. 8:26-27, a glossolalic activity, and therefore most likely identical to the speaking or singing in angelic languages, the glossolalia, in *TJ* 48-50 (even though, strikingly enough, the expression γλώσσαις λαλεῖν is lacking in *TJ*). In my opinion, therefore, David Flusser very properly remarks that the mystical hymns and praises in *TJ* possibly reflect the liturgy of a Jewish mystical group, which he then, to be true, without cogent arguments identifies as a second century C.E. Egyptian Jewish group[49]. An earlier dating and another provenance are equally possible. The fact that Flusser himself points out the affinity with the so-called 'angelic liturgy' in *4Q Serekh Shirot Olat ha-Shabbat* from the first century BCE[50], demonstrates that a Palestinian origin about the beginning of the Common Era can certainly not be excluded.

In a recent investigation into the origin of the expression 'speaking in tongues', Harrisville comes to the confident conclusion that it lies in pre-Christian Judaism, possibly even in Qumran. He points to passages like *1 Enoch* 71:11 and *Mart. Isaiae* 5:14 as instances of incomprehensible ecstatic speech (cf. perhaps also 4 Ezra 14:37 ff.), but also to other material that makes clear that the Jews of the Hellenistic period did not regard glossolalia as 'a category separate from the ecstatic *per se*'[51]. Ecstasy could express itself, as with the biblical prophets, in language varying from intelligible through hardly understandable to totally inarticulate and incomprehensible. In this connection it is very interesting to note that Lucian, in his portrait of Alexander the false prophet, says that at his first appearance this man girded himself with a gilded girdle and then uttered in ecstasy unintelligible sounds, such as may also be heard among Hebrews and Phoenicians (*Alex.* 12-13)[52]. Be that as it may, we can agree with Schaller that, although this writing cannot easily be attributed to one of the Jewish groups or movements known to us, there is no doubt that we have to do with a completely Jewish,

---

48   See O.S. Wintermute's translation in *OTP* I 514.
49   D. Flusser, Psalms, Hymns and Prayers, in M. E. Stone (ed.), *Jewish Writings* (n. 30) 564.
50   See J. Strugnell, The Angelic Liturgy at Qumran - 4Q Serek Shirot 'Olat Hashshabbat, in *Congress Volume Oxford 1959* (Suppl. to Vet. Test. 7), Leiden 1960, 318-345. C. A. Newsom, *The Songs of the Sabbath Sacrifice: Edition, Translation and Commentary*, Atlanta 1986.
51   R. A. Harrisville, Speaking in Tongues: A Lexicographical Study, *CBQ* 38 (1976) 35-48, *h.l.* 47; cf. also Bousset - Gressmann, *Religion des Judentums* (n. 43) 394 ff.
52   The motif of a golden or gilded girdle recurs time and again in a context of magic: golden girdles were worn by Kirke, Kalypso, Abaris, Empedocles; see Speyer, Gürtel (n. 31) 1238 f., 1243 f.

non-Christian writing[53], in which we find a melange of Jewish wisdom and mysticism and Hellenistic magic[54]. Although for ecstatic speech in general the Hellenistic world probably offered enough examples, for glossolalia we need not seek a Hellenistic origin[55]. We can state with relatively great confidence that, as regards glossolalia, the early Christians retained a Jewish form of religious experience.

As corroborative evidence we could point to an interesting passage in Ps-Philo where, to be true, nothing is said about ecstasy, but where all the other elements of *TJ* 48-50 appear in an undeniably Jewish context. In *LAB* 20:2-3 God appoints Joshua as the prophetic successor of Moses and says to him: '(Since Moses has died,) take his garments of wisdom and clothe yourself, and with his belt of knowledge gird your loins, and you will be changed and become another man' (. . .) And Joshua took the garments of wisdom and clothed himself and girded his loins with the belt of understanding. And when he clothed himself with it, his mind was afire and his spirit was moved, and he said to the people: . . .'. This combination of the reception of a girdle from or of a person who had been endowed with God's spirit and the ensuing inner change is found here again, now related to the prophetic figure of Joshua. It seems to me very improbable that one of both writings is dependent upon the other. Rather we have here a case of a non-interdependent use of this motif. One can imagine that the motif strongly appealed to our author who was heavily inclined to spiritualization, the more so since it offered him the opportunity to spiritualize the biblical remarks about the extraordinarily beautiful outer appearance of Job's daughters (42:15) by altering that into a beautiful inner self, a 'changed heart', as the author says it with the words of 1 Sam. 10:9 where it is said of Saul becoming ecstatic. So we may conclude that in the somewhat clumsily appended chs. 46-53 the author has adopted a piece of haggada in which Job 42:15 (on the exceptional inheritance of Job's exceptionally beautiful daughters) was the starting-point for the depiction of a scene in which, exceptionally too, women take the spiritual lead and become superior to men[56]. It is probable that this haggada originated in ecstatic-mystical circles of early Judaism of about the beginning of the Common Era, very probably also in a group in which women played a leading role by their greater ecstatic gifts and their superior

53   Schaller, *JSHRZ* III 3, 314-316.

54   See n. 52. H. C. Kee, Satan, Magic, and Salvation in the Testament of Job, *SBL Seminar Papers 1974*, Missoula 1974, I 53-76, sees the origin of *TJ* in an circle of Judeo-Greek merkavah mystics; but the element of 'throne-vision' does not play a prominent role in *TJ*. Peter Nicholls, *The Structure and Purpose of the Testament of Job*, unpublished dissertation, Jerusalem 1982, 258 aptly remarks; 'There are no points of contact between it (*TJ*) and the wide range of texts which deal with speculation about the merkabah. What evidence there is would suggest that the circle in which Test. Job arose had little interest in this form of mysticism'.

55   For ecstatic speech in Hellenistic religiosity see W. Bousset in *GGA* 163 (1901) 762 f.; Pfister, Ekstase, *RAC* 4 (1959) 944-987; E. Rohde, *Psyche* II, Leizig - Tübingen 1898 (repr. Darmstadt 1961), 18-22; R. Reitzenstein, *Poimandres* (n. 27), 55-59. Note also the restrictions made by Ch. Forbes, Early Christian Inspired Speech and Hellenistic Popular Religion, *Nov. Test.* 28 (1986), 257-270.

56   Nickelsburg, *Jewish Literature* (n. 16) 246, rightly says that Job's gift to his daughters 'ascribes a higher religious status to women than to men, surely a reversal of values in the comtemporary world'.

spiritual insight into heavenly reality. Other Jewish literature from antiquity does not give us much cause to think of women as leaders in Jewish circles. Nevertheless, we can assume, on the basis of epigraphic materials studied by Bernadette Brooten in her *Women Leaders in the Ancient Synagogue* (Chico 1982), that there were certain religious circles in which women played a or the leading part. It is thinkable or even feasible that such women often saw their position assailed and that hence they tried to strengthen it by creating haggada that legitimated their leading role (cf. *TJ* 46:2). Feminine authorship of the source adopted in chs. 46-53 cannot, therefore, be excluded[57].

The attempts made so far to locate this image of women into early Judaism have yielded nothing else than the theory of Therapeutic origin[58]. The Therapeutae are described by Philo in his *De vita contemplativa* as a Jewish monastic group in Egypt, the members of which, both men and women, are wholly devoted to ascesis, meditation, and religious meetings of which the central parts are allegorical interpretation of Scripture and community singing. It is conspicuous that women play a greater role in this than one would expect on the basis of other data on the position of Jewish women. Philo speaks of ecstatic experiences that occur in both groups and of alternate and combined singing of them during their meetings. Many of these women are widows, and widows are mentioned several times in *TJ*, once even as a singing group (14:2-3). It is my opinion that these agreements and similarities are too slight to base upon them a theory of Therapeutic origin of *TJ*[59]. Firstly, the agreements are only partial. For instance, as regards ecstasy and hymnic singing, *TJ* ascribes these only to women, not to both men and women. However conspicuous the position of women in the Therapeutic community may have been as compared to that in other Jewish circles, in the final analysis these women remain in a subordinate position; it is men who lead the community, it is men who read and expound Scripture, not women. Secondly, most other characteristics of this community are lacking in *TJ*, *sc.* praise of poverty, community of goods, frequent fasting, plain clothing, rejection of slavery, emphasis on virginity, etc. One should also take into consideration the fact that Philo's description of this group is of a dubious historical quality, being one of those well-known idealizing pictures of religious groups that we meet so often in Hellenistic literature[60].

For the motif of enhancing the role of a biblical woman in a positive sense one could also refer to the role of Rebecca in *Jubilees*[61]. In Genesis, Abraham is

---

57   Compare Athalya Brenner's suggestion of female authorship of parts of Song of Songs in her *The Israelite Woman*, Sheffield 1985, 49-50.
58   Defended by Kohler (n. 9), Spittler (n. 40), and M. Philonenko, Le *Testament de Job* et les Thérapeutes, *Semitica* 8 (1958), 41-53; idem, Le Testament de Job. Introduction, Traduction et notes, *Semitica* 18 (1968), 1-75, esp. 15 ff.
59   See Collins, Testaments (n. 30) 354, and esp. Schaller, *JSHRZ* III 3 (n. 12); Flusser, Psalms (n. 49) 564 n. 46, incorrectly states that Schaller *defends* the Therapeutic thesis.
60   See A.-J. Festugière, Sur une nouvelle édition du 'De Vita Pythagorica' de Jamblique, *Revue des études grecques* 50 (1937), 470-494, and P. W. van der Horst, *Chaeremon, Egyptian Priest and Stoic Philosopher. The Fragments collected and translated with explanatory notes*, Leiden 1984, 56-61.
61   P. W. van Boxel, The God of Rebekah, *SIDIC* IX (1976), 14-18.

already dead when Rebecca gives birth to Jacob and Esau, but in *Jub.* he is still living at that moment, and the author then explicitly says: 'Abraham loved Jacob, and Isaac loved Esau' (19:13), thus giving a patriarchal legitimation to Rebecca's love for Jacob. Her wile (Gen. 27) is legitimated theologically not only by Abraham's preference for Jacob, but also by God himself who sees to it that everything escapes Isaac's notice by his blindness (*Jub.* 26:18). The culminating-point of this long story, in which Rebecca is so prominent (*Jub.* 19 through 35), is the passage in which the Spirit descends upon her and she praises God, places her hands upon the head of Jacob and gives her matriarchal blessing both to him and to his posterity (*Jub.* 25:11-23), all this after Abraham and Isaac had already blessed Jacob (19:29; 22:11-13)! Finally, it is she who knows how to reconcile Isaac, Esau and Jacob to one another (*Jub.* 35). Here, too, we see a biblical woman who, by the Spirit of God, comes to truly matriarchal deeds. In spite of the great differences between these two writings in many other respects, there is a strong affinity on this point[62].

Finally, we will probably have to reconcile ourselves to the fact that for the time being we will not be able to situate *TJ* more precisely within early Judaism. Perhaps so much the better, because that broadens our vista on the pluriformity and multicolouredness of Judaism at the turn of our era. In this writing we see juxtaposed, but not without tension and discrepancy, on the one hand an image of women as creatures easy to lead astray and without insight, and, on the other hand, a picture in which women are gifted with the highest imaginable spiritual qualities, are sharing in the heavenly reality, and are taking the lead self-consciously thanks to this giftedness. We know from early Christian history that charismatic gifts could create strong emancipatory tendencies. It is instructive to see that, in this respect, too, Christianity could draw on Judaism.

SUMMARY

In *TJ* two images of women are presented that are diametrically opposed. On the one hand Job's first wife is presented, to be true, as a loyal and loving wife and mother, but apart from that as a creature that is easily led astray, does not have any spiritual insight and is characterized by a continuous lack of awareness of where God and Satan are at work. On the other hand there are Job's daughters (from his second wife, Dinah, Jacob's daughter), who play such a leading role in the final chapters as to reduce Job and his sons to the status of supernumerary actors. They are spiritually highly gifted, have insight into heavenly reality, speak the languages of the angels, and create a real reversal of roles in the story. The chapters on the daughters derive from another source than that on Job's wife, and probably had their origin in an ecstatic-mystical Jewish group in which women played a leading role.

---

62   One could also compare Judith's 'feminism', om which see G. W. E. Nickelsburg in M. E. Stone (ed.), *Jewish Writings* (n. 30), 46-52, esp. 49 f.

6. PORTRAITS OF BIBLICAL WOMEN IN PSEUDO-PHILO'S *LIBER ANTIQUITATUM BIBLICARUM*

In the recent spate of women's studies in the field of religion, Judaism too has received its share of attention.[2] But even though a considerable number of ancient Jewish authors and writings have been investigated from the point of view of their attitude towards women or their images of women,[3] Pseudo-Philo's LAB has not received the attention it deserves in this respect. It has to be said to the credit of Charles Perrot that he devoted a short paragraph to "le féminisme du Pseudo-Philon" as far back as 1976 in the Sources Chrétiennes commentary on LAB[4], but his brief remarks have not provoked the more detailed study that is necessary in order to do justice to the way this writing portrays several biblical women in its rewriting of the Bible story. The present paper is an attempt to make a first step in that direction. It will not deal with all women mentioned in LAB; I will focus on some of the more striking cases of enlargement and embellishment of the role of women in biblical stories. We will review the material in the order of the book.

The matriarchs can be passed over in silence since LAB does hardly more than just noting their existence, Rebecca not even being mentioned by name[5]. The first woman that is focused upon is Tamar, Judah's daughter-in-law

---

1   This is the expanded version of a paper read at the 44th meeting of the Society of New Testament Studies in Dublin, July 1989, and at the 10th conference of the World Union of Jewish Studies in Jerusalem, August 1989.

2   See I. M. Ruud, *Women and Judaism. A Select Annotated Bibliography*, New York - London, Garland, 1988.

3   E.g., W. C. Trenchard, *Ben Sira's View of Women*, Chico, Scholars Press, 1982. B. Halpern Amaru, Portraits of Biblical Women in Josephus' Antiquities, *JJS* 39 (1988) 143-170. J. R. Wegner, The Image of Woman in Philo, *SBL Seminar Papers 1982*, 551-563. J. R. Wegner, *Chattel or Person? The Status of Women in the Mishnah*, New York - Oxford, OUP, 1988. P. W. van der Horst, Images of Women in the Testament of Job, in M. A. Knibb and P. W. van der Horst (edd.), *Studies in the Testament of Job*, Cambridge, CUP, 1989, 93-116.

4   *Pseudo-Philon. Les Antiquités bibliques*, 2 vols., edd. D. J. Harrington, J. Cazeaux, C. Perrot, P.-M. Bogaert, Paris, Cerf, 1976, II 52-53.

5   Contrast Josephus' treatment of the matriarchs on which see J. L. Bailey, Josephus' Portrayal of the Matriarchs, in L. H. Feldman and G. Hata (edd.), *Josephus, Judaism, and Christianity*, Detroit, Wayne State University Press, 1987, 154-179; also B. Halpern Amaru's study mentioned in n. 2.

(Gen. 38). In a typically Pseudo-Philonic way, she is not mentioned where we would expect it, *sc.* in 8:9, but only in LAB's treatment of the story of Moses' birth in Exodus 1-2, *sc.* in 9:5.[6] There Amram raises a heavy protest against the decision of the elders of the people that they should no longer have intercourse with their wives in view of Pharao's measures. One of Amram's arguments for going on to create progeny is as follows:

"When our wives conceive, they will not be recognized as pregnant until three months have passed, as also our mother Tamar did. For her intent was not fornication, but being unwilling to separate from the sons of Israel she reflected and said, 'It is better for me to die for having intercourse with my father-in-law than to have intercourse with gentiles'. And she hid the fruit of her womb until the third month. For then she was recognized. And on her way to be put to death, she made a declaration saying, 'He who owns this staff and this signet ring and the sheepskin, from him I have conceived' [Gen. 38:25]. And her intent saved her from all danger."[7]

Several elements in this fragment call for comment. The first is the conspicuous appellation "our mother Tamar". As far as I know, there is no parallel in the Bible nor in the early Jewish literature to such an honourable title for either Tamar or any other woman from the Hebrew Bible. The only near-parallel is found in LAB 33:7, where after Deborah's death the people say in their lamentation, 'Behold there has perished a mother from Israel', with the words from Judg. 5:7. (To Deborah's exalted status in LAB we will return presently.) There can be little doubt that the expression 'our mother Tamar' is coined on the well-known expression 'our father Abraham'.[8] So what the author seems to imply here is that Tamar is not only not to be blamed for her behaviour but on the contrary to be seen as being on a par with the patriarchs, 'our fathers'. In his positive reappraisal of Tamar the author is not alone.[9] Several other ancient Jewish sources praise Tamar for her virtuous and pious action (Philo, the targumim, the midrashim).[10] But there is a clear difference in emphasis. In the other writings the emphasis is on the justification of Ju-

---

6   On this method of "nachholende Erzählung", which is such a frequent phenomenon in LAB, see O. Eissfeldt, Zur Kompositionstechnik des pseudo-philonischen Liber Antiquitatum Biblicarum, in his *Kleine Schriften* III, Tübingen, Mohr, 1966, 340-353.

7   I use throughout the translation by Daniel Harrington in J. H. Charlesworth's *Old Testament Pseudepigrapha* II, Garden City, Doubleday, 1985, 297-377.

8   See Josh. 24:3; *Avoth* 5:2, *Gen. R.* 39:1.6, 40:6, 41:8; Matt. 3:9, Luke 3:8, 16:24.30, John 8:53, Rom. 4:12.16.

9   See F. Petit, Exploitations non bibliques des thèmes de Tamar et de Genèse 38. Philon d'Alexandrie, textes et traditions juives jusqu'aux Talmudim, in *ALEXANDRINA. Mélanges Claude Mondésert*, Paris, Cerf, 1987, 77-115. For rabbinic evidence see [H. L. Strack-} P. Billerbeck, *Kommentar zum Neuen Testament aus Talmud und Midrasch* I, München, Beck, 1926, 15-18, with the critical comments by R. Bloch, "Juda engendra Pharès et Zara, de Thamar" (Matth. 1,3), in *Mélanges bibliques rédigés en l'honneur de André Robert*, Paris, Bloud & Gay, 1957, 381-389.

10   Josephus omits the story completely, see Petit, Exploitations 89.

dah's behaviour[11] (a common trait in much haggada on the patriarchs in general), whereas in LAB Judah is not even mentioned, the emphasis being completely on the justification, or rather the extolling, of Tamar's behaviour. It is not Judah that is 'our father', but Tamar is 'our mother', and this can only be meant as the highest praise of this woman and it elevates her to matriarchal status.[12] (In parentheses it may be added that in the question of whether Tamar was an Israelite or a Canaanite woman, a much debated issue in ancient Jewish sources, our author clearly sides with those who regard her as a member of the people of Israel.)

The second element to be noted is that of Tamar's hiding her pregnancy for three months. Genesis 38 only states that after three months Tamar was reported to Judah to be pregnant. The element of hiding for three months comes from Exodus 2, but there Jochebed hides the baby (Moses) for three months *after* its birth. Here these two motives have been fused together so as to make Tamar hide her pregnancy for three months, which is exactly what Jochebed is now also said to have done (LAB 9:12). There Jochebed "hid the child *in her womb* for three months", a statement which 'appears to result from the parallel with Tamar in LAB 9:5'.[13] Bauckham has demonstrated that this interpretation of Exodus 2:2 arose from a desire to explain an exegetical difficulty in the text of Exodus: "In view of Pharaoh's strict instructions in Exod 1:22 (cf. LAB 9:12), how could Jochebed have concealed the child after its birth?"[14] The parallel with Tamar in Genesis 38 "is invoked as scriptural authority for believing that the first three months of pregnancy can be concealed, but no more".[15] In other writings dealing with the three months of Exod. 2:2, the problem has been solved in a different way, namely by making Mo-

---

11   See Petit, Exploitations 92. The most glaring case of whitewashing is probably *Gen. R.* 85:8, where it is said that Judah did not feel like having intercourse with the harlot, but since the angel who is in charge of desire pressed him, he did so against his wish!

12   Bloch (see n. 8) demonstrates (in connection with Matt. 1:3) that in some Jewish writings the messianic aspects of Tamar's act receive emphasis.

13   Thus R. Bauckham, The Liber Antiquitatum Biblicarum of Pseudo-Philo and the Gospels as 'Midrash', in R. T. France and D. Wenham (edd.), *Gospel Perspectives* III, Sheffield, JSOT Press, 1983, 55 (33-76).

14   Bauckham, *ibid.*

15   Bauckham, *ibid.* In note 79 Bauckham discusses the possibility (suggested by L. H. Feldman in the Prolegomenon to the reprint of M. R. James' *The Biblical Antiquities of Philo,* New York, Ktav, 1971, p. XCIII) that words have fallen out in 9:12 by homoioteleuton so that the text originally may have read: "...she hid the child in her womb for three months. When she gave birth, she saw that he was a goodly child, and hid him for three months. For she could not hide him any longer ..." As Bauckham remarks, "This suggestion has the advantage of explaining *why* she concealed the first three months of pregnancy: so that the Egyptians should miscalculate her pregnancy and expect the birth three months too late (cf. *Exod. Rab.* 1:20). This miscalculation would give her three months, but only three months, after Moses' birth in which she could keep the birth secret. *Exod. Rab.* 1:20 (...) shows that the practical improbabilities of this suggestion would not have deterred Pseudo-Philo from suggesting it."

ses into a seven months' child, or rather a six months' child.[16]Our author does not do so, which is somewhat surprising in view of the fact that the haggadic tendency to create seven months' children from great biblical figures is not unfamiliar to him: in LAB 23:8 it is explicitly stated that Isaac was such an extraordinary child born in the seventh month. (The reasons behind this haggadic development, though fascinating enough, cannot be dealt with here; I have extensively discussed the relevant material in an article of 1978.)[17] However that may be, the parallel drawn here between Tamar and Moses' mother, her presentation as a model and her being called 'our mother' certainly suggests a raising of her status in the story.

The third element that calls for brief comment is the fact that Tamar is the first person in LAB to raise her voice against intermarriage with heathens, an important motif in LAB (see e.g. 18:13; 21:1; 30:1; 44:7; 45:3) which does not play a role in Genesis 38. It is not without importance to notice this, since we shall observe more often that our author has his most important or central religious ideas formulated by women (see, for example, below on Deborah and Jael). So we may conclude that in this very brief paragraph of Amram's speech we have found reason to be alert to his way of presenting biblical women.

I mention only in passing the three daughters of Kenaz (LAB 29:1-2), non-biblical personages deriving interest from the fact that they are the daughters of what seems to be Pseudo-Philo's most favourite haggadic character, Kenaz. They are said to receive as 'inheritance', albeit not from their father but from his successor Zebul, large portions of land in Palestine. Here the author draws undoubtedly on the stories about the inheritance of Selofchad's daughters in Num. 27:1-11 and 36:1-13. Still more striking, it is stated *not* that they are given to men as spouses but that men are given to them, which seems to be an intentional reversal to indicate their superior status. The whole passage is in a way reminiscent of the manner the 'inheritance' of the three daughters of Job (Job 42:15) is elaborated upon in the final chapters of the *Testament of Job* .[18]

But let us move quickly to what is the most relevant portion of LAB as regards our topic, chapters 30-33 on Deborah. Louis Feldman has recently discussed Josephus' portrait of Deborah.[19] In this article he says that, while the story of Deborah in Judges 4-5 is 786 words long, Josephus reduces the

---

[16] See P. W. van der Horst, Seven Months' Children in Jewish and Christian Literature from Antiquity, *Ephemerides Theologicae Lovanienses* 54 (1978) 346-360.

[17] See previous note.

[18] See P. W. van der Horst, Images of Women in the Testament of Job (n. 2), an earlier Dutch version of which is to be found in my *De onbekende god,* Utrecht, Rijksuniversiteit, 1988, 189-209.

[19] L. H. Feldman, Josephus' Portrait of Deborah, in A. Caquot, M. Hadas-Lebel, J. Riaud (edd.), *Hellenica et Judaica. Hommage à Valentin Nikiprowetzky,* Louvain - Paris, Peeters, 1986, 115-128.

story to 497 words for reasons of misogyny, but LAB devotes no less than 2,575 words to her.[20] This difference is very striking indeed. Right at the start the importance of Deborah is highlighted in LAB by the prediction of her rule - hers alone of all the judges - by God himself: "A woman will rule over them and enlighten (*illuminabit*) them for forty years" (30:2). The verb *illuminare* is used elsewhere in LAB (11:1-2; 12:2; 18:4; 19:6; 23:6.7.10; 33:1; 37:3; 51:3; 53:8) mostly with God or Moses as grammatical or logical subject (only once the Sages of Israel and Samuel are subject; in 33:1 Deborah herself is subject again). It is as if the author wants to say that like God himself and Moses, Deborah will be a light for her people; it is God who says so in the beginning (30:2) and it is Deborah who echoes God's words at the end (33:1). It is very probable that it is an intentional construction by the author to have thus distributed this pregnant terminology. When the story *stricto sensu* starts, the author states emphatically that "the Lord sent to them Deborah" (30:5), and immediately Deborah starts the first of her theological discourses, ending on the impressive note, "God is life" (30:7). And it seems to me to be an important fact that in this non-biblical speech the author has put together all the major themes of his theology: God's election of Israel, the giving of the Law, the sin-punishment-redemption scheme, the eternal covenant and the consequential indestructibility of Israel.[21] All of these are central and recurrent motifs in LAB, but here they are grouped together and succinctly but clearly formulated by Deborah in her programmatic maiden speech.

In ch. 31 the author has Deborah quote Job 38:3 to Barak ("Gird your loins like a man") and order him to attack Sisera. He does not get Barak to beseech Deborah to join him nor does he have Deborah reassure Barak that she will go with him (and so on), as in Judg. 4:8-9. It is worthwhile noting this, because Pseudo-Philo's contemporary and co-religionist Josephus does record Barak's request but is obviously so embarrassed by this biblical detail that he makes Deborah react to it with the indignant counter-question, 'Thou resignest to a woman a rank that God has bestowed on thee?' (*Ant.* 5:203)[22]. "Josephus here once again betrays his misogyny, since the indignation is caused by the fact that a man seeks to surrender to a woman a role that God has

---

20 Feldman, *ibid.* 120-121.

21 See on these themes, besides Perrot in vol. II of the Sources Chrétiennes edition (39-65), especially the series of recent essays by F. J. Murphy: Divine Plan, Human Plan: A Structuring Theme in Pseudo-Philo, *JQR* 77 (1986) 5-14; God in Pseudo-Philo, *JSJ* 19 (1988) 1-18; Retelling the Bible: Idolatry in Pseudo-Philo, *JBL* 107 (1988) 275-287; The Eternal Covenant in Pseudo-Philo, *JSP* 3 (1988) 43-57. In the last mentioned essay Murphy says that LAB does not show the fourfold scheme 'sin-punishment-repentance-redemption' since "God forgives Israel without demonstration of repentance on Israel's part" (46). Another important theme, esp. in Deborah's farewell speech in 33:1-5, is the impossibility of intercession by the deceased, on which see the important article by E. Reinmuth, Ps.-Philo, *Liber Antiquitatum Biblicarum* 33,1-5 und die Auslegung der Parabel Lk 16:19-31, *Novum Testamentum* 31 (1989) 16-38.

22 Compare the similar criticism of Deborah in b. *Meg.* 14b.

bestowed upon him."[23] Not so our author. Far from belittling Deborah's role, as Josephus consistently does, he has her firmly taking the lead and keeping it from beginning to end, even more so than in the Bible.

Sandwiched between the Deborah story is the narrative of Jael and Sisera. In the Bible, Jael's role is subordinate to that of Deborah; so it is in LAB. But, as compared to the account in Judges 4, LAB 31:3-9 aggrandizes her role in some respects. As is also the case in rabbinic literature[24], the erotic element in her action is strengthened (whereas Josephus omits any eroticizing detail in the story)[25] LAB stresses her beauty, also notes that she was elegantly adorned, and adds as a fine detail that she had scattered roses all over her bed, which made the simpleton Sisera sigh, 'If I am saved, I will go to my mother, and Jael will be my wife' (31:3). But the most significant addition in the Jael episode is Jael's prayer just before she kills Sisera (31:5). In that prayer, in which she reminds God of his election of Israel, she asks for a sign that God is with her and trustfully puts everything in God's hands. Of course this strongly reminds us of Judith 9, and it has repeatedly been observed that the Judith story, itself inspired by the Jael episode in Judges 4, has been one of the sources for Pseudo-Philo's rewriting of the Jael story in LAB. "Like Judith, Jael is a women of immense courage begotten of her trust in God."[26] Pseudo-Philo has made Jael much more a model of piety and trust in God than the biblical story does. But not only that, for by adding the element of seduction from Judith, he also wishes to emphasize that she put her qualities as a female into the service of the redemption of her people and God's people, Israel.

Back to Deborah. After the Jael episode, the Bible has the song of Deborah (Judges 5) and adds the very brief note that the land had rest for 40 years (5:31). And that is the end of the Deborah story. Josephus wholly omits the song and just remarks that Deborah died. LAB is completely different. First, it has a much longer song of Deborah than the biblical one. Second, that song is from beginning to end a new creation, which has very little in common with Judges 5. Third, the author seems to have intentionally reserved this song of Deborah for a bird's-eye view of Israel's history in which he relates some episodes omitted elsewhere but elaborately presented here because of their great significance to our author: the *Aqedah* (Gen. 22), especially, receives ample attention and haggadic treatment (32:2-5). The importance of the Aqedah for early Judaism has been the subject of several thoroughgoing investigations in recent times and need therefore not be dwelt upon here. Its relevance to Pseudo-Philo is apparent not only from the way he expands the

---

23 Feldman (n. 18) 124.

24 See e.g. b. *Meg.* 15a, *Yeb.* 103a, *Nazir* 23b, *Nid.* 55b.

25 Feldman (n. 18) 127.

26 G.W.E. Nickelsburg, Good and Bad Leaders in Pseudo-Philo's *Liber Antiquitatum Bibliocarum,* in G.W.E. Nickelsburg and J.J. Collins (edd.), *Ideal Figures in Ancient Judaism,* SCS 12, Chico, Scholars Press, 1980, 55 (49-65).

story of Gen. 22 but also from the fact that it is dealt with no less than three times in LAB: 18:5; 32:2-5; 40:2. Fourth, in her song, Deborah attributes to her victory a "paradigmatic quality"[27]: she says that from this day, on which the stars have fought on Israel's behalf, Israel should, in case of distress, call upon the heavenly bodies, "and they will form a delegation to the Most High, and He will remember that day and send the saving power of his covenant" (32:14). Fifth, in this speech - for it is more of a speech than a song - all LAB's major themes are again presented: Israel's election, the eternal covenant, the Lawgiving, the sin-punishment-redemption pattern. Sixth, LAB adds a whole new chapter (33) containing a farewell speech, in which Deborah terms herself *mulier dei*, 'woman of God', which Harrington has rightly called the feminist counterpart of the common expression 'man of God'[28], and in which she emphasizes that "I am enlightening (!) you as one from the female sex" (33:1) and that the people have to obey her as their mother. Then follows a lamentation of the people over Deborah's impending death, in which they say: "Behold now, mother, you will die, and to whom do you commend your sons whom you are leaving?" (It ends with the well-known words, 'Behold a mother from Israel has perished'). Seventh, there is the notice that the people mourned for her 70 days, which is a longer period of mourning than for any other person in the book including the favourite hero Kenaz, who is mourned for only 30 days, and which is equalled in the Bible only by the 70 days of mourning for the patriarch Jacob (Gen. 50:3)![29] Finally, in a later chapter (38:2), seven men who refuse to sacrifice to idols, refer to the commandments of 'our mother Deborah', just as Amram referred to 'our mother Tamar' (9:5).

Having seen all this one cannot but concur with Feldman's opinion that in LAB Deborah is "a mother in Israel fully comparable to the matriarchs, to the patriarchs, and to Moses."[30] Pseudo-Philo has reshaped this female biblical person into one of the central leader figures in Israel's history or into, as he put it himself, "a holy one (*sancta*) who exercised leadership in the house of Israel" (33:6). This has no parallel in any other ancient Jewish writing.

The next figure that deserves our attention is Jephtha's daughter, called Seila by the author (40:1), a name most probably to be explained as *She'ila*, 'she who is asked for/requested/demanded' (*sc.* by God) or 'she who is the object of the vow' (*sc.* by Jephtha, in 39:10).[31] It is Jephtha's vow to sacrifice to the Lord whoever meets him first on the way when he has defeated the Ammonites, that triggers off the whole dramatic sequence of events, as in Judges

---

27 Nickelsburg, *ibid.* 56.

28 Harrington in *OTP* II (n.6) 347 n. a.

29 But Bauckham 73 n. 69 rightly warns us not to rely on the accurate transmission of numbers in LAB.

30 Feldman, Josephus' Portrait (n. 18) 127.

31 See Perrot in the Sources Chrétiennes ed., vol. II 189.

11. But right from the start there is an important difference. Whereas the biblical account lets Jephtha's vow be inspired by the Spirit of the Lord (Judg. 11:29-31), in LAB the Lord sharply and angrily protests against this vow. In LAB 39:11 God distances himself from Jephtha's vow by saying:

"Behold Jephtha has vowed that he will offer to me whatever meets him first on the way; and now if a dog should meet Jephtha first, will the dog be offered to me? And now let the vow of Jephtha be accomplished against his own firstborn, that is against the fruit of his body, and his request against his only-begotten [daughter][32]. But I will surely free my people in this time, not because of him but because of the prayer that Israel prayed."

The problematic thing about God's utterance is that his anger is directed against the fact that Jephtha's carelessly formulated vow might have entailed the offering of an unclean sacrifice, *not* against the idea of offering Jephtha's child, since it is God himself who decrees beforehand that the vow shall be accomplished against his only daughter. As Philip Alexander recently put it, "It seems God prefers Seila dead rather than alive! One feels that the sacrifice of Seila had a deep significance for the author of LAB: it has become the feminine counterpart of the *aqedat yizhak*."[33] This becomes apparent in the immediately following scene. Upon hearing about her destiny, Seila's first reaction is to draw an analogy between her sacrifice and that of Isaac, which had such an importance for our author.[34] She says:

"Do you not remember what happened in the days of our fathers when the father placed the son as a holocaust, and he did not refuse him but gladly gave consent to him, and the one being offered was ready and the one who was offering was rejoicing?" (40:2).

She emphatically asks her father not to annul anything of what he has vowed but to carry it out, and she stresses her willingness to die and her wish that her death will be acceptable to the Lord (40:3). That this reaction of Seila represents the summit of wisdom is made abundantly clear by the author in the following scene in which this young woman outshines all the wise men of the people of Israel, who do not know how to respond to her words about her situation. The author then has God say the following:

"Behold now I have shut up the tongue of the wise men of my people for this generation so that they cannot respond to the word of Jephtha's daughter, in order that my word be fulfilled and my plan that I thought out not be foiled.

---

[32] I add this word in brackets to Harrington's translation since his rendering does not make clear that the Latin text has the feminine form *unigenitam*.

[33] P. S. Alexander, Retelling the Old Testament, in *It Is Written: Scripture Citing Scripture (Essays in Honour of Barnabas Lindars)*, Cambridge, CUP, 1988, 110 (99-121).

[34] This is the third time the *aqedah* episode is referred to; see above. Cf. also G. Delling, Von Morija zum Sinai (Pseudo-Philo Liber Antiquitatum Biblicarum 32, 1-10), *JSJ* 2 (1971) 4-5 (1-18). The parallel between Isaac and Seila was also suggested by the fact that in the Bible both persons are called *yahid/agapetos*, the only child of their father (Gen. 22:2, Judg. 11:34).

And I have seen that the virgin is wise in contrast to her father and perceptive in contrast to all the wise men who are here. And now let her life be given at his request and her death will be precious before me always, and she will go away and fall into the bosom of her mothers" (40:4).

One should notice the irony in these words: God himself declares that Seila is the wisest person of the whole people and that this woman is wiser than all men together. Accordingly, says God, when she dies, she will not fall into the bosom of her fathers, which is the more usual expression, but into 'the bosom of her mothers', again one of those feminizations of male-centered formulas, comparable to the phrase 'woman of God' for Deborah in 33:1. When Nickelsburg states, "In a curious turn, the judge who has saved Israel is discredited, but his daughter's willingness to die becomes a *post-facto* means to God's favor and a public example to the people, as Isaac had predicted that his own willingness to die would be",[35] that is correct in itself but it is an understatement. What we have here is in fact a second *aqedah*, completely on a par with the first, but this time it is a woman who is the protagonist. And because Seila was indeed sacrificed, whereas Isaac was not, one feels inclined to say, 'Behold, something greater than Isaac is here' (unless one takes the reference to Isaac's blood in 18:5 to imply that the author of LAB believed that Isaac had actually been sacrificed, like Seila; in that case there is a complete parity between the two).[36]

The other major ingredient in LAB's story of Jephtha's daughter is Seila' lament. While the Bible only says that she bewailed her virginity upon the mountains (Judg. 11:38), LAB puts into her mouth a highly remarkable composition, which "in the language it uses and the emotions it portrays (...) stands in sharp contrast to everything else in (...) LAB."[37] It is easily the most poetic, the most pathetic, and the most moving part of LAB, in which the author dwells passionately on human emotions. Its contents have been more extensively studied than anything else in LAB, so there is no need to dwell on it for long.[38] It has been amply demonstrated that there is influence of Greek lamentation traditions here, with elements not only from Sophocles' *Antigone* and Euripides' *Iphigeneia Aulensis* but also from themes in epitaphs, especially the idea of the netherworld as a bridal chamber (40:6). It may suffice to refer to the conclusion of the most important investigation,

---

35 Nickelsburg, Good and Bad Leaders 57-58.

36 On the (mostly late) traditions concerning Isaac's blood and death see esp. Sh. Spiegel, *The Last Trial. On the Legends and Lore of the Command to Abraham to Offer Isaac as a Sacrifice: The Akedah,* New York: Pantheon, 1967.

37 M. Alexiou - P. Dronke, The Lament of Jephtha's Daughter: Themes, Traditions, Originality, *Studi medievali* (3rd. ser.) 12 (1971) 819 (819-863).

38 See, besides the lengthy study of Alexiou and Dronke mentioned in the previous note, also M. Philonenko, Iphigénie et Sheila, in *Les syncrétismes dans les religions grecque et romaine,* Paris, Cerf, 1973, 165-177, and I. Fröhlich, Historiographie et aggada dans le Liber Antiquitatum Biblicarum du Pseudo-Philon, *Acta Antiqua Academiae Scientiarum Hungaricae* 28 (1980) 353-409, esp. 394-401.

where it is stated that one can say with certainty that the author of LAB knew a long unbroken Greek tradition of laments for girls who had died young or laments put into the mouths of these young girls themselves, in which the elegiac language was deeply imbued with the language of epithalamia.[39]

Now at first sight the fact that Seila raises such a dramatic lament seems to be not completely compatible with - and so to detract from - the heroic stance towards her fate in her first reaction.[40] One may surmise that the author's eagerness to create this artful specimen of a typically Greek lament and adopt it into his story has made him unaware that in so doing he had created a certain tension between the first and second part of the Seila episode. But this should not be exaggerated. His prime examples in the tradition upon which he drew, Iphigeneia and Antigone, were famous heroines, and in spite of the emotional character of the lament, "it has more of a heroine's dignity than of sentimentality."[41] The human touch this lament adds to the story and the unfailing steadfastness to have herself sacrificed in spite of her great grief, only help to make clear what a superb human being and model of faith Seila is. When compared to the rabbinic traditions about Jephtha's daughter there is nothing to be found there that even remotely resembles this remarkable picture.[42] Again, like in the cases of Tamar and Deborah, we may conclude that the author has done his utmost to put this woman on the same level as the patriarchs, in this case especially Isaac. It is clear, anyhow, that this procedure of aggrandizing the role and importance of women is not restricted to one isolated case. We can rightfully speak of 'the feminism of Pseudo-Philo'.

When we look for further evidence, we do not find any other such convincing instances of this 'feminism'. There are some striking elements in the picture of Eluma, which is the name of Manoah's wife and Samson's mother in LAB. This name is unique in haggadic literature, and since its meaning is unknown, it is unclear what the author wanted to express by it (cf. Seila), if anything at all.[43] The major addition to the story of Samson's birth is the dispute between Manoah and Eluma over who is responsible for the couple's childlessness. An intriguing element in this dispute is the fact that Manoah says to his wife that it is she who is the sterile one and therefore asks her to let him go (*dimitte me*) so that he may take another wife(42:1), which seems to imply that the wife could or even should take the initiative in a divorce pro-

---

[39] Alexiou-Dronke, Lament 825.851.

[40] See e.g. the note by Chr. Dietzfelbinger in his German translation of LAB in the series *JSHRZ* II 2, Gütersloh, Mohn, 1975, 213 n. 5a.

[41] Alexiou-Dronke, Lament 823.

[42] For references see L. Ginzberg, *The Legends of the Jews* IV, Philadelphia, Jewish Publication Society, 1913, 44-47, with notes in vol. VI (1928) 203-204.

[43] The name closely resembles the enigmatic name Elymas in Acts 13:8; for a survey of possible derivations see E. Haenchen, *Die Apostelgeschichte*, Göttingen, Vandenhoeck & Ruprecht, 1968, 341-2 n. 1, and Bauer-Aland, *Wörterbuch zum NT*, s.v. Is there a connection with Arabic '*alima*, 'to have insight'?

ceeding. It is interesting that this seems to run counter to most (not all) other evidence on Jewish divorce procedures we have. Perhaps we should not read that much in the two words *dimitte me,* but the matter deserves closer scrutiny than it can receive here.[44]

Also new is her prayer to God on the roof, which is followed by the appearance of an angel of the Lord. This appearance, or rather the biblical story of the two successive appearances of the angel to Manoah's wife without her husband being present, has evoked haggadic elaborations in which the main element is Manoah's intense jealousy: both Josephus and rabbinic literature testify to this.[45] This motif of jealousy is completely absent in LAB, which follows more the biblical line.[46]

Finally, one might point to LAB's treatment of Hannah, Samuel's mother in chs. 50-51. Let us briefly look at some significant additions. In 50:2 the author says that Hannah had feared God from her youth, which is repeated later in her own prayer (50:4). Then he elaborates upon the provoking and irritating words of Peninnah. After Hannah's prayer in the house of the Lord in Shiloh, the author reports her soliloquy in which he has her say: " I know that neither she who has many sons is rich nor she who has few is poor, but whoever abounds in the will of God is rich." Hannah's song in 1 Sam. 2 is rendered in LAB in a form which is almost as free a composition as Deborah's song in ch. 32, but its contents are nevertheless more related to Hannah's situation than is the case in Deborah's hymn.

---

44 Cf. e.g. Josephus, *Ant.* 15:295, "Salome sent him (Costobarus) a document dissolving their marriage, which was not in accordance with Jewish law. For it is (only) the man who is permitted by us to do this, and not even a divorced woman may marry again on her own initiative unless her former husband consents." Cf. *Ant.* 18:136 and 20:143. But contrast Mark 10:12. See in general G. Delling, Ehescheidung, *Reallexikon für Antike und Christentum* IV (1959) 707-719, and G. Mayer, *Die jüdische Frau in der hellenistisch-römischen Antike,* Stuttgart, Kohlhammer, 1987, 78-84. Vol 4 of the *Jewish Law Annual* (1981) is completely devoted to 'The Wife's Right to Divorce" in Judaism. On the question of this right see esp. the defence of its historical probability by B. J. Brooten, Konnten Frauen im alten Judentum die Scheidung betreiben?, *Evangelische Theologie* 42 (1982) 65-80, and the same, Zur Debatte über das Scheidungsrecht der jüdischen Frau, *ibid.* 43 (1983) 466-478. That *dimittere* is a term used in divorce contexts cannot be denied.

45 For references see L. H. Feldman, Josephus' Version of Samson, *JSJ* 19 (1988) 171-214.

46 A nice haggadic trait is found in 44:2, where the mother of the idolatrist Micah, who is nameless in Judg. 17:2, is called Dedila, undoubtedly a transcriptional error for Delila, Samson's Philistine harlot mentioned just before in 43:5. She is one of the really very few women who play a less than positive role in LAB (cf. Peninnah in ch. 50). The identification of named with unnamed persons in the Bible is common in the haggadah; cf., e.g., in LAB the identification of Jacob's daughter, Dinah, with Job's wife in 8:7-8.

Although we could point out some other elements which are of relevance for our topic (e.g., the God-sent dreams and visions of Miriam (9:10) and pharaoh's daughter (9:15), the appellation 'sons of Leah' for the Israelites (10:4)[47], etc.[48]), the most important evidence has now been reviewed. And the question to be raised now is: What is the implication of all this, and what is its explication? Unfortunately, this question can hardly be given a satisfactory answer. It is clear that the author attributes a prominence to some biblical women that goes far beyond what they are accorded in either the Bible or elsewhere in the post-biblical tradition. What would have led him to do so? When investigating recently the *Testament of Job* for its images of women, especially those of Job's daughters, I came to the conclusion that the final 7 chapters of this book could hardly have been written by a man and I suggested that it must have originated in a Jewish religious movement in which women played the leading role.[49] The main reason for that conclusion was the complete reversal of roles that takes place in these chapters: the women are the leaders, the persons with insight and spiritual gifts, the men, on the contrary, are just the reverse. Does LAB present us with a similar black-and-white picture? Not at all. The heroes of the book are Abraham, Isaac, Moses, Kenaz; Tamar, Deborah, Seila, and to a lesser extent Jael[50]: 4 men and 3 (or 4) women. There is no blackening of men (although the picture of Jephtha and Israel's sages in his time verges on it), but there is a considerable 'upgrading' of women. Does that suffice to assert that here we must have another case of female authorship? I do not think so. The only thing one can say is that it can never be excluded that LAB is the writing of a female author.[51] But even if we do not go that far, we surely have to establish that the portraits of a number of biblical women in LAB are of such a nature as to point in the direction of an author one of whose concerns it was to ascribe to women a greater and much more important role in Israel's history than they were accorded in the Bible, *sc.* as great and as important a role as had the patriarchs and Moses. That he/she did this with an eye on his/her actual situation can hardly be doubted, and this is a point where further research is to be done. For if this author was a man, he was a rare bird in ancient Judaism.

---

[47] If that is the correct text; see Perrot *ad loc.* in his commentary.

[48] See Perrot's short list list referred to in n. 3 above.

[49] See my Images of Women in the Testament of Job (n.2 above).

[50] To be sure, Tamar is not allotted much space, but even in the short paragraph 9:5 she is endowed with a remarkable distinction.

[51] It seems to me that nothing justifies the assumption that the 'feminist' passages are interpolations since all of them are integral parts to the story.

7. THE MEASUREMENT OF THE BODY. A CHAPTER IN THE HISTORY OF ANCIENT JEWISH MYSTICISM

INTRODUCTION

One of the most conspicuous features of Judaism in its setting in the ancient world was undoubtedly that it was a religion without images. That there was no image worship among the Jews struck many outsiders (see *e.g.* Strabo, *Geographica* XVI 2, 35)[1]. This deviance of normal ancient practice had, of course, its basis in the unequivocal Biblical injunctions in the Decalogue (Exodus 20:4-5; Deuteronomy 5:8-9). Nonetheless, in the Bible itself we see already traces of a debate over the question of whether or not this God, who can and may only be worshipped without an image, does have a shape and can be seen. When we compare Deuteronomy 4:12-15 ('the Lord spoke to you out of the midst of the fire; you heard the sound of words, but saw no form; there was only a voice .... You saw no form on the day that the Lord spoke to you at Horeb') to Exodus 24:10-11 (referring to the same scene: 'they saw the God of Israel, ... they beheld God, and ate and drank'), or Exodus 33:20 (God says to Moses: 'You cannot see my face, for man shall not see me and live') to Numbers 12:8 (God says to Moses: 'With him I speak mouth to mouth, ... he beholds the form of the Lord'), it is clear that on the issue of the possibility of seeing (a form of) God there was no unanimity in ancient Israel. Moreover, some of the prophets had actual visions of the deity (whilst other prophets were more of an exclusively auditive type), e.g. Isaiah, who says in 6:1 'I saw the Lord sitting upon a throne, high and exalted', and Ezekiel, who describes a similar vision in which he saw 'a likeness as it were of a human form', which was 'the appearance of the likeness of the glory of the Lord', sitting on a throne (Ezekiel 1:26-28). Especially these two last-mentioned passages formed the starting point of a long tradition of visionary mystical literature in post-biblical Judaism[2]. Beside a current of increasing spiritualization and abstraction in the concept of deity there grew this mystical trend, or rather trends. For within the mystical movement there was much variety. There were those who experienced visions of the heavenly dwellings, the hosts of angels, the throne of God[2a], but who stopped short of visualizing the deity itself (*e.g. Apocalypse of Abraham* 18:12 - 19:4: the visionary sees the throne, fire around the throne, and angels, but 'I saw no one else there'). There were others who did see the deity and concentrated on its beauty, on the basis of passages like Isaiah 33:17, Zachariah 9:17, Song of Songs 1:16 (e.g. Hekhaloth Rabbati par. 253f.). Finally, there were those who focused on the magnitude of the deity, especially on the basis of Psalm 147:5, 'Our Lord is great, and abundant in power', which was taken to mean that God was very big, even gigantic. This type of mysticism is called *Shiur Qomah* (*SQ*).

The *SQ* literature, the investigation of which is still in its infancy[3], is characterized by an excessive indulgence in an almost provocative anthropomorphism, which is the reason why there has always been bitter antagonism against it in more rationalistic Jewish circles. The name *Shiur Qomah* itself, meaning 'the measurement of the body' (*sc.* of God)[4], indicates that it is really God's body, in all its parts and members, that the mystic wanted to become familiar with. In *SQ* literature the members of God's body are enumerated with their sizes, always astronomical, and their names, always magical or at least mesmerizing, like mantras. The function of this kind of treatises probably was that their repeated recitation induced a hallucinogenic state in the mystic (furthered also by fasting and by putting the head between the knees), so that in the end he attained the desired vision of God's body[5].

When and where did *SQ* originate?[6]. We don't exactly know. Since the middle of the nineteenth century scholars have advanced theories concerning the time of origin of SQ varying from the second or first century B.C.E. to the eighth century C.E. One of the problems is that all the manuscripts are late, (almost) all of them dating after 1000 C.E., and that there are no unambiguous references to or quotations from *SQ* before the post-talmudic period, *i.e.* before the sixth century C.E. The strongest argument in favour of a much earlier dating seems to be the supposed influence of *SQ* on Elchasai, a Jewish-Christian prophet from about 100 C.E., who describes an angel, most probably Christ, of enormous dimensions, 96 miles long, 24 miles wide, etc. (see Hippolytus, *Refutatio* IX, 13, 2; Epiphanius, *Panarion* XIX 4, 1). But quite apart from the fact that the 96 miles of Elchasai and the 100.000.000.000 parasangs of *SQ* are really incomparable quantities, the other essential *SQ* element, the names of God's limbs, is wholly lacking in Elchasai[7]. Another passage often adduced to prove the antiquity of *SQ* is 2 Enoch 39:6: 'You, you see the extent of my body, the same as your own; but I, I have seen the extent of the Lord, without measure and without analogy, who has no end'. Admittedly, this parallel is closer than Elchasai's passage, but apart from the fact that the dating of the Slavonic *Enoch* is itself notoriously problematic and highly uncertain, the names are lacking again[8]. Moreover, as the most recent authority on *SQ* remarks: 'The complete absence of any citations from the *Shiur Qomah* in the collection of mystic data in the second chapter of Tractate Hagigah in both the Palestinian and the Babylonian Talmuds suggests, at least *ex silentio*, that those traditions were unknown to the redactor of those sections of the Talmuds'[9]. It is not of much help to argue that *Hekhalot*-mysticism is demonstrably early, possibly even pre-Christian, for it can be shown that there have been, probably for a long time, *Hekhalot*-traditions without any *SQ* elements. Several *Hekhalot*-recensions do not have any *SQ* passages[10]. Although certainty is impossible in this matter, it is safe, for the time being, to date *SQ* to the early post-Talmudic or gaonic period[11]. That the attribution of the *SQ* revelations to some famous second century C.E. rabbis (Aqiva, Ishmael, Nathan) is pseudepigraphic has never been contested.

SQ texts are extant in 34 manuscripts of various dates and provenances, representing 7 recensions, all of which go back to a now lost 'Urtext'[12]. Although lost, we may come very close to it in one particular manuscript which was very recently published, British Library ms. 10675. It is not only the oldest *SQ* manuscript (possibly 10th cent.); contrary to other mss. or recensions, it is titled *Shiur Qomah*; it is the only ms. to present *SQ* alone; it contains the sections that are common to all the recensions. All this adds up to the not improbable hypothesis that this ms. is either a copy of the Urtext or at least very close to it[13]. It's Hebrew text is translated here for the first time[14].

TRANSLATION

Shiur Qomah

1.   With the help of the Rock and His redemption, with the aid of Heavens,

2.   with the help of the Lord, we will begin and finish. My help is from the Lord, the maker of heavens and earth[15].

3.   I will begin to write the measure of the body (*shiur qomah*). All Israel has

4. a portion in the world to come, as it is said: 'And your people, all of them righteous,

5. will inherit the earth forever; (they are) the shoot that I planted, the work of my hands,

6. designed for glory'[16].

7. Rabbi Ishmael said[17]: 'I saw

8. the King of the kings of kings, the Holy One,

9. blessed be He, sitting on a high and exalted throne, and His soldiers

10. were standing before Him on His right and on His left side[18]. Then spoke to me the Prince

11. of the presence, whose name is Metatron[19], Ruah, Pisoqonyah[20], Pasqon,

12. Itimon, Hagaon, Igron, Sigron, Danigron, Meton,

13. Mekon, Hastas, Hasqas, Sartam, Haskam, Hiqron,

14. (...)na, Rabba, Bantasazantaf.'[21].
    Rabbi Ishmael says:

15. 'What is the measure of the body of the Holy One, blessed be He,

16. who is hidden from all mankind (litt. creatures)?' The soles of His feet[22]

17. fill the entire universe, as it is said: 'The heavens

18. are my throne and the earth is my footstool'[23]. The length of His soles is

19. 30.000.000 parasangs[24]. The name

20. of His right foot is[25] Parsamyah, Atraqat, Shamah, and

21. the name of His left foot is Agometz. From His foot till

22. His ankle (the distance is) 10.000.500 parasangs

23. in its height (on the right side) and thus also on the left side. The name of His right ankle

24. is Tsagmiyah Tasasqam, the name of the left one

25. is Astamets. From His ankle(s) till His knees

26. (the distance is) 190.005.200

27. parasangs in its height (on the right side) and thus

28. also on the left side. The name of His right calf is Qanagago Mahadyah Tasasqam,

29. the name of the left one is Memgehawwaziya

30. (...)zaziyah. From His knees till His thighs

31. (the distance is) 120.000.000 parasangs

32. and 1.200 parasangs in its height (on the right side) and thus

33. also on the left side. The name of His right knee is Stamgagats
    Yahamay

34. and of the left one Magahanoriya. The name of

35. His right thigh is Shashtesatparnasay and of the left one

36. Tephagnihaziza. From His thighs until His neck (the distance is)

37. 240.000.000 parasangs. And the name of His loins[26] is

38. Astanah (...)dadyah. And on His heart stand seventy names[27]:

39. Tsats, Tsedeq, Tsehiel, Tsur, Tsevi, Tsaddiq, Sa'af, Sahats,

40. Tsevaoth, Shadday, Elohim, Ziv, Yah, Yah, Yahweh, Tsah, Dagol,

41. Adum, Sasas, A'a, Wa'a, Aya, Ah, Hav, Yah, Hu, Wekhu,
    Tsatsats,

42. (...)faf, Nets, Hah, Hay Hay Hay, Hehavav, Aravoth, Yav, Hah,
    Wah, Mamam,

43. (...)nan, Hawu, Yah, Yahah, Hafets, Qatsats, Ay, Za, Tsa'a, Za,
    A'a,

44. (...)hah, Qasher, Buzakh, Nitar, Ya, Ya, Yod, Hon, Paf, Ra'u,
    Yay,

45. (...)af, Waw, Waru, Bavav, Bavav, Tatat, Baphakh, Palal, Sis,
    Otiotav[28].

46. Blessed be the name of the glory of His Kingdom forever and
    ever. Blessed be the name of the glory of His Kingdom forever
    and ever.

47. Blessed be the name of the glory of His Kingdom forever and
    ever[29]. His neck is

48. 130.000.800 parasangs

49. in its height. The name of His neck is Sangihu Yavah Tiqats. The
    circumference of His head is

50. 3.000.000.033

51. and one third (parasangs), something which the mouth cannot
    express

52. and which the ear cannot hear[30]. Atar Hodriya

53. Astiyah is its name. His beard is 11.500

54. parasangs. Hadaraq Semya is its name. The appearance of the
    cheeks

55. is like the image of the spirit and like the form of the soul, and
    no soul

56. is able to recognize (it)[31]. Like *tarshish*[32] is the shining of His
    splendour, a bright light[33]

57. in the middle of the darkness, and a cloud and mist surround

Him[34]. All the princes

58. of the presence and the seraphs are before Him like a jar. We have in our hands no measure (than?)

59. (...) of[35] the names that are revealed to us. The name of the nose

60. is Lagbagtsiya, indeed Gagtaphiya is its name. His tongue extends

from one end of the world to

61. the other end, as it is said: 'He makes known his words to Jacob, his statutes and decrees

62. to Israel'[36]. Isasgyhu'ya is its name. The width of His forehead [is 130.000.800 parasangs][37](?)

63. Its name is Mesasgihu Na'aya. On His forehead are written 72

64. letters[38]: yyhw, hyh, ywh, wyh, h', hy, hy, hy, h', hh, wwh, yyhw,

65. wh, wyhw, hh, yh, y', h', yh, yhw', hw, hw, yyhyw, hyh,

66. wyh, yhw, h', h', hyh, wyh. The black of His right eye is

67. 11.500 parasangs, and thus also of His left eye. And the name of

68. His right (eye) is Uriq At Tisum, and the name of its prince is Rahbiel[39].

69. And the name of His left (eye) is Metatgariamtsia. And the sparks that go forth (from them)

70. shine to all creatures. The white which is in His right eye is 20.000 (parasangs)

71. and thus also of His left (eye). The name of[40] the right (white of the eye) is Padarnaphsya and of the left one

72. (...)uqtsatya. From His right shoulder to His left shoulder (the distance is)

73. 160.000.000 parasangs, and the name of the

74. right shoulder is Metatgia'a Anagats and of the left one Tatmahangiya,

75. and that one still has another name, Shalmahingiya. From His right arm till His left

76. arm (the distance is) 120.000.000 parasangs. His arms

77. are folded. The name of His right arm is Gevarhazazyatakhsi[41], and of His left one

78. Metatgahagtsiqu. The fingers of His hands are 100.000.000

79. parasangs, each individual finger, that is, also of the left hand.

80. (The names of the fingers) of the right hand are Tatmah,

Tatsmats, Gagmuh, Gagshemesh, and Gagshash, and of

81. the left one Tatsmats, Tatmah, Agagmats, Ugmah, and Shoshnas.

82. And thus you have to count from the big one onwards[42]. The palms of His hands are

83. 40.000.000 parasangs, also at the left side. The name of

84. the right one is Zazya Etgaray and of the left one Sheqizazya.

85. His toes are 100.000.000 parasangs,

86. 20.000.000 parasangs for each toe, that is[43], also on the

87. left side. (The names) of the right (toes) are Adumats, Asumath, Darmenath, Kevat (...)

88. (...)ramon, and of the left (toes) Yeshnayin, Baznayin, Hatsmat, Ahuz, and Tahamum.

89. (And thus) like with the hands you begin to count[44]. Therefore He is called the great,

90. mighty, and awsome God[45], as it is said: 'For the Lord your God is God

91. and the Lord of Lords, the faithful God, who keeps His covenant and (shows) His loving kindness

92. to those who love Him and keep His commandments for a thousand generations'[46]. But he[47] said to me:

93. 'I will tell (you) the calculation of the parasangs, how much their measure is[48]. Each parasang

94. is three miles, and each mile is 10.000 cubits[49]

95. (and) each cubit is two spans [in His span], and His span fills the whole

96. world, as it is said: 'Who measured the waters with the hollow of his hand and gauged the heavens with

97. His span (etc.)'[50].
    Rabbi Nathan[51], a student of Rabbi Ishmael, says:

98. 'Even (of) the nose he gave me the right measures and also (of) the lip and also

99. (of) the cheeks. The appearance of the face and the appearance of the cheeks is like the measure and form

100. of a soul. No creature is able to recognize it even though he gave me

101. the measurement of the forehead. The width of the forehead is like the height of the neck, and also the shoulder like the length

102. of the nose. The length of the nose is like the length of the little finger[52]. The heigth of the cheeks

103. is like half of the circumference of the head. And so is the size of every[53] man. His lip is about

104. 770.000 parasangs. The name of His upper lip is Gevarhatya

105. and the name of His lower lip is Hasharhiya. His mouth is a consuming fire, whatever He says.

106. (...)sadarsa is its name. And whatever He desires, the Spirit in His mouth says it. The crown on His head

107. is 500.000 by 500.000 (parasangs). Its name is Israel. And the precious

108. stone that is between its horns is engraved: 'Israel is my people, Israel is my people'.

109. '(My) beloved[54] is fair and ruddy. His head is gold, fine gold, his locks are palm fronds, his eyes

110. are (like) doves beside brooks of water, his cheeks are like beds of spices, etc.'

111. 20.000.000 parasangs[55]. And everyone who does not conclude with this biblical verse,

112. Lo, he errs[56]. '(Like) banks sweetly scented, his lips are lilies,

113. dropping liquid myrrh. His hands are rods of gold, his legs are pillars

114. of marble, his conversation is sweetness, he is altogether lovable, such is my friend, such is my beloved'.

115. Antaya Tahon Yahon is good and pure. Yod Yod Yod Yah Yah Yah Hasiv

116. (Ya)h YHWH in the place of Yah Yah[57]. 'Holy Holy Holy is the Lord of hosts,

117. the whole earth is full of His glory'[58]. His eyebrows are like the measure of the height of His eyes. The name of

118. His right eye[s][59] is Hadarzulad, and of His left one Ephdah Tsetsihu.

119. The height of His ears is like the heights of His forehead. The name of His right (ear) is

120. Etstahiya and the name of the left (ear) is Metatutstsiya. It turns out that the entire measurement

121. is 100.000.000.000 parasangs in height and

122. 10.000.000.000 parasangs in width[60].
Rabbi Ishmael said: 'When I said

123. this thing[61] before Rabbi Aqiva[62], he said to me: 'Everyone who

124. knows the measurement of the body of his Creator and the glory

of the Holy One,

125. blessed be He, who is hidden from all mankind, it is certain for him

126. that he is a son of the world to come[63] and that they will lengthen his days in this

127. world'[64]. Rabbi Ishmael said: 'I and Aqiva are guarantors

128. in this matter, but only if he recites this as a *mishnah*

129. every day'[65].

Blessed be the Lord forever. Amen and Amen.

NOTES

1   See for further passages M. Stern, *Greek and Latin Authors on Jews and Judaism* I, Jerusalem 1974, 306.

2   On this literature in general see G. Scholem, *Major Trends in Jewish Mysticism*, New York 1941. One of the earliest exemplars of a post-biblical vision of God is discussed in my 'Moses' Throne Vision in Ezekiel the Dramatist', *Journal of Jewish Studies* 34 (1983) 21-29. For visions of god as a literary genre in early Judaism see also C. Rowland, 'The Visions of God in Apocalyptic Literature', *Journal for the Study of Judaism* 10 (1979) 137-154.

2a   The heavenly palaces are called *hekhaloth*, the throne *merkavah*, hence in current terminology one often speaks of *merkavah* or *hekhalot* mysticism and literature.

3   The most important studies are M. Gaster, 'Das Schiur Komah' (orig. 1893), in his *Studies and Texts* II, New York 1928 (repr. 1971), 1330-1353. Scholem, *Major Trends* (n.2.) 63-67. Scholem, *Jewish Gnosticism, Merkabah Mysticism, and Talmudic Tradition*, New York 1960, 36-42 (addenda on pp. 129-131 in the 2nd ed. of 1965). Scholem, *Von der mystischen Gestalt der Gottheit*, Zürich 1962, 7-47. Scholem, 'Shiur Qomah', *Encycl. Jud.* 14 (1972) 1417-18. I. Gruenwald, *Apocalyptic and Merkavah Mysticism*, Leiden 1980, 213-217. The best study to date is M.S. Cohen, *The Shi'ur Qomah. Liturgy and Theurgy in Pre-Kabbalistic Jewish Mysticism*, Lanham-London 1983. Cohen also prepared the text-edition: *The Shiur Qomah. Texts and Recensions*, Tübingen 1985. Cohen's first book will be referred to as Cohen (1983), the edition as Cohen (1985).

4   Extensive discussion of this name in Cohen (1983) 77-81.

5   Cohen (1985) 3: 'the authenticity of the original experience allowed the tangible results of that experience - the facts and the figures - to serve as the meditative spring-board for others' mystic jour-neys'.

6   Detailed discussion in Cohen (1983) 51-76. A survey of other scholars' opinions *ibid.* 13-41.

7   This is insufficiently taken into account by J.M. Baumgarten, 'The Book of Elkesai and Merkabah Mysticism', *Journal for the Study of Judaism* 17 (1986) 212-223. The matter is not discussed by G.P. Luttikhuizen, *The Revelation of Elchasai*, Tübingen 1985.

8   Two other frequently referred to passages in this connection, *sc.* Irenaeus' quotation from Marcus the gnostic in *Adversus Haereses* I 14, 1-3 and Origen's remark in his *Prologus in Canticum* (*Patrol. Lat.* 13, 63), have still less probative value than the passages

9   referred to in the text. Cohen's (1983, 23 ff.) criticisms of Scholem on this point are convincing.
9   Cohen (1983) 52.
10 This can now be easily verified by a glance in P. Schäfer's *Synopse zur Hekhalot-Literatur*, Tübingen 1981, esp. pp. 158-162.
11 See J. Maier, *Geschichte der jüdischen Religion*, Berlin-New York 1972, 201. Cohen (1983) 51 ff.
12 Cohen (1983) 43-49; Cohen (1985) 1-26. The idea of a *merkavah-* 'Urtext' has rightly been dropped by Schäfer, *op.cit.* (n. 10) V-VII, but for *SQ* the situation is different, as Cohen (1985) has pointed out.
13 On this ms. see Cohen (1985) 5-6; his edition *ibid.* 192-195. That the text of this ms. was regarded as holy writ is indicated by the fact that several letters in it are decorated with coronets, like in ritually proper Torah scrolls.
14 For reasons of space a commentary to this text cannot be given here. We have restricted ourselves here to a very limited number of elucidating notes. Parallels in other *SQ* recensions and in *Hekhalot*-texts can be found in Cohen's apparatus. Brackets (...) indicate either a gap in the ms. or necessary supplements.
15 These two liturgical lines are given in the ms. in abbrevation, *i.e.* of each word only the first letter has been written.
16 Lines 3-6 are a quotation of Mishna, *Sanhedrin* 10:1 (including the scriptural quote Is. 60:21), which constitutes the standard formula used to introduce a liturgical reading of the Mishna treatise *Avoth*. So our writing is clearly presented as a liturgical text.
17 Rabbi Ishmael and still more so his contemporary Rabbi Aqiva (see 123) are mentioned elsewhere as the leading mystic tradents of their generation, *e.g.* Babyl. Talmud, *Hagigah* 14b *et al.*
18 A combination of Isaiah 6:1 and 1 Kings 22:19.
19 On Metatron, the highest angel ('Prince of the presence [lit. "face"]' is the angel who serves in front of God), see the litera- ture mentioned by Cohen (1983) 203 n. 9, esp. H. Odeberg, *3 Enoch or the Hebrew Book of Enoch*, Cambridge 1928 (repr. New York 1973), 79-146. There follow 17 or 18 other names. More often Metatron is said to have 70 names (cf. ll. 38-45). Most of these names, like the names of God's limbs from l. 20 onwards, are incomprehensible. For an extensive list of names of angels (269!) see J. Michl, Engel (V), *Reallexikon für Antike und Christentum* 5 (1962) 200-239.
20 The ms. has *ruhphi soqonyah*. On the basis of parallel versions I have corrected to *ruah pisoqonyah*, which in its turn is probably a paleographical corruption of *ruah pisqonit*, which is how an inter- ceding spirit (*ruah* = spirit) or angel is called in Bab. Talmud, *Sanhedrin* 44b, where it is also said that his names are Pisqon, Itmon, and Sigron; cf. ll. 11-12.
21 One expects a quote of Metatron's words, which is lacking. Either it has dropped out or these lines are displaced and should be read before 93 ff., where the subject of 'he spoke' must be Metatron.
22 This way of describing a body going from the feet upwards was well-known in Graeco-Roman literature, see S.J.D. Cohen, 'The Beauty of Flora and the Beauty of Sarai', *Helios* n.s. 8 (1981) 41-53; but, as Cohen (1983) 109 remarks: 'Such a descriptive technique could reasonably be expected from one who experienced his God while standing at the base of the throne and looking up'.
23 Isaiah 66:1, the first Biblical *locus probans* to support the anthro- pomorphic gigantism.
24 A parasang is roughly 5,5 kilometers, but in 93-5 it will become clear that a divine parasang is infinitely longer than a human one.

Therefore, it is clear, as Scholem, *Major Trends* (n. 2) 64, says, that 'it is not really intended to indicate by these numbers any concrete length measurements'. The numbers are rather meant as an 'essentially inconceivable notion upon which the mystic might focus for the sake of his meditative technique', Cohen (1983) 10.

25   It should be added here that not only the vocalization of these *nomina magica (theurgica)* is very uncertain (hence the many conventional a's), but also the consonantal stock, since the textual corruption of *SQ* manuscripts is at its worst in the names of the limbs, as a comparison of the 34 mss. shows. The names sometimes have clearly recognizable theophoric elements. 'One can never be sure that the name was constructed in the first place for any but its phonological value', Cohen (1983) 103. The names may have originated in glossolalic experiences (See F. Dornseiff, *Das Alphabet in Mystik und Magie*, Leipzig 1925 (repr. 1975), 54-55). That glossolalia was not unknown in early Judaism seems certain, see my 'The Role of Women in the Testament of Job', *Nederlands Theologisch Tijdschrift* 40 (1986) 273-289, esp. 285-287.

26   Understandably the author passes over the size of God's genitalia.

27   The heart is the only inner organ mentioned. The list of names of God that follows contains besides known Hebrew words (for 'righteousness', 'rock', etc.) and Biblical names of God (Shadday, Elohim, Yahweh), especially a whole series of words based on various permutations of the Holy Name (YHWH) and of *'ehyeh* (Exod. 3:14 *'ehyeh 'asher 'ehyeh* = I am who I am). Everyone who has read Greek or Coptic magical papyri recognizes this type of name lists, or rather sound lists. See Dornseiff, *Alphabet* (n. 25) 35-51.

28   The final 'name', Otiotav, means, 'his letters', which refers to the letters of YHWH and 'HYH (see note 27).

29   This *berakhah* (blessing) is repeated thrice, but the second time only in abbreviation, like the liturgical formula in 1-2. This liturgical doxology is part of a daily recited prayer.

30   This is a rabbinic expression (see *e.g. Sifre Numbers* 102, *Shevuoth* 20b, *Rosh ha-Shana* 27a), which is reminiscent of 1 Corinthians 2:9.

31   On these lines see the comments of Scholem, *Von der mystischen Gestalt* (n. 3) 17.

32   The ms. reads *Ktr shysh zwhr*. This, if connected with the preceding words, yields: 'no one is able to gaze upon the crown which is the splendor etc.' (one also has to assume then that, after *shysh*, *nw* has dropped out before *zw*, a common paleographical error). But I feel inclined to correct the ms. according to the other versions which read *ktrshysh*, 'like tarshish', a word of uncertain meaning (here probably a precious stone) that occurs also in Ezechiel 1:16 and Song of Songs 5:14, which are important *Merkavah* and *SQ* chapters (see 109-114).

33   I read *nura* ('fire' or 'light', an Aramaism), not *nora* ('awesome').

34   Contrast the Christian *Visio Dorothei* (Pap. Bodmer 29) 14, where it is said that *no* clouds surround him.

35   The text is in disorder here. Other versions have something like 'we have nothing (or: no measure) in our hands save the names ...'. Gruenwald, *Apocalyptic* (n. 3) 215, suggests that this implies that the names are meant to replace and indicate the measures of the limbs. But I cannot see how the measures can be derived from the names. Moreover, as Cohen (1983) 29 remarks, all the recensions which give the names also give the measurements.

36   Psalm 147:19. It is hard to see how this quotation proves the preceding statement. It may have been quoted among other reasons

because Ps. 147 was the SQ Psalm *par excellence* because of verse 5 'Our Lord is great/big'; see the introduction above; Gruenwald, *Apocalyptic* (n. 3) 216 n. 15 and especially the discussion by Cohen (1983) 114 f.

37 Line 62 is at the end of a leaf, which is why probably the next sentence, indicating the measure, has dropped out. I have supplemented it from other versions.

38 Other versions have '70 letters', another instance of the well-known '70 or 72' question which is also met in the traditions on the origin of the Septuagint and the mission of Jesus' seventy (two) disciples in Luke 10:1. The letters are again permutations of the Holy Name YHWH and of 'HYH (Ex. 3:14); see n. 27.

39 Why only the right eye has a guardian angel is unclear. In some other versions his name is Rahmiel, 'God is my love'.

40 I rad *shl* (of) instead of the ms.'s *shn* (tooth) which makes no sense.

41 I assume that this name is a paleographically mangled form of Begadhuzya Takhsi (metathesis of *beth* and *gimel*, misreading *daleth* as *resh* and *vav* as *zayin*), the first part of which is obviously constructed on an alphabetic principle (b, g, d, h, v/u, z, being the second through seventh letters of the alphabet, with *ya* added); see Scholem, *Jewish Gnosticism* (n. 3) 37 n. 4. The second part, Takhsi, might be a transcription of the Greek word *taxei*, 'in order', *sc.* the order of the alphabet.

42 *I.e.*, the names mentioned are to be attributed to the fingers in this order beginning with the thumb.

43 Note the difference with 79-80.

44 See line 82 with note 42.

45 *Sc.* in Deuteronomy 10:17.

46 Deuteronomy 7:9 with a minor variant reading and a major addition, *sc.* 'Lord of Lords'.

47 *Sc.* Metatron, see note 21.

48 The following two lines make clear that the preceding indications of length are not human but divine measures, which are infinitely larger. Cohen (1983) 108 remarks: 'It seems clear that this conversion table is a fixed literary pericope inserted here by the editor to take some of the sting out of the text (...) by multiplying the dimensions from the merely immense to the incalculably vast'. In the other recensions there are several variants of this conversion table.

49 Read *'mh* instead of the ms.'s *'mr*.

50 Isaiah 40:12.

51 A famous scholar from the 2nd half of the 2nd century C.E.

52 This short sentence is the only SQ passage that seems to have a parallel in the Babylonian Talmud, *Bekhorot* 44a, but there in a wholly different context, where the appropriate proportion of nose to little finger indicates the point at which nose-length may be considered a defect of sufficient gravity to invalidate a priest's right to serve in the temple. See Cohen (1983) 218.

53 Read *kl* instead of the ms.'s *kn*.

54 Lines 109-114 are a conspicuously long quote from Song of Songs 5:10-16, with various omissions, metatheses, and mistakes (and an interruption, see n. 56). The 'beloved' of the Biblical text is interpreted as God and the quote functions as a sort of Biblical confirmation of the validity of anthropomorphic mysticism. See the discussion of the use of this passage in SQ by Cohen (1983) 111-2.

55 It is unclear of what this figure is a measurement, possibly of the precious stone mentioned in 107-8.

56 Curiously enough, the Biblical quotation is interrupted by the warning that the mystic will not attain his goal (for which see line 126) if he will not conclude his spiritual exercises by reciting these verses from Song of Songs.

57 The meaning of 115-116a is unclear. Actually one expects the quote from Song of Songs to be the end of the text or at least the passage from 117-122 to come before this quote. The order of the text in its present state does not seem to me to be the original one.

58 Isaiah 6:3, from the prophet's vision of God!

59 The scribe mistakenly repeated the plural of the previous sentence (in the Hebrew text the words 'his eyes' and 'his eye(s)' follow immediately upon one another).

60 The 10:1 proportion between height and width seems too thin for a normal man, as Cohen (1983) 222 n. 22 correctly remarks. It is clear that this total figure is not arrived at by adding up the previously mentioned measures.

61 'This thing' is the *SQ*.

62 See note 17.

63 For the expression cf. Luke 16:8 and 20:34, with the comments in P. Billerbeck, *Kommentar zum Neuen Testament aus Talmud und Midrasch* II, München 1924, 219.

64 Here it is clearly stated that the reward of the mystic will be not only other-worldly but also this-worldly.

65 The rewards promised by Aqiva will only be realized if there is daily exercise by the mystic, although it is not clear what exactly is meant by reciting something that is not a *mishnah* as a *mishnah*. Cohen (1983) 223 surmises that 'the mystic is being enjoined to recite the text in the fashion of a *mishnah*, *i.e.* out loud, orally'.

8. THE SAMARITAN DIASPORA IN ANTIQUITY

The existence of a Samaritan diaspora in antiquity is much less well-known than that of a large Jewish diaspora in the ancient world. The Jewish diaspora is already known from the Bible. We know from the Old Testament that as early as the eighth century B.C., when the Northern Kingdom of Israel was conquered by the Assyrians and its population partly deported, Israelites began to live outside their own country. This situation worsened after the conquest of Judaea by the Babylonians in the sixth century, and still further after later conquests, all of which went hand in hand with deportations. Hence in the New Testament, in Acts as well as in the Epistles, we find Jews everywhere outside Palestine, scattered over the world, from Persia to Spain (see e.g. Acts 2:9-11). That the majority of the Jews today still live outside the state of Israel, is a well-known fact. However, neither from the Bible nor from modern history have we become acquainted with a Samaritan diaspora. In the Bible we meet Samaritans only in the area of Samaria, and, if outside that area, then at least within Palestine. And also in the present day situation we meet Samaritans only within the state of Israel: the very small Samaritan community (ca. 600 members) lives in Nablus and in Holon (a little town to the south of Tel Aviv). So the most important sources of information about Samaritans for most people of our time, the Bible and the present situation, both suggest that Samaritans lived and live only within the borders of Israel. This small contribution has the modest intention of correcting this picture as far as the ancient world is concerned. Both literary and archaeological data demonstrate that in the post-biblical period there was a considerable Samaritan diaspora analogous to the Jewish dispersion.[1] We will present firstly the most important literary data which in principle have been known already for a long time, and after that the epigraphical material that surfaces here and there especially in recent times. We will limit ourselves to material outside Palestine.[2]

---

[1] In a sense the distinction between Jews and Samaritans in antiquity is artificial because, in spite of the growing distance between the two communities, from a religio-historical point of view Samaritans should be regarded as a Jewish sect. See for instance S. Safrai, *Die Wallfahrt im Zeitalter des zweiten Tempels*, Neukirchen 1981, 111-120.

[2] That is to say that we will not pay attention to inscriptions that have been found outside of Samaria but inside Israel. The interested reader can be referred to *inter alia* G. Reeg, Die samaritanischen Synagogen, in: F. Hüttenmeister - G. Reeg, *Die antiken Synagogen in Israel*, 2 vols., Wiesbaden 1977, II 533-550. B. Bagatti, Phasga, *Dictionnaire de la Bible, Suppl.* VII (1966) 1129-1132. A. Hamburger, A Graeco-Samaritan Amulet from Caesarea, *Israel Exploration Journal* (=*IEJ*) 9 (1959) 43-45. J. Kaplan, Two

We commence, however, with a remark of a methodological nature. It is only recently that one has become aware of the fact that when our sources speak about *Samareis, Samar(e)itai, Samaritani,* and the like, it is not always Samaritans that are referred to. For the reference can also be to 'Samarians'. Samarians is a modern term reserved for inhabitants of the city or the region of Samaria, and these are in many - perhaps even in most - cases not Samaritans; Samaritans are members of the Samaritan religious community. This terminological distinction - which was mostly not made in antiquity[3] - is of the greatest importance for our investigation. For if this distinction is not made, the data about both categories become confused and the picture of the Samaritans is completely blurred. Recently Rita Egger has convincingly demonstrated that Josephus has always been unjustly accused of vehemently anti-Samaritan sentiments because the researchers had not seen that most of the places in his works where he mentions *Samareis,* do not deal with Samaritans at all but with inhabitants of Samaria, that is Greeks and Phoenicians in many cases.[4] That implies for our subject that data for the study of the Samaritan diaspora are only relevant if we also have other indications (apart from the term used) that we are dealing with a member or members of the Samaritan religious community. Unfortunately only rarely is an ancient author or scribe aware of this problem of terminological ambiguity: an exception is the papyrus (to be mentioned below) of which the scribe unambiguously states that the two people concerned were *Samaritai tên thrêskeian,* 'Samaritans by faith'.[5]

We do not know when, why, and where the Samaritan diaspora began. The Samaritans themselves say that their dispersion started when in 712 B.C. the

---

Samaritan Amulets, *IEJ* 17 (1967) 158-162. J. Kaplan, A Second Samaritan Amulet from Tel Aviv, *IEJ* 25 (1975) 157-159. A. Zertal, The Samaritans in the District of Caesarea, *Ariel* 48 (1979) 98-116. R. Reich, A Samaritan Amulet from Nahariya, *Revue Biblique* 92 (1985) 383-388. For a complete list of Samaritan amulets both inside and outside Palestine see now R. Pummer, Samaritan Amulets from the Roman-Byzantine Period and their Wearers, *Revue Biblique* 94 (1987) 251-263.

3   A survey of ancient terms for Samaritans is given by H. G. Kippenberg, *Garizim und Synagoge. Traditionsgeschichtliche Untersuchungen zur samaritanischen Religion in der aramäischen Periode,* Berlin-New York 1971, 33-34 n.1.

4   R. Egger, *Josephus Flavius und die Samaritaner* (NTOA 4), Freiburg - Göttingen 1986. Sometimes Egger goes too far in her zeal to find Samarians instead of Samaritans. For some instances and criticisms see my article 'Novum Testamentum et Orbis Antiquus': aantekeningen bij een nieuwe reeks, *Nederlands Theologisch Tijdschrift* 42 (1988) 60-66.

5   I cannot agree with Alan D. Crown when he states that we need not make the distinction between Samaritans and Samarians since the ancient sources don't do that either. Consequently, his article on the Samaritan diaspora in A. D. Crown (ed.), *The Samaritans,* Tübingen 1989, 195-217, is marred by a lack of methodological strictness. Nathan Schur's brief survey of the evidence in his *History of the Samaritans,* Frankfurt 1989, 54-56, is useful for a first orientation but also very incomplete.

Northern Kingdom was partly deported.[6] But since one can only speak of Samaritans once this religious community begins to define itself over against the Jewish mother-religion - and that happened only after the Exile - the beginnings of this diaspora must be looked for in a later period. The first document that informs us about it is Josephus' *Antiquitates*.[7] In *Ant*. XII 7-10 he tells that Ptolemy I Soter (end of the 4th cent. B.C.) "took many captives both from the hill country of Judaea and the district round Jerusalem and from Samaria and those on Garizim and brought them all to Egypt and settled them there"(7). Later Ptolemy favours the Jews more than others so that "their descendants had quarrels with the Samaritans because they were determined to keep alive their fathers' way of life and customs, and so they fought with each other, those from Jerusalem saying that their temple was the holy one, and requiring that the sacrifices be sent there, while the Shechemites wanted these to go to Mount Garizim" (10).[8] Here we clearly have to do with a conflict between two religious communities, a conflict that, also in Hellenistic Egypt, will escalate later. For in *Ant*. XIII 74-79 Josephus tells us about a violent quarrel during the reign of Ptolemy VI Philometor (180-145) between Jews and Samaritans in Alexandria over the question of whether the temple in Jerusalem or the one on Garizim was in accordance with the Law of Moses. Both parties ask the king himself to make a decision. Ptolemy follows the principle of *audi et alteram partem* and listens to speakers of both parties. But it is the champion of the Jewish cause who is able to convince the king with proof from the Torah and also on the basis of the fact that "all the kings of Asia had honoured the temple with dedicatory offerings and most splendid gifts, while none had shown any respect or regard for that on Garizim, as though it were not in existence"(78). Thereupon the Samaritan pleaders were put to death.[9]

---

6   See A. D. Crown, The Samaritan Diaspora to the End of the Byzantine Era, *Australian Journal of Biblical Archaelogy* 2 (1974/75) 107ff. For our purposes also Crown's *Bibliography of the Samaritans*, Metuchen 1984, is of great use (Crown is currently working on an updated version of this bibliography).

7   In *Ant*. XI 345 we read that Alexander the Great, after his meeting with Sanballat at Sichem, orders the latter's soldiers to go with him to Egypt where he will give them a piece of land in the Thebais. I do not take account of this passage since for various reasons it is suspect as a historical source.

8   Translation by Ralph Marcus in the LCL.

9   In medieval Samaritan chronicles this story is told as well, but then with the outcome reversed! See J. A. Montgomery, *The Samaritans*, Philadelphia 1907 (repr. New York 1968), 76-77. On the possible occasion for the conflict A. Schlatter remarks: "Schon die jährlichen Geldsendungen an die Tempel gaben Anlass zu Konflikten mit den Behörden, die eine Entscheidung des Königs nötig machen konnten" (*Die Theologie des Judentums nach dem Bericht des Josephus*, Gütersloh 1932, 77). But see now on both the Samaritan versions of this conflict and on the possible reasons for it Egger, *Josephus Flavius und die Samaritaner* (see n. 4) 95-101.

That there were Samaritans in Egypt already from early Hellenistic times is confirmed indirectly by the mention of a village called *Samareia* (in the Fayum) in Greek papyri from Egypt from the end of the third century B.C.[10] In one of these papyri, a contract from 201 B.C. (CPJ 22), all six witnesses are called *Ioudaioi*; in two others (CPJ 28 and 128) we find names like Jo(h)annes, Jonathan, Jacobus, Haggai, and Sambathion, which were, at least in this early period, typically Jewish names. There can be little doubt that these 'Jews' themselves named their village Samaria after the city or area where they came from. So they may have been Samarians, but the conflicts mentioned by Josephus (see the previous paragraph) make it rather probable that they were Samaritans.[11] Absolute certainty in this matter, however, is impossible. It is very probable that Egyptian inhabitants or at any rate non-Samaritan inhabitants of this village called themselves *Samaritai*, so that in Egypt this term received the additional meaning of 'inhabitant of the village of Samareia'. It was possibly this situation which induced the scribe of a divorce deed in 586 A.D. (CPJ 513) to call the man and the woman concerned for clarity's sake *Samaritai tên thrêskeian* (Samaritans by faith). So this divorced couple from Hermoupolis shows us that as late as the end of the sixth century Samaritans still lived in Egypt.[12] This is confirmed, moreover, by the fact that Eulogius, patriarch of Alexandria from 580-607, presided over a disputation between two rival groups of Samaritans (who no doubt lived in Alexandria) and afterwards promulgated a *Decree against the Samaritans*.[13]

In *Antiquitates* XVIII 167, Josephus reports that Herod Agrippa I, when in financial problems in Rome, borrowed from a freedman of the emperor Tiberius, a *Samareus genos,* one million drachmas. From this passage some have concluded that around the turn of our era a Samaritan community must

---

10 See V. A. Tcherikover - A. Fuks - M. Stern, *Corpus Papyrorum Iudaicarum*, 3 vols., Cambridge (Mass.), 1957-1964, nos. 22.28.128.

11 See M. Smith, *Palestinian Parties and Politics that Shaped the Old Testament*, New York - London 1971, 189. A. Kasher, *The Jews in Hellenistic and Roman Egypt*, Tübingen 1985, gives a survey of all data on this village.

12 CPJ 514, a papyrus from Nessana with an account from ca. 600 A.D., also mentions a *Samaritês*, but there is too little context to conclude anything from it. That Samaritans still lived in Egypt, especially in Cairo, till the late Middle Ages, appears from several later sources; see Crown, *AJBA* 2 (n.6) 117; also E. Schürer, *The History of the Jewish People in the Age of Jesus Christ* III 1, rev. ed. by G. Vermes *et al.*, Edinburgh 1986, 60 n.63.

13 See Photius' excerpt in *Bibliotheca* 230 (285a; ed. Henry, V p. 60). In later times, especially in the 12th century, there seem to have developed friendly relationships between Jews and Samaritans in Egypt; see A. Cowley, Samaritana I, *Jewish Quarterly Review* 16 (1904) 474-483.

have existed in Rome.[14] That may quite well have been the case, in view of the large numbers of Jews in Rome by that time, but it cannot be concluded from this passage directly.[15] After all, the man may have been a Samarian. Now one has tried to support the view that he was a Samaritan by pointing to the fact that Justin Martyr, in *I Apol*. 26, states that Simon Magus, who created a furore in Rome during Claudius' reign, was worshipped as God by almost all Samaritans, which would indicate the presence of a great number of Samaritans in Rome in the first half of the first century. That conclusion is incorrect for two reasons. Firstly, Justin does not say that Simon was worshipped by Samaritans-in-Rome. Secondly, even if that were the case, then one need assume that he writes not about Samaritans but about Samarians, for in view of what we know about Samaritan religion in the first century, it would seem to be ruled out that members of this religious community would have regarded someone like Simon as a god.[16] Moreover, this whole passage in Justin contains incorrect statements and does not inspire confidence as a historical source.[17] To be sure, it is definitely not improbable that there were Samaritans in Rome in the first century, but neither Josephus nor Justin can be adduced as witnesses. There certainly are witnesses for Samaritan presence at Rome, but these are of a much later date. Now it must be said that most literary data about the Samaritan diaspora are late, that is from the time after Constantine. In this striking fact lurks a problem, as has rightly been surmised that pagan authors usually made no distinction between Jews and Samaritans, the consequence being that possibly much (for us unrecognizable) information about Samaritans is hidden in what they write about *Ioudaioi/Iudaei*. (Similarly, information about Samaritans may be hidden in material that we have to leave out of account for reasons of necessary methodological strictness because we have no means to determine whether authors are speaking about Samaritans or Samarians.) Be that as it may, as concerns Rome we have in Cassiodorus' *Variae* (sc. *epistulae*, a collection of deeds and letters from kings of the fifth and sixth centuries) a letter from the East-Gothic king Theodoric (early sixth cent.), in which he complains that in Rome there is a *Samareae superstitionis populus* which asserts that a building that originally was a Samaritan synagogue, has been illegally annexed by the Christian church in order to serve as a church-buil-

---

14 So e.g. H. G. Kippenberg, *Garizim und Synagoge* (n.3) 146; on pp. 145-150 Kippenberg gives a useful (but incomplete) survey of the evidence for a Samaritan diaspora that was known till 1970.

15 See Egger, *Josephus Flavius* (n. 4) 143-148.

16 See B. W. Hall, *Samaritan Religion from John Hyrcanus to Baba Rabba*, Sydney 1987, who argues that Justin here undoubtedly refers to Samarians (46-47; cf. 102ff.). On pp. 262-275 Hall convincingly demonstrates that Simonianism has been from beginning to end a predominantly pagan and not a Samaritan movement.

17 See for instance, in the same paragraph, the notorious remark about the inscription *Simoni deo sancto*. See further the discussion in Egger 143-148.

ding henceforth (*Var.* III 45).[18] Theodoric does not believe this, but a glance at the legislation of the later Roman Empire will make clear that these Samaritans most probably have not exaggerated.[19]

The passages in this legislation that explicitly refer to Samaritans will now briefly pass in review.[20] What we will be dealing with is imperial decrees from the period 390 - 535 A.D., which are to be found in the *Codex Theodosianus* (with the *Novellae*) and the *Codex Justinianus*. In *Cod. Theod.* XIII 5, 18 (A.D. 390) Jews and Samaritans are exempted from the so-called *navicularia functio*, i.e. a supply of ships enforced by the state for general public interest.[21] This first mention of Samaritans in a Roman law book protectis them from unfair burdens. But things change to the worse under Theodosius II. *Cod. Theod.* XVI 8, 28 (A.D. 426)[22] decrees that Jews and Samaritans who have become converts to Christianity should never be disinherited by their parents or put at a disadvantage in other ways in matters of inheritance. *Novella* 3 (A.D. 438)[23] forbids Jews, Samaritans, pagans and heretics to exercise any judicial authority over Christians or to have any dignitary function whatsoever, nor may synagogues be built any longer[24] *Cod Iust.* I 5, 12 (A.D. 527)[25] again excludes all Jews, Samaritans, Manichaeans, and other heretics from all government services and military functions. *Cod. Iust.* I 5, 13 (A.D. 527)[26] decrees that orthodox Christian children from Jewish, Samaritan or heretical parents are fully entitled to be heirs, so may not be disinherited. *Cod. Iust.* I 5, 17 (A.D. 527)[27] decrees that Samaritan synagogues should be destroyed and that those who rebuild them will be severely punished; Samaritans may only leave heritages to orthodox

---

18 The emendation *Samareae* for the *amarae* of the mss. has been generally accepted, rightly I think.

19 See now especially A. Linder, *The Jews in Roman Imperial Legislation*, Detroit - Jerusalem 1987, Index s.v. Samaritans.

20 Besides Linder's work (see previous note), a very useful tool is P. R. Coleman-Norton, *Roman State and Christian Church*, 3 vols., London 1966, Index s.v. Samaritans.

21 See C. Pharr, *The Theodosian Code and Novels and the Sirmondian Constitution*, Princeton 1952, 394.

22 Coleman-Norton no. 392 (pp. 638-639).

23 Coleman-Norton no. 429 (pp. 711-715).

24 At the end this novella is summarized as follows: *Haec lex specialiter iubet ut nullus Iudaeus, nullus Samaritanus ad nullum militiae aut administrationis honorem possit accedere neque defensoris officium nulla ratione suscipere neque carceris esse custodes, ne forsitan sub specie cuiuslibet officii Christianos vel etiam sacerdotes sub quacumque occasione iniuriis audeant fatigare, ne supra scripti qui inimici legis nostrae sunt legibus nostris aliquos aut condemnare aut iudicare praesumant, nullam denuo audeant construere synagogam*, etc. (ed. Mommsen-Meyer III p.11).

25 Coleman-Norton no. 567 (pp.995-999).

26 Coleman-Norton no. 570 (pp. 1003-1004).

27 Coleman-Norton no. 574 (pp. 1007-1008).

Christian persons. *Cod. Iust.* I 5, 18 (A.D. 527)[28] summarizes the prohibitions of previous laws pertaining to the Samaritans' being invested with high offices. *Cod. Iust.* I 5, 19 (A.D. 529)[29] again forbids the disinheritance of Christian children by their Samaritan parents. *Cod. Iust.* I 5, 21 (A.D. 531)[30] forbids Jews, Samaritans and heretics to act as witnesses against Christians in lawsuits, but allows them to testify against their own co-religionists. *Cod. Iust.* I 10, 2 (A.D. 534)[31] forbids Jews, Samaritans and pagans to hold Christian slaves.

This very concise survey of measures against Samaritans, Jews, heretics, and pagans makes clear that the legislators definitely did not regard the Samaritans as a 'quantité négligable', as an insignificant sect that was withering away somewhere in a corner of Palestine. On the contrary, the fact that Samaritans are so often explicitly mentioned and the fact that several of these edicts were directed to prefects of Italy, Egypt, and other areas is an indirect proof that Samaritans were present throughout the Roman Empire in late antiquity.

Although we do not strive to make an exhaustive presentation of all data, we mention yet some other literary sources. The writer(s) of the *Historia Augusta* (end of the 4th cent.) cite(s) in the *Vita Saturnini* a (to be sure completely fictitious) letter by the emperor Hadrian[32], in which he voices criticisms against the population of Egypt. In this letter we read the following sentence: "There is no archisynagogos, no Samaritan, no Christian priest there, who is not an astrologist, not a diviner, not a charlatan". Even if this is not a historical document, it nevertheless demonstrates how a writer of the fourth century imagined the religious composition of the Egyptian population.

Procopius, *Anecdota* 27:26-31, writes that in the reign of Justinian (527-565) there was in Constantinople a senator of high repute, Faustinus, who had become Christian in name but had in fact remained a Samaritan (a kind of Marrano Samaritano avant la date). This senator was accused before Justinian of hostility towards Christians and condemned to exile, but he was

---

[28] Coleman-Norton no. 575 (pp. 1008-1012).

[29] Coleman-Norton no. 599 (pp. 1047-1048).

[30] Coleman-Norton no. 622 (pp. 1099-1100).

[31] Coleman-Norton no. 647 (p. 1162).

[32] E. M. Smallwood, *The Jews Under Roman Rule,* Leiden 1976, 512, regards it as a "piece of non-history". On p. 504 she passes the same verdict on a remark in the *Vita Heliogabali* 3:5 that this emperor would have said that the cults of Jews, Samaritans and Christians should be united with the pagan cults. See on both passages M. Stern, *Greek and Latin Authors on Jews and Judaism* II, Jerusalem 1980, 627-628 and 636-641. Cf. H. Dessau, Die Samaritaner bei den Scriptores Historiae Augustae, in *Festschrift zu C.F. Lehmann-Haupts sechzigstem Geburtstage,* Wien-Leipzig 1921, 124-128. Kippenberg, *Garizim* (n. 3) 147, rightly remarks that from *Vita Hel.* 3:5 one can at least deduce that the Samaritan religion played a role of some importance in fourth century Rome.

able to bribe Justinian so that the verdict was not carried out. This passage has given rise to the suspicion, rightly I suppose, that in the early Byzantine period there must have been more crypto-Samaritans in government service.

Damascius tells in his *Vita Isidori,* fragments 141-144 (p. 196 ed. Zintzen), that Proclus' successor as head of the Academy in Athens, Marinus, was originally a Samaritan, who under the influence of Greek philosophy had become an apostate and adopted paganism. This Marinus wrote *inter alia* commentaries on Plato's *Philebus* and *Parmenides,* an introduction to Euclides' *Data,* and a *Vita Procli.*[33]

Zacharias Rhetor, in his *Historia Ecclesiastica* III 5 (a work only partly preserved in Syriac), reports that under the emperor Marcianus' reign Romans and Samaritans fought side by side against the Christians, monophysites that is.[34] In view of the fact that this event took place at Neapolis (Nablus) in Palestine, it seems reasonable to assume that the author refers to members of the religious community of the Samaritans, not to Samarians.

That Samaritans also lived in Sicily is apparent from some letters of Gregory the Great (end of the 6th cent.) to bishops on that island, in which he says that the Samaritans there should not be allowed to circumcise their slaves (*Ep.* VI 33) and that Christian slaves of Samaritans there should be redeemed (*Ep.* VIII 21).

The passage in the Babylonian Talmud that is sometimes adduced as proof for a Samaritan diaspora in Babylonia (*Gittin* 45a), cannot bear the burden of this proof. The passage reports disputes between Abaye and Rav Chisda and Couthim (=Samaritans), but in view of recent theories about the unreliability of the Talmud as a historical source, it has rightly become doubtful to draw such conclusions from this material (although in itself it is far from improbable that Samaritans lived in southern Iraq in the Talmudic period).

As far as the non-literary material is concerned, we have to begin with the most recent and spectacular find, because that is the most ancient epigraphical testimony for a Samaritan diaspora. In 1980 two Samaritan inscriptions were found on the little island of Delos.[35] Both inscriptions, dating respecti-

---

33 See on this passage J. R. Masullo, *Marino di Neapoli: Vita di Proclo,* Napoli 1985, 17 n.15, and Stern, *op. cit.* (n. 32), II 673-675. On p. 675 Stern says: "The emergence of a Samaritan philosopher in the second half of the fifth century C.E. accords well with the general impression given by the sources of the strength of the Samaritan element both in Palestine and outside it in the Byzantine period". On p. 309 Stern remarks that Galen, in his commentary on the sixth book of Hippocrates' *Epidemica* (this commentary has been preserved only in an Arabic translation), utters criticisms of Rufus of Samaria whom he calls a Jew. Stern assumes that this Rufus was probably a Samaritan because presumably Galen could not make a distinction between Jews and Samaritans and Jews did not live in Samaria in the second century. This is of course very questionable.

34 ed. W. Brooks, CSCO 38, p. 159.

35 See Ph. Bruneau, 'Les Israélites de Délos' et la juiverie délienne, *Bulletin de correspondance hellénique* 106 (1982) 465-504, which is the editio princeps. An English

vely from the third to second and from the second to first century B.C., do not speak about Samaritans *expressis verbis,* but they they do speak about "the Israelites on Delos who pay their first offerings to the sanctuary (of) Argarizin". The mention of *Argarizin* leaves no room for doubt. These Delian Samaritans honour a certain Sarapion of Cnossos and Menippus of Heraclea for their benefactions towards the community, possibly the building of a synagogue.[36] The interesting thing about these inscriptions is not only that they are witnesses of a very early presence of Samaritans on Delos, but also that they make very probable that as early as the second century B.C. Samaritans lived in Crete (Sarapion of Cnossos).[37]

Another spectacular discovery from recent times is an inscription from a Samaritan synagogue in Thessalonica of the fourth, possibly the fifth century.[38] In this inscription of 20 lines one finds first a *berakhah* in Samaritan Hebrew (*barukh 'elohenu le'olam*), then in Greek the priestly blessing from Numbers 6:22-27, with a dozen deviations from the Septuagint that probably derive from a Samaritan revision of the Septuagint (not necessarily the *Samareitikon*), then again a *berakhah* in Samaritan Hebrew (*barukh shemo le'olam*), and finally a Greek dedication to Siricius from Neapolis (Nablus), possibly the rhetorician Siricius who was a teacher of rhetoric in Athens in the fourth century, although it is not certain whether this rhetor was a Samaritan or not.[39]

---

translation of the inscriptions is given by A. T. Kraabel, New Evidence of the Samaritan Diaspora Has Been Found on Delos, *Biblical Archaeologist* 47 (1984) 44-46.

[36] Bruneau (n. 35) extensively discusses all the problems. For *Argarizin* see now R. Pummer, ARGARIZIN: A Criterion for Samaritan Provenance?, *Journal for the Study of Judaism* 18 (1987) 18-25.

[37] This interpretation is not undisputed; see P. W. van der Horst, The Jews of Ancient Crete, *Journal of Jewish Studies* 39 (1988) 183-200. From which of the 10 known Heraclea's Menippus came is unknown. Bruneau 479 mentions in this connection an inscription (*Inscriptions de Délos* 2616) of ca. 100 B.C. in which a certain *Praylos Samareus* is mentioned who has contributed to the building of the Sarapieion of Delos. This will have been a Samarian rather than a Samaritan.

[38] This inscription was discovered already at the beginning of the fifties, but only published in 1968 by B. Lifshitz and J. Schiby, Une synagogue samaritaine a Thessalonique, *Revue Biblique* 75 (1968) 368-378. See also Lifshitz' edition and discussion in his Prolegomenon to the reprint of J. B. Frey, *Corpus Inscriptionum Iudaicarum* I, New York 1975, 70-75. Additions and corrections by E. Tov in *Rev. Bibl.* 81 (1974) 394-399, and J. D. Purvis in *Bulletin of the American School of Oriental Research* 221 (1976) 221-223.

[39] For a discussion of other aspects of this inscription I refer the reader to (apart from the publications mentioned in the previous note): J. and L. Robert, Bulletin épigraphique, *Revue des études grecques* 82 (1969) 476-478 and G. H. R. Horsley, *New Documents Illustrating Early Christianity* I, Macquarie 1981, 108-110. An inscription that is similar in many respects is the one from Imwas (Emmaus) in Reeg, *Samar. Synag.* (n. 2) 603-609.

To remain in Greece for yet another moment, the *Corpus Inscriptionum Graecarum* 2891-2893 (= *Inscriptiones Graecae* 10219-10221) contains 3 Athenian funerary inscriptions of a certain *Ammia Samareitis*, a *Theodora Samaritis*, and one more Samaritan (the text is badly damaged) - or are they Samarians, for in view of our criterium we have to leave open whether we have to do with Samarians or with Samaritans in this case. The same applies to the anonymous *Samaritês* in *IG* II2 2943 (also from Athens).[40]

Further we have to mention a Samaritan amulet from Corinth (albeit one from the ninth to eleventh century)[41], for that gives us occasion to point to the fact that such amulets, always inscribed with short quotations from the Pentateuch, have been found on several sites: Damascus, Tyrus, etc., but most of them in Israel.[42] Quite recently, however, Pummer has pointed out that there is reason to be very cautious in regarding these amulets as proof of Samaritan presence in the sites where they have been discovered. For most of these amulets have been found in Jewish and Christian tombs and there are several indications that the wearers of these phylacteria were not Samaritans but persons who asked Samaritans to make these amulets for them because of their supposed magical (apotropaic) power. "Samaritan amulets from Roman-Byzantine times are therefore 'Samaritan' only in the sense that they were produced or partially inscribed by Samaritans".[43] So we will have to leave them out of consideration and focus on other inscriptions.

To be sure, there are not many of these that unequivocally refer to Samaritans. If we leave aside 7 inscriptions from Damascus, because they do not belong to antiquity[44,] we can mention a Greek epitaph from Hipponion (South Italy) which records that this is the grave of *Antiochos Samaritanos*, according to Louis Robert a Samaritan inscription, but that is very questionable[45]; further a tomb-inscription *Samaritôn eleutherôn* from Tyre, with

---

[40] See J. and L. Robert, *ibid.* (n. 39) 478: "Il faut (...) relever que dans tous ces cas on peut se demander s'il s'agit de gens de confession samaritaine (...) ou des colons grecs de Samarie".

[41] J. Kaplan, A Samaritan Amulet from Corinth, *IEJ* 30 (1980) 196-198.

[42] For a complete dossier see Pummer, Samaritan Amulets (n.2) 260-263 (with bibliography).

[43] Pummer 257.

[44] A. Musil, Sieben samaritanische Inschriften aus Damaskus, *Sitzungsberichte der philologisch-historischen Klasse der kaiserlichen Akademie der Wissenschaften in Wien* 147, Wenen 1904, 1-11. Musil says that, if they are not a forgery, they must be from some period before 1000. I had no access to S. Yonick, The Samaritan Inscriptions from Siyagha, *Studii Biblici Franciscani Liber Annuus* 17 (1969) 162-221.

[45] See *Notizie degli scavi* 1921, 485, and L. Robert, *Hellenica* III, Paris 1946, 97. Later Robert has become more cautious in this respect, see *REG* 82 (1969) 479 (quoted above in note 40).

the same problem[46]; inscriptions from Rhodos (*IG* XII 1, 716; XII 8, 439)[47], Sicily (*IG* XIV 336), Kaunos in Caria where in a building inscription a number of women are mentioned as *Sikimitai*[48], and Iran.[49] In all these inscriptions from the Hellenistic and Roman periods the editors wanted to see "un nouveau témoignage de la diaspora samaritaine"[50], but we have to defer our verdict. *Possibly* we have to do with Samaritans here, but as long as we do not have additional criteria that guarantee such an identification, it should remain a *non liquet*, except in the case of the Carian *Sikimitai* since Sichem is the old name of the holy place of the Samaritan community.

The situation is identical in the papyri. Apart from the unequivocal *Samaritai tên thrêskeian* in CPJ 513 (see above), we find 6 other papyri (ranging from the second to the seventh century A. D.) where persons are called *Samaritês* or *Samareus* but we are not able to say whether or not they deal with Samaritans.[51]

Let us draw some conclusions. It will have become clear that much of the material that has often been adduced as evidence for a Samaritan diaspora cannot serve such a purpose. It cannot be excluded that that material deals with Samaritans, but it may be about Samarians as well. Nevertheless, there remains enough evidence: the inscriptions from Delos and Thessalonica, some papyri, passages in Josephus and several church-fathers, and the decrees in the legislative corpora. All that evidence makes abundantly clear that from the third century B.C. to the seventh century A.D. members of the Samaritan religious community had settled themselves in all parts of the ancient world. About the size of that diaspora we know very little. It will have been very small, of course, in the third century B.C., but in the later Roman Empire much bigger. Ancient sources report that during the great revolt of the Samaritans in Palestine against the Byzantine emperor in 529 some 100.000 Samaritans were killed.[52] Even if this number is exaggerated, it is nevertheless indicative of a very sizeable Samaritan community in Palestine. A prominent Samaritanologist, Alan Crown, estimates the number of Palestinian Samaritans in late antiquity to have been ca. 300.000 and the

---

46   See J. P. Rey-Coquais, *Inscriptions grecques et latines découvertes dans les fouilles de Tyr (1963-1974) I: Inscriptions de la nécropole*, Paris 1977, no. 168.

47   *IG* XII 8, 439 is mistakenly recorded there as an inscription from Thasos; see Robert in *REG* 82 (1969) 477-478.

48   Robert, *REG* 67 (1954) 169-171 (no. 229).

49   Robert, *Comptes Rendus de l'Académie des Inscriptions et Belles Lettres* 1967, 281-297.

50   Robert, *REG* 67 (1954) 171.

51   See the enumeration of these papyri by M.Nagel, *Un Samaritain dans l'Arsinoite au IIe siècle après J.C.*, *Chronique d'Egypte* 49/98 (1974) 356-365.

52   M. Avi-Yonah, *Geschichte der Juden im Zeitalter des Talmud*, Berlin 1962, 251ff.

number of Samaritans in the diaspora ca. 150.000.[53] This remains guesswork, but we can be sure that there must have been a very considerable Samaritan diaspora, without any doubt consisting of many tens of thousands. In the course of the Middle Ages this diaspora disappeared, partly by a gradual process of christianization, partly by islamization, in many cases probably by a kind of 'marranization'.[54]

---

[53] Crown, Samaritan Diaspora (n. 6) 118. See also *Encycl. Jud.* XIV (1972) 736.

[54] I owe thanks to Prof. Hans G. Kippenberg who commented on an earlier draft of this article and to Dr. Judith Frishman who corrected my English.

9. THE JEWS OF ANCIENT CRETE

The history of Cretan Jewry in antiquity is largely unknown to us. This is due not only to the scarcity of our sources but also to the fact that this history seems to have been a rather uneventful one. This is in keeping with the history of the island itself, for it can be said that from the late Hellenistic period to the Early Middle Ages Crete enjoyed a unique period of peace and had practically no 'history', inasmuch as until the seventh century C.E. 'nothing regarded as worthy of note by the ancient authors happened'.[1] Although the scarce literary and epigraphical data[2] do not grant us more than occasional glimpses of the Jewish communities in Crete, it is nonetheless worthwhile assembling the material available in order to try to make a dossier as complete as possible, something that has not been done so far.[3]

Before surveying the evidence, let us ask how and when the Cretan diaspora originated. We can only guess at the answer to this question but it may be an educated surmise. We know that during the Maccabaean revolt many Jews fled from Palestine to other countries like Egypt and Syria. It is not improbable that some of them may have taken refuge in Crete since that would tie in very well with a passage in I Maccabees to be discussed presently. Some may have come by way of Egypt, for an inscription from Crete reveals that Ptolemy VI Philometor (180–145 B.C.E.) sent troops to Gortyn in Crete[4] in the middle of the sixties of the second century B.C.E., and it is well known from various sources that Philometor used a great many Jews in his military operations, often in leading positions.[5] Admittedly, this does not constitute compelling proof that the Cretan diaspora started in the sixties of the second century B.C.E., but it is a hypothesis that gains some support from I Macc. 15:22–3.

---

[1] I. F. Sanders, *Roman Crete. An Archaeological Survey and Gazetteer of Late Hellenistic, Roman and Early Byzantine Crete* (Warminster, 1982), 1.

[2] There are no remains of ancient synagogues in Crete.

[3] For incomplete and summary statements on Cretan Jewry see Sanders, *Roman Crete* (n. 1) 43; M. Stern, 'The Jewish Diaspora', in *The Jewish People in the First Century* (CRINT I 1) (Assen, 1974), 160; S. Marcus, 'Crete', *Enc. Jud.* 5 (1972), 1088–9; E. Schürer, G. Vermes, F. Millar and M. Goodman, *The History of the Jewish People in the Age of Jesus Christ* III.1 (Edinburgh, 1986), 69; U. Baumann, *Rom und die Juden* (Bern and Frankfurt, 1983), 240 n. 12.

[4] M. Guarducci (ed.), *Inscriptiones Creticae*, 4 vols. (Rome, 1935–1950), IV no. 195. Ptolemy probably sent his troops to assist Gortyn in its war against Cnossos.

[5] P. M. Fraser, *Ptolemaic Alexandria* I (Oxford, 1972), 83 with notes in vol. II (1972), 163–4. For other Ptolemaic officials on Crete see *ibid.* I 66, 101. It is notable that there were also many Cretans in Ptolemaic service in Egypt (*ibid.* 66, 70, 81, 88 f., 101, 180, 614 f.), which indicates the strong ties between Egypt and Crete.

This passage immediately follows upon a letter written in 140 B.C.E. by Lucius, consul in Rome, to Ptolemy VIII Euergetes in which he asks him to refrain from waging war upon the Jews whom he calls 'our friends and allies' (15:17). After having quoted the letter, the author of I Macc. adds:

(22) καὶ ταῦτα ἔγραψεν Δημητρίῳ τῷ βασιλεῖ καὶ ᾿Αττάλῳ καὶ ᾿Αριαράθῃ καὶ ᾿Αρσάκῃ (23) καὶ εἰς πάσας τὰς χώρας καὶ Σαμψάμῃ καὶ Σπαρτιάταις καὶ εἰς Δῆλον καὶ εἰς Μύνδον καὶ εἰς Σικυῶνα καὶ εἰς τὴν Καρίαν καὶ εἰς Σάμον καὶ εἰς τὴν Παμφυλίαν καὶ εἰς Λυκίαν καὶ εἰς ῾Αλικαρνασσὸν καὶ εἰς ῾Ρόδον καὶ εἰς Φασηλίδα καὶ εἰς Κῶ καὶ εἰς Σίδην καὶ εἰς ῎Αραδον καὶ Γόρτυναν καὶ Κνίδον καὶ Κύπρον καὶ Κυρήνην.

(22) He wrote the same letter to King Demetrius and to Attalus and to Ariarathes and to Arsakes, (23) and to all the following countries: to Sampsame and the Spartans, to Delos and to Myndos and to Sicyon and to Caria and to Samos and to Pamphylia and to Lycia and to Halicarnassus and to Rhodos and to Phaselis and to Cos and to Side and to Aradus and Gortyn and Cnidus and Cyprus and Cyrene. (I Macc. 15:22–3)

These lines form an interesting document for the spread of the diaspora in the middle of the second century B.C.E.[6] For our purpose it is remarkable that, whereas in the case of other islands the name of the whole island is mentioned (Samos, Rhodos, Cos, Cyprus), only in the case of Crete is the name of one single city mentioned, which happens to be Gortyn, where Ptolemy VI Philometor had sent his troops a quarter of a century before. This adds probability to my hypothesis that the military operation of Philometor may have marked the beginning of Jewish settlement in Crete, especially in Gortyn, which was also the birthplace or residence of one of the very few Jews about whom more is known than merely the name, as will be seen later (see below on Sophia, pp. 198–200).[7]

Although we will reserve the epigraphical evidence for Cretan Jewry for the latter part of this study, it seems appropriate to deal at this point with an inscription which may indicate that in approximately the same period there were also Samaritans in Crete. It is a recently published inscription from the island of Delos and runs as follows:[8]

[6] See the commentary on this passage by J. A. Goldstein, *I Maccabees* (Garden City, 1976), 496–500. It is obvious that these lines list not just names of allies, but countries and cities where Jews are living and in danger of being attacked.

[7] In a private communication Professor Martin Hengel suggested that Jewish settlement in Crete may have started already in the third century B.C.E., in view of the fact that elsewhere in Greece (Attica, Cyprus) there is evidence of Jewish presence from *ca.* 300 B.C.E. onwards (see the references in his *Juden, Griechen und Barbaren* (Stuttgart, 1976), 121) and that there is also a third century B.C.E. epitaph (in Gaza) of a Cretan officer in Ptolemaic service (*SEG* 8, 269; see *Judentum und Hellenismus* (Tübingen, 1973²), 26 with note 77), which may be indicative of contacts between Crete and Jewish Palestine in that period.

[8] Ph. Bruneau, 'Les Israélites de Délos et la juiverie délienne', *Bulletin de correspondence hellénique* 106 (1982), 465–504. At pp. 468–9 Bruneau presents a photo and a transcription with translation of the inscription.

1. οἱ ἐν Δήλῳ Ἰσραελεῖται οἱ ἀ-
2. παρχόμενοι εἰς ἱερὸν Ἀργα-
3. ριζεὶν στεφανοῦσιν χρυσῷ
4. στεφάνῳ Σαραπίωνα Ἰάσο-
5. νος Κνώσιον εὐεργεσίας
6. ἕνεκεν τῆς εἰς ἑαυτούς.

The Israelites of Delos who contribute their offerings to the temple (of) Argarizin (or: to the sacred mountain Garizin) crown with a golden crown Sarapion, the son of Iason, from Cnossos for his benefaction towards them.

There is no doubt that the Israelites who pay their temple-taxes to the *hieron Argarizin*[9] are the religious community of the Samaritans, who describe themselves as Israelites in order to distinguish themselves from those called *Ioudaioi* who had their own synagogue nearby on Delos.[10] These Samaritans honour Sarapion from Cnossos in Crete for his benefactions to the community. An earlier Samaritan inscription built into the same wall of what may have been a Samaritan synagogue records the honouring of a certain Menippus of Heraclea for having erected and dedicated at his own cost a building probably for the community.[11] What Sarapion's gift to the community was, we do not know, but the relevant point is that he was most likely a Samaritan believer from Crete, whether he was only born in Cnossos or still lived there when he acted as a benefactor to the Delan Samaritans.[12] That he had a very pagan-sounding name is no proof that he cannot have been a Samaritan believer. The Jewish prosopography of Ptolemaic and Roman Egypt shows that several Jews bore theophoric names containing the elements 'Isis' and 'Horus',[13] so a Samaritan name with the element 'Sarapis' need not be surprising. Of course, the possibility can never be ruled out that the Samaritans honoured pagan benefactors, but it is much more probable that a religious community honours a co-religionist. In that case, we may assume that in the second century

---

[9] For *Argarizin* = 'the mountain of Garizim' see also Pseudo-Eupolemus, fragment 1, *ap.* Eusebius, *Praep. Evang.* IX 17, 5. Originally *har Garizim*, it is written as one word in Samaritan sources (e.g. *argarizim* in the Greek translation of the Samaritan Pentateuch). Cf. also Josephus' use of *Argarizin* in *Bell.* I 63, which derives from a Samaritan source; see R. Egger, *Josephus Flavius und die Samaritaner* (Freibourg and Göttingen, 1986), 294–6. See further C. R. Holladay, *Fragments from Hellenistic Jewish Authors* I (Chico, 1983), 183 n. 21, and R. Pummer, 'ARGARIZIN: A Criterion for Samaritan Provenance?', *JSJ* 18 (1987), 18–25, who fails to discuss *Bell.* I 63. Bruneau, *art. cit.* (n. 8), 477, refers to *ΤΟΥΡΓΑΡΙΖΙΝ* on the Madaba map (*tur* being Aramaic for 'mountain').

[10] See Bruneau (n. 8), *passim*.

[11] See Bruneau (n. 8), 471 f. The inscription is damaged so we do not know what Menippus built and dedicated.

[12] Bruneau (n. 8), 481: 'le plus probable est que Sarapion et Ménippos soient eux-mêmes Samaritains'. This is doubted by A. T. Kraabel, 'New Evidence of the Samaritan Diaspora has been found on Delos', *Biblical Archeologist* 47 (1984), 44–6.

[13] See V. A. Tcherikover, A. Fuks and M. Stern, *Corpus Papyrorum Judaicarum* III (Cambridge, Mass., 1964), 167–96.

B.C.E. there were Samaritans in Crete, which should cause no astonishment in view of the extent of the Samaritan diaspora.[14] Since the editor dates the inscription between 150 and 50 B.C.E. on palaeographical grounds, and since it was probably written before the destruction of the sanctuary of Mount Garizim in 129 B.C.E., it is plausible to suppose that Sarapion lived in Cnossos around the middle of the second century B.C.E.

The next piece of evidence in chronological order dates from more than one and a half centuries later. In the early forties of the first century C.E., the Jewish philosopher Philo of Alexandria wrote his *Legatio ad Gaium* where he quotes at length a letter from Agrippa to the Emperor Caligula, in which the former says that Jerusalem has settled colonies in almost every country of the world.

> καὶ οὐ μόνον αἱ ἤπειροι μεσταὶ τῶν Ἰουδαϊκῶν ἀποικιῶν εἰσιν, ἀλλὰ καὶ νήσων αἱ δοκιμώταται, Εὔβοια, Κύπρος, Κρήτη.

> And not only are the mainlands full of Jewish colonies but also the most highly esteemed of the islands, Euboia, Cyprus, Crete. (*Leg.* 282)

The difference from the earlier testimonies is striking. Here it is no longer a few cities that are mentioned, like Gortyn and Cnossos: it is stated that the greater islands, Crete included, are *full of* Jewish settlements. That the Cretan diaspora had expanded considerably in the meantime is confirmed by a few other testimonies in the last quarter of the first century C.E.

In one of his many stories of Jews who had been deceived by an impostor, Josephus tells about a Jewish fraud who pretended to be the prince Alexander whom King Herod had put to death (*Bellum* II 101 ff.). This man gave out that the executioners sent to kill both him and Aristobulus had stolen them away out of compassion, substituting in their stead the corpses of persons who resembled them. So, contrary to the rumours, he was still alive.

> τούτοις γοῦν τοὺς ἐν Κρήτῃ Ἰουδαίους ἐξαπατήσας καὶ λαμπρῶς ἐφοδιασθεὶς διέπλευσεν εἰς Μῆλον.

> With this tale he completely deceived the Jews in Crete, and, being magnificently furnished with supplies, he sailed across to Melos. (II 103)

In Melos and elsewhere, and finally in Rome, the Pseudo-Alexander succeeded in gathering a large following among the Jews, but the Emperor Augustus unmasked him as an impostor.[15] Whereas this story took place at the beginning of the first century, the same Josephus tells us in his autobiography that in the second half of the seventies he divorced his wife and took another.

---

[14] See e.g. A. D. Crown, 'The Samaritan Diaspora to the End of the Byzantine Era', *Australian Journal of Biblical Archaeology* 2 (1974/75), 107–23, and my article 'De Samaritaanse diaspora in de oudheid', *Nederlands Theologisch Tijdschrift* 42 (1988), 134–44.

[15] The same story is found in Josephus, *Ant.* XVII 324–338.

μετὰ ταῦτα ἠγαγόμην γυναῖκα κατῳκηκυῖαν μὲν ἐν Κρήτῃ, τὸ δὲ γένος
Ἰουδαίαν, γονέων εὐγενεστάτων καὶ τῶν κατὰ τὴν χώραν ἐπιφανεστάτων.

Thereafter I married a woman who was Jewish by birth and had settled in
Crete. She came of very distinguished parents, indeed the most illustrious
people in that country. (*Vita* 427)

These two passages demonstrate that Cretan Jewry had not only become
numerous, as Philo had already shown, but also that some of them were
probably well-to-do and belonged to the upper class of the island.

Contemporary with Josephus' testimonies, two passages in the New
Testament, though not very illuminating, nevertheless offer corroborative
evidence. In a text comparable to I Macc. 15 and Philo (discussed above),
the author of Acts enumerates a large number of countries from which
diaspora Jews went on pilgrimage to Jerusalem, where they witnessed the
manifestations of the Holy Spirit. Acts 2:9–11:

(9) Πάρθοι καὶ Μῆδοι καὶ Ἐλαμῖται καὶ οἱ κατοικοῦντες τὴν Μεσοποταμίαν,
Ἰουδαίαν τε καὶ Καππαδοκίαν, Πόντον καὶ τὴν Ἀσίαν, (10) Φρυγίαν τε καὶ
Παμφυλίαν, Αἴγυπτον καὶ τὰ μέρη τῆς Λιβύης τῆς κατὰ Κυρήνην, καὶ οἱ
ἐπιδημοῦντες Ῥωμαῖοι, (11) Ἰουδαῖοί τε καὶ προσήλυτοι, Κρῆτες καὶ
Ἄραβες, ἀκούομεν λαλούντων αὐτῶν ταῖς ἡμετέραις γλώσσαις τὰ μεγαλεῖα
τοῦ θεοῦ.

(9) Parthians and Medes and Elamites and residents of Mesopotamia, Judea
and Cappadocia, Pontus and Asia, (10) Phrygia and Pamphylia, Egypt and
the parts of Libya belonging to Cyrene, and visitors from Rome, both Jews
and Proselytes, (11) Cretans and Arabs, we hear them telling in our own
tongues the mighty works of God. (RSV)

In spite of Otto Eissfeldt's theory that the placing of 'Cretans and Arabs'
after the summarizing 'Jews and proselytes' indicates that these two words
should not be interpreted literally but as a general statement meaning '(Jews
and proselytes) from West to East',[16] I still think it legitimate also to take
the sentence at its face value as meaning that Jews were living in Crete too.
This is what is implied in the second New Testament text in the
pseudo-Pauline letter to Titus, written to a Christian community in Crete,
where we read in 1:10–14:

(10) Εἰσὶν γὰρ πολλοὶ ἀνυπότακτοι, ματαιολόγοι καὶ φρεναπάται, μάλιστα
οἱ ἐκ τῆς περιτομῆς, (11) οὓς δεῖ ἐπιστομίζειν, οἵτινες ὅλους οἴκους
ἀνατρέπουσιν διδάσκοντες ἃ μὴ δεῖ αἰσχροῦ κέρδους χάριν. (12) εἶπέν τις ἐξ
αὐτῶν, ἴδιος αὐτῶν προφήτης· Κρῆτες ἀεὶ ψεῦσται, κακὰ θηρία, γαστέρες
ἀργαί. (13) ἡ μαρτυρία αὕτη ἐστὶν ἀληθής. δι᾽ ἣν αἰτίαν ἔλεγχε αὐτοὺς

---

[16] O. Eissfeldt, 'Kreter und Araber', *Theol. Lit. Zt.* 72 (1947), 207–12. See now also G.
Schneider, *Die Apostelgeschichte* I (Freiburg, 1980), 253, and R. Pesch, *Die Apostelgeschichte* I
(Neukirchen, 1986), 106.

ἀποτόμως, ἵνα ὑγιαίνωσιν ἐν τῇ πίστει, (14) μὴ προσέχοντες Ἰουδαϊκοῖς μύθοις καὶ ἐντολαῖς ἀνθρώπων ἀποστρεφομένων τὴν ἀλήθειαν.

(10) For there are many insubordinate men, empty talkers and deceivers, especially the circumcision party; (11) they must be silenced, since they are upsetting whole families by teaching for base gain what they have no right to teach. (12) One of themselves, a prophet of their own, said: 'Cretans are always liars, evil beasts, lazy gluttons'. (13) This testimony is true. Therefore rebuke them sharply, that they may be sound in the faith, (14) instead of giving heed to Jewish myths or to commands of men who reject the truth. (RSV)

Although the passage concerns Jews who have become Christians, it is also an indirect testimony to Jewish presence in Crete. The author of the epistle accuses what he calls literally 'those of the circumcision', i.e. Jewish converts, of perverting the truth of the gospel by taking notice of Jewish fables or myths and human commandments, and he tries to blacken them by applying to them a quotation from a poem of Epimenides about the objectionable character of the Cretans.[17] This shows that, as in Asia Minor and Syria, in Crete, too, tensions ran high between Christians of Jewish and Gentile origin. For the present purpose it is not necessary to enter into the details of this controversy. We would however record the appearance around the turn of the first to the second century of the first signs that Christianity made converts among Cretan Jews. This is the beginning of a process of which we find the sad apogee in the final literary document concerning Cretan Jewry.

But before discussing that last testimony, we will by way of interlude look at a curious text from the beginning of the second century C.E. In the famous fifth book of his *Histories*, Tacitus relates the fall of Jerusalem in 70, but before doing so makes the following remark:

> quoniam famosae urbis supremum diem tradituri sumus, congruens videtur primordia eius aperire. Iudaeos Creta insula profugos novissima Libyae insedisse memorant, qua tempestate Saturnus vi Iovis pulsus cesserit regnis. argumentum e nomine petitur: inclutum in Creta Idam montem, accolas Idaeos aucto in barbarum cognomento Iudaeos vocitari.

> As I am now to record the final days of a famous city, it seems appropriate to inform the reader of its origins. The Jews are said to have been refugees from the island of Crete who settled in the coastal area of Africa in the stormy days when, according to the story, Saturn was dethroned and expelled by the aggression of Jupiter. This is a deduction from the name Iudaei: that word is to be regarded as a barbarous lengthening of Idaei, the name of the people dwelling around the famous mount Ida in Crete. (*Hist.* V 2, 1–3)

---

[17] On the problem of the attribution of this verse see especially C. Spicq, *Les Epitres Pastorales* II (Paris, 1969), 608 f. (there lit.), and M. Dibelius and H. Conzelmann, *Die Pastoralbriefe* (Tübingen, 1966), 101–3.

This curious passage seems to be the product of a mixture of blurred historical reminiscences, folk etymology, the equation of Shabbath with the day of Saturnus, and fantasy. The reminiscences may concern the very early contacts between Palestine and Crete in the age of the so-called Sea Peoples (*ca.* 1200 B.C.E.), when most probably the Philistines invaded Palestine from Crete.[18] It is not improbable that the Philistines were expelled from Crete (*Creta insula profugos!*), and that therefore until late antiquity the god Marnas in the originally Philistine city of Gaza was identified with *Zeus Cretagenes* (Zeus who was born in Crete).[19] This unhistorical identification of Philistines/Palestines with 'Judaeans' induced the folk-etymological equation of *Iudaei* and *Idaei*, a well-known type of 'aetiological' etymology of which a famous other but similar example is Vergil's derivation of *Iulus* from *Ilus*, the founder of Ilium = Troy, which is meant to link the founding of Rome with that of Troy.[20] On the connection between Saturnus and the Jews and especially the Jewish sabbath, the 'day of Saturn', several ancient authors make their comments. Since these can easily be found in Stern's *Greek and Latin Authors on Jews and Judaism*,[21] they need not detain us here. All these elements, perhaps with the admixture of the story that Cretans—like Jews—abstained from eating pork,[22] may have created this fanciful theory of the Cretan origin of the Jews. It does not add to our knowledge of Jewish history in Crete, however.

From the period from the beginning of the second to the fifth century C.E. we have no literary evidence on Cretan Jewry. Rabbinic literature yields no data, neither does Christian literature. It is possible only to speculate. Thus a considerable influx of Jews into Crete from Cyrene (ancient Libya) may have occurred in the years 115–117, when the great revolt erupted there and elsewhere in North Africa. There had been close connections between Crete and Cyrene ever since Rome united the two administratively to form one province in the sixties of the first century B.C.E. It is known that during the revolt many Jews fled to the islands, and it is probable that many of them went to Crete.[23]

Now we turn to the final and most dramatic piece of relevant evidence extant: the *Historia Ecclesiastica* of Socrates, composed in about 440, a work designed to continue the story of Eusebius' *Historia Ecclesiastica*,[24] and covering the events from the accession of Constantine to the year

---

[18] On this problem see W. Fauth in H. Heubner and W. Fauth, *P. Cornelius Tacitus. Die Historien* V (Heidelberg, 1982), 20–2 (there lit.).

[19] See G. Mussies, 'Marnas', *ANRW* II 18 (forthcoming).

[20] Vergil, *Aen.* I 267 f. See A. M. A. Hospers-Jansen, *Tacitus over de Joden* (Groningen, 1949), 112. For other instances see M. Stern, *Greek and Latin Authors on Jews and Judaism* II (Jerusalem, 1980), 33.

[21] See the references in vol. III (Jerusalem, 1984), 147.

[22] See the references in Stern, vol. I (Jerusalem, 1974), 559.

[23] See S. Applebaum, *Jews and Greeks in Ancient Cyrene* (Leiden, 1979), 292 f., and H. Z. (J. W.) Hirschberg, *A History of the Jews in North Africa* I (Leiden, 1974), 39.

[24] See G. F. Chesnut, *The First Christian Histories* (Paris, 1977), 167–89.

438/439. In one of the final chapters of the book (VII 38) he writes as follows:[25]

Περὶ δὲ τὸν χρόνον τοῦτον πολλοὶ τῶν ἐν Κρήτῃ Ἰουδαίων ἐχριστιάνισαν διὰ πάθος τοιόνδε· ἀπατεών τις Ἰουδαῖος ὑπεκρίνατο εἶναι Μωϋσῆς. πεπέμφθαι δὲ ἔλεγεν ἐκ τῶν οὐρανῶν ὅπως ἂν τοὺς τὴν νῆσον οἰκοῦντας Ἰουδαίους ἐκβάλῃ διὰ τῆς θαλάσσης ἀγαγών. αὐτὸς γὰρ εἶναι ἔλεγεν ὁ καὶ τὸν Ἰσραὴλ πάλαι διὰ τῆς Ἐρυθρᾶς θαλάσσης σώσας. ἐφ᾽ ὅλον οὖν ἐνιαυτὸν περιῄει καθ᾽ ἑκάστην τῆς νήσου πόλιν καὶ τοὺς ἐν αὐταῖς οἰκοῦντας Ἰουδαίους τὰ τοιαῦτα πιστεύειν ἀνέπειθε. παρῄνει τε πάντα τὰ χρήματα καὶ τὰ κτήματα καταλιπεῖν. ἄξειν γὰρ αὐτοὺς διὰ ξηρᾶς τῆς θαλάσσης εἰς τὴν γῆν τῆς ἐπαγγελίας ὑπισχνεῖτο. οἱ δὲ ταῖς τοιαύταις ἐλπίσι βουκολούμενοι πάντων μὲν τῶν ἔργων ἠμέλουν. κατεφρόνουν δὲ καὶ ὧν ἐκέκτηντο, τοῖς ἐπιτυχοῦσιν ἀφέντες λαμβάνειν αὐτά. ἐπειδὴ δὲ ἦν ἡμέρα ἦν ὁ ἀπατεὼν Ἰουδαῖος ἐσήμαινεν, ἡγεῖτο μὲν αὐτός, ἠκολούθουν δὲ οἱ σύμπαντες ἅμα γυναιξὶ καὶ τῇ μικρᾷ ἡλικίᾳ. ἄγει οὖν αὐτοὺς ἐπί τι ἀκρωτήριον ἐπὶ τῆς θαλάσσης ἐκνεῦον, καὶ κυβιστᾶν κατ᾽ αὐτῆς ἐκέλευε. τοῦτο οὖν ἐποίουν οἱ πρότεροι τῷ κρημνῷ προσπελάσαντες καὶ εὐθὺς ἔθνησκον, τοῦτο μὲν τοῖς κρημνοῖς προσρηγνύμενοι, τοῦτο δὲ καὶ εἰς τὸ ὕδωρ ἀποπνιγόμενοι. καὶ πλείους ἂν διεφθάρησαν εἰ μὴ θεοῦ προνοήσαντος παρέτυχον ἄνδρες Χριστιανοί, ἁλιεῖς τε καὶ ἔμποροι. οἳ τοὺς μὲν πνιγομένους ἀνέλκοντες ἔσωζον, τότε τῆς ἀνοίας αἴσθησιν ἐν τῷ κακῶς πάσχειν λαμβάνοντας. τοὺς δὲ ἄλλους ἀνεῖργον ῥίπτειν ἑαυτοὺς μηνύοντες τὴν ἀπώλειαν τῶν πρότερον ῥιψάντων ἑαυτούς. οἳ καὶ γνόντες τότε τὴν ἀπάτην ἐμέμφοντο μὲν τὴν ἄκριτον ἑαυτῶν πίστιν, τὸν δὲ ψευδο-Μωϋσῆν ἀνελεῖν σπεύδοντες συλλαβεῖν οὐ δεδύνηνται· ἀφανὴς γὰρ ἐγένετο, ὑπόνοιάν τε πάρεσχε τοῖς πλείοσιν ὡς εἴη δαίμων ἀλάστωρ ἀνθρώπου σχῆμα ὑποδύς, ἐπὶ λύμῃ τοῦ ἐκεῖ ἔθνους αὐτῶν. διὰ δὲ τόδε τὸ πάθος πολλοὶ τότε τῶν ἐν τῇ Κρήτῃ Ἰουδαίων χαίρειν τῷ Ἰουδαϊσμῷ φράσαντες τῇ πίστει τοῦ χριστιανισμοῦ προσεχώρησαν.

At about that (same) time many of the Jews in Crete became Christians because of the following incident. A Jewish impostor pretended to be Moses. He said he had been sent from heaven in order to evacuate the Jews who lived on the island by leading them through the sea. For he said he was the same person who also saved Israel through the Red Sea long ago. During a whole year he went around along every town of the island, and the Jews who lived therein he tried to persuade to believe such things. He exhorted them to leave behind all their money and possessions. For he promised to lead them through the dry sea to the land of promise. Those who let themselves be cheated with such hopes began to neglect all their tasks. And they also despised what they

[25] The text printed is that from Migne's *Patrologia Graeca* 67, 825–8 (with minor corrections). Unfortunately, the new edition by P. Périchon for the series *Sources Chrétiennes*, although announced long ago (see Périchon's article 'Pour une édition nouvelle de l'historien Socrate: les manuscrits et les versions', *Recherches de science religieuse* 53 (1965), 112–20), has never appeared. See also the three-volume edition with annotations by R. Hussey, *Socratis Scholastici Ecclesiastica Historia* (Oxford, 1853), text in vol. II, pp. 822–4; Hussey has no annotations to this chapter. A. C. Zenos' English translation was unavailable to me.

possessed, and let it be taken away by any chance person. When the day designated by the Jewish impostor arrived, he himself led the way and all the others followed with their wives and little children. He brought them to a promontory that stood as a precipice above the sea and ordered them to plunge into it. Those who first reached the edge did so, and they died straight away, partly because they dashed against the cliffs, partly also because they drowned in the water. And more people would have been killed if not by God's providence some Christian fishermen and merchants would have been there. These saved some who were drowning by dragging them up. Only then, when they were suffering so badly, they realized their folly. They kept the others off from throwing themselves down by telling them about the deaths of those who threw themselves down before. Then they too realized the fraud and blamed themselves for their uncritical belief. But when they eagerly wanted to kill the pseudo-Moses, they could not lay their hands on him; for he had disappeared. And this raised in many the suspicion that he had been an avenging demon who had taken on human disguise in order to outrage their people there. By this incident many of the Jews who then lived on Crete took leave of Judaism and embraced the Christian faith. (*Hist. Eccl.* VII 38)[26]

Several elements in this passage need to be discussed.[27] As regards the reliability of the story, it should be said that, although on the one hand Christian bias may be responsible for some exaggeration (*many* of the Jews following the impostor), especially in the happy ending (*many* of them becoming Christians), on the other hand it was to be expected exactly in this period, as we shall see presently, that messianic hopes would run high. So there can be little doubt that the kernel of the story is historical. The period in question can be fixed fairly exactly. The *terminus ante quem* is 438/439 C.E., the final year dealt with by Socrates, the *terminus a quo* is 431/432, since the story immediately preceding it recounts events which took place during the consulship of Bassus and Antiochus, who became consuls in 431. So most probably the time can be placed in the first half or the middle of the thirties of the fifth century C.E. Strikingly enough, this is the first messianic movement known since the Bar Kochba revolt exactly three centuries before. That messianic risings no longer occurred after the shattering defeat of the second revolt is not surprising, but why did they recur, in both pacifistic-quietistic and belligerent ways, from *ca.* 430 onwards? For the

[26] For Latin versions of this story see *inter alios* Cassiodorus, *Historia Tripartita* XII 9 (*Patrol. Lat.* 69, 1210 f. or *CSEL* 71, 677 f.); several other Latin authors are enumerated by B. Blumenkranz, *Juifs et chrétiens dans le monde occidental 430–1096* (Paris and La Haye, 1960), 244 n. 139.

[27] Extremely brief discussions of this passage are given by M. Seligsohn in *Jew. Enc.* 9 (1905) 64; S. W. Baron, *Social and Religious History of the Jews* V (New York, 1957), 168.367; B. Blumenkranz, *op. cit.* (n. 26), 244.

movement was only the first in a long series ranging from our pseudo-Moses to Shabbetai Zvi.[28]

There are clear reasons for the resurgence of messianic expectations in this period. First, ever since the destruction of the Temple, Jews had prayed for and expected the defeat of Rome and the ascendancy of the Jewish people consequent upon it.[29] 'In the fifth century these hopes reached their fever point. The Empire was breaking up; the long-anticipated collapse was about to take place.'[30] Rome had been conquered and sacked by the Visigoths in 410. The years following saw other invasions in Italy and elsewhere. In 430 North Africa was overrun by the Vandals. And in 433 Attila's rise to power in the Hunnish kingdom was the beginning of a new and tremendous threat to the power of Rome. Second, there was an enormous deterioration in the conditions of life for the Jews in the first third of the fifth century. Roman, i.e. Christian, oppression intensified. Theodosius II (408–450) abolished the Jewish patriarchate and closed the few remaining rabbinic schools. This emperor, who deposed the patriarch Gamliel, also forbade the construction of new synagogues and ordered the destruction of existing ones. In 438 he even issued a statute in which Jews, defined as enemies of the Roman laws and of the supreme majesty, were forbidden to hold any high office. Thus in the twenties and thirties of the fifth century, their civil inferiority, and discrimination against them, were legally sanctioned. This in itself would have been already enough to kindle messianic sentiments.[31]

But quite apart from these factors, older traditions predicted that the messiah would come sometime in the fifth century. As may be observed in Talmud Bavli, *Avoda Zara* 9a–b, *Sanhedrin* 97a–b and 99a, and in parallel passages, calculations varied from 365 to 400 (or more) years after the destruction of the Temple; that is to say, somewhere from *ca.* 435 onwards. Rav Ashi, who lived in the beginning of the fifth century, even sought to avert any evil consequences which might follow upon the failure of this

---

[28] For a list of messianic movements frim the fifth through the twelfth centuries see K. H. Bernhardt, 'Zu Eigenart und Alter der messianisch-eschatologischen Zusätze im Targum Jeruschalmi I', in *Gott und die Götter. FS E. Fascher* (Berlin, n.d. (1958?)), 79. For the same period see further A. H. Silver, *A History of Messianic Speculation in Israel from the First through the Seventeenth Centuries* (Boston, 1959 (repr. of 1927)), 25–80; H. H. Ben-Sasson, 'Messianic Movements', *Enc. Jud.* 11 (1972), 1420–2. Ben-Sasson and Silver both·wrongly date the appearance of the Cretan Moses to the middle of the fifth century.

[29] See Silver, *op. cit.* (n. 28), 27–9 for references. For a general survey of Jewish attitudes toward Rome in antiquity see G. Stemberger, *Die römische Herrschaft im Urteil der Juden* (Darmstadt, 1983).

[30] Silver, *op. cit.* (n. 28), 29.

[31] See J. Juster, *Les Juifs dans l'Empire Romain* I (Paris, 1914), 162–7, vol. II (1914), 101–3; M. Simon, *Verus Israel. A Study of the Relations Between Christians and Jews in the Roman Empire* (Oxford, 1986), 224–33; A. M. Rabello, 'Theodosius II', *Enc. Jud.* 15 (1972), 1101–2. It should be added that Theodosius' measures sometimes had only regional application or were later mitigated. The question why it was only in Crete that they created an uprising cannot be answered.

messianic hope by saying that before the eighty-fifth jubilee, i.e. 440–490 C.E., one should *not* expect him, afterwards one *may* expect him (*Sanh.* 97b).[32] It was inevitable that the worsening circumstances fertilized these messianic speculations exactly in the early thirties of the fifth century. No wonder that in an age of eschatological ferment someone claiming to be a new God-sent Moses found a ready audience.

The next point to be noted is that the event described follows a pattern well-known from similar messianic movements in the first century C.E.[33] A constitutive element in it is the idea that the eschatological liberation will be similar to the exodus from Egypt. 'Jewish prophecy—and particularly Jewish eschatological prophecy—foresees the future as re-creation of the past.'[34] Already the prophet Micah had said: 'As in the days when you came out of the land of Egypt, I will show them marvellous things' (7:15, RSV). This 'exodus' motif in the eschaton recurs in most messianic movements of the Imperial period and later times, and of course the figure of a new Moses was integral to this expectation.[35] 'It was perfectly natural that a people whose very identity had been forged in the recitation of the exodus deliverance should treasure the memory of Moses and look for rescue in their own periods of crisis in terms of a repetition of the exodus events.'[36] A second element that played a role here is the prediction in Deut. 18:15–18 of the appearance of a prophet like Moses, although this motif is less explicit in our sources.[37] If the evidence is studied, especially from Josephus,[38] it will be seen that recurring traits of these first century movements are the exodus into the desert, the usually sizeable following, and the expectation of miracles promised by the pretender. Now since there is no desert in Crete, the first could not play a part in our story. It was therefore replaced by the theme of being led dryshod through the sea to

---

[32] Silver, *op. cit.* (n. 28), 26 f. See on these passages also E. E. Urbach, 'Redemption and Repentance in Talmudic Judaism', in R. J. Zwi Werblowski and C. J. Bleeker (eds.), *Types of Redemption* (Leiden, 1970), 197 ff.

[33] P. W. Barnett, 'The Jewish Sign Prophets A.D. 40–70: Their Intentions and Origins', *NTS* 27 (1980/81), 679–97; R. A. Horsley, 'Popular Messianic Movements Around the Time of Jesus', *CBQ* 46 (1984), 471–95; *idem*, 'Popular Prophetic Movements at the Time of Jesus', *JSNT* 26 (1986), 3–27; M. Hengel, *Die Zeloten* (Leiden, 1976²), 119 f., 235 ff., 255 ff., 296 ff. See now also R. A. Horsley and J. S. Hanson, *Bandits, Prophets and Messiahs: Popular Movements in the Time of Jesus* (New York, 1986). Horsley's careful distinction between messianic and prophetic movements is relevant for the study of the various first century charismatic types, not for out passage of the fifth century.

[34] H. Jacobson, 'Visions of the Past: Jews and Greeks', *Judaism* 35 (1986), 468; cf. *ibid.* 479: 'Jews consistently saw themselves, both in large (i.e., the Jewish nation) and in small (individuals), as re-experiencing, re-creating or re-living the history of earlier Jews.' Jacobson argues that in this respect there is a striking difference between Jews and Greeks.

[35] See J. Jeremias, 'Moses', *TWNT* 4 (1942), 852–78, esp. 860–8; D. L. Tiede, *The Charismatic Figure as Miracle Worker* (Missoula, 1972), 178–207.

[36] Tiede, *op. cit.* (n. 35), 178 f.

[37] Jeremias, *art. cit.* (n. 35), 860 f.

[38] E.g. *Bell.* II 258–263; VI 285; VII 437–441; *Ant.* XVIII 85–87; XX 97 f., 167–172, 188.

Palestine. The miracle of deliverance is present in the form of the exodus miracle *par excellence*, the passage through the sea. The large following is also included. As these movements in the first century appeared to re-enact the great divine act of liberation from biblical history, so our pretender and his followers acted out this pattern of liberation according to the historical-eschatological typology and thus participated in the new and anticipated divine action.[39] Hence we see that after four centuries the pattern is still essentially unchanged, the only real new element being that the pretender called himself Moses. Another difference is, of course, that the movement did not end in massacre by the ruling authorities, which was the common disastrous ending of the first century movements according to Josephus. The recurrence of this ancient pattern in the story under discussion seems to prove that the Cretan Jews fostered the old traditions of their people.

The final question to be raised in this connection is whether the event recorded by Socrates implied the end of Cretan Jewry as the author wishes us to believe. As a matter of fact, apart from an inscription which may derive from the same period, and which will be discussed presently, no reports whatsoever exist on Jews or Judaisim in Crete between the first half of the fifth century and the eleventh century.[40] Furthermore, reports from *ca.* 1000 C.E. onwards suggest that Cretan Jews formed only a very small group by then. What had happened in the intervening five or six centuries, we do not know. The only Cretan Church father of some significance, Andrew of Crete, who worked in the first half of the eighth century, makes very negative and scathing remarks concerning the Jews, but these are so much the stock invectives known from other Christian writers that Andrew probably borrowed them from his predecessors. They cannot be used to shed light on the situation of the Cretan Jews of that time.[41] Whether or not the events related by Socrates marked the ending of ancient Cretan Jewry, we have to record that it constitutes the last piece of extant evidence for a long period.

To turn lastly to the epigraphical material, one piece of inscriptional evidence, the recently published Samaritan inscription from Delos, has been discussed above, and we will now limit ourselves to evidence from Crete itself. A search of the 1936 edition of vol. I of J.-B. Frey's *Corpus Inscriptionum Iudaicarum* reveals nothing. In the 1975 reprint, B. Lifshitz has added a prolegomenon with quite a number of new inscriptions, three of

---

[39] These formulations are borrowed from Horsley, *JSNT* 26 (1986), 7 f. (see n. 33).

[40] For the later Middle Ages see e.g. I. Lévi, 'Les Juifs de Candie de 1380 à 1485', *REJ* 26 (1893), 198–208; S. Schwarzfuchs, 'A propos des juifs de Crète et de Nègrepont', *REJ* (3rd. ser.) 2 [119] (1961), 152–8; L. J. Weinberger, *Jewish Poets in Crete* (Cincinnati, 1985).

[41] See Andreas Cretensis, *Homiliae* 2 (PG 97, 821C), 3 (845C–D), 8 (964B–C), 10 (1024C), etc.

which are from Crete.[42] Before presenting these, we first have to discuss briefly the difficult problem of how to tell a Jewish from a non-Jewish inscription. In his *Corpus Papyrorum Iudaicarum*, Victor Tcherikover lists the following criteria:[43] a papyrus is Jewish (a) if the word *Ioudaios* or *Hebraios* occurs in it; (b) if technical terms like 'synagogue' or 'sabbath' appear in it; (c) if it originates from what are known to have been places of exclusively Jewish settlement; (d) if it contains Jewish names. Now, unfortunately, the first three criteria cannot be applied to any Cretan inscription, with one exception, and in applying the fourth criterion we move on extremely slippery ground. For, as Ross Kraemer reminds us, there are very few names 'which can be demonstrated to have been used only by Jews, and never by Christians or pagans, whether in the same or other geographic areas'.[44] As will be seen, both Bandy (see n. 42) and Lifshitz designate inscriptions as Jewish only on the basis of a name which could as well be regarded as Christian or pagan, whereas they do not mention some inscriptions from the corpus *Inscriptiones Creticae* which on the same principle could be accepted as Jewish.

To begin with the first category, Bandy's first 'Jewish' inscription (from the fifth century C.E.) runs as follows (*Inscr. Cret.* IV no. 509):

$$[\kappa]\hat{v}\rho\iota\ \Sigma\alpha\tau\acute{v}\rho\omega\ \Theta\epsilon o[\delta o\acute{v}]$$
$$[\lambda o]v\ \acute{\iota}\epsilon\rho\epsilon\hat{v},\ M\omega\sigma\hat{\eta}\ \acute{a}\rho\chi\omega\nu[\tau\iota]$$
$$[\zeta\eta\tau]\acute{\eta}\sigma\alpha\sigma\langle\iota\rangle\ \acute{\epsilon}\nu\ \pi\acute{o}\nu o\iota\varsigma$$
$$[\pi o\lambda\lambda]o\hat{\iota}\varsigma\ \sigma\omega\tau\eta\rho\acute{\iota}\alpha\nu.$$

[This burial-place belongs to] lord Satyros, a priest, son of Theodoulos, (and) to Moses, a ruler who (both?) sought salvation with many toils.[45]

Bandy regards the inscription as Jewish because of the occurrence of the name Moses and the mention of the offices ἱερεύς, 'priest', and ἄρχων, which he suggestively translates by 'head of the synagogue'. However, as Lifshitz aptly remarks, 'the name of Moses is extremely rare in Jewish inscriptions and very frequent in Christian epigraphy'.[46] It should be added that ἱερεύς may be the title of a Christian official, and that ἄρχων, although it can designate a Jewish official, may be a secular ruler of some kind.[47] That is

---

[42] In the forty years in between both Margareta Guarducci's *Inscriptiones Creticae* (4 vols.; Rome, 1935–1950) and Anastasios C. Bandy's *Greek Christian Inscriptions from Crete* (Athens, 1970; with an appendix on Jewish inscriptions) were published.

[43] V. A. Tcherikover and A. Fuks, *Corp. Pap. Jud.* I (Cambridge, Mass., 1957), XVII–XX.

[44] R. S. Kraemer, 'Hellenistic Jewish Women: The Epigraphical Evidence', *SBL 1986 Seminar Papers* (Atlanta, 1986), 191 (183–200).

[45] I correct Bandy's translation where I do not agree with him; see Bandy, *op. cit.* (n. 42), 140. His addition ⟨ι⟩ may be questioned.

[46] Prolegomenon to the *CII* reprint (New York, 1975), p. 89.

[47] See for both the Jewish religious and the secular meanings W. Bauer, *A Greek–English Lexicon to the New Testament*, rev. ed. by W. F. Arndt, F. W. Gingrich and F. W. Danker (London, 1979²), 113 f.

to say, Bandy may be right and Lifshitz may be right; we just do not know.[48]

Curiously enough, the critical sense that Lifshitz displayed in this case seems to leave him in another case. For his own first inscription, a tombstone regarded by him as Jewish, runs as follows (*Inscr. Cret.* II no. 8):

$$\Sigma\alpha\nu\beta\dot{\alpha}\theta\iota(\varsigma)$$
$$\text{'}E\rho\mu\hat{\eta} \ \mu\nu\dot{\alpha}\text{-}$$
$$\mu\alpha\varsigma \ \chi\dot{\alpha}\rho\iota\nu$$

Sanbathis (set up this stone) for Hermes, for the sake of his memory.[49]

Lifshitz assumes that the inscription is Jewish because of the occurrence of the name Sanbathis, which is one of the hellenized forms of the Hebrew name Shabbetai. He is certainly right in stating that this name was very common among Jews. But he could have known the very instructive excursus on 'The Sambathions' by Menachem Stern in the *Corpus Papyrorum Judaicarum*,[50] where it is proved beyond any reasonable doubt that, whereas in the Hellenistic period this name was by and large a typically Jewish name, in the Roman and Byzantine periods a great many non-Jews adopted it without being aware of its original connotation.[51] Stern's evidence is from Egypt, but it is attested from Crete as well that the names Sanbathion and Sanbathis were used by pagans and Christians.[52] If Lifshitz would have been as critical in this instance as in the case of Bandy's first inscription, he would have omitted it, for the inscription is not from the Hellenistic period. However, it should be said once more that there is no way of attaining any certainty regarding inscriptions which do not exhibit, in addition to names, explicitly Jewish symbols like the menorah or Christian symbols like the cross or alpha and omega. That is to say, Guarducci's large corpus of Cretan inscriptions may well include a number of Jewish ones which we cannot recognize as such. What, for instance, is one to say of graffiti with names like *Avdias*, which is almost certainly the transcription of *Obadia* (*Inscr. Cret.* II.xxiii.28.34.52); or of inscriptions containing the name *Zaulos*, which can hardly be other than a scribal variant of *Saulos* (*Inscr. Cret.* II.xii.23 and IV 223B); or of inscriptions with

---

[48] Except Lifshitz, also B. Nystrom, '*Inscr. Cret.* IV 509: An Ancient Christian Priest?', *ZPE* 50 (1983), 122, regards this inscription as non-Jewish.

[49] I correct an error in Lifshitz's transcription; he prints $\chi\dot{\alpha}\zeta\iota\nu$.

[50] *CPJ* III (Cambridge, Mass., 1964), 43–56.

[51] In the Hellenistic period the usual Greek form of the name was $\Sigma\alpha\beta\beta\alpha\theta\alpha\dot{\iota}$ / -$\alpha\hat{\iota}o\varsigma$ or $\Sigma\alpha\mu\beta\alpha\theta\alpha\hat{\iota}o\varsigma$ / -$\tau\alpha\hat{\iota}o\varsigma$, in Imperial times it became $\Sigma\alpha\mu\beta\alpha\theta\dot{\iota}\omega\nu$ / -$\tau\dot{\iota}\omega\nu$ (masc.) and $\Sigma\alpha\mu\beta\dot{\alpha}\theta\iota o\nu$ or $\Sigma\alpha\mu\beta\alpha\theta\dot{\iota}\varsigma$ / $\Sigma\alpha\beta\beta\alpha\tau\dot{\iota}\varsigma$ (fem.); later hypocoristica are $\Sigma\alpha\mu\beta\hat{\alpha}\varsigma$ (masc.) or $\Sigma\dot{\alpha}\beta\beta\eta$ (fem.). Details in Stern (n. 50).

[52] *Inscr. Cret.* II.xxiv.12. For more evidence of the non-Jewish use of the names Sambathis etc. see H. Solin, 'Juden und Syrer im westlichen Teil der römischen Welt. Eine ethnisch-demographische Studie mit besonderer Berücksichtigung der sprachlichen Zustände', *ANRW* II 29, 2 (Berlin and New York, 1983), 587–789, esp. 645 n. 145 and 679.

names like *Simon* and *Ioannes* (*Inscr. Cret.* II.xv.4 and 5; I.xxv.8); or of the numerous inscriptions in which names like *Eirena* or *Theodoros* or *Dositheos* are found (*Inscr. Cret.*, Indices *s.vv.*)? They may be Jewish, but some or all may be pagan or Christian, like the inscriptions with names such as Moses and Sanbathis. We have to reconcile ourselves to the fact that there are no means of distinguishing between Jewish and non-Jewish inscriptions on the basis of names alone when other indicators are absent. This sad conclusion leaves us with only two inscriptions regarded as Jewish by both Bandy and Lifshitz and by other other scholars as well.[53]

The first is a tombstone and is not very revealing. The accumulation of three typically Jewish names in three successive generations makes it highly probable that it is a Jewish inscription. It runs (*Inscr. Cret.* I.v.17):

$$
\begin{array}{l}
\text{Ἰώσηφος} \\
\text{Θεοδώρου} \\
\text{Ἰούδα τῶ υ} \\
\text{ἰῶ αὐτοῦ} \\
5 \quad (μ)νείας χάρι \\
\quad ν· ἐτῶν α.
\end{array}
$$

Josephus, son of Theodorus, (set up this stone) for Judas his son as a memorial. (He lived) one year.[54]

This inscription from the third or fourth century C.E. was found in an area at Kassanoi called ἐβροί (= ἐβραῖοι), 'where there was reputed to be a Jewish cemetery'.[55] But it is not only this element that makes it probable that we have to do with a Jewish inscription. An additional factor is that although, as we have seen, 'Jewish' names need not in themselves indicate a Jewish origin, in this case a Jewish origin is made extremely probable by the fact that the father's name is recorded (line 2), which is an element lacking in all Christian inscriptions of Crete.[56]

Although I am convinced that this inscription is Jewish, it must be admitted that it leaves room for doubt to the extreme sceptic. Fortunately, the final piece of epigraphical evidence does not. Again, it is a sepulchral

---

[53] There is a possibility that *Inscr. Cret.* IV no. 518 (Bandy's no. 35) is a Jewish inscription, but it may be Christian, and the interpretation is highly uncertain. The text (which is probably hexametric) runs:

$$
\begin{array}{l}
\text{...].[...} \\
\text{...]θεναι [...} \\
\text{...] θεσμοῖς [..]μ[...} \\
\text{...]ας ἀγορεύ[σ]ων} \\
5 \quad \text{...]α αμιν. Θεὸς αὐτὸς} \\
\text{...]τασσάμενος ἱερήα} \\
\text{...]κεν εὐσ[ε]βίη [..] η} \\
\text{...]ιερα [...}
\end{array}
$$

[54] See Bandy, *op. cit.* (n. 42), 142, where he prints a photo of the inscription.
[55] Bandy, *ibid.*
[56] Bandy, *ibid.*

inscription, from Kastelli Kissamou, which was dated by Bandy to the first or second century C.E., but by the great epigraphist Louis Robert to the fourth or fifth century C.E.[57] This dating is also defended by Lifshitz and by Brooten in her meritorious dissertation.[58] The text runs as follows (*CII* I² 731c):

> Σοφία Γορτυνί
> α πρεσβυτέρα
> κὲ ἀρχισυναγώ
> γισσα Κισάμου ἔν
> 5 θα. Μνήμη δικέας
> ἰς ἐῶνα. Ἀμήν.

Sophia of Gortyn, elder and leader of the synagogue of Cissamos, (lies) here. The memory of the righteous one be for ever. Amen.

There is an illuminating difference between the interpretation of this inscription by Bandy and the one by Brooten. Bandy adopts the traditional theory that 'elder' and 'leader of the synagogue' are 'honorary titles' (143) bestowed upon Sophia because her husband (not she herself) held the offices of elder and head of the synagogue. It was Brooten who was the first to break through this traditional androcentric interpretation.[59] She convincingly interpreted a whole series of inscriptions concerning Jewish women in such a way that it became obvious that titles like πρεσβυτέρα and ἀρχισυναγώγισσα were not honorary titles but indicated real functions.[60] She writes on our inscription: 'There is no *internal* reason for believing that Sophia of Gortyn received the titles through her husband. If here husband were the source of her titles, why is she not called Sophia the wife of X? The image of Sophia of Gortyn emerging from the inscription (...) is of a very important figure in the Jewish community of Cissamos. She was not only an elder, but also head of the synagogue. There is no evidence that she was married.'[61] 'Important for the interpretation of *presbytera* is its parallelization with *archisynagogissa*, which makes it unlikely that *presbytera* is

[57] This inscription is not in *Inscr. Cret.* It was first published by Bandy in *Hesperia* 32 (1963), 227–9, and afterwards in his *Greek Christian Inscriptions* (n. 42), 143. Jeanne and Louis Robert discussed it in their 'Bulletin épigraphique', in *Revue des études grecques* 77 (1964), 413, and Lifshitz in the Prolegomenon to *CII* I 88.

[58] B. J. Brooten, *Women Leaders in the Ancient Synagogue* (Chico, 1982), 11 f., 41.

[59] It should be said, however, that in the same year (1982) the late I. F. Sanders adopted the same interpretation of the inscription as Brooten by taking it at face value; see his *Roman Crete* (n. 1), 43: 'One of these [inscriptions] includes the only evidence for the organisation of the faith, the dead person, Sophia of Gortyna, being an elder and leader of the synagogue at Kissamos.'

[60] It is very much to the point when Susanne Heine writes: 'Wer, wie bewuszt oder unbewuszt immer, Frauen in höheren Ämtern und Funktionen nicht wahrhaben will, neigt nicht nur dazu, weibliche Vornamen zu übersehen, sondern auch dazu, das Amt dann, wenn eine Frau es bekleidet, abzuwerten' (*Frauen der frühen Christenheit* (Göttingen, 1986), 98).

[61] Brooten, *op. cit.* (n. 58), 12.

simply a term meant to distinguish Sophia the elder from a Sophia the younger.'[62] Brooten's research has made several things clear. First, a number of inscriptions leave no doubt that in some communities, especially in the diaspora, there were female elders; they probably had financial, possibly educational responsibilities. Second, there are a number of inscriptions that mention women as heads of a synagogue. In these, no husbands are mentioned; and it is highly significant that in those instances where wives of (male) *archisynagogoi* are mentioned, they do not bear this title. That is to say, the traditional theory that regards this title as 'honorific' when a woman is the bearer has no leg to stand on. *Archisynagogissai* were indeed female leaders of a synagogue. They were probably active in administration and exhortation. 'They could have worked in a team of two or three synagogue heads, for we have seen than the number was not necessarily restricted to one. Or perhaps they served alone. (...) Sophia of Gortyn, both elder and head of the synagogue, must have been very actively involved in the affairs of the synagogue. Was it her long years of work that convinced even the most sceptical that a woman was capable of filling that office? Family ties, long years of involvement, largesse—these have often played a role in attaining various offices and seem as likely in the case of women as of men.'[63]

Brooten has been quoted at length because her conclusions shed a striking light on Cretan Jewry in late antiquity. The comparable inscriptions she adduces make very probable indeed that in diasporic situations women could rise to high positions and even to leadership in Jewish communities.

Quite independently from her, my own research has led me to identical conclusions along very different lines.[64] Needless to say, it is not possible to draw generalizing conclusions for the whole of Crete from one sepulchral inscription in Kastelli Kissamou, but it can at least be asserted that in some quarters of Cretan Jewry in the later Roman period emancipatory tendencies made the most of their chances so that women were able to attain to positions of leadership. That such women were at odds with strict rabbinic rules is obvious.[65]

Some final remarks. It is self-evident that the material at our disposal does not allow for a history of the Cretan Jews in antiquity to be written. Although it can never be excluded that new documents may emerge, it has

---

[62] Brooten, *op. cit.* (n. 58), 41. See now also R. S. Kraemer, 'A New Inscription from Malta and the Question of Women Elders in the Diaspora Jewish Communities', *HTR* 78 (1985), 431–8.

[63] Brooten, *op. cit.* (n. 58), 32–3.

[64] P. W. van der Horst, 'The Role of Women in the Testament of Job', *Nederlands Theologisch Tijdschrift* 40 (1986), 273–89.

[65] See e.g. L. Swidler, *Women in Judaism. The Status of Women in Formative Judaism* (Metuchen, 1976); M. Küchler, *Schweigen, Schmuck und Schleier. Drei neutestamentliche Vorschriften zur Verdrängung der Frauen auf dem Hintergrund einer frauenfeindlichen Exegese des Alten Testaments im antiken Judentum* (Freiburg and Göttingen, 1986).

to be recognized that the chances are small. New literary sources can hardly be expected and papyrological evidence from Crete itself will not be found; only a few fresh inscriptions (an epitaph or two) may reasonably be expected. The small corpus of evidence will in consequence probably remain small and not allow us to arrive at general conclusions. A recent historian of Crete observes of the Jews that 'the literary references depict a peaceful, rich community, if somewhat gullible',[66] solely on the basis of two passages in Josephus and Socrates. This is too sweeping a statement when in fact from these passages all that can be deduced is that in the first century there were rich Jews living in Crete and that in the first and fifth centuries many Jews put their unthinking trust in an impostor. Similarly, the inscription on Sophia of Gortyn does not permit us to conclude that Jewish women in Crete found it easy to reach leading positions; the case of Sophia was probably exceptional. When the afore-mentioned historian maintains that the Jewish community was peaceful, we can more easily agree with him since there is no evidence to the contrary. The fact that we have no reports on Cretan Jewry between say 100 and 430 C.E. may indicate that in the second through fourth centuries the Jews reached a high degree of integration into Cretan society, a situation that was probably only disrupted by the legal measures of Theodosius II.[67] As was said in the beginning, the evidence yields no more than occasional glimpses of the history of this community, but these are without doubt interesting and sometimes even fascinating.[68]

---

[66] Sanders, *Roman Crete* (n. 1), 43.

[67] Compare the situation of several Jewish communities in Asia Minor, e.g. Sardis, on which see A. T. Kraabel, 'Paganism and Judaism: The Sardis Evidence', in A. Benoit *et al.* (ed.), *Paganisme, Judaisme, Christianisme. Mélanges offerts à Marcel Simon* (Paris, 1978), 13–33.

[68] This article is the expanded version of a paper read at the July 1987 meeting of the European Association for Jewish Studies in Berlin. It may be added here that I have left out of account all legendary material from the Christian apocrypha such as the story that after Jesus' execution, Tiberius had Annas and Caiaphas arrested and brought to Rome, but on the way Caiaphas died. When they wanted to bury him in Crete, the earth refused to receive his body, and they had to cover it with stones (see e.g. M. R. James, *The Apocryphal New Testament* (Oxford, 1924), 153). Until the nineteenth century there was near Cnossos a site called 'the tomb of Caiaphas'; for details see N. A. Bees, *Die griechisch-christlichen Inschriften des Peloponnes* (Athens, 1941), 41 with n. 2.

10. Jews and Christians in Aphrodisias in the Light of Their Relations in Other Cities of Asia Minor

In his *Legatio ad Gaium* 214, Philo says about the Jewish people that "it is spread abroad over all the continents and islands so that it seems to be not much less than the indigenous inhabitants".[1] In *Bellum* II 398, Josephus has Agrippa say to the Jews: "There is not a people in the world which does not contain a portion of our nation"; and in *Bellum* VII 43, he states that the Jewish people is "densely interspersed among the native populations of every portion of the world". The third Sibyl predicts in a *vaticinium ex eventu* that "the whole earth and every sea will be filled with you", i.e. the Jewish people (*Or. Sib.* III 271). And the pagan geographer Strabo is quoted by Josephus as saying: "This people has already made its way into every city, and it is not easy to find any place in the habitable world which has not received this nation and in which it has not made its power felt" (*Antiquitates* XIV 115). Finally I quote the well-known words of the philosopher Seneca who is reported by Augustine as saying about the Jews: "Meanwhile the customs of this accursed race have gained such influence that they are now received throughout all countries of the world. The vanquished have given laws to the victors" (*victi victoribus leges dederunt*; in *De Civ. Dei* VI 11).[2]

These testimonies by both Jewish and pagan authors - still more could be added - make abundantly clear that the Jewish diaspora at the beginning of our era must have been very sizeable and extensive. No one doubts that indeed in the first century A.D. most countries of the Mediterranean world contained Jewish communities. On the exact numbers of this diaspora, however, opinions differ widely. The total Jewish population of the early Roman Empire has been calculated by some to have been two million, by others more than eight million, by others somewhere in between. In fact nobody knows exactly.[3] But even if we take a not too unsafe middle course and estimate the total number of Jews at five million and if we assume that no

---

1   Cf. also *Legatio* 281-2.

2   On the passages by Strabo and Seneca see M. Stern, *Greek and Latin Authors on Jews and Judaism* I, Jerusalem: The Israel Academy of Sciences and Humanities, 1974, nos. 105 and 186.

3   See S. W. Baron, Population, *Encyclopaedia Judaica* XIII (1972) 870-872, and also Baron's *A Social and Religious History of the Jews* I, New York - Philadelphia 1952, 170.

more than one and a half to two million lived in Palestine, we have a diaspora of three to three and a half million. If one million Jews lived in Egypt, we have two to two and a half million left for the rest of the Roman Empire. Then it is a reasonable guess that also about one million Jews lived in Asia Minor. Even if that number were somewhat too high, we yet know for certain that the diaspora in Asia Minor was very large. Seventy-five years ago Juster could enumerate 70 cities of Asia Minor in which a Jewish presence was attested.[4] Several of his instances were dubious - Juster was well aware of that - but even in a much more critical recent survey (in the revised edition of Schürer's *History*)[5] some 50 places in Asia Minor are mentioned in all of which it is certain that Jews lived in the Imperial period. And of course we know only a fraction of the reality.[6]

If we now draw the circle closer and look at the region of ancient Caria (the south-western part of Asia Minor)[7], we see that Jewish presence is attested there early, although we do not know anything about numbers. In 1 Macc. 15 we read that the Roman consul Lucius asks king Ptolemy VIII Euergetes in a letter of 140/139 B.C. to refrain from waging war upon Jews, whom he calls 'our friends and allies' (15:17). After quoting that letter, the author of 1 Maccabees adds that this consul wrote letters of similar intent to quite a number of other kings and countries, including the province of Caria, undoubtedly because Jews lived there.[8] And indeed, Jewish communities are attested there in at least 8 cities: Hyllarima, Priene, Miletus, Iasus, Halicarnassus, Cnidus, Myndus, and Aphrodisias.[9] Evidence for the first seven cities has been available for a long time. For Aphrodisias the evidence has turned up only very recently, but important and very striking evidence it is.

Aphrodisias had since time immemorial been a site of the cult of the mother-goddess, later called Aphrodite by the Greeks when they came there,

---

4 J. Juster, *Les Juifs dans l'Empire Romain* I, Paris: Geuthner, 1914, 188-194.

5 E. Schürer, *The History of the Jewish People in the Age of Jesus Christ* III 1, rev. ed. by G. Vermes, F. Millar and M. Goodman, Edinburgh: Clark, 1986, 17-36.

6 See for a discussion of the evidence F. Blanchetière, Le juif et l'autre: la diaspora asiate, in R. Kuntzmann and J. Schlosser (edd.), *Études sur le judaïsme hellénistique*, Paris: Cerf, 1984, 41-49.

7 On Caria see L. Robert, *La Carie: histoire et géographie historique* II, Paris: Maisonneuve, 1954. All Robert's works are of the greatest importance for the study of Asia Minor; see esp. *Hellenica* I-XIII, Paris: Maisonneuve, 1940-1965, and his collected contributions in *Bulletin épigraphique (1938-1977)*, 12 vols., Paris: Les Belles Lettres, 1972-1979, and in *Opera Minora Selecta*, 4 vols., Amsterdam: Hakkert, 1969-1974. Much of Robert's work was done in co-operation with his wife Jeanne Robert.

8 On the problem of the authenticity of this document see Schürer, *History* (n. 5) I (1973), 194-7, and J. A. Goldstein, *I Maccabees*, Garden City: Doubleday, 1976, *ad loc.*

9 See Schürer, *History* (n. 5) III 24-26; Juster, *Juifs* (n. 4) 191.

and it had been a renowned centre of pilgrimage[10]. Probably up till the third century B.C. the site was no more than a sanctuary, a *temenos*, not a city. It emerges as a city only in the Hellenistic period, and it begins to flourish in the first century B.C., not least because of the privileges bestowed upon it by Augustus (and later also by other emperors).[11] In the first three centuries of our era, Aphrodisias was a prestigious city and an important religious, literary, scientific, and artistic centre. The novelist Chariton, the physician Xenocrates, the philosophers Alexander and Adrastus (both Peripatetic scholars) and all the famous sculptors of the so-called school of Aphrodisias added to the fame of the city as a centre of culture.[12] As late as the end of the fifth or the beginning of the sixth century, the Neoplatonist Asclepiodotus, a student of Proclus, lived in Aphrodisias and was one of its highly esteemed inhabitants.[13] The strong tradition of worship of both Aphrodite and the Emperors - note that the claim of the Julio-Claudian dynasty to descent from Venus-Aphrodite created a special bond between the Emperors and Aphrodisias - was tenacious in this city[14] and we can observe that paganism remained a vital force there till far into the post-Constantinian period. Testimony to this - apart from literary references[15] - is to be found in numerous inscriptions from the fourth through sixth centuries a number of which were already known long ago but a great number of which have been found only in the last three decades.[16] Since the beginning of the sixties this splendid city has been excavated in an exemplary way by the Turkish-Ame-

---

[10] For this paragraph I much rely upon K. T. Erim, *Aphrodisias, City of Venus Aphrodite*, New York: Facts on File Publications, 1986, esp. 25-35.

[11] See J. Reynolds, *Aphrodisias and Rome*, London: The Roman Society, 1982, passim. For a later period see Ch. Roueché, Rome, Asia and Aphrodisias in the Third Century, *Journal of Roman Studies* 71 (1981) 103-120.

[12] On the 'school of Aphrodisias' see Erim, *Aphrodisias (n. 10)* 133-152.

[13] On Asclepiodotus see esp. L. Robert, *Hellenica* IV, Paris: Maisonneuve, 1948, 115-126. The pertinent inscriptions are in MAMA VIII (1962) nos. 486-487(see n. 16), now reprinted in Roueché, *Aphrodisias in Late Antiquity* (see n. 18) nos. 53-54.

[14] On the Emperor cult in Aphrodisias see Erim, *Aphrodisias* (n. 10) 106-123, and S.R.F. Price, *Rituals and Power: The Roman Imperial Cult in Asia Minor*, Cambridge: CUP, 1984, Index s.v. Aphrodisias.

[15] See esp. the pertinent passages in the *Vita Severi* of Zacharias Scholasticus discussed by Robert (n. 13) and by Roueché, *Aphrodisias* (n.18) 85-93; Roueché, *ibid.* 47-52 and 63-66, discusses the tenacity of paganism in this city till the sixth century.

[16] Earlier collections include: Th. Reinach, Inscriptions d'Aphrodisias, *Revue des études grecques* 19 (1906) 99-150 and 205-298; H. Grégoire, *Recueil des inscriptions grecques-chrétiennes d'Asie Mineure*, Paris: Leroux, 1922, 87-94 (nos. 246-281); Monumenta Asiae Minoris Antiqua VIII, edd. W. M. Calder and J. M. R. Cormack, Manchester: Manchester University Press, 1962, 72-147 (nos. 405-615), with the elaborate and incisive critique by L. Robert in his *Hellenica* XIII, Paris: Maisonneuve, 1965, 109-238 (cf. *Gnomon* 37, 1965, 380-388). Older and minor collections are mentioned by Erim, *Aphrodisias* (n. 10) 187-8.

rican archaeologist Kenan T. Erim, and now, after almost 30 years, about 20% of the city has been unearthed.[17] During the digging campaigns many new and important inscriptions have been uncovered, which are in the process of being edited at the moment.[18]

One of the most sensational finds (in 1976) was a huge marble block or pillar almost three meters high and approximately 45 centimeters wide, inscribed on two sides with a long Greek inscription of 86 lines. The text was published in 1987 by Joyce Reynolds and Robert Tannenbaum with an elaborate commentary.[19] It most probably dates from the beginning of the third century A.D. The greatest part of the text consists of names. Some 125 persons are mentioned in it as donors or contributors to the local synagogue or rather to an institution of the synagogue, which is identified tentatively by the editors as the community's soup-kitchen, from which any needy person could obtain a daily portion, a charitable institution prescribed for every community by the Mishnah. (The Mishnah's *t.t.* is *tamhuy,* the inscription speaks of *patella,* both words meaning literally 'plate' or 'dish').[20] I leave aside for the moment the question raised by the editors of whether or not the introduction of such an institution in a city of western Asia Minor should be regarded as a sign of control over diaspora communities by Mishnaic rabbis (they point, for example, to the Talmudic story of rabbi Meir's mission to Asia Minor as an *apostolos/shaliah* in b. *Megilla* 18b; cf. t. *Meg.* 2:5).[21] I want to focus here on a more important matter, and that is the division of the names into three categories. The 125 names of the benefactors are subdivided into three categories: 68 are Jews (although they are not explicitly so described, the overwhelming preponderance of Biblical and Hebrew Jewish names, often even in ungrecisized, *i.e.* undeclinable forms, leaves no room for another conclusion), 3 are called proselytes, and 54 are called 'Godfearers', *theosebeis.* This strikingly high percentage of Godfearers, in a list of benefactors and contributors to a Jewish institution, is the great surprise of this inscription.

---

[17] See Erim's *Aphrodisias* (n. 10), where at pp. 184-193 an exhaustive bibliography is given.

[18] So far published are the inscriptions pertaining to the city's relationship with Rome up till 250, see Reynolds' monograph mentioned in n. 11; further the Jewish inscriptions by J. Reynolds and R. Tannenbaum, *Jews and Godfearers at Aphrodisias* Cambridge: The Cambridge Philological Society, 1987. Ch. M. Roueché, *Aphrodisias in Late Antiquity,* London: The Roman Society, 1989, contains *inter alia* the Christian inscriptions. Another volume by Reynolds and Roueché is in preparation.

[19] See the previous note. For a short and popular report on the inscription see R. F. Tannenbaum, Jews and God-Fearers in the Holy City of Aphrodite, *Biblical Archaeology Review* 12,5 (1986) 54-57.

[20] On this institution see S. Krauss, *Talmudische Archaeologie* III, Leipzig: Fock, 1912, 66-74, esp. 68; Schürer, *History* (n. 5) II (1979) 437.

[21] Reynolds - Tannenbaum, *Jews* (n. 18) 81.

What is a Godfearer (in Greek θεοσεβής or σεβόμενος (τὸν θεόν) or φοβούμενος (τὸν θεόν), in Latin metuens or, with the Greek loanword, *theosebes*)? A Godfearer is a pagan "who is attracted enough to what he has heard of Judaism to come to the synagogue to learn more; who is, after a time, willing, as a result, to imitate the Jewish way of life in whatever way and to whatever degree he wishes (up to and including membership in community associations, where that includes legal study and prayer); who may have had held out to him various short codes of behaviour to follow, but does not seem to have been required to follow any one; who may follow the exclusive monotheism of the Jews and give up his ancestral gods, but need not do so; who can, if he wishes, take the ultimate step and convert, and is, whether he does or not, promised a share in the resurrection for his pains".[22] Some of them called themselves, or were called, Jews, although they were not so *stricto sensu*.[23]

We know from the Book of Acts and from Josephus that in most cities of the ancient world synagogues had sympathizers in the form of a body of permanent or semi-permanent catechumens. Josephus even reports, with characteristic exaggeration, that most of the pagan women of Damascus belonged to this category, and that also in Syrian Antioch the number of sympathizers was extremely great (*Bellum* II 560, VII 43-45).[24] It was among these Godfearers that Paul made most of his early converts, according to Acts. If we leave out of account Josephus' exaggerating reports, neither from Acts nor from inscriptional evidence is it possible to gauge the extent of this phenomenon of pagans sympathizing in various degrees with Judaism. Now we have for the first time, and unexpectedly, an indication of the degree of influence of the synagogue on local pagans in a middle-sized city of Asia Minor. And we have to bear in mind that this inscription records only the names of the contributors to the new building, that is, probably of only a part of the more well-to-do citizens among the Godfearers. Even so there are 54 of them listed. As a matter of fact we can see that the employment of the Godfearers, of which some 22 are given in the inscription, co-

---

22 Reynolds-Tannenbaum, *Jews* (n. 18) 65. All relevant sources and modern studies of the phenomenon of Godfearers can be found in their notes 167-289 at pp. 72-77. Add the references in L. H. Kant, Jewish Inscriptions in Greek and Latin, *ANRW* II 20, 2, Berlin-New York: W. de Gruyter, 1987, 688-9 nn. 101-110 and in L. H. Feldman, *Josephus and Modern Scholarship*, Berlin-New York: W. de Gruyter, 1984, 732-4. Important is Marcel Simon's article Gottesfuerchtiger in *Reallexikon fuer Antike und Christentum* XI (1981) 1060-1070.

23 If, that is, Hommel's interpretation of *SEG* 4, 441, the famous theater inscription from Miletus, is correct; see H. Hommel, Juden und Christen im kaiserzeitlichen Milet, in his *Sebasmata* II, Tübingen: Mohr, 1984, 200-230.

24 On these and other cases of 'adherence' and 'conversion' in Josephus see S. J. D. Cohen, Respect for Judaism by Gentiles According to Josephus, *Harvard Theological Review* 80 (1987) 409-430. Cohen discusses Josephus' varying and ambivalent attitude towards both phenomena.

vers a wide range of occupations only very few of which indicate lower social status.[25] Most remarkable is the fact that nine of them are *bouleutai*, city councillors. In the later Roman Empire, this office implied heavy financial obligations and could only be exercised by the wealthy of a city. So what we are now able to see is that, in Aphrodisias at least, the Jews attracted large numbers of local gentiles - again, the people recorded form undoubtedly only a part of the total group of Godfearers - and persons of high standing and great influence at that. When pagan local magistrates heartily support and partly pay for the foundation of a Jewish institution, one cannot but conclude that the Jewish community of that city was influential in a degree which hitherto could hardly have been imagined. "Its members appear to have been self-confident, accepted in the city, and evidently able to attract the favourable attention of many gentile fellow Aphrodisians".[26] The Jews of this city do not appear to be half-paganized syncretists, as far as we can judge from the fact that they meet the Mishnaic requirement that every community must have a soup-kitchen and from the fact that many of them bear Biblical and/or Hebrew names. The members of the community seem strongly bound to their own traditions, but nevertheless they had such an influence upon their fellow citizens that these give financial support to an institution of the synagogue. Indeed, some of them are even members of the community's private association for study of the Torah and worship; for, besides three proselytes, two Godfearers are mentioned as members of the local δεκανία τῶν φιλομαθῶν τῶν καὶ παντευλογούντων (I 3-5).[27] So these were no longer outsiders. Moreover, the important fact that 3 persons are explicitly called proselytes, so have become full members of the Jewish community, in a period in which Jewish proselytism was forbidden by imperial decree, is a strong testimony of the powerful influence of the Jewish community in Aphrodisias.[28]

The other Jewish inscriptions of the city are less revealing and also of much later date than the main one (fifth through sixth centuries). Some are no more than graffiti, representing traditional symbols like *menoroth, ethrogim, lulavim*, and the like (nos. 3-6 in the Appendix in Reynolds-Tannenbaum). Interesting is the fact that in the Sebasteion, after the cessation of the imperial cult activities, some of the doorjambs at entrances to the *tabernae* - the Sebasteion seems to have been converted for use as shops - have had *menoroth* incised upon them while others carry crosses, a situation which is remi-

---

25 Reynolds-Tannenbaum, *Jews* (n. 18) 116-123, esp. 119-122.

26 Erim, *Aphrodisias* (n. 10) 131.

27 The formula δεκανία τῶν φιλομαθῶν τῶν καὶ παντευλογούντων is a nice illustration of the early Jewish idea of 'study as worship', on which see the book with that title by B. T. Viviano (Leiden: Brill, 1978).

28 For the imperial decrees on proselytism see M. Simon, *Verus Israel. A Study of the Relations Between Christians and Jews in the Roman Empire (AD 135-425)*, Oxford: OUP, 1986, 99-100.

niscent of that in Sardis, where in the early Byzantine period there was be-hind the synagogue a market-street with Jewish and Christian shops side by side. We will return to Sardis later. Still more intriguing is the small in-scription for seat-reservation in the Odeum which runs: τόπος Βενέτων Ἑβραίων τῶν παλαιῶν = 'seat for the elderly Jewish Blues' (no. 1 in the Appendix in Reynolds-Tannenbaum), the Blues being a well-known circus faction. The use of *Hebraioi* rather than *Ioudaioi* points to a period not be-fore the sixth century, and in that century the circus factions of Blues and Greens surely have a Christian context.[29] There are some other indications of connections between Jews and Blues in the later Roman Empire, al-though the often made assertion that it was the Greens who were most anti-Semitic is debatable.[30] The exact nature of this connection of Jews and Blues is unknown, unfortunately.

That a synagogue has not been found in Aphrodisias is without significance, because 80% of the city is still unearthed. Further excavation might well re-veal the community's synagogue(s). But even if it is not discovered, that does not mean that it never existed. We know, for example, from literary sources that Ephesus had one or more synagogues, but in this extensively excavated city such a building has never been found. The reason is most probably that synagogues were either completely changed for use as chur-ches[31] or so completely demolished as to become unrecognizable. But let us hope that further digging at the site will bring us a surprise as great as the inscription was.

Although much more could be said about the implications of the inscription, it is time to turn to Christianity in Aphrodisias. Unfortunately, we know next to nothing about Christianity in this city in the pre-Constantinian pe-riod. The earliest testimony we have is the notice in the *Martyrologium Sy-riacum* for April 30 and in the *Martyrologium Hieronymianum* for May 3 about the martyrdom of two Christian inhabitants of Aphrodisias, Rhodo-pianus and Diodotus, during the persecution of Diocletian in the early fourth century.[32] They are said to have been lynched by their fellow citizens. But the historical value of this notice can hardly be established and must remain somewhat doubtful.[33] If historical at all, it does not give the impression of a

---

29 A. Cameron, *Circus Factions. Blues and Greens at Rome and Byzantium,* Oxford: Cla-rendon Press, 1976, 126-156.

30 Cameron, *Circus Factions* 149-151. Reynolds and Tannebaum, *Jews* 132, do not share Cameron's scepticism about the Jews-Blues connection.

31 M. Simon, *Verus Israel* (n. 28) 225ff. mentions many instances.

32 See H. Achelis, *Die Martyrologien, ihre Geschichte und ihr Wert,* Berlin:Weidmann, 1900, 40, 137. *Acta Sanctorum* XIV 386, cf. XII 759-760; also V. Schultze, *Altchristli-che Städte und Landschaften* II 2, Gütersloh: Bertelsmann, 1926, 161.

33 See Achelis, *Martyrologien* (n. 32) 138 *et passim.* Roueché, *Aphrodisias* (n.18) 15-16, also speaks of the 'confused account of two martyrs' and of the 'highly unsatisfac-tory tradition' about these martyrs.

large scale persecution but rather of a small scale riot. A more certain[34] witness to Christian presence in our city is the fact that a certain Ammonius, bishop of Aphrodisias, was one of the signatories at the council of Nicaea in 325.[35] It is perhaps not without significance that 11 years before, at the council of Ancyra, there was no bishop of Aphrodisias or Caria, whereas bishops were present there from all the neighbouring districts.[36] The impression that Christianity made a relatively late appearance in Aphrodisias, perhaps even as late as the end of the third or the beginning of the fourth century, is further strengthened by the fact that no Christian inscription from the city is earlier than the second half of the fourth century.[37] Corroborative evidence comes from the other cities of Caria. For, strikingly enough, while in all districts of western Asia Minor Christianity is attested in either the first or second or at the latest the third century, only in the district of Caria the situation is different.[38] For all cities of Caria for which Christian presence is attested, the earliest testimonies, both literary and epigraphic, are from 325 or later.[39] Whereas, as Harnack says, in the pre-Constantinian period Asia Minor was the Christian country *par excellence*, the district of Caria with its capital Aphrodisias is a striking exception. It is hard to give a satisfactory explanation for this difference. Was it the tenacity of the Aphrodite cultus and the imperial cult that made it so hard for Christianity to become rooted in the Aphrodisian soil? Or was it the strong Jewish presence in the city that caused the church to have so little success there? Or was it the combination of these pagan and Jewish factors? We will come back to this question at the end of this paper.

The later history of Aphrodisian Christianity is not very relevant to our to-

---

34 Although not completely certain, since E. Honigmann published a Greek manuscript with a list of Church-Fathers at Nicaea that mentions Ἀμμώνιος Ἀφροδικείας (Ammonius of Aphrodikia), which it is hard to consider as a scribal error for Ἀφροδισιάδος see his Recherches sur les listes des Pères de Nicée et de Constantinople, *Byzantion* 11 (1936) 429-439.

35 See A. von Harnack, *Mission und Ausbreitung des Christentums in den ersten drei Jahrhunderten* II, 4. Aufl., Leipzig: Hinrich, 1924, 784; Schultze, *Städte* (n. 32) 161. Roueché, *Aphrodisias* (n.18) 322-326, gives a complete list of bishops of the city.

36 See J. D. Mansi, *Sacrorum conciliorum nova et amplissima collectio* II, Paris-Leipzig 1901 (=repr. of Florence 1759), 534. *Ibid.* 695 and 700 Ammonius from Aphrodisias is mentioned at Nicaea.

37 See the collections in Grégoire's *Recueil* and in MAMA mentioned in n. 16, and Roueché, *Aphrodisias* (n.18), *passim*.

38 See Harnack, *Mission* (n. 35) 732-785 for Asia Minor, 784 for Caria; Schultze, *Städte* (n. 32), *passim* for Asia Minor, esp. 157-187 for Caria. The massive study by F. Blanchetiere, *Le christianisme asiate aux IIeme et IIIeme siecles*, Lille 1981, confirms the picture sketched above: it presents no data about Caria.

39 This applies even to the Carian harbour-city Miletus, for the three references to this city in the New Testament do not imply that there was a Christian community there (Acts 20:15.17; 2 Tim. 4:20).

pic. In the last two decades of the fourth century we find its bishop Eumenius present at the council of Constantinople; we find a statue with an honorary inscription to Aelia Flavia Flaccilla, the wife of the emperor Theodosius I; we find some other inscriptions none of which, unfortunately, sheds any light on the relations of Christians and Jews. Probably in the middle or second half of the fifth century the great temple of Aphrodite was converted for use as a church.[40] In the fifth and sixth centuries vehement controversies over monophysitism are reported in the city- in the sixth century two bishops were deposed because of their monophysite stance. It was only in the seventh century that the name of the city was changed into 'Stauropolis' instead of the pagan-sounding theophoric name it had borne for over 1000 years.[41]

Since the evidence for Judaism and Christianity in Aphrodisias does not enable us to draw conclusions about their interrelationship, we have to look elsewhere for evidence that may throw light on it.

Let us first have a look at close-by Sardis. Since the Second World War the most sensational archaeological discovery in Asia Minor as far as Judaism is concerned, is the synagogue of Sardis.[42] The building deserves our greatest attention in more than one respect. First, it is of very big size, measuring ca. 20 x 85 meters, and could contain approximately 1000 persons. Second, it was not a free-standing building, but an integral part of a monumental Roman bath and gymnasium complex. Third, the building was probably already a synagogue in the third century A.D., but its present form with its sumptuous decorations dates from the second quarter of the fourth century, which is to say that during and after Constantine the Jews of Sardis had full opportunity to enlarge and embellish the building into what is now the largest ancient synagogue we know. Moreover, changes and renovations to the building went on unhindered till the second half of the sixth century, and the synagogue remained in use till the seventh century when the whole city was abandoned. Fourth, the more than eighty inscriptions reveal that many Jews in Sardis had high civic status in the fourth century and later, for we come

---

[40]   Erim, *Aphrodisias* (n. 10) 57. Roueché, *Aphrodisias* (n.18) 153-154, even suggests the sixth century as the time of conversion from temple to church. For the inscription honouring Theodosius' wife see Roueché no. 23 (pp. 45-46).

[41]   For references see Schultze, *Städte*(n. 32) 162-164, and Roueché, *Aphrodisias* (n.18) 144-146 and 149-150.

[42]   See A. R. Seager and A. T. Kraabel, The Synagogue and the Jewish Community, in G. M. A. Hanfmann (ed.), *Sardis from Prehistoric to Roman Times*, Cambridge (Mass.): Harvard University Press, 1983, 168-190; also A. T. Kraabel, The Diaspora Synagogue: Archaeological and Epigraphic Evidence since Sukenik, *ANRW* II 19,1, Berlin-New York: W. de Gruyter, 1979, 483-488 (477-510); both publications give further bibliography. For the inscriptions from the synagogue see L. Robert, *Nouvelles inscriptions de Sardes,* Paris 1964, esp. 39ff. Cf. also Kraabel's Paganism and Judaism: The Sardis Evidence, in *Paganisme, Judaïsme, Christianisme. Mélanges offerts à Marcel Simon*, Paris: Boccard, 1978, 13-33.

across 9 *bouleutai*, 1 *comes*, 1 *procurator,* and 1 archivist of the city; and it is their status in the city and its administration that is emphasized in the inscriptions rather than their status within the Jewish community. With respect to other Jews it can be said that their professions do not differ in any way from those of the gentile Sardians (there were for example three Jewish goldsmiths). Fifth, a number of *theosebeis* are mentioned as contributors to the synagogue. As Thomas Kraabel remarks, "The importance of the discovery of the Sardis synagogue is simply that it reveals a Jewish community of far greater wealth, power, and self-confidence than the usual views of ancient Judaism would give us any right to expect".[43] The Jewish community in Sardis was "still a minority, but a powerful, even a wealthy one, of great antiquity in a major city of the Diaspora, controlling a hugh and lavishly decorated structure on 'Main Street' and able to retain control of it as long as the city existed".[44] Jews had lived in Sardis from the third century B.C. onwards.[45] Josephus' testimonies give the impression that they were faithful to their ancestral traditions[46]: they ate kosher food and transmitted the annual half-sheqel tax to the temple in Jerusalem, a privilege often contested by the gentiles but guaranteed them time and again by the Roman government (Josephus, *Ant.* XIV 232-5. 259-61; XVI 171).[47] The new evidence from the synagogue, too, does not give any indication of syncretism on the part of the Jews. Nonetheless, they evidently developed good relationships with their gentile fellow citizens and became more and more integrated into the life of the city, without there being signs of pagan anti-Semitism at Sardis in the Imperial period.

Christianity is also attested early in Sardis. Revelation 3:1-6 is clear evidence of Christian presence there in the first century. And from the second century we have bishop Melito's homily *On Pascha*[48] which demonstrates both the influence of Jewish traditions and anti-Jewish polemic. This polemic is so fierce that one gets the impression that it arises from a sense of powerlessness over against the Jews in Sardis. When, finally, in the middle of the fourth century the Christians start to build a church there, it is not a very small one but nonetheless a far smaller one than the synagogue that had recently been rebuilt and enlarged. All this seems to point in a certain direc-

---

43   Kraabel in *Sardis* (n. 42) 178.

44   Kraabel in *ANRW* II 19,1 (n.42) 488.

45   Kraabel in *Sardis* (n. 42) 179.

46   On the loyalty of the Jews of Asia Minor to their own traditions, see S. Safrai, *Die Wallfahrt im Zeitalter des zweiten Tempels*, Neukirchen: Neukirchener Verlag, 1981, 87-91.

47   For the problems of sending the temple-tax from Asia Minor to Jerusalem the notorious Flaccus affair is revealing; see Cicero, *Pro Flacco* 66-69, with the comments by Stern, *GLAJJ* I (n. 2) 193-201.

48   S. G. Hall, *Melito of Sardis, On Pascha*, Oxford: Clarendon Press, 1979, is a useful edition with translation and bibliography.

tion. Judaism in Sardis was, till the end of antiquity, stronger than Christianity. "The strength of Sardis Jews and pagans together appears to have counterbalanced the Christians, resulting in a greater stability and security for the Jews here than was usually the case in this period".[49] It seems probable that Jews and pagans joined forces against the Christians in Sardis' final religious conflict. As Kraabel has remarked, such a coalition would help to explain how the synagogue building remained Jewish and was not expropriated, not even under the later emperors by whose decrees Christians so often felt entitled to annex Jewish places of worship.[50] The Sardis synagogue would have made a fine church, but not one piece of evidence for Christianity has been found within it.[51]

Is there a parallel with Aphrodisias here? It is again Kraabel who tentatively suggests this when he remarks on the Aphrodisias inscription: "These new data suggest that the Jews of this well-known Roman city may have been as influential as those of Sardis, and that other ancient cities in this area may also have had Jewish minorities, perhaps substantial ones, evidence for which has yet to be unearthed".[52] But we are not completely without evidence. We do have both literary and epigraphic data that strongly suggest that in several cities of Asia Minor Judaism had such a strong foothold as to act as a counterforce against Christianity.

In Acmonia (Phrygia) magistracies were held by Jews in the third century A.D. and in nearby Eumenia Christians held the same positions at the same time.[53] But the Christian and Jewish inscriptions from both cities are sometimes indistinguishable since there are so many Jewish elements, sometimes strikingly typical ones, in the Christian inscriptions. As a matter of fact there seems to have been such a great deal of interaction between the Jews of Acmonia and the Christians of Eumenia that the distinctions between both groups were often blurred.[54] And it is this blurring of the distinctions that was a cause of concern and a great threat for Church leaders in Asia Minor from apostolic times onward. It was in the heart of Asia Minor more than

---

[49] Kraabel in *Sardis* (n. 42) 180.

[50] See A. Linder, *The Jews in Roman Imperial Legislation*, Jerusalem-Detroit: Israel Academy of Sciences - Wayne State University Press, 1987, Index s.v. synagogues. On the generally moderate tone of the imperial legislation concerning the Jews see A. H. M. Jones, *The Later Roman Empire (284-602)* II, Oxford: Blackwell, 1964, 944-950.

[51] Thus Kraabel in *ANRW* II 19,1 (n. 42) 488.

[52] Kraabel in *Sardis* (n. 42) 181. Cf. also his remark , "other Jewish communities of the western Diaspora were closer to Sardis than they are to the traditional view", in: The Roman Diaspora: Six Questionable Assumptions, *Journal of Jewish Studies* 33 (1982) 460 (445-464).

[53] A.R.R. Sheppard, Jews, Christians and Heretics in Acmonia and Eumenia, *Anatolian Studies* 29 (1979) 169-180.

[54] See, besides Sheppard's article (n. 53), also L. Robert, *Hellenica* XI-XII, Paris: Maisonneuve, 1960, 414-439.

anywhere else that the power and influence of Judaism made itself felt, both with Christians and with pagans. When the influence exercised upon gentiles was strong, Christianity had to face a double front. When the influence exercised upon Christians was strong, the church had to face the danger of the judaizing of its own members. That both things did occur so that Judaism was a threat to the existence of the church in a double sense, is not open to doubt.[55]

When we return to Acmonia, we see that already in the third quarter of the first century A.D. a high-standing lady of a very influential family of pagan priests, Julia Severa, probably a priestess herself too, openly supported financially the large Jewish community of the city (*Corpus Inscriptionum Iudaicarum* 766).[56] In Tralles we see that Capitolina, "une dame d'une grande famille" as Louis Robert called her[57], became *theosebes* and donated a staircase to the local synagogue (*CIG* 2924).[58] In Hierapolis (Phrygia) the city's association of purple-dyers took upon itself responsibility for memorial ceremonies for their Jewish members (*CII* 775-7). And many more instances could be given of this kind of pagan-Jewish co-operation[59], but let me point to only one more striking testimony. In the *Acta Pionii* we read about the martyrdom of Pionius in Smyrna in 250 A.D. In chapters 13-14 Pionius launches an attack on the Jews that is more vehement than his attack on his pagan persecutors. Why is that? It appears from his words that the Jews of Smyrna, of whom we know that they formed a prominent and influential community in the city[60], tried to make proselytes among persecuted Christians. A conversion to Judaism was of course as efficacious in avoiding martyrdom as a sacrifice to idols. Even in the Diocletian persecution the Emperor explicitly exempted the Jews from the necessity of offering sacrifice, thus confirming an old privilege of Judaism. And, as Marcel Simon has observed, "it is very difficult to believe that Jewish attempts to

---

[55] I leave aside the Jewish factor in Quartodecimanism. For the Jewish element in Christianity in Asia Minor see e.g. S. E. Johnson, Asia Minor and Early Christianity, in J. Neusner (ed.), *Christianity, Judaism, and Other Greco-Roman Cults (FS M. Smith)*, II, Leiden: Brill, 1975, 77-145.

[56] W.M. Ramsay, *Cities and Bishoprics in Phrygia* I 2, Oxford: Clarendon Press, 1897, 649-651; also Sheppard, Jews (n. 53) 170.

[57] L. Robert, *Etudes Anatoliennes. Recherches sur les inscriptions grecques de l'Asie Mineure*, Paris: Boccard, 1937, 409-412. Cf. Hommel, Juden (n. 23) 206.

[58] Several scholars have already drawn attention to the fact that it is especially pagan women who seem to have felt attracted to Judaism; see Simon, *Verus Israel* (n. 28) 326-7; Schürer, *History* (n. 5) III 162-3. Conversion to Judaism by women will be the subject of a forthcoming study by Ross Kraemer, according to Cohen, Respect (n. 24) 430.

[59] Notice also that Josephus reports in *Ant.* XIV 110 that pagan *sebomenoi* in Asia (and Europe) enriched the temple in Jerusalem with their donations.

[60] See R. Lane Fox, *Pagans and Christians*, Harmondsworth: Viking, 1986, 479ff. for the evidence.

convert persecuted Christians were made without the cognizance of the Roman authorities. (...) It looks as if the state, in its desire to eliminate Christianity by making apostates and not martys, accepted the two recognized religious categories, Jewish and pagan, and left to the defecting Christians themselves the choice".[61] If Simon is right, and we have reason to believe he is, then we see here one of the most threatening consequences for the church of the Jewish-pagan coalition. And if Robin Lane Fox is right in his surmise that the 'Great Sabbath' (mentioned in *Acta Pionii* 2:1) which marked the occasion of the persecution, is the festival of Purim which the Jews in Smyrna celebrated together with the pagans who celebrated their Dionysia at the same time, then we see a bizarre form of that coalition in an easy relationship between a Jewish and a gentile festival, which the church had to face.[62]

The second aspect, the influence of Judaism upon Christianity and the consequential blurring of the distinction between the two religions, can be seen in various manifestations. We must limit ourselves here. We already mentioned the inscriptions from Eumeneia, but the clearest evidence is still the 8 homilies against the Jews by John Chrysostom in the year 386/7[63]. To be sure, they deal with the situation in Antioch on the Orontes in Syria, just outside Anatolia, but that does not seriously impair the argument. From Chrysostom's vehement invectives against Christians who go to the synagogue on sabbath, who have themselves circumcised, who celebrate Jewish Pesach, who keep Jewish food laws, who fast together with the Jews, etc., etc., - it becomes more than clear that as late as the end of the fourth century many Christians were being strongly attracted by Judaism. If the Jews are painted so black, it is because to too many Christians they appear not sufficiently unattractive. "The most compelling reason for anti-Semitism was the religious vitality of Judaism".[64] How strong this vitality was in Asia Minor becomes especially evident from several canons of the council of Laodicea (Phrygia) which was held somewhere in the third quarter of the fourth century.[65] In canon 29 it is stated: "It is forbidden that Christians live like Jews

---

61 Simon, *Verus Israel* (n. 28) 111.

62 Fox, *Pagans* (n. 60) 486-7. Note that *Codex Theodosianus* XVI 8,18 (from 408) prohibits the Jews to mock Christianity on Purim by burning Haman's effigy on a cross! See Linder, *Jews* (n. 50) 236-8.

63 W.A. Meeks and R.L. Wilken, *Jews and Christians in Antioch in the First Four Centuries of the Common Era*, Missoula: Scholars Press, 1978, 83-126 *et al*. R. Brändle, Christen und Juden in Antiochien in den Jahren 386/87. Ein Beitrag zur Geschichte altkirchlicher Judenfeindschft, *Judaica* 43 (1987) 142-160, has a very useful bibliography.

64 Simon, *Verus Israel* (n. 28) 232. Cf. also E. M. Smallwood, *The Jews Under Roman Rule*, Leiden: Brill, 1976, 508.

65 The exact date of this synod is unknown, though most scholars incline to date this meeting to the sixties of the fourth century. The text of the canons can be found in Mansi (n. 36) II 563-573 and also in E. J. Jonkers, *Acta et symbola conciliorum quae*

(ἰουδαΐζειν) and rest on sabbath; they should work on that day. They should prefer the Lord's day to rest on, if possible, since they are Christians. If they turn out to be judaizers, let them be accursed (*anathema*) by Christ." Canon 38 runs as follows: "It is forbidden to take unleavened bread from the Jews or to participate in their godless acts." Canon 37 forbids any participation in the festivals of the Jews or heretics, and canon 36 warns the clergy against making *phylakteria*, which are probably *tefillin* used as magical apotropaic amulets.[66] These canons can only be explained on the assumption that keeping the sabbath, celebrating Pesach and other Jewish religious festivals, etc., were not marginal but frequently occurring and tenacious phenomena among Christians in Asia Minor in the second half of the fourth century. John Chrysostom's and Aphraat's testimonies make it highly probable that this assumption is correct.[67] Only the fact that Judaism continued to make itself strongly felt and to make effective propaganda throughout the first five centuries of our era makes it explicable that during these centuries there was a persistent tradition of judaizing in the church of Asia Minor which defied all the anathemas of the church authorities. Marcel Simon put it well: "The anti-Jewish bias of official ecclesiastical circles was counterbalanced by equally marked pro-Jewish sentiments among the laity and among some of the clergy too. Or rather, it is the existence of the pro-Jewish sentiments among the laity that is the real explanation of Christian anti-Semitism".[68]

We can only guess at the causes or the reasons for the attraction which Judaism exercised on both pagan and Christian minds and for the success its propaganda had.[69] That Jews could present their religion as an enlightened philosophy with lofty ethics will certainly have made Judaism one of the more attractive of the Eastern cults in the Roman Empire. The rather detailed code of behaviour that Scripture and halakha contained must have been envisioned as a stabilizing factor in life by a good many people. Also the Jewish charitable institutions will have been a source of attraction. For many Christians, the argument that the commandments in the Torah were after all God's words may have carried more weight than the often tortuous argumentations to the effect that God had abolished his own Law. Be that as it may, not only in Asia Minor but also in the rest of the Empire, Judaism and Christianity struggled with one another over the pagan soul. In the practical sphere the two religions fought over the pagan clientele that Ju-

---

saeculo quarto habita sunt, Leiden: Brill, 1954, 86-96.

[66] On the great reputation of Jewish magic in antiquity see Simon, *Verus Israel* (n. 28) 339-368, esp. 361 on the magical use of phylacteries/tefillin. Some scholars regard also canon 35 (against *angelolatreia*) as directed against judaizing practice.

[67] On Aphraat see J. Neusner, *Judaism, Christianity, and Zoroastrianism in Talmudic Babylonia,* Lanham-New York-London: University Press of America, 1986, 199-228.

[68] Simon, *Verus Israel* (n. 28) 232.

[69] See e.g. Schürer, *History* (n. 5) III 53ff.

daism had built up for itself and whose attention the church tried to gain. In the third century the early Christian Latin poet Commodian addresses judaizing pagans as follows (*Instructio* I 24, 11-14):

"Why do you go so often to the synagogue, so ambivalently?
In the hope that He, whom you will deny thereafter, will be merciful to you?
You come out (of the synagogue) and you are looking for idols again!
You want to live between both (religions), but that will be the cause of your destruction"[70]

The effect of such appeals we do not know. We do know that real success was only achieved when after 312 the pagan-Jewish coalition gradually had to give way to an Empire-Church alliance which used its power to paralyze Judaism in its propagandistic efforts.[71]

Let us go back to Aphrodisias. We do not know more now about the situation in that city, but perhaps we can put our evidence now in a wider context. That context is Asia Minor as a bone of contention between Judaism and Christianity. At the beginning of that struggle, Judaism had an enormous headstart. It had been present in the area since the third centurey B.C., it held to older and much more venerable traditions than Christianity did, it had won official recognition and protection of the emperors, it had established itself and was integrated in all the cities of Anatolia, it had risen high on the social and sometimes political ladder, it had won wide adherence among the population of all Asia Minor, in some cities these adherents, the *theosebeis,* were socially high-ranking persons and magistrates in positions of influence, and there was little anti-Semitism in the country. This almost undefeatable position had to be faced by the church.[72] In several areas of the country Christianity grew roots relatively easily, but in others it did not succeed in outshining the attractiveness of Judaism until compulsory measures against the Jews guaranteed its success. Sardis is a striking example of the enduring vitality of the Jewish religion in the fourth and fifth centuries. Although it must remain somewhat speculative, there can hardly be serious doubts that the late appearance and success of Christianity in the province of Caria and its capital Aphrodisias is due to the very strong position Judaism had built up there in co-operation with the gentiles. The new inscription from that city helps us to explain the nature of the obstacles Christianity had to overcome before it could achieve its final triumph in Asia Minor.

---

70   The Latin text can be found in the CCSL edition by J. Martin (1960), 19.

71   Simon, *Verus Israel* (n. 28) 290ff. See the title of E. Mary Smallwood's inaugural lecture: *From Pagan Protection to Christian Oppression* (Belfast 1979). I have not seen Smallwood's lecture but I owe the reference to Kraabel's article mentioned in n. 52.

72   Compare W.H.C. Frend's characterization of the position of early Christianity in Carthage as "a situation in which Christianity was something of an upstart, thrusting rival confronted by a long established Jewish community", in: Jews and Christians in Third Century Carthage, in *Paganisme, Judaïsme, Christianisme (n.* 42) 192 (185-194).

By way of appendix, I present an English translation of one of the *Instructiones* by Commodian, which well illustrates the propaganda efforts Christians made in order to lure Godfearing pagans away from the synagogue.[73]

INSTRUCTIO I 37 : *To pagans who judaize*

What? Do you want to be half Jew, half pagan?
Then you will not escape the judgement of Christ after your death!
You were errant as a blind one yourself, and now you associate with blind people, you fool!
So the blind leads the blind into the pit.
You do not know where you are going and you will come back unknowing.
Those who want to learn go to the learned in order to come back learned, but you go to another kind of people from whom you cannot learn anything!
(For) when you come out (of the synagogue), you go to the idols again.
Ask in the first place what has been commanded in the Law,
and let them tell you whether it is allowed to worship the gods.
But they do not know what is the principal goal of our existence.[74]
And because they are guilty of the same fault (as you),
they tell you nothing but amazing things about God's commandments.
So, blind ones as they are, they lead you with them into the pit.
They are deadly persons! It would be too much to report all about them; otherwise I would run short of space for my ploughs, since I am restricted.
The Almighty did not want them to recognize their King,
and He withdrew from those who were stained with such a crime.
He delivered himself to us and moreover gave us a new Law.
That is why they bark now against us, but deserted by their King.
And if you think that hope is to be found with them,
then you err completely, if you worship both God and the idols.[75]

---

73 The text translated is Martin's (see n. 70), p. 31. A useful discussion is K. Thraede, Beiträge zur Datierung Commodians, *Jahrbuch für Antike und Christentum* 2 (1959) 96-100 (90-114), who presents a German translation at p. 113. I also consulted the Italian translation with commentary by A. Salvatore, *Commodiano. Instructiones, libro primo* , 2 vols., Napoli: Libreria Scientifica Editrice, 1965-66.

74 The Latin of this line is very obscure and the exact meaning must remain highly uncertain.

75 I wish to express my thanks to Ms. Dr. J. Reynolds and Ms. Dr. Ch. Roueché for some helpful information and Dr. J. N. Pankhurst for his correction of my English.

11. "LORD, HELP THE RABBI". THE INTERPRETATION OF SEG XXXI 1578B

The latest volume of the *Supplementum Epigraphicum Graecum* (XXXI, 1981, published in 1984) contains an item that, though insignificant at first sight, may turn out to be of some importance. It is a graffito, dating from the middle of the fourth century C.E., scratched upon a column of an early Byzantine bath in Cyrene. The text runs:

βοήθησον, κύριε, τοῦ ῥαββί.

It was first published in 1981 by the Italian archeologist Stucchi, who also added an interpretation that is now adopted by the editors of *SEG*.[1] Stucchi assumes that it is a Christian inscription and that *rabbi* means here 'maestro interprete della dottrina', 'vescovo della communità' (p. 218). Although Stucchi does not give any justification of this interpretation, he may have seen three reasons for it. First, the graffito is one of a group of three graffiti (by three different hands) on the column, the other two being almost certainly Christian.[2] Second, there are no other Jewish inscriptions in Cyrene or other places of ancient Libya from this period.[3] Third, Lampe's lexicon of Patristic Greek *s.v.* ῥαββί gives as a meaning 'title of a Christian priest'.[4] Let us weigh the pros and cons of this interpretation.

First some general remarks about the text of the inscription are in order. It is a type of inscription that is well known. There are many inscriptions, pagan, Jewish, and Christian, that invoke a deity, its name in the vocative being followed by βοήθησον (or βοήθει) plus the name(s) of the person(s) to be helped.[5] As a matter of fact, the other two inscriptions on the column run as follows: κύριε, βοήθησον τοῦ 'Ιανουαρίω (1578a) and κύριε, βοήθησον

---

[1] S. Stucchi, *Divagazioni archeologiche* II, Roma 1981, 215–23.

[2] *SEG* XXXI 1578a and c, actually republications of *SEG* IX 187–188; cf. *SEG* XVIII 755, and see the discussion of these inscriptions by J. Reynolds, 'The Christian Inscriptions of Cyrenaica', *Journal of Theological Studies* n.s. 11 (1960), 284–94, esp. 286. The column was found in 1928, inscriptions *a* and *c* were published in 1930, inscription *b* was deciphered only in 1980; for details see Stucchi (n. 1) 215 ff.

[3] G. Lüderitz, *Corpus jüdischer Zeugnisse aus der Cyrenaika*, Wiesbaden 1983, 59: 'Jüdische Inschriften später als 115 n. Chr. sind sonst aus der antiken Cyrenaika bisher nicht bekannt'. Unfortunately, Lüderitz does not know our inscription.

[4] G. W. H. Lampe, *A Patristic Greek Lexicon*, Oxford 1968, 1214.

[5] For some instances see the references in J. H. Moulton and G. Milligan, *The Vocabulary of the Greek Testament*, London 1930, 113, and W. Bauer, W. F. Arndt, F. W. Gingrich and F. W. Danker, *A Greek-English Lexicon of the New Testament*, London 1979², 144. Cf. Matthew 15:25—κύριε, βοήθει μοι. More instances in Stucchi (n. 1) 217, and in E. Segelberg, 'God Help His Soul', in *Ex Orbe Religionum. Studia Geo Widengren oblata* II, Leiden 1972, 173.

Ἀναστασίῳ τοῦ ἔχοντος τὰς περεστεράς (sic, 1578c).[6] The only difference in the formulation of our inscription is the inverted order of nominative and imperative. As to the genitive instead of the usual dative after βοηθεῖν, it has to be noted that this is just one of the many instances of replacement of the dative by either genitive or accusative due to the gradual disappearance of the dative from later Greek usage.[7]

At first sight this inscription looks like an invocation of God by a Jew on behalf of his rabbi (or by a rabbi on behalf of himself). How strong are the arguments for a Christian origin? Let us begin with Lampe's lemma ῥαββί. As a proof for the existence of 'rabbi' as the title of a Christian priest Lampe refers to only one passage, sc. John of Damascus' *Epistula de confessione* 9. In this letter the author exhorts monks to be humble and modest even if they have authority to confess a person,

> μηδὲ κατὰ τῆς ψυχῆς ὑμῶν [sc. μάχεσθαι] διὰ κενοδοξίαν ἢ φιλοδοξίαν ἢ
> ἐμπορίαν ἢ ἀναισθησίαν. γίνεται γὰρ διὰ τὸ ῥαββὶ καὶ πατέρες καλεῖσθαι
> ἀλλοτρίους ἀναδέχεσθαι λογισμούς. μή, παρακαλῶ, μὴ ἀναισχύντως οὕτως
> ἁπλῶς τὴν τῶν ἀποστόλων ἀξίαν ἁρπάζωμεν.[8]

Lampe's reasoning must have been that, if the author exhorts his monks not to let themselves be called rabbi or father, these must have been titles of address in his church. Two critical remarks are in order here. First, it should be indicated that modern research has proved that this epistle is not at all from the pen of John of Damascus but was written by Simeon the New Theologian.[9] That makes the distance, both geographical and chronological, between this document and our inscription still greater: not Damascus in the first half of the eighth century but Asia Minor at the beginning of the eleventh century. A local usage in Asia Minor around 1000 C.E. can hardly be used to shed light on circumstances in Cyrene six and a half centuries earlier. Second, and of much greater importance, is the observation that in this passage the relevant words are nothing but an allusion to Matthew 23:7-9. There Jesus says to his disciples about the Pharisees:

> (φιλοῦσιν) ... καλεῖσθαι ὑπὸ τῶν ἀνθρώπων ῥαββί. ὑμεῖς δὲ μὴ κληθῆτε
> ῥαββί. εἷς γάρ ἐστιν ὑμῶν ὁ διδάσκαλος, πάντες δὲ ὑμεῖς ἀδελφοί ἐστε.
> καὶ πατέρα μὴ καλέσητε ὑμῶν ἐπὶ τῆς γῆς. εἷς γάρ ἐστιν ὑμῶν ὁ πατὴρ
> ὁ οὐράνιος.

There can be no doubt that it is this passsage that the author of the epistle is referring to. If an eleventh century author admonishes his readers to be

---

[6] See note 2, and Reynolds, *JTS* 11 (1960) 286 n. 5 for interpretation. More details in Stucchi (n. 1) 217 ff.

[7] P. Humbert, *La disparution du datif en Grec*, Paris 1930.

[8] Text in *MG* 95, 293B; also in K. Holl, *Enthusiasmus und Bußgewalt beim griechischen Mönchtum*, Leipzig 1898, 118.

[9] The relevant literature is mentioned by B. Altaner and A. Stuiber, *Patrologie*, Freiburg 1978[8], 529.

humble by means of a reference to this text of the Gospel, can one deduce from that the existence of 'rabbi' as the 'title of a Christian priest'? The answer must be no. So this lemma in Lampe's lexicon should be deleted.

Another point to be discussed is the absence of any other Jewish inscriptions from Cyrenaica later than 115 C.E. In that year the great Jewish revolt began in Northern Africa which in less than two years ended with the almost complete annihilation of North African Jewry.[10] Does this preclude the existence of a Jewish community, however small, in fourth century Cyrene? Again the answer must be no. The history of modern Germany has shown that relatively shortly after the great calamity of the Holocaust Jews settled again in that country. This could have happened also in ancient Cyrene, the more so when two centuries or more had lapsed in the meantime. As *CPJ* III nos. 451–480 show, there were Jews living in Egypt in the period between 117 and 337 C.E., albeit few, even though Egyptian Jewry, too, had been almost exterminated in the war. As a matter of fact, we do have some evidence which points to the presence of Jews in Cyrene after the great revolt under Trajan. In a Vatican papyrus containing the data of a cadastral reform in Marmarika, a district of Libya, at the end of the second century, a large number of names occur. Gert Lüderitz, who has thoroughly studied personal names of pagans and Jews in ancient Cyrene, comes to the conclusion that in all likelihood some of the persons mentioned in the cadastral registers were Jews. As he admits, complete certainty cannot be attained in this matter, but detailed onomastic study of Cyrenaic Jewry makes it highly probable that Jews were involved in this land reform.[11] Still more indubitable is the evidence from Procopius who reports (in the first half of the sixth century) that Jews had lived in the town of Boreion/Boreum for a long time. They asserted, says Procopius, that their local temple had been built by King Solomon, but the Emperor Justinian had it changed into a church (*De Aedificiis* VI 2, 21–23).[12] There is no doubt that this 'temple' was the local synagogue, for Justinian had decreed that all African synagogues were to be

---

[10] On this war see A. Schlatter, *Geschichte Israels von Alexander dem Großen bis Hadrian*, Stuttgart 1925³, 370–3; E. Schürer, *A History of the Jewish People in the Age of Jesus Christ (175 B.C.–A.D. 135)*, rev. and ed. by G. Vermes and F. Millar, vol. I, Edinburgh 1973, 529–34 (vol. III, Edinburgh 1986, 60–2, deals with the evidence for the Jewish diaspora in ancient Cyrene); J. Maier, *Grundzüge der Geschichte des Judentums im Altertum*, Darmstadt 1981, 98–106; P. Schäfer, *Geschichte der Juden in der Antike*, Stuttgart and Neukirchen 1983, 155–7. The most comprehensive monograph is S. Applebaum, *Jews and Greeks in Ancient Cyrene*, Leiden 1979.

[11] Lüderitz, *Corpus* (n. 3) 165–77, gives all the details. Note especially the names Annianos, Eirenaios, and Iason.

[12] Lüderitz, *Corpus* (n. 3) 161–3. Procopius' text is as follows:

Βόρειον δὲ ἡ πόλις Μαυρουσίοις γειτνιῶσα βαρβάροις φόρου ὑποτελὴς οὐ γεγένηται ἐς τόδε τοῦ χρόνου. οὐδέ τινες πώποτε δασμολόγοι ἢ φορολόγοι ἐς αὐτὴν ἵκοντο, ἐξ οὗ γεγόνασιν ἄνθρωποι. οἱ δὲ Ἰουδαῖοι ᾤκηντο ἐκ παλαιοῦ αὐτῶν ἄγχιστα. οὗ δὴ καὶ νεὼς ἦν ἀρχαῖος αὐτοῖς, ὅνπερ ἐσέβοντό τε καὶ ἐτεθήπεσαν μάλιστα, δειμαμένου τοῦτο Σολομῶνος, ὥσπερ φασί, βασιλεύοντος Ἑβραίων τοῦ ἔθνους. ἀλλὰ καὶ αὐτοὺς ἅπαντας Ἰουστινιανὸς βασιλεὺς μεταγνῶναί τε τὰ πάτρια ἤθη, καὶ Χριστιανοὺς γεγονέναι διαπραξάμενος, τοῦτον δὴ τὸν νεὼν ἐς ἐκκλησίας μεθηρμόσατο σχῆμα.

transformed into churches (*Novella* 37:8 ... *neque synagogas eorum stare concedimus, sed ad ecclesiarum figuram eas volumus reformari*). This proves that in the first half of the sixth century there were Jews in Cyrene, and Procopius' statement implies that they were not newcomers in his time. Our inscription from the middle of the fourth century is halfway through the period of more than three centuries that lie between the Vatican papyrus and Procopius. It adds probability to the assumption of a continuous presence of Jews in ancient Cyrene, however small their communities may have been.

Finally, the fact that the graffito stands between two other ones, most probably Christian inscriptions, does not prove, or even make probable, that it, too, must be Christian. We do not know the history of the column on which these graffiti were scratched. But if it belonged to the local public bath frequented by pagans, Jews, and Christians, and if Christians inscribed on it intercessions for their local leaders or for themselves, why could not Jews do the same? There is nothing to prevent us from taking this inscription at its face value and regarding it as Jewish.

Theoretically there are two other possibilities. First, it might be argued that we have here a pagan inscription. In that case, one has to take the genitive τοῦ ῥαββί not *pro dativo* but as possessive genitive to κύριε, and to translate it, 'Help, Lord of the rabbi'. The inverted order of the vocative and imperative as compared to the other inscriptions that have κύριε, βοήθησον κτλ. may lend some support to this suggestion. One can imagine a pagan in a troublesome situation seeking help from his gods without result, invoking at his wits end the nameless god of the Jews. He may have heard the local rabbi speaking about the mighty acts of his κύριος. Hence, when he calls on this powerful god, he identifies him as κύριος τοῦ ῥαββί. In that case, βοήθησον has no object, but that is not without parallels.[13] Invocation of the god of the Jews by pagans is very common in e.g. the magical papyri.

Second, it might be suggested that it is a Christian inscription with a prayer for help for a rabbi who had become a Christian. It is conceivable that when a personality such as a rabbi became a church member, people in the Christian community continued to call him 'the rabbi'. In such a situation a Christian prayer like 'Lord, help the rabbi' is not unthinkable.

As I said, these are theoretical possibilities that cannot be ruled out entirely. It has to be stressed, however, that both alternative interpretations presuppose the existence of a Jewish community in Cyrene; and if that is the case, then it is much less artificial to regard the inscription as Jewish. This view would seem to me to be the least far-fetched and by far the most likely.

This conclusion is of some importance in three ways. First, it would mean that we have now evidence of the existence of a Jewish community in Cyrene in the fourth century, which is proof of a greater continuity of Jewish presence in that area. Second, we have made a small but not altogether unimportant correction to Lampe's Patristic Lexicon. Third, we have added

---

[13] See LSJ *s.v.* for other instances of the absolute use of βοηθεῖν.

a new instance to the very infrequent occurrences of the word 'rabbi' in Greek in Jewish inscriptions.[14]

Appendix

My colleague, Professor T. Baarda, suggested the possibility that the 'rabbi' of the inscription might be Jesus. He drew my attention to a small papyrus fragment of an apocryphal Gospel published by Hans Lietzmann in *Zeitschrift für die neutestamentliche Wissenschaft* 22 (1923) 153–4. In this papyrus (*Pap. Berolinensis* 11710), which dates from the sixth or seventh century C.E., we read part of a dialogue between Nathanael and Jesus in which Nathanael addresses Jesus as ῥαμβιού and Jesus is called ὁ ῥαμβίς, with the typically Egyptian μβ for ββ.[15] Lietzmann remarks that this is the only time, outside the New Testament, that Jesus is called 'rabbi' in early Christian literature. If one takes into account that Nathanael's address of Jesus as rabbi is caused here by the fact that in the Gospel of John 1:49 Nathanael calls Jesus 'rabbi', one should be very careful in assuming that 'rabbi' has ever been a christological title. In my view that is very improbable and cannot elucidate the inscription discussed above.

---

[14] There are, of course, many instances of the use of 'rabbi' in Hebrew and Aramaic inscriptions, as may be gathered from J. B. Frey's *Corpus Inscriptionum Iudaicarum*. But in Jewish inscriptions in Greek, the terms used most of the time are νομομαθής, νομοδιδάσκαλος, διδάσκαλος. We find ῥαββί only in three inscriptions: nos. 736 from Cyprus (in the form ῥαββή), 951 from Jaffa (in the form ῥεβί), and 1052 from Beth Shearim (in the form ῥιββί). In Jewish inscriptions in Latin we find three times the form *rebbi*: in nos. 568 from Salerno, 611 from Venosa and 665a from Merida in Spain (the latter published on pp. 57–8 of the Prolegomena by B. Lifshitz to the reprint of vol. I of Frey's *Corpus*, New York 1975). In Jewish Greek literature the word ῥαββί does not occur at all. In Christian literature, apart from the 16 instances in the NT, it hardly occurs. There are some instances in the *Acta Pilati* (15:6, 16:3, *et al.*) and in the *Narratio de rebus Persicis* (pp. 2 and 34 in the ed. by E. Bratke, *Das sogenannte Religionsgespräch am Hof der Sassaniden*, TU 19:3, Leipzig 1899). See further the papyrus mentioned in the Appendix to this article. An almost complete survey of the inscriptional evidence for 'rabbi' in Hebrew, Aramaic, Latin and Greek of the first seven centuries C.E. can be found in S. J. D. Cohen, 'Epigraphical Rabbis', *JQR* 72 (1981/82) 1–17. Our item *SEG* XXXI 1578b should be added to his list.

[15] The enigmatic vocative ῥαμβιού is explained by my colleague Dr G. Mussies as ῥαμβὶ ιου = ῥαββὶ Ἰησοῦ, a somewhat unusual form of this *nomen sacrum*.

12. The Interpretation of the Bible by the Minor Hellenistic Jewish Authors

Introduction

In this contribution, not all minor Hellenistic Jewish authors will be dealt with. Excluded are all pseudepigrapha because they constitute a class of their own and are discussed elsewhere in this volume, as is also Aristobulus.[1] Some borderline cases, like Thallus and Theophilus, have also been omitted either because their Jewish identity is uncertain or because their tiny fragments do not yield much of importance. We have restricted ourselves to the nine authors from whom quotations or excerpts have been preserved via Alexander Polyhistor in the ninth book of bishop Eusebius' *Praeparatio Evangelica* (henceforth *PE*), written in the first quarter of the fourth century c.e.[2]

Alexander Polyhistor[3] was a prolific writer in the genre of geographical-historical periegesis. According to the Suda (*s.v.* Ἀλέξανδρος ὁ Μιλήσιος, ed. Adler 1, p. 104) he was brought as a captive from Miletus to Rome in the time of Sulla, but regained his liberty in 82 b.c.e.; he died in Italy as an aged man somewhere after 40 b.c.e.[4] Innumerable books came from his pen (συνέγραψε βίβλους ἀριθμοῦ κρείττους, Suda *s.v.*), e.g. on the history of Egypt, Babylonia, India, Crete, Libya, Phrygia, Lycia (Αἰγυπτιακά, Χαλδαϊκά, Ἰνδικά, Κρητικά, Λιβυκά, Περὶ Φρυγίας, Περὶ Λυκίας), etc.[5] He was not an original and independent author, for most of his work seems to have consisted of

---

[1] On Aristobulus see Borgen, 'Philo of Alexandria', 274-79 (Philo and His Predecessor Aristobulus).

[2] Some fragments or parts of them are quoted also in Clemens Alexandrinus' *Stromateis*. The texts are most conveniently accessible in Denis, *Fragmenta*, 175-228 (Denis prints the text from Mras' edition of Eusebius' *PE* in GCS 43, 1, Berlin 1954, but without app. crit.). The historians can now best be consulted in Holladay, *Fragments* 1.

[3] On Alexander Polyhistor see Freudenthal, *Hellenistische Studien*; Susemihl, *Geschichte* 2, 356-64; Christ-Schmid-Stählin, *Geschichte der griechischen Litteratur* 2/1, 400-01; Lesky, *Geschichte*, 873; Stern, *GLAJJ* 1, 157ff.; *Der Kleine Pauly* s.v. 1, 252. The fragments of his historical work have been collected in Jacoby, *FGH* 3 A no. 273.

[4] His pupil, the grammarian Hyginus, had his *floruit* during Augustus' reign. Alexander must have lived from ca. 110/105 to ca. 35/30 b.c.e.. See Unger, 'Wann schrieb Alexander Polyhistor?', and the same, 'Die Blüthezeit'.

[5] He also wrote some works in the field of the history of philosophy and grammar; see Christ-Schmid-Stählin, *Geschichte der griechischen Litteratur* 2/1, 401.

excerpts and quotations from other authors. But in this manner he became one of the most important mediators of knowledge of the history of oriental peoples to later Greek and Latin authors in the West. For us he is most interesting as the author of a work *On the Jews* (Περὶ 'Ιουδαίων), which is unfortunately lost, but part of which has been preserved in the quotations made from it by Eusebius of Caesarea in his *PE*. As in his other works, here too Alexander gives quotations (sometimes lengthy) from or summaries of the works of other authors, in this case Jewish ones.

The question of trustworthiness need not be raised when Alexander is quoting poetry; he probably does not alter metrical texts. But when he paraphrases or summarizes prose texts, how reliable is he? The impression is that he has sometimes misunderstood his sources (so that, for example, he makes David the son of Saul), but that in general he has been quite faithful to them.[6] However, it should be borne in mind that in the present case there have been at least five stages of possible corruption of the texts concerned:

1. The transmission of the texts between the autographs and their arrival on Alexander's desk.
2. Alexander's partial rewording or rephrasing of them.
3. The transmission of Alexander's text until it arrived in Eusebius' hands.
4. Eusebius' partial rewording or rephrasing of Alexander's text.
5. The transmission of Eusebius' text through the ages during which it underwent manifold corruption.[7]

These factors should make us somewhat diffident and prevent us from making too apodictic or definitive statements on the material under discussion (especially as to numbers and dates).

Problems of dating and provenance will not be discussed. For most of the authors concerned one could say that their dates cannot be fixed exactly. At any rate it is clear that all of them wrote before Alexander Polyhistor compiled his work *On the Jews* and after the translation of the Pentateuch into Greek. That is to say, they worked somewhere between, say, 250 and 50 B.C.E., most of them probably in the second cent. B.C.E.[8] Their provenance probably was often Alexandria, sometimes Palestine, but certainty is impossible in many cases.[9]

---

[6] See Freudenthal, *Hellenistische Studien*, 16-35.
[7] See for the textual history of *PE* the introduction to Mras' edition, vol. 1, XIII-LIV, and Holladay, *Fragments* 1, 9-13.
[8] See Holladay, *Fragments* 1, 4.
[9] On Jewish Greek literature in Palestine, see Hengel, *Judentum und Hellenismus*, 161-90 (ET 1, 88-102; 2, 59-71).

Poets

EZEKIEL THE DRAMATIST

Ezekiel[10] is the only Jewish playwright known to us from antiquity. He is an important and characteristic example of what could happen when biblical tradition and Greek literary form merged: the content is scriptural story, but the genre is Hellenistic drama.[11] Although he probably wrote more pieces (Clement of Alexandria, *Strom.* 1:23, 155 calls him 'the writer of Jewish tragedies'), portions (which total only 269 iambic trimeters) have been preserved from only one play. It is titled *Exagoge* ('Ἐξαγωγή) and deals with the exodus story. The LXX text of Exodus 1-15 is followed fairly closely, sometimes almost literally, but there are some significant deviations, varying from minor details to whole non-biblical scenes. In several of these passages one can easily see motifs that recur in later aggadic literature as well, and it is often difficult to say whether Ezekiel depends upon the same sources as the later aggada or that the later aggadists depend upon Ezekiel, the latter being a possibility that one should not dismiss too quickly.[12]

A few of the minor variations will illustrate this point. In the Prologue (vv. 1-65) Moses summarizes the events of Exod 1-2. In v. 21 he says that when the Egyptian princess noticed Moses' basket, she immediately took hold of the child. The biblical text, both the Hebrew and the Greek, have her send her maidservant to fetch it (Exod 2:5). In the Talmud, however, there is a discussion on the question of whether it was the princess herself or one of her maids who took up the child (*B.T. Sota* 12b). And, indeed, the targums Onkelos and Pseudo-Yonatan have the princess do it herself, as does one of the paintings in the Dura-Europos synagogue as well.[13] Ezekiel is our earliest witness to this tradition.

In vv. 60-62 Zippora, a daughter of one of the local rulers, tells Moses that he is in Libya where the black Ethiopians live.[14] So, Zippora is supposed to be an Ethiopian woman. Here, again, Ezekiel works within the framework of Jewish exegesis. In Num 12:1 it is said that Moses had an Ethiopian wife. Targum

---

[10] See Nickelsburg, 'Bible Rewritten', 125-30 (Ezekiel the Tragedian); Robertson in Charlesworth, *OTP* 2, 803-19. Schürer, *History* (rev. ed.) 3/1, 563-65.

[11] Ezekiel's play happens to be the only dramatic piece of the Hellenistic period of which substantial portions have been preserved; everything else is lost except for tiny fragments. Although Ezekiel is heavily influenced by the classical tragedians Aeschylus, Sophocles, and Euripides, his play has several Hellenistic features, e.g. the total abandonment of the unity of time and place. The play probably was divided into five acts, each of which had a different setting. See Jacobson, *Exagoge*, 28-36, and the older literature mentioned in his 'Two Studies' 167, notes.

[12] It is very significant, for instance, that the major non-biblical scene, vv. 68-89, occurs in a Hebrew translation in the aggadic collection of Jellinek, *Bet ha-Midrasch* 5, 159.

[13] See Vermes, 'Bible and Midrash', 90-91; Jacobson, *Exagoge*, 76.

[14] On this apparent geographical oddity see my 'De joodse toneelschrijver', 99; Jacobson, *Exagoge*, 85f.

Neofiti 1 explicitly says there: this Ethiopian woman is no one else than Zippora. The same tradition is found in Demetrius (*PE* 9:29, 1-3) and elsewhere, and it seems to be connected with the legend found in Artapanus and Josephus that Moses stayed for some time in Ethiopia.[15] The apologetic motive is, of course, to avoid the idea that Moses was polygamous.

In vv. 165-66 it is said that the gold, silver and garments that the Jews received from the Egyptians (Exod 11:2; 12:35) are given as payment for all the work the Jews had done for the Egyptians. This apologetic expansion of the scriptural text is also frequently found in rabbinic literature. Obviously, the biblical text was embarrassing to the Jews since it seemed to imply that the Jews borrowed or stole things from the Egyptians without ever returning them. There is evidence that on the basis of this report in Exodus pagans accused the Jews of theft.[16] In the Talmud (*B. T. Sanhedrin* 91a) we read: 'The Egyptians came in a lawsuit against the Jews before Alexander of Macedon. They pleaded thus: Is it not written "And the Lord gave the people favour in the sight of the Egyptians and they lent them gold, etc." (Exod 12:36)? Then return us the gold and silver which you took'. In the ensuing debate between them and Gebiha ben Pesisa the latter refuted them on the basis of Exod 12:40 ('the sojourning of the children of Israel who dwelt in Egypt was 430 years') and said: 'Pay us for the toil of 600.000 men whom you enslaved for 430 years!'. The same anti-Jewish (Egyptian) interpretation of Exod 11:2; 12:35-36 is also reflected in *Esther Rabba* 7:13.[17] 'One can readily understand Ezekiel's introduction of this *apologia* since his Greek audience might well have been regularly subjected to this argument by anti-Semitic native Egyptians'.[18] Here, as elsewhere, Ezekiel avoids or omits all incidents that might cast a bad light on the Jews or Moses.

Now we turn to the most puzzling passage of the preserved fragments, the most extensive non-biblical scene, vv. 68-89. Here Moses says that he dreamt about a great throne on the top of mount Sinai, whereupon a noble man (*i.e.* God) was seated with a crown on his head and a sceptre in his left hand. He beckoned Moses with his right hand, gave the crown and sceptre to him, and summoned him to sit on the great throne which He himself left. From God's throne Moses saw all of heaven and earth, and all the heavenly bodies made obeisance to him. Then he awoke. Moses' father-in-law, Raguel, interprets the dream as predicting that Moses will establish a great throne and become a leader of men, and that he will be able to see 'what is, what was, and what will be'.

---

[15] Jacobson, *Exagoge*, 86ff.; Levy, 'Moïse en Éthiopie', 201-11; Vermes, 'La figure de Moïse', 74; Ginzberg, *Legends* 6, 90 n. 488; Rajak, 'Moses in Ethiopia'; Runnals, 'Moses' Ethiopian Campaign'.

[16] Jacobson, *Exagoge*, 126ff.

[17] Cf. further, *Jub.* 48:18-19; Philo, *Mos.* 1:141-42; *Avot de-R. Natan* A 41, p. 132-33; perhaps Wisdom 10:17?

[18] Jacobson, *Exagoge*, 127. See also Le Déaut, *Targum du Pentateuque* 2, 30 n. 92; Ginzberg, *Legends*, 5, 436-37 n. 233.

This scene has been explained in very divergent ways, I will mention only two important recent opinions which are very opposed to one another. The first one[19] sees in this scene a polemic against notions of Moses' divinization and cosmic kingship, and against throne-mysticism. Consequently, it represents, according to this interpretation, a playing down of anything supernatural in Moses. Many other stories of heavenly ascension by Moses speak of a real ascension, not a visionary one nor in a dream. 'Ezekiel deliberately chose to portray the "ascension" as an imaginary event'.[20] The reason for this conscious rejection of the legend that Moses actually ascended to heaven and beheld God is to be found in the Bible itself. In Num 12:6-8 God says: 'If there is a prophet among you, I the Lord make myself known to him in a vision, I speak with him in a dream. Not so with my servant Moses; he is entrusted with all my house. With him I speak mouth to mouth, clearly, and not in dark speech; and he beholds the form of the Lord'. The fact that in Ezekiel's text God does make himself known to Moses in a vision and speaks to him in a dream makes all this an irrelevant event.

Whereas according to this interpretation Ezekiel is critical of traditions concerning Moses' exaltation, the other interpretation[21] maintains that it is precisely Ezekiel who is one of the earliest champions of such traditions exalting Moses. This interpretation regards the scene not only as one of the earliest post-biblical *merkava* – visions, of which there are so many in the later *hekhalot* – literature (based on Ezek 1), but also as one of the earliest examples of the post-biblical Jewish idea of a vice-regent or plenipotentiary of God: the Old Testament figure of 'the angel of the Lord' could become identified with a human being who achieved a divine status and became God's helper or the mediator between God and men or the highest angel. This person received charge over the world and came close to being an anthropomorphic hypostasis of God himself. That Moses was qualified for such a position was suggested, *inter alia*, by the fact that he is twice called 'god' in Exodus (4:16 and 7:1), and that by God himself. Another serious candidate was, of course, Enoch (Gen 5:24: 'Enoch walked with God. Then he vanished because God took him away'). Hence the most striking parallels to this scene are found in the Enochic literature, especially in the Hebrew Book of Enoch *(3 Enoch)* where Enoch is identified with the highest angel, Metatron (*i.e.*, probably, 'he with whom God shares His throne'). Metatron is called 'the little YHWH' (12:5), which is exactly what Moses is in Ezekiel's play.[22] There probably was even a certain rivalry between Moses and Enoch in this function, but it should be added that they were not the only ones who were identified with the angel of the Lord. The

[19] Jacobson, 'Mysticism and Apocalyptic', and *Exagoge*, 89-97.
[20] Jacobson, 'Mysticism and Apocalyptic', 277.
[21] Van der Horst, 'De joodse toneelschrijver'; 'Moses' Throne-Vision'; 'Some Notes'. Now also Rowland, *Christian Origins* 37, and Fossum, *Name of God*, 191 n. 348.
[22] It should be remembered that in Exod 23:21 God says of the 'angel of the Lord': 'My Name is in Him'.

theme of Moses' divine kingship over the universe is also found elsewhere, in Philo in such a pronounced way that 'the analogy between Moses and God (. . .) approaches consubstantiality'.[23] (Naturally, all this is an important chapter in the prehistory of christology.) The implication of this interpretation is that, for Ezekiel, Moses still is 'an active and present power'[24] who rules the world in God's name, as his plenipotentiary. This is boldly expressed by making God leave his throne, giving it to Moses.[25]

The first mentioned interpretation cannot be entirely ruled out, but the problem is that the play itself does not give any indication that this scene should be so interpreted. The supposed subtle reference to Num 12:6-8 could not have been understood by his Greek audience (and hardly by his Jewish), and since the play drew its biblical material only from Exod 1-15, it is difficult to imagine how Num 12:6-8 could have been brought in somewhere. Moreover, Ezekiel would completely overshoot his mark if he represented the hero of his play as a kind of megalomaniac dreaming about his exaltation to divine cosmic kingship. If that was what Ezekiel wanted to say, he could have made the point by having Raguel say so in his interpretation of the dream. But, on the contrary, Raguel says that Moses will establish a great throne and be a great prophet (thereby indicating, incidentally, that he has not yet grasped the full meaning of the vision, a well-known literary device). Just as the prohibition of animal-worship in Exod 20:4-5 did not inhibit Ezekiel's contemporary Artapanus from presenting Moses as the founder of the Egyptian animal cult, so Num 12:6-8 did not prevent Ezekiel from giving his view of Moses in the form of a dream-vision (thus using a dramatic form well-known from his classical predecessors).[26]

The other great non-biblical scene, depicting the appearance of a phoenix at the exodus, can only be dealt with very briefly.[27] Recent study of the myth of the phoenix has shown that the common element in stories about the appearances of this miraculous bird is that it indicates an important turning-point in history.[28] The accent always falls on the symbolism of the phoenix as inaugurator of a new era. In a sixth cent. c.e. Coptic sermon (which contains much older tradition) it is also reported that 'at the time that God brought the children of Israel out of Egypt by the hand of Moses, the phoenix showed itself on the temple of On, the

---

[23] Meeks, *Prophet-King*, 104f. The above-said is based upon Meeks' *Prophet-King*, his article 'Moses as God and King'; Segal's *Two Powers in Heaven*, and his article 'Ruler of this World'; and upon Fossum, *Name of God*. Detailed evidence can be found in my three articles mentioned in n. 21.

[24] The phrase is Goodenough's who uses it for Philo's view of Moses (*By Light, Light*, 233).

[25] What is meant here is the same as what Jesus says in Matt 28:18 ἐδόθη μοι πᾶσα ἐξουσία ἐν οὐρανῷ καὶ ἐπὶ γῆς.

[26] See Kappelmacher, 'Zur Tragoedie', 78-80; Starobinski-Safran, 'Un Poète', 220; Snell, *Szenen*, 170ff.

[27] See my 'De Joodse toneelschrijver', 110-12; Jacobson, *Exagoge*, 157-66.

[28] See Van den Broek, *The Myth of the Phoenix*. Collins (*Athens*, 209f.) misses the point because he does not know Van den Broek's work.

city of the sun'.[29] The exodus is the beginning of a new era in world-history, marked by the manifestation of the fabulous phoenix.

It is clear from all this that Ezekiel's deviations from the biblical text serve one purpose: the glorification of Moses and of the people and Israel. Detractions by anti-Semitic propaganda probably inspired him to emphasize the nobility of this people and its first leader, even the divine status of the latter, whose heavenly enthronement validates the nation of the Jews as divinely established.[30]

PHILO THE EPIC POET

This author[31] wrote a lengthy epic of at least 14 (or 4?) books, *On Jerusalem*, in what is sometimes almost unintelligible Greek. This obscurity may be due partly to the author's own tortuous style and diction,[32] partly to faulty transmission of the text. Only 24 lines (hexameters) are extant. The first fragment deals with the binding of Isaac, the second with Joseph's rule over Egypt, the third with the water-supply of Jerusalem. This time not drama but epic, more exactly epic on the history of a city,[33] is the Greek genre used to convey the biblical story.

It is important to notice that in the first book of this poem on the history of Jerusalem the story of Gen 22 is dealt with, since this implies the equation of the *land* Moriah (Gen 22:2) with the *mount* Moriah, probably already hinted at in 2 Chr 3:1,[34] and explicitly stated in later tradition, e.g. *Jub.* 18:13; Josephus, *Ant.* 1:226, 7:333; targums Onkelos and Ps.-Yonatan *ad* Gen 22:2; *Gen. Rabba* 55:7 (p. 591-92); etc.[35] According to current opinion, it is only in vv. 8-10 that the *Akeda* is mentioned.[36] However, I believe that already in v. 2, where Abraham is said to be 'famous especially by reason of the knot of the bonds' ('Αβραὰμ

---

[29]   Van den Broek, *The Myth of the Phoenix*, 47. In Ezekiel the bird appears at Elim (Exod 15:27); so probably the Coptic sermon does not derive the motif from Ezekiel.

[30]   See Fallon, *The Enthronement*, 48. It has to be emphasized here that since Manetho (beginning of the third cent. B.C.E.; see Stern, *GLAJJ*, 1, 62ff.) there was a continous tradition of anti-Semitic versions of the exodus story; see Gager, *Moses* 113-33, and my *Chaeremon*, 49f.

[31]   See Nickelsburg, 'Bible Rewritten', 118-21; Attridge in Charlesworth, *OTP* 2, 781-84. Probably he is not identical with Philo the Elder (mentioned by Josephus, *Ag. Ap.* 1:218, and Clemens Alexandrinus, *Strom.* 1:141, 3); see Walter 'Philon der Epiker'; Wacholder, 'Philo (the Elder)'; Schürer, *History* (rev. ed.) 3/1, 559-61. Unfortunately, about another Jewish epic poet, Sosates, called the 'Jewish Homer', we know next to nothing; see Cohen, 'Sosates, the Jewish Homer', and Van der Horst, 'Korte notities' 102-03.

[32]   Schürer, *Geschichte* 3:498 'bis zur Unverständlichkeit schwülstig und geschraubt'. Walter, 'Philon, der Epiker', 141 refers to an unpublished paper by J. Atwell and J. Hanson who compare Philo's style to that of Apollonius Rhodius' *Argonautica* and Rhianus' *Messeniaca*, both third cent. B.C.E. epics; see already Gutman, 'Philo the Epic Poet', 60-63.

[33]   On this genre see Ziegler, *Das hellenistische Epos*, 18ff.; Gutman, 'Philo the Epic Poet' 38f., 59ff.

[34]   See Williamson, *1 and 2 Chronicles*, 203f.

[35]   See Fohrer, 'Morija', 1239; Barrois, 'Moriah', 438f.; Bowker, *Targums*, 230.

[36]   See e.g., most recently, Walter, 'Philon der Epiker', 149.

κλυτοηχὲς ὑπέρτερον ἄμματι δεσμῶν), reference is made to the *Akeda* (rather than to the making of the covenant in Gen 17).[37] Vv. 5-7 fit in well with this interpretation: 'with a loud voice the Blessed One stopped the kindling (of the wood) and made his (Abraham's) fame immortal' (ἔκκαυμα βριήπυος αἰνετὸς ἴσχων / ἀθάνατον ποίησεν ἐὴν φάτιν). These lines are best explained as a free rendering of Gen 22:11-12. 16-18, comparable with the later aggadic accounts as reflected in the targums *ad loc.* and *Gen. Rabba* 56:7ff. (p. 602ff.).

Aggadic elements come to the fore even more clearly in the description of Abraham as the one who left the splendid enclosure of the giants (4-5 λιπόντι . . . ἀγλαὸν ἕρκος αἰνοφύτων).[38] This most probably refers to the equation of the giants of Gen 6:4 with the rulers of Babel who planned and executed the building of the tower under Nimrod (Gen 10:8-12 combined with 11:1-9) and who tried to coerce Abraham to join in their enterprise; see for instance *Jub.* 10; Josephus, *Ant.* 1:113-14; Ps-Eupolemus, fragm. 1; Ps-Philo, *LAB* 6; *B.T. Pesahim* 118a; *PRE* 24.[39]

The second short fragment, on Joseph as ruler of Egypt, does not exhibit specific aggadic traits,[40] unless they are hidden in the very obscure 5th line in which Joseph is said to be δινεύσας λαθραῖα χρόνου πλημμυρίδι μοίρης ('unraveling the secrets of fate in the flood of time'?), perhaps a reference to his onirocritic activities in Gen 40 and 41.

The third fragment contains a rather unclear description of a part of the water supply system of Jerusalem.[41] Its astonishing features are emphasized (vv. 1 and 7). A comparable enthusiasm for this system is also reflected in Sir 50:3 and especially in *Ep. Arist.* 89-91.[42] As this account is not based on the text of the Bible, it may be an eye-witness account, but it may also derive from literary sources similar to (those of) *Ep. Arist.* The tendency to underline the magnificence of Jerusalem and to eulogize Abraham is similar to the one manifesting itself in Ezekiel's picture of Moses and Israel.

THEODOTUS

Like Philo, Theodotus wrote an epic about the history of a city, Shechem. Because of this theme and because the author calls Shechem 'a holy city' (ἱερὸν

---

[37] See also Collins, *Athens*, 45, and Attridge in Charlesworth, *OTP* 2, 783.

[38] For this translation of αἰνόφυτοι see Mras *ad loc.* and Walter, 'Philon der Epiker', 149.

[39] Other rabbinic texts in Strack-Billerbeck, *Kommentar* 2, 95; 3, 34-35. Walter, *ibid.*; Holladay, *Fragments* 1, 178 n. 5. See also below, n. 120.

[40] The theory of Dalbert (*Theologie*, 34-35) and Gutman ('Philo the Epic Poet', 59) that Joseph is described here as a god is rightly refuted by Walter, *ibid.* 150 n. c.

[41] On this system see Kosmala, 'Jerusalem' 825-27, and Jeremias, *Rediscovery of Bethesda* (non vidi); also Amiran, 'Water Supply' and Mazar, 'Aquaducts'.

[42] Walter, *ibid.*, 142-43. A remote pagan parallel is Frontinus' *De aquis urbis Romae.*

ἄστυ, fragm. 1) he has often been held to be a Samaritan.[43] But nowadays there is a growing consensus that he was not: there is no clear pro-Samaritan tendency in the poem; Garizim is not mentioned; and the murder of the Shechemites by Jacob's sons (Gen 34) is not condemned (as in Gen 49:5-7) but viewed as an act commanded by God against the godless (ἀσεβεῖς, fragm. 5) inhabitants of Shechem; and 'holy city' is a traditional Homeric expression.[44] But these facts do not disprove that Theodotus was a Samaritan. Against the consensus it may be argued that the Samaritans of Theodotus' time, as Pentateuchal Jews, did not claim to be descendants of the Shechemites (who were all murdered), but of the Israelites left in the land at the time of the Assyrian exile, and of the priests who came back to teach the Assyrian colonists to worship the God of Israel (2 Kings 17). The Jews partly accepted these claims. The Shechemites of Hellenistic times can, therefore, easily be supposed to praise Simeon and Levi and to represent them as heroes who by their violent deed liberated the 'holy city' from its former wicked inhabitants. So Theodotus may have been a Samaritan author after all.[45]

The 47 lines that are extant (*PE* 9:22, 1-11) are partly a description of Shechem's surroundings and a summary of Jacob's history, especially with Laban (Gen 29-30, without aggadic embellishments: fragm. 1-3), and partly a free poetic rendering of Gen 34 (fragm. 4-6) in Homeric style. There are some interesting agreements with Josephus' presentation of the same story in *Ant.* 1:337-41,[46] and also with *Jub.* 30, Judith 9:2-4, *Test. Levi* 5-7. For example, Dina is said to have gone to Shechem because there was a festival (fragm. 4 – *Ant.* 1:337). It is not both Simeon and Levi who thought out their murderous plan, but only Simeon (fragm. 4 – Judith 9:2), as in *Test. Levi* 5 it is only Levi. In fragm. 5 their act is justified as being in accordance with God's will, just as in *Jub.* 30:23-25 it is counted to them as righteousness; also in *Test. Levi* 5:3-4; 6:8; Josephus, *Ant.* 1:341, and *Jos. As.* 23:14, we find attempts to unburden the two brothers. Philo praises their role in *On the Migration of Abraham* 224 and *On the Change of Names* 195 and 200. Cf. also *Gen. Rabba* 80:8. 10 (p. 960-61, 964-66); 97 (p. 1206-07). In fragm. 6 it is not only said *that* they killed Hamor and Shechem, which is the only thing mentioned in Gen 34:26, but *how* they killed them is also described, and who killed whom: Simeon kills Hamor, Levi kills Shechem; in *Test. Levi* 6:4 first Levi kills Shechem, then Simeon kills Hamor. It is also noteworthy that, whereas Gen 34 only states that the brothers say: 'We cannot give our sister to a man who is uncircumcised', Theodotus has

---

[43] Freudenthal, *Hellenistische Studien*, 99f. Schürer, *Geschichte* 3:499f. But see now, Schürer, *History* (rev.ed.) 3/1, 561-63; since then many other scholars, see Walter, 'Theodotus der Epiker' 158 nn. 24, 25; Pummer, 'Genesis 34', 177 n. 2; Fallon in Charlesworth, *OTP* 2, 785ff.

[44] Kippenberg, *Garizim*, 83f.; Collins, 'The Epic of Theodotus', 91ff.; Walter, *ibid.* 157-61. Cf. e.g. Homer, *Odyssey* 1:2.

[45] See M. Smith, *Palestinian Parties*, 188-89 (with nn. 207-17). For this paragraph I owe several important hints to Prof. Morton Smith, for which I am very grateful.

[46] Josephus may have known Theodotus' work, however.

Jacob say: 'It is not allowed (οὐ θεμιτόν) to the Hebrews to marry sons or daughters from elsewhere, but only such ones as declare to belong to the same people'. This wording, especially οὐ θεμιτόν, is reminiscent of a similar addition to the text that targums Neofiti, Onkelos and Ps.-Yonatan make in v. 7 (in a comparable context): it is לא כשר, 'not allowed', to do such a thing. The poem evidently insists on the prohibition of mixed marriages with the uncircumcised Gentiles.

The poem is often thought to be a piece of ideological justification of the anti-Samaritan policy of John Hyrcanus I (135-104 B.C.E.)[47] – this ruler destroyed the temple on mount Garizim in 129 and devastated Shechem in 109 B.C.E. –, since an anti-Samaritan interpretation of the story of Gen 34 could be very helpful in justifying his acts of violence against the Samaritans.[48] Indeed, the procedure to re-interpret biblical texts in an anti-Samaritan way is also used elsewhere: It has been demonstrated that in the course of the textual transmission of the Hebrew Bible, scribes made subtle changes in several texts so that they received an anti-Samaritan edge.[49] But if, as has been argued above, the consensus that Theodotus was not a Samaritan author is wrong, the poem should be read as a piece of Samaritan propaganda, in which the author presents the ancestors of the Samaritans as zealous Jews.[50] Theodotus had an obvious desire to purge the character of these forefathers from negative traits.[51]

Historians

DEMETRIUS

Demetrius, the so-called chronographer, is almost certainly the earliest Jewish author we know to have written in Greek.[52] He is interesting in that he tries to mould biblical material into both the Hellenistic genre of the description of the history of a non-Greek people by one of its members in a way that could meet

---

[47]   Walter, 'Theodotus der Epiker', 159-61; Collins, *Athens*, 48; Collins, 'The Epic of Theodotus'. Pummer, 'Genesis 34' rightly emphasizes that not every treatment of Gen 34 with a positive valuation of the patriarchs' deed is *per se* anti-Samaritan polemic.

[48]   Kippenberg, *Garizim*, 85-87, 93.

[49]   Tournay, 'Quelques relectures'. Tournay dates most of the examples of 'relectures antisamaritaines' to the 2nd cent. B.C.E. A relatively simple instance is, e.g., Hosea 14:9 where MT has אפרים מה לי עוד לעצבים, LXX τῷ Ἐφραιμ τί αὐτῷ ἔτι καὶ εἰδώλοις; Here LXX's αὐτῷ = לו is original, MT's לי is an anti-Samaritan correction. For the reverse process cf. Joshua 24:1 in Mt and LXX.

[50]   Smith, *Palestinian Parties*, 189. Van der Horst, 'Korte notities' has to be corrected on this point.

[51]   Pummer, 'Genesis 34', 180. The same tendency is also noticeable in Artapanus' account (fragm. 2) of Joseph's move to Egypt: he is not sold by his brothers, but goes of his own accord.

[52]   Walter, 'Demetrios', 282. He worked in the last half or quarter of the third cent. B.C.E. For literature on Demetrius see Holladay, *Fragments* 1:57f. J. Hanson in Charlesworth, *OTP* 2:846-47; Attridge, 'Historiography' 161-62; Schürer, *History* (rev. ed.) 3/1, 513-17. On Demetrius, Artapanus and Eupolemus, see Van der Horst, 'Schriftgebruik'.

scientific criticism and into the genre of *erotapokriseis*. The somewhat unwieldy definition of the first-mentioned genre refers to the works of people like the Egyptian Manetho, the Babylonian Berossus, the Roman Fabius Pictor (and, from a later period, the Phoenician Philo of Byblos and the Jew Josephus), and others. When at the beginning of the Hellenistic era new, especially oriental, peoples came within the horizon of the Greeks, these peoples competed with one another in trying to win the ear of their Hellenistic masters. Adopting Greek modes of reasoning, they tried to remedy the ignorance of the Greeks concerning their respective peoples, their history, wisdom, and especially their antiquity. They tried to trace their own origin back to remotest antiquity in order not to appear to be the imitators of other people.[53] Proudly aware of the greater antiquity of their people over against the Greeks (the implication being that Greek culture was dependent upon theirs), they made various chronological calculations (and exaggerations) when presenting their respective national histories, thereby using Greek forms of historical thinking, but following their national sources. This is the cultural framework in which the Jewish historian Demetrius' work *On the Kings of Judaea* (if that was its title, which is uncertain)[54] has to be placed.[55] An additional factor in this case may have been a growing critical attitude of some hellenized Jews themselves towards their Bible. Over against that, the credibility of the biblical record had to be defended and established.[56] As Berossus and Manetho did for their peoples, so Demetrius gave a matter-of-fact abridgement of the biblical materials from Abraham (or Adam?) to at least the end of the kingdom of Juda (in 586 B.C.E.), skilfully placing everything in an accurate chronological framework. *Mutatis mutandis* one may compare this also with works like *Jubilees* and *Seder Olam Rabba* where similar calculations occur.[57]

The second-mentioned genre is the *erotapokriseis*.[58] This is a literary style in which the theme is dealt with in the form of questions and answers (κατὰ πεῦσιν καὶ ἀπόκρισιν; also called ἀπορίαι καὶ λύσεις or ζητήματα καὶ λύσεις, 'problems and solutions'). This form was applied especially in scientific literature, particularly in the exegesis of Homer. Demetrius uses it in a rather loose, unsystematic way.[59] Not much of his materials are dealt with in this way, but occasionally problems created by the biblical accounts are introduced

---

[53]   See Bickerman, 'The Jewish Historian Demetrios'. A later Jewish example is Justus of Tiberias, fragm. 2 (Holladay, *Fragments* 1:383).

[54]   See Walter, 'Demetrios', 280.

[55]   See Fraser, *Ptolemaic Alexandria* 1:690-94, esp. 693.

[56]   Collins, *Athens*, 29.

[57]   See M. Gaster, 'Demetrius and Seder Olam'. On Hellenistic biblical chronologies see Wacholder, *Eupolemus*, 97ff.

[58]   Dörrie – Dörries, 'Erotapokriseis'.

[59]   On the unsystematic use of *erotapokriseis* see Dörrie – Dörries, *ibid.*, 343-45; they also refer to Philo's *Quaestiones in Genesim et Exodum*.

in question-and-answer form (fragm. 2, 3, and 5; see below). Polyhistor's abridgement may of course have erased other examples of this form.

The substantial fragm. 2 (*PE* 9:21, 1-19)[60] first gives a discussion of Jacob's age when he left for Haran (comparable with *B.T. Megilla* 17a) and (omitting Gen 28-29) then presents the exact dates and chronological sequence of the births of Jacob's sons (each ten months after the other or simultaneously from both mothers or maidservants). Then he mentions Jacob's struggle with an 'angel', whereas both the Hebrew and the Greek ot (Gen 32:25) have just 'man'. This modification, which occurs here for the first time, is current in all later aggadic literature: Targum Ps.-Yonatan says it was an angel in the shape of a man, targum Neofiti says it was Sariel with the appearance of a man, *Gen. Rabba* 77:2 (p. 910-12) and 78:1 (p. 916-18) says it was Michael or Gabriel.[61] The influence of post-biblical angelology is noticeable here. There follows a short account of Simeon's and Levi's revenge for the raping of Dina by Shechem (Gen 34), unlike Theodotus without any embellishments, but with the exact ages of all persons concerned indicated: Dinah 16 years and 4 months, Levi 20 years and 6 months, Simeon 21 years and 4 months, and Jacob 107 years. This again shows his almost grotesque preoccupation with chronology.

When dealing with the Joseph story in Gen 37-50, Demetrius again omits many scenes, so that it becomes no more than a series of disconnected events.[62] He raises two questions. First, why did it take 9 years before Joseph, who lived in wealthy circumstances in Egypt, sought to rescue his father from the famine-ridden Canaan to Egypt? The answer is: 'Because Jacob was a shepherd, as were Joseph's brothers too. But being a shepherd is considered something disgraceful by the Egyptians. That it was for this reason that he did not send for his father is made clear by himself. For when his relatives came to him, he said to them that if the king would invite them and ask them what kind of work they did, they were to say that they were cattle-keepers' (fragm. 2; *PE* 9:21, 13). Obviously Demetrius interpreted, in an almost rabbinic fashion, the lxx text of Gen 46:31-34 in such a way as if it meant to say that shepherd (ποιμήν) and cattle-keeper (κτηνοτρόφος) indicate different kinds of work. The second question raised is: why did Joseph give Benjamin at dinner five times as much as to his other brothers (Gen 43:34), whereas obviously Benjamin could never consume so much meat? The answer is: 'He did this because six (mss: seven)[63] sons had been born to his father by Leah and only two by Rachel, his mother. Therefore he gave Benjamin five portions and he himself took one: together

---

[60] Fragm. 1 is not dealth with, not only since the attribution to Demetrius by Freudenthal (*Hellenistische Studien*, 14f., 36) is very uncertain – it is quoted anonymously in *PE* 9:19,4 –, but also because it is nothing but a very short summary of Gen 22 without any aggada, contrary to Philo the epic poet and all later *akeda* literature.

[61] See also *PRE* 37; for other instances Ginzberg, *Legends* 1:384ff., 5:305; Vermes, 'The Archangel'. Josephus, *Ant.* 1:331-34, has φάντασμα in 331 and 334, ἄγγελος in 333.

[62] But how much of this is due to Polyhistor? See Fraser, *Ptolemaic Alexandria* 1:691.

[63] On this text-critical problem see Holladay, *Fragments* 1, 84-85 nn. 34-37.

that was six (MSS: seven)[64] portions, just as many as Leah's sons had got. (. . .) So the house of his mother was put on a par (with Leah's house)' (*ibid.* 14-15). Compare another solution in *Gen. Rabba* 92:5 (p. 1143).

The fragment closes with a computation of the number of years from the creation till Jacob's arrival in Egypt (3624 years), a genealogy from Jacob to Moses, and a calculation of the length of Israel's sojourn in Egypt (215 years) and of the time-lapse from Abraham's departure from Ur till the exodus (430 years). This last number (430) is given in the Hebrew text of Exod 12:40 as the time of Israel's stay in Egypt, in the LXX however as the time of Israel's stay in Egypt and Canaan. The latter reading is presupposed non only by Demetrius but also by the apostle Paul (Gal 3:17) and *Seder Olam Rabba* 3; Josephus has 215 years in *Ant.* 2:318, but in 2:204 he speaks of 400 years of oppression of the Israelites in Egypt (from Gen 15:13), thus indicating how the biblical texts created chronological problems to the Jews. This becomes still more apparent in *Mekhilta de-Rabbi Yishmael, Pisha* 14, p. 50 (*ad* 12:40) where both biblical passages, Exod 12:40 and Gen 15:13, are quoted and opposed and where it is asked, 'How can both these passages be maintained?'. *Exod. Rabba* 18:11 (*ad* 12:40) says about the 430 years: 'that is from the time that the decree was pronounced (*sc.* Gen 15), for they were only 210 years in Egypt'.[65] Again we see how Demetrius, sensitive as he was to the requirements of scientific historiography, attempted to solve problems of biblical chronology which could undermine faith in the reliability of the Scriptures.

Similar problems are treated in Fragm. 3 (*PE* 9:29,1-3). In fragm. 2 Moses' genealogy was presented as: Abraham – Isaac – Jacob – Levi – Kehat – Amram – Moses (Moses being the seventh in that line); in fragm. 3, however, the genealogy of Moses' wife, Zippora, is: Abraham and Keturah – Jokshan – Dedan – Raguel – Jethro – Zippora (the LXX inserted Raguel into the text of Gen 25:1-4, and Demetrius took him to be the father of Jethro),[66] and here Zippora is the sixth in the line. How she could be a contemporary of Moses, is the problem. The solution given is that Abraham begat Isaac when he was 100 years, and Jokshan when he was 142 years; this time-gap being a generation, Zippora could be Moses' contemporary. The fragment continues by stating that, since Abraham sent the sons of his concubines to the East (Gen 25:6), Aaron and Miriam could say that Moses had taken an Ethiopian wife (Num 12:1), the implication being that Ethiopia lies in the East[67] and that Zippora is identical with Moses' Ethiopian wife, a motif we have already met in Ezekiel the dramatist. No doubt Demetrius' concern was to show that Moses was not

---

[64]   On this text-critical problem see Holladay, *Fragments* 1, 84-85 nn. 34-37.
[65]   See Heinemann, '210 Years of Egyptian Exile'.
[66]   Freudenthal, *Hellenistische Studien* 42-44; Fraser, *Ptolemaic Alexandria* 3, 960 n. 91.
[67]   Cf. Gen 2:13. The ancients often located Ethiopia in the East, even as far as India; see *OCD s.v.* Ethiopia, and above, n. 14.

polygamous and did not marry outside his own people (cf. Theodotus, fragm. 4, *PE* 22, 6), a relevant issue in diaspora-Judaism.[68]

Fragments 4-6 are very brief, fragm. 5 (*PE* 9:29, 16) being especially worth mentioning in the present context.[69] There the question is raised how the Israelites could have weapons (implied, e.g., in Exod 17:8-13), whereas they left Egypt unarmed. The answer is: probably they took arms from the drowned Egyptians who drifted ashore. Ezekiel, *Exagoge* 210, and Josephus, *Ant.* 2:321, also say that the Israelites were unarmed, Josephus adding later (2:349) that they got their weapons from the dead Egyptians. Exod 13:18 says that the Israelites left Egypt חמשים. This is often translated 'armed, equipped for battle', but the exact meaning is quite uncertain. Although most ancient versions take it to mean 'armed' here, the LXX read 'the fifth generation', obviously deriving it from חמש, 'five'. This may have induced Demetrius, Ezekiel, Josephus and others to deny the Jews weapons, thus causing the problem discussed here by Demetrius.[70] Discussion of the meaning of the word is still visible in *Mekhilta, Beshallah* 1, p. 77-78.[71]

Compared to other, later Jewish Hellenistic historians (Eupolemus, Artapanus, etc.) Demetrius is remarkably sober in his descriptions of biblical personalities. No exaltation of Moses, no glorification of Abraham or such like is to be expected from him. 'There is a dryness and lack of adornment of substance and style which is in marked contrast to all other Jewish historiography, in which the figures of early biblical history take on some of the wondrous qualities bestowed on non-biblical figures in the contemporary world'.[72] There is also no evidence of the tendency towards syncretism which we will meet in his successors. The main emphasis is on the credibility of the Bible as a historical record, although he was not a literalist and did not hesitate to modify the text when a passage contradicted his chronological schemes.[73]

ARTAPANUS

A striking contrast with the academic chronographer Demetrius is formed by the 'historian' Artapanus.[74] His Persian name suggests that he was a Jew of

---

[68] Collins, *Athens*, 28.

[69] Although being quoted anonymously, like fragm. 1, it almost certainly is from Demetrius. On fragm. 6 and rabbinic parallels see Wacholder, *Eupolemus* 101 with n. 17, and the notes by Holladay, *Fragments* 1, 90-91 nn. 92-97.

[70] See Jacobson, *Exagoge*, 216 n. 53; Holladay, *Fragments* 1, 89 n. 88; and my 'Some Notes'.

[71] See the excellent examination of the problem by Le Déaut, 'A propos'.

[72] Fraser, *Ptolemaic Alexandria* 1, 693; cf. also Dalbert, *Theologie*, 27.

[73] Wacholder, *Eupolemus*, 103 n. 25 says that 'the idea that the non-legal texts (even the Pentateuch) of Scripture were authoritative and unalterable is evidently post-Maccabean'.

[74] Literature on Artapanus in Fraser, *Ptolemaic Alexandria* 2, 983 n. 177; Walter, 'Artapanos', 126; Holladay, *Fragments* 1:199-201; J.J. Collins in Charlesworth, *OTP* 2:896; add: Droge, 'Interpretation' 151-57; Attridge, 'Historiography' 166-68.

mixed descent or a proselyte.[75] The longest and most important of the three fragments preserved (fragm. 3 = *PE* 9:27, 1-37) is a kind of 'Life of Moses',[76] running from his birth to the exodus (Exod 2-16). Two shorter fragments deal with Abraham (fragm. 1) and Joseph (fragm. 2). The most striking thing about these three fragments is that they deviate from the biblical accounts much farther than those of other Jewish historiographers and that most of the aggadic embellishments do not have exact parallels in contemporary or later Jewish midrashic literature. To be sure, fragm. 1 (*PE* 9:18, 1) has an aggadic element that does have parallels: Abraham came to Egypt, remained there twenty years,[77] and taught the pharao astrology. So, contrary to what was often asserted in antiquity, this important science was originally a Jewish, not an Egyptian invention. Also Ps-Eupolemus (fragm. 1 = *PE* 9:17, 3-4) makes Abraham the inventor of astrology, and Ps-Hecataeus (II), fragm. 1 (= Josephus, *Ant.* 1:167), again makes him the teacher of this 'Chaldaean art' to the Egyptians. These traditions were probably based upon Gen 15:5. In some Jewish circles Abraham's astrological knowledge was considered a mark of his greatness, especially among syncretistic Jews, but in more conservative circles this idea was so scandalous that they presented it as a pre-conversion practice, which he later abandoned; see e.g. *Jub.* 12:16ff.; Philo, *On Abraham* 68-71 and 81-83; *Sib. Or.* 3:221-30.[78]

The second fragment (*PE* 9:23,1-4) presents Joseph, who after his voluntary (!) voyage to Egypt became right away its administrator or governor, as an organizer of a radical landreform on behalf of the weak and the poor (contrary to Gen 47). So he, too, like Abraham, is a benefactor of the Egyptian people.[79]

The third fragment is too long to be summarized here. The first half (*PE* 9:27,1-20) is an almost wholly non-biblical account of Moses' deeds in Egypt. Artapanus calls him Μώϋσος (instead of Μωϋσῆς) and says that the Greeks called him Mousaios, the mythical Greek poet and teacher of Orpheus.[80] Since according to tradition Orpheus brought culture and religion from Egypt to Greece (e.g. Hecataeus of Abdera *apud* Diodorus Siculus 1:96, 4ff.), the

---

[75] On other Jews with Persian names see Mussies, 'The interpretatio judaica of Thot-Hermes' 92.

[76] The real title of the work probably was *On the Jews*; see Fraser, *Ptolemaic Alexandria* 1, 704 with n. 177, and esp.: Holladay, *Theios Aner*, 215-16 n. 98.

[77] On the midrashic chronology implied here see Wacholder, 'How long did Abraham stay in Egypt?'; he refers to several other calculations in early Jewish literature (*Jub.* 13:11; *1QGenAp* 20:18; *Seder Olam Rabba* 1).

[78] Knox, 'Abraham'; Vermes, 'Life of Abraham', 79ff.; Collins, *Athens*, 35; Walter, 'Pseudo-Orpheus', 225 n. 47; Mayer, 'Aspekte' 123ff.; Mayer says: 'Der Topos "Abraham als Astrolog" lebt von der Authorität, die die populäre wie die wissenschaftliche Astrologie bzw. Astronomie im zweiten vorchristlichen Jahrhundert besonders in Ägypten genossen'. Cf. Georgi, *Gegner*, 67-73.

[79] Similar land reforms are attributed to Sesostris, Isis and Osiris in Diodorus Siculus 1; see Holladay, *Fragments* 1, 228 n. 18.

[80] Usually Musaeus is Orpheus' disciple, but Artapanus reverses the relation; see Kern, *Orphicorum fragmenta*, 50-51; Denis, *Introduction*, 255 n. 43; West, *Orphic Poems*, 39-40.

implication is that Moses is the ultimate source of Greek culture.[81] But there is more: Moses appears to be the inventor of 'many useful things': ships, instruments for quarrying, hydraulic machinery, weapons of war, hieroglyphs, philosophy; he divides the country into 36 districts and assigns to each district its titulary deity (cats, dogs, ibises, etc.). All this made him a favourite among the people (cf. Exod 11:3), especially among the priests who honoured him as a god and called him Hermes, the Greek name of the Egyptian god Thoth. Then follows a long story of pharao's jealousy of Moses' popularity and the ambushes he lays to put Moses out of the way, all of them unsuccesful.[82] (In one of the attacks on him, Moses kills his assailant out of self-defence, clearly a favourable rendering of the story in Exod 2:12, more or less comparable to *Exod. Rabba* 1:29, where the same embarrassment is perceivable. Josephus, *Ant.* 2:254ff., simply omits the story). When Moses is put into jail by the pharao, the doors open of their own accord to set Moses free. He enters the palace, wakes up the king, and when thereupon the kings asks him to tell him the name of his God, Moses whispers the holy Name into the ear of the pharao who collapses consequently. An Egyptian priest who scorns the Name dies. The rest of the story more closely follows the biblical text, although not without many minor midrashic additions (e.g. Moses' staff plays a much greater role than in Exodus).[83]

Several remarks are in order here. First, Artapanus' remarkably great freedom in dealing with the biblical tradition probably is inspired partly by his desire to present Moses in a way that is in direct opposition to the account of Moses given by Manetho (or similar anti-Semitic Greco-Egyptian writers), who present(s) the Jewish leader as the embodiment of hostility to Egypt who attacks their temples and homes, etc. Artapanus' picture of Moses is that of a great teacher to whom the Egyptians owe their culture, their religion, the arts of war and peace, and the basic economy of the country.[84] 'By demonstrating the dependence of Egyptian culture on the Jews, he not only establishes the priority of the latter, but at the same time proves their benevolent as opposed to their malevolent posture'.[85] It is this concern which makes him go even as far as attributing to Moses the establishment of the Egyptian animal-cult, in spite of

---

[81]   Collins, *Athens* 34; Holladay, *Fragments* 1, 232 n. 45; Schalit, 'Artapanus' 646: 'In view of the fact that, like Herodotus and Plato, Artapanus sees in Egyptian civilization the origin of all civilization, it may be said that he regards Moses as the father of universal civilization'.

[82]   In this context Artapanus reports Moses' war with the Ethiopians and his prolongued stay in Ethiopia, a motif which occurs with many variations in several other sources; see above n. 15.

[83]   See Tiede, *Charismatic Figure*, 170ff. It should also be noted that pharao, the Egyptian princess and many other persons, the names of which are not given in the Bible, receive a name here. On this well-known process see Heller, 'Die Scheu vor Unbekanntem'; for the NT Metzger, 'Names for the Nameless'.

[84]   Fraser, *Ptolemaic Alexandria* 1, 705.

[85]   Holladay, *Theios Aner*, 217.

Exod 20:4-5.[86] It should also be borne in mind that the claim that someone was a 'first inventor' (πρῶτος εὑρετής) was very prestigious in antiquity.[87] In this case it certainly helped to serve the glorification of the Jewish people and its history.

Moses is identified with Thoth-Hermes, the Egyptian god of science and culture. True, the identification is explicitly said to have been made by the Egyptian priests (just as the equation with Musaeus is made by the Greeks) and it has a strong Euhemeristic ring about it[88] which relativizes Egyptian religion, but one cannot say that Artapanus distances himself from this divinization of Moses.[89] As we have seen before, in 'heterodox' circles divinization of Moses did occur (see above on Ezekiel Tragicus); and we also know of Rabbinic speculations regarding the identity of Joseph and the Egyptian god Sarapis[90] (compare Ps-Eupolemus' equation of Enoch and Atlas, PE 9:17, 9). The equation of Moses and Thoth-Hermes was possible because there were several contact-points between the two: Thoth as architect of temples – Moses as the one who passed on God's instructions for the making of the Tabernacle; Thoth as giver of laws and as judge – Moses as lawgiver and judge; Thoth as founder of (local) cults – Moses as the giver of cultic prescriptions; Thoth as the inventor of language and writing and as scribe of the gods – Moses as the first man in the Bible who is said to have written and who was called 'scribe' (sc. of God) in later tradition; Thoth's holy bird is the ibis – ibises help Moses during his Ethiopian campaign (Josephus, Ant. 2:246ff.); Thoth as a great magician – Moses as a great magician (according to pagan tradition); etc.[91] Besides these parallels with Thoth there are other ones with traditional Egyptian benefactors who gained immortality and divine status because of their benefits to men, especially Sesostris (Hecataeus in Diodorus Siculus 1:53-58), but also Isis and Osiris.[92] The equation of Moses with Egyptian divine personalities shows that, as so often, here too the lines between what is Jewish or Jewish syncretistic and pagan are not easily drawn.[93]

---

[86] That Jews abhorred the cult of animals needs no further documentation; see Holladay, Fragments 1, 234 n. 51. N.B.: the LXX inserted the Egyptian sacred bird, the ibis, into the lists of unclean birds in Lev 11:17 and Deut 14:16. Contrast Artapanus in PE 9:27, 4.

[87] Thraede, 'Erfinder'.

[88] Euhemerus (± 300 B.C.E.) developed the theory that the gods had originally been great leaders or kings to whom mankind had shown their gratitude for their helpful deeds by worshipping them as gods.

[89] Here I disagree somewhat with Holladay, Theios Aner, 227.

[90] See Mussies, 'The interpretatio judaica of Sarapis'.

[91] Detailed evidence in Mussies, 'The interpretatio judaica of Thot-Hermes'.

[92] Tiede, Charismatic Figure, 146-77; Holladay, Theios Aner, 209ff.; idem, Fragments 1, 232-33 n. 46. See above n. 78.

[93] See Tiede, Charismatic Figure, 105ff. Freudenthal's theory (Hellenistische Studien, 146ff., 162ff.) – based on the half-Jewish half-pagan character of these fragments – that Artapanus' work was a 'Trugschrift' and that he was identical with Ps-Aristeas and Ps-Hecataeus, has been effectively refuted; see e.g. Fraser, Ptolemaic Alexandria 2, 983 n. 179.

Many elements still ask for some comment, but I single out the 'Türöffnungs-wunder' and the tremendous power of the holy Name. Doors opening of their own accord (αὐτομάτως) is a motif found in Greek literature from Homer onwards; when opening in order to liberate someone from prison, Euripides' *Bacchae* is our earliest instance.[94] Well-known are the stories of such liberation miracles in the Acts of the Apostles (5:17ff; 12:6ff; 16:25ff).[95] In Jewish litera-ture there are instances of doors opening automatically, but none of them in order to liberate someone. Josephus relates, among several prodigia preceding the destruction of the temple, that its doors opened of their own accord in the middle of the night (*War* 6:293; it is also reported by Tacitus, *Hist.* 5:13),[96] and there are other stories about spontaneous opening of the temple doors in rabbinic literature, but none of these in the context of a liberation (not even the story about the opening of Akiva's prison-gates in *Midrash Prov.* 9:2, p. 31a/b).[97] The fact that the Greek stories of liberations by automatical opening of doors often occur in a Dionysiac context (in the *Bacchae* it is Dionysus who is so liberated) might suggest that Artapanus' story has a point directed against the Dionysus cult in Alexandria.[98] Alongside this typically Greek motif, the next paragraph in the story has a more typically Jewish motif in that it relates the destructive power depending upon the use or abuse of the tetragrammaton. Not only pharao lost consciousness (or died?; the text is unclear) when he heard the Name, but the priest who treated contemptuously the tablet upon which Moses (or pharao) wrote this Name, died a terrible death. 'The Name was endowed with power. The Name and the Power were synonyms'.[99] Acts 4:7 says: 'By what *power* or by what *Name* have you done this?' The *shem ha-meforash* was believed to be extremely powerful and effective both *in bonam* and *in malam partem*. *Exod. Rabba* 1:29-30 (*ad* 1:12 and 14) raises the question, 'with what did Moses slay the Egyptian' (. . .)? The Rabbis say that he pronounced God's name against him and thus slew him' (a tradition also reported by Clemens Alexandrinus, *Strom.* 1:154,1: 'the initiated say that Moses killed him by only a word'). In *1 Enoch* 69:14 the angel requests Michael 'to show him the hidden Name in order that he might enunciate it in the oath so that those might quake before that Name and oath'. In *B.T. Bava Batra* 73a Rabba says that seafarers told him that a stormy sea can be subsided by beating it with clubs on which is engraven: 'I am that I am, Yah, the Lord of Hosts, Amen'. People frequently used the Name on amulets and for incantations, as the Greek magical papyri amply demonstrate, and it does not matter whether the Name is pronounced by

---

[94] See Weinreich, 'Türöffnung' 45ff., 118ff.
[95] Discussed in Weinreich, 'Türöffnung' 147ff.
[96] Weinreich, 'Türöffnung' 109ff.
[97] Strack-Billerbeck, *Kommentar* 2, 707.
[98] On which see Fraser, *Ptolemaic Alexandria* 1, 201-12.
[99] Urbach, *The Sages* 1:124.

a Jew or by a heathen because the effective power lies in the Name itself.[100] Hence the Rabbis developed halakha for the use of the Name in writing and speaking.[101]

So we see how Artapanus uses side by side typically Greek and typically Jewish elements in order to emphasize the superiority of Moses and of Moses' religion. In the anti-Semitic atmosphere of Ptolemaic Egypt, where people like Manetho were no exception, this Jewish writer felt free to embellish and enrich the biblical story drastically with motives that were designed to enhance the prestige of his people and to bolster their ethnic pride.

EUPOLEMUS

Eupolemus[102] is a fascinating example of how a mid-2nd cent. B.C.E. member of an influential priestly family in Jerusalem could be critical of the biblical traditions and rewrite them in order to magnify the great figures of Israel's past, especially Solomon. Eupolemus is probably identical with the Eupolemus, son of John, mentioned in 1 Macc 8:17f. (cf. 2 Macc 4:11) as the man whom Judas Maccabee sent as an ambassador to Rome in order to conclude a Roman-Jewish friendship-treaty, in 161 B.C.E..[103] His work *On the Kings in Judaea* was written in Greek, a fact that demonstrates that being an adherent to the Maccabees need not be identical with being anti-Greek.[104]

In the first fragment (*PE* 9:26,1) Eupolemus says that Moses was the first wise man, that he gave the alphabet to the Jews and that the Phoenicians received it from the Jews and the Greeks from the Phoenicians.[105] Moses was also the first lawgiver. This picture of Moses as cultural benefactor and founder of civilization is reminiscent of Artapanus and is found, *mutatis mutandis*, also in Philo's *Life of Moses* 2:1ff. and Josephus' *Ag.Ap.* 2:154ff.

The long second fragment (*PE* 9:30, 1-34, 18) first summarizes Jewish history from Moses to Saul[106] but then focuses on David and especially on Solomon. The territory conquered by David, according to Eupolemus, not only exceeds the biblical account but is also anachronistic (e.g. the country of the Nabataeans is mentioned) and probably reflects the political situation during the Maccabees; the description of the land promised to Abraham's descendants in *Genesis*

---

[100] See e.g. *P.T. Yoma* 3:7, 40d: 'Samuel once heard, as he was passing, a Persian cursing his son by the Name and he died'.

[101] See esp. Urbach, *The Sages* 1, 124-34, 2, 733-40; and Fossum, *Name of God*, ch. 3.

[102] Bibliography in Holladay, *Fragments* 1:105-07; Fallon in Charlesworth, *OTP* 2:864. Add: Bartlett, *Jews* 56-71, and Attridge, 'Historiography', 162-65.

[103] Wacholder, *Eupolemus*, 4-21.

[104] For other instances of Jerusalem priests writing in Greek see Wacholder, *Eupolemus*. 274ff. and Van der Kooij, 'On the Place of Origin'.

[105] The origin of the alphabet was a much-discussed theme in antiquity; see Wacholder, *Eupolemus*, 81f., and Droge, 'Interpretation' 142-43.

[106] This summary omits the period of the judges (contrast Ps-Philo, *LAB*!) and calls Saul David's father; both the omission and the mistake may be due to Alexander Polyhistor, however.

Apocryphon 21:8-29 roughly reflects 'the utopian borders of the Davidic empire as reported by Eupolemus'.[107] These descriptions reflect a midrashic version of Israel's early history in the light of the situation under the Maccabees. David also subdues Suron, *i.e.* Hiram,[108] and concludes a pact of friendship with Ouaphres, the Egyptian pharao, both non-biblical episodes – maybe Eupolemus derived the name Ouaphres from Jer 51:30 LXX (MT 44:30) where a pharao Ouaphre is mentioned who lived at least 4 centuries after David.[109] Both Suron and Ouaphres play an important role in the then following account of the building of the temple by Solomon. After a peaceful (!) transfer of David's kingship to Solomon when the latter is twelve – see 1 Kgs 2:12 LXX cod. A; *Seder Olam Rabba* 14; *Sifrei Deut.* 357 (p. 426) – the building activities begin when Solomon is thirteen (*bar mitswa* ?).[110] The first thing he does is to write letters to Suron (cf. 1 Kgs 5:2-6 and 2 Chr 2:2-9) and to Ouaphres in order to procure enough manpower for the task. These letters and the replies by both kings are fully quoted by Eupolemus, as if from an archival document.[111] Solom writes severely, as if to client kings, the others submissively, to 'the great king' (they themselves are addressed as just kings), as if Solomon were an emperor with subordinate vassal-kings. Then follows a remarkably detailed description of the construction of the temple that deviates from the biblical account in many respects. E.g., the dimensions of the sanctuary are larger than in 1 Kgs and 2 Chr (neither do they fit in with those in Ezekiel, the *Temple Scroll* from Qumran, Josephus, or the Mishna treatise *Middot*); the amount of gold and silver spent in the interior is so fantastically exaggerated (4.600.000 talents) that even the high figures of 1 Chr are left far behind (e.g., the two bronze pillars are gilded with pure gold a finger thick, 34:7); also measures of items of furniture and tools in the temple (altar, laver, king's podium) are modified or aggrandized; new items are added, e.g. an elaborate 'scare-crow system' for protecting the temple from defilement by birds: here, as elsewhere, he retrojects elements from the temple of Zerubbabel or Herod (see *Temple Scroll* 46:1-4; Josephus, *War* 5:224; *M. Middot* 4:6) into Solomon's time. But other elements have been

---

[107] Wacholder, *Eupolemus*, 138; Hengel, *Judentum und Hellenismus*, 172. n. 274 (ET 2, 64 n. 282); Fitzmyer, *The Genesis Apocryphon*, 146ff. Note also that David's major enemies, the Philistines, are not mentioned by Eupolemus; in the second cent. B.C.E. they were non-existent.

[108] On this curious transcription see Wacholder, *Eupolemus*, 135ff.

[109] Holladay, *Fragments* 1, 141 n. 23.

[110] Wacholder, *Eupolemus*, 155. The Bible says: in his *fourth* year (1 Kgs 6:1; 2 Chr 3:2), which is clearly corrected by Eupolemus. Josephus, *Ant.* 8:211, makes him fourteen years.

[111] On these letters Wacholder, *Eupolemus*, 155ff. Josephus, *Ant.* 8:55, says that the Solomon – Hiram correspondence was still extant in his days in a Tyrian archive. There is a rabbinic tradition that Solomon wrote to pharao Necho for men to assist with the temple building. Necho sent men that he knew would die within a year. By the Holy Spirit Solomon recognized the trick and sent them back immediately (*Num. Rabba* 19:3; *Eccles. Rabba* 7:23, 1). Whether this is an independent tradition or meant to satirize Eupolemus is uncertain; see Wacholder, *Eupolemus*, 168. Very probably Eupolemus invented the correspondence with the Pharao. 'His aim is to demonstrate to his second century B.C. readers that the ancestors of the Ptolemaic and Seleucid kingdom were respectively friendly and subservient to the interests of Jerusalem' (Bartlett, *Jews*, 68).

brought into conformity with the Tabernacle, obviously because he felt a need for harmonization between these. In fact, however, Eupolemus may have been describing neither Solomon's temple nor Moses' Tabernacle nor Zerubbabel's or Herod's temple, but a futuristic temple, out of dissatisfaction with the contemporary one.[112] Curiously enough, when describing the size of the offerings at the dedication of the temple, his figures are considerably smaller than the biblical ones (compare 34:16 with 1 Kgs 8:62, 2 Chr 7:4). In general it can be said that if Eupolemus follows the biblical data at all, he either prefers Chr or (less frequently) he harmonizes Chr and Kgs. But more often he either abbreviates or expands by adding from other sources (or his own imagination), thus treating the biblical text as 'a mere starting point rather than as an authoritative history'.[113] In the same period we can see a similar procedure in the book of *Jubilees*, also 'rewritten Bible' in accordance with the contemporary religious outlook. In Eupolemus' case, this outlook is clearly a priestly one. The temple is the focus of Jewish history; it is the religious, economic and political centre of the people; and its fabulous wealth serves to underline its spiritual value.

A short glance at fragments 4 and 5. Fragm. 4 (*PE* 9:39,1-5) reports, *inter alia*, that Jeremiah saved the ark and the two tablets it contained from being transported to Babylon. Almost the same tradition is found in 2 Macc 2 and *Lifes of the Prophets, Jer* 9-10; and also, although without mentioning Jeremiah, in *M. Shekalim* 6:1, *T. Shekalim* 2:18, *B.T. Yoma* 53b; and in *Para. Ier.* 3:8-20, albeit there without explicit mention of the ark. Here again the concern for the temple, especially for its holiest object, is apparent. It is not impossible that Eupolemus is the originator of this tradition concerning Jeremiah. His purpose 'seems to be to indicate that in spite of the destruction of the Temple in 587 B.C.E., continuity was assured by the secret preservation of the Ark and of the commandments'.[114]

The fifth fragment (*Strom.* 1:21, 141, 4-5) is very much like Demetrius' chronography. It calculates the time from Adam to 158/157 B.C.E. as 5.149 years (*i.e.*, the creation took place ca. 5.307 B.C.E.) and from the exodus to 158/157 as 2.580 years (*i.e.*, the exodus took place ca. 2.738 B.C.E.[115] These numbers neither agree with MT nor with LXX. They also disagree with Demetrius, and it is unknown how Eupolemus came to this calculation. There were of course more than one exegetical and chronological systems in this period, as is attested by a remark in Clement of Alexandria, *Strom.* 1:141, 1-2 (immediately preceding

---

[112]   Wacholder, *Eupolemus*, 196-201. Josephus' description of Solomon's temple sticks much closer to the biblical data; see Faber van der Meulen, *Das Salomobild*, 122-47.

[113]   Wacholder, *Eupolemus*, 250.

[114]   Bartlett, *Jews*, 71.

[115]   Wacholder, *Eupolemus*, 111ff. There have been several attempts at emendation of these numbers in order to get them in more accordance with either LXX or MT, without much success; see also Holladay, *Fragments* 1, 154f. nn. 118-20.

this excerpt from Eupolemus). The tendency to make the Jewish people older than the Greeks – and hence more venerable – is the same as in Demetrius.[116]

PSEUDO-EUPOLEMUS

'Pseudo-Eupolemus'[117] is a misleading designation since one of the two fragments has been attributed erroneously to Eupolemus by Alexander Polyhistor (*PE* 9:17, 1-9), and the other has been transmitted anonymously (*PE* 9:18, 2); so they are no pseudepigrapha *stricto sensu*.[118] Both deal primarily with Abraham. Ps-Eupolemus uses not only biblical but also aggadic traditions and Greek and Babylonian mythological traditions as well, and interweaves these. Hesiod, Berossus and the Bible are intermixed, with some Samaritan elements added. Kronos and Asbolus are incorporated into the genealogy of Gen 10 as is also the Babylonian Belus (= Bel); Enoch is identified with Atlas; and Abraham is received as a guest at mount Garizim ('Αργαριζίν), which is interpreted as 'mount of the Most High'. This syncretistic concoction cannot derive from the real Eupolemus for whom the Jerusalem temple was of such a central importance. If the author was a Samaritan, he is important as representing Samaritan midrashic traditions from a period much earlier than most of the other Samaritan literature (which is of the fourth cent. c.e. and later). It points to an open-minded and universalist attitude among (at least some) early Samaritans, who, like other Hellenistic Jews, tried to heighten their own tradition by establishing kinship with other nations of great distinction.[119]

Fragm. 1 states that the tower of Babel was built by the giants who were saved from the flood, a theory based upon a combination of LXX Gen 6:4; 10:8; 10:10 and 11:1ff. that we already met in Philo the epic poet.[120] Like Artapanus, Ps-Eupolemus claims Abraham to be the inventor of astrology, but the Patriarch seems to share this distinction with Enoch, of whom, curiously enough, in the same fragment Abraham says that he was the discoverer of that science and that he, Abraham, received it from him. In *Jub.* 4:17 the discovery of astronomy is attributed to Enoch; his knowledge of the heavenly bodies is stressed in *1*

---

[116] Wacholder, *Eupolemus*, 243-46, presents a convenient synopsis of Eupolemus and OT passages, showing where Eupolemus is original and introduces new elements.

[117] Bibliography in Holladay, *Fragments* 1, 166-67; R. Doran in Charlesworth, *OTP* 2:879; add: Droge, 'Interpretation' 146-51, and Prato, 'Babilonia'.

[118] Some scholars doubt whether the two fragments come from the same author; see Doran in Charlesworth, *OTP* 2:874. Doran even believes that fragm. 1 is from the real Eupolemus.

[119] See Wacholder, 'Pseudo-Eupolemus'; Hengel, *Judentum und Hellenismus* 162-69 (ET 1:88-92, 2:59-63); Walter 'Pseudo-Eupolemos' 137-40; Holladay, *Fragments* 1:158-65. On the Hellenistic elements see esp. Prato, 'Babilonia'.

[120] See above p. 526 with n. 39. Cf. also Josephus, *Ant.* 1:113ff., and Ps-Philo, *LAB* 6:3ff., and some rabbinic parallels noted by Wacholder, 'Pseudo-Eupolemus' 89 n. 45, and by Ginzberg, *Legends* 1:179, 5:198, 201, 213.

Enoch (43-44; 72-82) and *2 Enoch* (11-17).[121] The borderline between astronomy and astrology was always fluid in antiquity (the distinction, if existent at all, was mostly no more than that between theoretical and applied science), and although most Jewish authors from antiquity reject astrology, there certainly was great interest and even the practice of it in some circles[122] who justified their stance by retrojecting this practice onto the great heroes of the past (cf. Artapanus, fragm. 1; Ps-Hecataeus (II) *apud* Josephus, *Ant.* 1:167). In our fragment Abraham teaches astrology to the Phoenicians and Egyptians, who are grateful for it. Skipping his presentation of the war of the kings in Gen 14, I mention Abraham's reception into the temple of mount Garizim, translated as 'mountain of God Most High' (ὄρος ὑψίστου), clearly intended to legitimize the Samaritan cult near Shechem.[123] The following line probably says that it was there, not in Jerusalem, that Abraham received gifts from Melchisedek. Only after this scene Ps-Eupolemus tells the story of Gen 12 with the typically aggadic emphasis on the miraculous protection of Sarah's chastity ('the king was unable to have intercourse with her') also found in *Genesis Apocryphon* 20:1-32; Josephus, *Ant.* 1:162-65; Philo, *On Abraham* 96-98; *Gen. Rabba* 40:2 (p. 388-90); etc.[124] Then follows the genealogy in which Bel (identified with Kronos)[125] is the father of Canaan, who is the father of Cush (identified with Asbolus, see Hesiod, *Scutum* 185), who is the brother of Mizraim, the father of the Egyptians. This same Bel is said (in fragm. 2) to have escaped the flood (= Noah) and to have built the tower of Babel as one of the giants (= Nimrod). Here either two different traditions with different identifications are combined (although the extreme brevity of the account suggests that Alexander Polyhistor may have misunderstood things when abbreviating the text of the anonymous author) or we have to assume that Ps-Eupolemus indeed made the striking identification of Noah and Nimrod. Texts like *Genesis Apocryphon* 2:1ff. and *1 Enoch* 106:8ff. at least seem to imply that there were Jews who believed that Noah was a child of the antediluvian giants.[126] In any event, the text shows that early Samaritan aggada went very far in combining pagan

---

[121]   All this and much more was derived from the intriguing Gen 5:24 ('Enoch walked with God, and he was no more, for God took him away'). For further aggadic developments see Kasher, *Encyclopedia* 1, 174-7; Ginzberg, *Legends* 1:125-42, 5:152-66; Milik's Introduction to his *The Books of Enoch* (1976). The basis of his identification with Atlas was the Greek tradition about Atlas as the discoverer of astrology; see Wacholder, 'Ps-Eupolemus' 96 n. 83.

[122]   Hengel, *Judentum und Hellenismus* 432-38 (ET 1, 236-39 2, 159-61); Wächter, 'Astrologie'; Charlesworth, 'Jewish Astrology'. On this passage see Droge, 'Interpretation', 149f.

[123]   Kippenberg, *Garizim*, 83: 'Dieses Heiligtum ist nicht etwa erst 150 Jahre alt, sondern schon Abraham fand es in Phoenizien vor'.

[124]   Holladay, *Fragments* 1, 184 n. 24; Hengel, *Judentum und Hellenismus*, 165 n. 248 (ET 2, 61 n. 256).

[125]   On the reasons for this identification see Wacholder, 'Ps-Eupolemus' 90f.

[126]   Wacholder, 'Ps-Eupolemus' 94 distinguishes between two giants, Belus I – Kronos – Noah, and Belus II – Nimrod. *Ibid.* 99 Wacholder discusses the possibility that there has been a belief that Noah was the offspring of the 'sons of God' of Gen 6:1-4. Hengel, *Judentum und Hellenismus*, 163 with n. 237 (ET 1, 89; 2, 60 n. 244), says that Noah = Nimrod here.

mythology with biblical traditions, but that in Euhemeristic fashion. This religious outlook is close to that of Artapanus and Cleodemus-Malchus. 'It finds its identity in a glorified tradition, but one that is placed in a cosmopolitan, syncretistic setting'.[127]

CLEODEMUS – MALCHUS

The only surviving fragment of the work of this historian[128] (*PE* 9:20, 3-4 = Josephus, *Ant.* 1:240-41) deals primarily with Abraham's descendants through Keturah. The genealogical data of Gen 25:1-6 are reshuffled and expanded somewhat. Three grandsons of Abraham, Asshurim, Epha, and Epher (so MT) are promoted to the status of sons, now called Assouri, Apher, and Aphras.[129] The first of course is the ancestor of the Assyrians, the other two of the Africans. Apher and Aphras join Heracles in his battle against the Libyan giant Antaeus.[130] Heracles then marries Aphras' daughter. Their son, Diodorus, is the father of Sophon, ancestor of the Sophakes and king of Libya.[131] The most striking feature is the attempt to forge a genealogical link between Abraham and the Greek mythological hero Heracles; in Cleodemus' version Heracles marries Abraham's granddaughter.[132] There is also a clear tendency to make several peoples descend from Abraham and so to create kinship between the Jews and other peoples. This trend also comes to the fore in the well-known letter supposedly sent by the Spartan king to the Jerusalem highpriest stating that a document has come to light which shows that Spartans and Jews are kinsmen, descended alike from Abraham (1 Macc 12:21).[133] By this device the diaspora Jews wanted to make clear to the native inhabitants of the countries where they lived as 'guests' that they were their equals.[134] Here again, as in Artapanus and Ps-Eupolemus (although Artapanus lacks the genealogical element), we observe the free and unconcerned interweaving of pagan mythology

---

[127]   Collins, *Athens*, 39. Note the contrast to Theodotus.
[128]   Bibliography in Holladay, *Fragments* 1, 250; Doran in Charlesworth, *OTP* 2, 886.
[129]   There are numerous orthographical variants of these names, both in Josephus and in Eusebius.
[130]   See Diodorus Siculus 4:17, 4-5 and many other passages collected by J.G. Frazer in his *LCL* edition of Apollodorus' *Bibliotheca*, vol. 1, p. 222f. n. 2.
[131]   The line Heracles – Sophax – Diodorus (in this order!) occurs also in a book by the first cent. B.C.E./C.E. historian-king Juba of Mauretania; see *FGH* 275T10 (= Plutarch, *Sertorius* 9:8).
[132]   A comparable idea is reported by Epiphanius, *Panarion* 55:2, 1, where he states that some (Jews?) say that Heracles is the father of Melchisedek.
[133]   Cf. Josephus, *Ant.* 12:226 and 13:164. See Cardauns, 'Juden und Spartaner'; older literature in the *LCL* edition of Josephus, vol. 7, p. 769 (App. F).
[134]   Walter, 'Kleodemos Malchas' 116f. does the attractive suggestion that the prominence of Africa/Libya in the fragment may indicate that the author lived in or near Carthago. On the North-African Diaspora see Stern, 'The Jewish Diaspora' 133-37. It is interesting to note that Ezekiel the dramatist identifies Midian and Libya and Ethiopia (*Exagoge*, 60-62) and that in Gen 25:4 the two sons mentioned by Cleodemus as the ancestors of the Libyans are the sons of Midian. This can hardly be accidental.

and biblical tradition in order to posit Abraham as a kind of universal ancestor and so to trace other cultures to Jewish origins.[135]

ARISTEAS

Only one short fragment of Aristeas' work *On the Jews*[136] is extant (*PE* 9:25, 1-4). It summarizes in a few lines the story of Job, following the LXX including the epilogue to this translation (42:17b-e).[137] There are only a few aggadic elements. The fragment begins by saying that Esau married Bassara and fathered a son Job, who was first called Jobab. Jobab is an Edomite king from Bozrah, mentioned in Gen 36:33, and Aristeas certainly mistook the LXX's ἐκ Βοσορρας for the name of his mother, Basarra. The same name of the mother is also mentioned in LXX Job 42:17b where the identification of Job with the Edomite king Jobab is also explicitly stated;[138] but there Esau is not Job's father, but grandfather. It should also be noted that Job is thus placed in the patriarchal period, a tradition also found in Ps-Philo, *LAB* 8:8 and *Test. Job* 1:6. Finally it is said that God admired his imperturbability or fortitude (ἀγασθέντα τὴν εὐψυχίαν αὐτοῦ).[139] This non-biblical element can be compared to *11QtargJob* 38:3 where it is said that God turned to Job in love for his attitude in his misfortunes.[140] We see here the beginnings of the post-biblical Job tradition which is more elaborated in the *Testament of Job* and (in a lesser degree) in *11QtargJob*.[141]

Conclusions

For reasons of space the present survey had to be a selection in more than one sense. First, not all (not even all minor) Hellenistic Jewish authors have been dealt with. Second, from these authors only a selection of the motifs and elements relevant to the study of their use of Scripture has been presented, and very briefly at that. One hopes that it was enough to get a clear idea of the fascinating variety of ways in which they appropriated the biblical traditions and tried to reshape them in Greek literary modes. There has been much complaint about the low literary level of these attempts, but one should not underestimate

---

[135]   Holladay, *Fragments* 1, 246f. Sandmel, *Philo's Place*, 56, says: 'Insofar as one can see, there are no specifically 'Jewish' qualities to Abraham'.
[136]   Bibliography in Holladay, *Fragments* 1, 265; Doran in Charlesworth, *OTP* 2, 858.
[137]   Unless the author of the epilogue used Aristeas' work, which would seem to be less probable since he says that he translated the epilogue from the Syriac book (ἑρμηνεύεται ἐκ τῆς Συριακῆς βίβλου), a targum?; see Fitzmyer, *Wandering Aramean* 167; contra Walter, 'Aristeas', 293.
[138]   This identification is also found in the later *Testament of Job* 1:1.
[139]   Dalbert, *Theologie*, 67-70; Collins, *Athens*, 31.
[140]   Fitzmyer, *Wandering Aramean*, 177, n. 16.
[141]   Aristeas presents Job more as a patient sufferer than as a critical questioner.

how great and many the problems were that had to be solved by these pioneers.[142]

The variety not only of literary forms but also of religious outlooks of these hellenized Jews is so great that they can hardly be reduced to a common denominator. Nevertheless it is possible to sketch some motives that were common to several or most of them in their use of biblical traditions. It can be said that it was a special concern to strengthen the Jewish self-consciousness by repeated assertions that several inventions of major cultural importance, e.g. astrology or the art of writing (be it in hieroglyphs or in alphabet), were made by Abraham and/or Moses and were therefore in fact Jewish discoveries. Because Moses was regarded as the author of the Tora, and his books were the oldest and hence most prestigious of all books, many cultures, including Greek civilization, were regarded as ultimately dependent upon Moses. In authors not discussed here, it is sometimes more explicitly stated that the great Greek philosophers drew all their wisdom from the books of Moses (Aristobulus, fragm. 3 = *PE* 13:12, 1, and *Aristeas to Philocrates* 30 and 313-16, go so far as to postulate the existence of an early pre-LXX translation of the Pentateuch in order to substantiate this claim).[143] In view of this idea it is all the more conspicuous that in none of the fragments we find any emphasis on the central significance of the Tora as a book of commandments and laws. Moses is *not* presented as the man to whom God has revealed all these commandments and prohibitions on Sinai; he is presented as the first wise man or the wise man par excellence, as an inventor, as a cultural benefactor, as a great king, even as a cosmic ruler with divine status, but hardly as a lawgiver. The striking absence of a central role of the Tora is one of the most notable features of this literature and gives an impression of a world that is entirely different from the early rabbinic world. Early Hellenistic Jewish literature and early rabbinic literature are worlds apart, connected by nothing but the wish to be Jewish and to remain so. The ways in which this wish took shape show a high degree of discrepancy. Illustrative is the fact that, as far as we can judge from these few fragments and as far as the Pentateuch is concerned, these writers concentrated on the non-halakhic parts of the Tora, Genesis and the first half of Exodus, whereas the early rabbinic literature (e.g. the Tannaic midrashim *Mekhilta, Sifra, Sifrei*) focused exactly on the other parts of the Pentateuch. Even when compared to Philo and Josephus, these earlier authors show a significant lack of interest in halakhic matters. Again, however, it should be remembered that this might just be a distorted picture because Alexander Polyhistor may have left out such

---

[142] See Amir, 'Wie verarbeitete das Judentum' 153.
[143] See the discussion of these passages by Fraser, *Ptolemaic Alexandria* 2, 956. n. 72.

matters. In view of the whole atmosphere of the fragments, however, that would seem to me to be less likely.[144]

In spite of the above-said, we have seen that many of the fragments exhibit aggadic traits and elements that occur also in later midrashim or aggadic passages of the halakhic literature. It has often been too easily assumed that the Hellenistic Jewish authors are in such cases dependent upon early aggadic traditions as reflected in these later sources. That may be correct in some cases, but, as already said, we should not deny the possibility that many motifs in later aggada derive from these Hellenistic authors. This has to be decided from case to case, although often a decision will not be possible. Much work remains to be done here.

The Greeks were aware that oriental historians writing in Greek tried to glorify their respective peoples.[145] That is certainly true of our authors. The glorification of Israel's past, of its heroes and their achievements, is the most conspicuous trait of this literature. No doubt, this has to be seen against the background of anti-Jewish sentiments, especially in Alexandria but also elsewhere.[146] But it was not only as a corrective of and *apologia* against anti-Semitic stories about Moses and others[147] that they wrote their versions, but also as a means to prevent strongly hellenized co-religionists from giving up Judaism altogether. They tried to do this by showing that it is worthwile to be a member of the people of Abraham and Moses since these were the founders of human culture. Whether they ever convinced a pagan, or a Jew on the verge of apostasy, remains unknown.[148] At any rate, later Church Fathers were happy to have these writings at their disposal which could serve their own apologetical purposes. Thanks to these learned Christians we can now catch glimpses of the free and creative ways in which these Jewish pioneers (Samaritans included) used and even rewrote their Bible in an attempt to respond to the changed political, social, and religious situation of their times.

Bibliography

The fundamental work on Alexander Polyhistor and our authors (although mainly dealing with historians, not with the poets) still is FREUDENTHAL, *Helle-*

---

[144]   Collins, *Athens* 51: 'We must emphasize that a significant segment of Hellenistic Judaism did not think primarily in terms of the law or ethical practices, but found its identity in the often fantastic stories of ancestral heroes who outshone the best of the Greeks, Babylonians, and Egyptians'. On the gradually increasing importance of the Mosaic laws in Hellenistic Judaism see Mack, 'Under the Shadow of Moses', esp. 310f.

[145]   *FGH* 609T11 . . . τὸ ἴδιον ἔθνος θελόντων δοξάσαι . . . Georgi, *Gegner* 139, rightly says 'dasz das Selbstbewusztsein der Apologeten, das auf die Fragen der hellenistischen Welt eine Antwort zu haben meint, nicht einfach mit billiger Aufschneiderei verwechselt werden darf'.

[146]   See Sevenster, *The Roots of Pagan Anti-Semitism*, with the corrections by Gager, *Origins*.

[147]   Gager, *Moses*, 113-33; Stern, *GLAJJ*, *passim*.

[148]   That educated Greeks and Romans were highly critical of Oriental claims to great antiquity for their cultures can be seen in Cicero, *De Divinatione* 1:19, 36.

nistische Studien 1-2. Good general introductions are (in chronological order): SUSEMIHL, *Geschichte* 2, 644-56; SCHÜRER, *Geschichte* 3, 468-82, 497-503, 512-22 (see now the revised English edition by VERMES-MILLAR-GOODMAN: *History* 3/1, 513-31, 559-66); VON CHRIST-SCHMID-STAEHLIN, *Geschichte der griechischen Litteratur* 2/1, 588-608; GUTMAN, *Beginnings, passim*; DENIS, *Introduction*, 239-83; HENGEL, 'Anonymität', 234-44; CHARLESWORTH, *The Pseudepigrapha and Modern Research, passim*; COLLINS, *Athens*, 27-51; DROGE, 'Interpretation', 135-59.

The only complete edition of our authors is found in MRAS (ed.), *Eusebius' Werke*, 8/1. Mras' text is conveniently reprinted (but without app. crit.) in DENIS (ed.), *Fragmenta*, 175-228. The historians are now available in HOLLADAY, *Fragments, 1: The Historians*, an excellent edition with app. crit., English translation, introduction and explanatory notes; Vol. 2, with poets, philosophers, etc. is soon to be published. For Ezekiel we now have the fine new edition by SNELL in his *Tragicorum graecorum fragmenta* 1, 288-301. Poets and historians alike are now available in English translation in the various contributions to CHARLESWORTH, OTP 2, 775-920.

Ezekiel: There are three commentaries on Ezekiel, all of them with edition of the Greek text: WIENEKE, *Ezechielis Iudaei poetae Alexandrini fabulae*; FORNARO, *La voce fuori scena*; JACOBSON, *The Exagoge of Ezekiel*. Wieneke and Fornaro are useful for text-critical and grammatical points, but Jacobson was the first to interpret the play against its aggadic background (for some corrections and additions see VAN DER HORST, 'Some Notes').

Philo Epicus: basic discussions can be found in GUTMAN, 'Philo the Epic Poet' and WALTER, 'Philon der Epiker', with some corrections on Gutman.

Theodotus: relevant is the discussion between COLLINS, 'The Epic of Theodotus', and PUMMER, 'Genesis 34'. For a good survey see WALTER, 'Theodotus der Epiker'.

Demetrius: important discussions are FRASER, *Ptolemaic Alexandria*, 1, 690-94; 2, 958-63 (notes); BICKERMANN, 'The Jewish Historian Demetrios'; further WALTER, 'Demetrios'; HOLLADAY, *Fragments* 1, 51-91.

Artapanus: the only monograph on Artapanus is MERENTITIS, 'Ὁ Ἰουδαῖος λόγιος Ἀρτάπανος καὶ τὸ 'ἔργον αὐτοῦ, (*non vidi*, but see Walter's very critical review in *Helikon* 3 [1963] 789-92); good discussions are WALTER, 'Artapanos', and HOLLADAY, *Fragments* 1, 189-243.

Eupolemus: The standard work on Eupolemus is WACHOLDER, *Eupolemus*. See further especially HOLLADAY, *Fragments* 1, 93-156; also BARTLETT, *Jews in the Hellenistic World* 56-71.

Pseudo-Eupolemus: again the standard discussion is by WACHOLDER, 'Pseudo-Eupolemus'; but cf. the corrections by WALTER, 'Zu Pseudo-Eupolemos'. See further especially HOLLADAY, *Fragments* 1, 157-87.

Aristeas: the best studies are WALTER, 'Aristeas', and HOLLADAY, *Fragments* 1, 261-75.

Cleodemus-Malchus: again the reader is best referred to WALTER, 'Kleodemos-Malchas', and HOLLADAY, *Fragments* 1, 245-59.

BIBLIOGRAPHICAL DETAILS

Y. Amir, Wie verarbeitete das Judentum fremde Einflüsse in hellenistischer Zeit?, *Judaica* 38 (1982) 150-63

R. Amiran, The Water Supply of Israelite Jerusalem, in Y. Yadin (ed.), *Jerusalem Revealed*, Jerusalem 1975, 75-8

H. W. Attridge, Historiography, in M. E. Stone (ed.), *Jewish Writings of the Second Temple Period* (Compendia II 2), Assen - Philadelphia 1984, 157-84

G. A. Barrois, Moriah, *Interpreters Dictionary of the Bible* 3 (1962) 438-9

J. R. Bartlett, *Jews in the Hellenistic World*, Cambridge 1985

E. J. Bickerman, The Jewish Historian Demetrius, in his *Studies in Jewish and Christian History* II, Leiden 1980, 347-358

(H.L. Strack-) P. Billerbeck, *Kommentar zum Neuen Testament aus Talmud und Midrasch* I-IV, München 1922-28

P. Borgen, Philo of Alexandria, in Stone, *Jewish Writings* (see above) 233-82

J. Bowker, *The Targums and Rabbinic Literature*, Cambridge 1969

R. van den Broek, *The Myth of the Phoenix According to Classical and Early Christian Traditions*, Leiden 1972

B. Cardauns, Juden und Spartaner. Zur hellenistisch-jüdischen Literatur, *Hermes* 95 (1967) 317-24

J. H. Charlesworth, Jewish Astrology in the Talmud, the Pseudepigrapha, the Dead Sea Scrolls, and Early Palestinian Synagogues, *Harvard Theological Review* 70 (1977) 183-200

--, *The Pseudepigrapha and Modern Research*, Missoula 1981 (2nd ed.)

-- (ed.), *The Old Testament Pseudepigrapha* 1-2, Garden City 1983-85

W. von Christ - W. Schmid - O. Stählin, *Geschichte der griechischen Litteratur* II 1, München 1920 (6th ed.)

S. J. D. Cohen, Sosates, the Jewish Homer, *Harvard Theological Review* 74 (1981) 391-96

J. J. Collins, The Epic of Theodotus and the Hellenism of the Hasmoneans, *Harvard Theological Review* 73 (1980) 91-104

--, *Between Athens and Jerusalem. Jewish Identity in the Hellenistic Diaspora*, New York 1986

P. Dalbert, *Die Theologie der hellenistisch-jüdischen Missionsliteratur*, Hamburg 1954

A. M. Denis, *Introduction aux pseudépigraphes grecs d'Ancien Testament*, Leiden 1970

--, *Fragmenta pseudepigraphorum quae supersunt graeca una cum historicorum et auctorum judaeorum hellenistarum fragmentis*, Leiden 1970

H. Dörrie - H. Dörries, Erotapokriseis, *Reallexikon für Antike und Christentum* 6 (1966) 342-70

A. J. Droge, The Interpretation of the History of Culture in Hellenistic-Jewish Historiography, *SBL Seminar Papers 1984*, Chico 1984, 135-159

H. E. Faber van der Meulen, *Das Salomobild im hellenistisch-jüdischen Schrifttum*, Kampen 1978

F.T. Fallon, *The Enthronement of Sabaoth. Jewish Elements in Gnostic Creation Myths*, Leiden 1978

J. A. Fitzmyer, *The Genesis Apocryphon from Qumran Cave I: A Commentary*, Rome 1971 (2nd ed.)

--, *A Wandering Aramean*, Ann Arbor 1979

G. Fohrer, Morija, *Biblisch-Historisches Handwörterbuch* 2 (1964) 1239

P. Fornaro, *La voce fuori scena. Saggio sull' Exagogê di Ezechiele con testo greco, note e traduzione*, Torino 1982.

J. E. Fossum, *The Name of God and the Angel of the Lord. Samaritan and Jewish Concepts of Intermediation and the Origin of Gnosticism*, Tübingen 1985

P. M. Fraser, *Ptolemaic Alexandria* I-III, Oxford 1972

J. Freudenthal, *Hellenistische Studien 1-2: Alexander Polyhistor und die von ihm erhaltenen Reste jüdäischer und samaritanischer Geschichtswerke*, Breslau 1874-75

J. G. Gager, *Moses in Greco-Roman Paganism*, New York 1972

M. Gaster, Demetrius and Seder Olam, in his *Studies and Texts* II, New York 1928, 650-659

D. Georgi, *Die Gegner des Paulus im 2. Korintherbrief*, Neukirchen 1964

L. Ginzberg, *The Legends of the Jews* I-VII, Philadelphia 1909-38

E. R. Goodenough, *By Light, Light. The Mystic Gospel of Hellenistic Judaism*, New Haven 1935

Y. Gutman, Philo the Epic Poet, *Scripta Hierosolymitana* 1 (1954) 36-63

--, *The Beginnings of Jewish Hellenistic Literature* I-II, Jerusalem 1958-63 (Hebr.)

J. Heineman, 210 Years of Egyptian Exile, *Journal of Jewish Studies* 22 (1971) 19-30

B. Heller, Die Scheu vor Unbekanntem, Unbenanntem in Agada und Apokryphen, *Monatsschrift für Geschichte und Wissenschaft des Judentums* 80 (1936) 170-184

M. Hengel, Anonymität, Pseudepigraphie und "literarische Fälschung" in der jüdisch-hellenistischen Literatur, in *Pseudepigrapha* I (Entretiens de la Fondation Hardt XVIII), Vandoeuvres 1972, 229-308

--, *Judentum und Hellenismus*, Tübingen 1973 (2nd ed. = *Judaism and Hellenism* I-II, Philadelphia 1974)

C.R. Holladay, *Theios Aner in Hellenistic Judaism*, Missoula 1977

--, *Fragments from Hellenistic Jewish Authors I: The Historians*, Chico 1983

P. W. van der Horst, De joodse toneelschrijver Ezechiël, *Nederlands Theologisch Tijdschrift* 36 (1982) 97-112

--, Moses' Throne Vision in Ezekiel the Dramatist, *Journal of Jewish Studies* 34 (1983) 21-9

--, Some Notes on the *Exagoge* of Ezekiel, *Mnemosyne* (ser. IV) 37 (1984) 354-375

--, *Chaeremon: Egyptian Priest and Stoic Philosopher. The Fragments Collected and Translated with Explanatory Notes*, Leiden 1984, 1987 (2nd ed.)

--, Korte notities over vroeg-joodse epiek, *Nederlands Theologisch Tijdschrift* 39 (1985) 102-9

--, Schriftgebruik bij drie vroege joods-hellenistische historici: Demetrius, Artapanus, Eupolemus, *Amsterdamse Cahiers voor Exegese en Bijbelse Theologie* 6 (1985) 144-161

--, Pseudo-Phocylides, in Charlesworth, *OTP* 2 (see above) 565-582

H. Jacobson, Two Studies on Ezekiel the Tragedian, *Greek, Roman and Byzantine Studies* 22 (1981) 167-78

--, Mysticism and Apocalyptic in Ezekiel the Tragedian, *Illinois Classical Studies* 6 (1981) 272-93

--, *The Exagoge of Ezekiel*, Cambridge 1983

F. Jacoby (ed.), *Die Fragmente der griechischen Historiker* 3A1-2, Leiden 1964

A. Jellinek, *Bet ha-Midrasch. Sammlung kleiner Midraschim und vermischter Abhandlungen aus der ältern jüdischen Literatur* I-VI (in 2 vols.), Jerusalem 1967 (3rd ed.)

J. Jeremias, *The Rediscovery of Bethesda*, Louisville 1966

A. Kappelmacher, Zur Tragoedie der hellenistischen Zeit, *Wiener Studien* 44 (1924-25) 69-86

M. M.Kasher, *Encyclopedia of Biblical Interpretation* I, New York 1953

O. Kern, *Orphicorum Fragmenta*, Berlin 1922 (repr. 1963)

H. G. Kippenberg, *Garizim und Synagoge. Traditionsgeschichtliche Untersuchungen zur samaritanischen Religion der aramäischen Periode*, Berlin - New York 1971

W. L. Knox, Abraham and the Quest for God, *Harvard Theological Review* 28 (1935) 55-60

A. van der Kooij, On the Place of Origin of the Old Greek of Psalms, *Vetus Testamentum* 33 (1983) 67-74

H. Kosmala, Jerusalem, *Biblisch-Historisches Handwörterbuch* 2 (1964) 820-825

R. Le Déaut, *Targum du Pentateuque* I-V, Paris 1978-81

--, A propos du Targum d'Exode 13,18: La Torah, arme secrète d'Israel, in N. Carré et al. (edd.), *De la Torah au Messie. Mélanges H. Cazelles*, Paris 1981, 525-33

A. Lesky, *Geschichte der griechischen Literatur*, Bern 1971 (3. Aufl.)

I. Lévy, Moïse en Éthiopie, *Revue des études juives* 53 (1907) 201-11

G. Mayer, Aspekte des Abrahambildes in der hellenistisch-jüdischen Literatur, *Evangelische Theologie* 32 (1972) 118-127

A. Mazar, The Aquaducts of Jerusalem, in Y. Yadin (ed.), *Jerusalem Revealed*, Jerusalem 1975, 79-84

W. A. Meeks, *The Prophet-King. Moses Traditions and the Johannine Christology*, Leiden 1967

--, Moses as God and King, in J. Neusner (ed.), *Religions in Antiquity*, Leiden 1968, 354-71

J. T. Milik, *The Books of Enoch*, Oxford 1976

G. Mussies, The interpretatio judaica of Sarapis, in M. J. Vermaseren (ed.), *Studies in Hellenistic Religions*, Leiden 1979, 189-214

--, The interpretatio judaica of Thoth-Hermes, in M. Heerma van Voss et al. (edd.), *Studies in Egyptian Religion Dedicated to Jan Zandee*, Leiden 1982, 89-120

G. W. E. Nickelsburg, The Bible Rewritten and Expanded, in Stone, *Jewish Writings* (see above) 89-156

G. L. Prato, Babilonia fundata dai giganti: il significato cosmico di Gen. 11,1-9 nella storiografia dello Pseudo-Eupolemo, in V. Collado - E. Zurro (edd.), *El Misterio de la Palabra. Homenaje a L. A. Schökel*, Madrid 1983, 121-146

R. Pummer, Genesis 34 in Jewish Writings of the Hellenistic and Roman Periods, *Harvard Theological Review* 75 (1982) 177-88

T. Rajak, Moses in Ethiopia: Legend and Literature, *Journal of Jewish Studies* 29 (1978) 111-22

C. Rowland, *Christian Origins*, London 1985

D. Runnalls, Moses' Ethiopian Campaign, *Journal for the Study of Judaism* 14 (1983) 135-56

S. Sandmel, *Philo's Place in Judaism*, Cincinnati 1956

A. Schalit, Artapanus, *Encyclopaedia Judaica* 2 (1972) 646-7

E. Schürer, *Geschichte des jüdischen Volkes im Zeitalter Jesu Christi* I-III, Leipzig 1901-1909 (4th ed.)

--, *The History of the Jewish People in the Age of Jesus Christ* I-III (4 vols.), rev. ed. by G. Vermes, F. Millar, M. Black, M. Goodman, Edinburgh 1973-1987.

A. F. Segal, *Two Powers in Heaven. Early Rabbinic Reports About Christianity and Gnosticism*, Leiden 1977

--, Ruler of This World. Attitudes About Mediator Figures and the Importance of Sociology for Self-Definition, in E. P. Sanders (ed.), *Jewish and Christian Self-Definition* II, London 1981, 245-268

J. N. Sevenster, *The Roots of Pagan Anti-Semitism in the Ancient World*, Leiden 1975

M. Smith, *Palestinian Parties and Politics That Shaped the Old Testament*, New York 1971

B. Snell (ed.), *Tragicorum Graecorum Fragmenta* I, Göttingen 1971

--, *Szenen aus griechischen Dramen*, Berlin 1971

E. Starobinski-Safran, Un poète judéo-hellénistique: Ézékiel le Tragique, *Museum Helveticum* 31 (1974) 216-24

M. Stern, *Greek and Latin Authors on Jews and Judaism* I-III, Jerusalem 1974-1984

F. Susemihl, *Geschichte der griechischen Litteratur der Alexandrinerzeit* I-II, Leipzig 1891-92

K. Thraede, Erfinder (geistesgeschichtlich), *Reallexikon für Antike und Christentum* 5 (1962) 1191-1278

D. L. Tiede, *The Charismatic Figure as a Miracle Worker*, Missoula 1972

R. Tournay, Quelques relectures bibliques antisamaritaines, *Revue Biblique* 71 (1964) 504-36

G. F. Unger, Wann schrieb Alexander Polyhistor?, *Philologus* 43 (1884) 528-31

--, Die Blüthezeit des Alexander Polyhistor, *Philologus* 47 (1889) 177-83

E. E. Urbach, *The Sages. Their Concepts and Beliefs* I-II, Jerusalem 1975

G. Vermes, La figure de Moïse au tournant des deux testaments, in H. Cazelles (ed.), *Moïse, l'homme de l'alliance*, Paris-Tournay 1955

--, The Life of Abraham, in his *Scripture and Tradition in Judaism*, Leiden 1973, 67-126

--, Bible and Midrash: Early Old Testament Exegesis, in his *Post-Biblical Jewish Studies*, Leiden 1975, 59-91

B. Z. Wacholder, Pseudo-Eupolemos' Two Greek Fragments on the Life of Abraham, *Hebrew Union College Annual* 34 (1963) 83-113

--, How Long Did Abraham Stay in Egypt?, *Hebrew Union College Annual* 35 (1964) 43-65

--, Philo (the Elder), *Encyclopaedia Judaica* 13 (1972) 407-8

--, *Eupolemos. A Study of Judaeo-Greek Literature*, Cincinnati 1974

L. Wächter, Astrologie und Schicksalsglaube im rabbinischen Judentum, *Kairos* 11 (1969) 181-200

N. Walter, Zu Pseudo-Eupolemos, *Klio* 43-45 (1965) 282-90

--, Artapanos, Eupolemos, Pseudo-Eupolemos, Kleodemos-Malchas, in *Jüdische Schriften aus hellenistisch-römischer Zeit* I 2, Gütersloh 1976

--, Aristeas, Demetrios, *idem* III 2, Gütersloh 1975

--, Philon der Epiker, Theodotos der Epiker, Pseudo-Orpheus, *idem* IV 3, Gütersloh 1983

O. Weinreich, Türöffnung im Wunder-, Prodigien- und Zauberglauben der Antike, des Judentums und Christentums, in his *Religionsgeschichtliche Studien*, Darmstadt 1968, 38-290

M. L. West, *The Orphic Poems*, Oxford 1983

J. Wieneke, *Ezechielis Poetae Judaei Alexandrini fabulae quae inscribitur ΕΞΑΓΩΓΗ fragmenta*, Münster 1931

H. G. M. Williamson, *1 and 2 Chronicles*, London 1982

K. Ziegler, *Das hellenistische Epos. Ein vergessenes Kapitel griechischer Dichtung*, Leipzig 1966 (2nd ed.)

13. NIMROD AFTER THE BIBLE

In percentage terms the early chapters of Genesis have always been more productive of haggada than most other parts of the Bible. Some short and enigmatic verses in those chapters, especially, have been rich sources for midrashic speculation. Famous instances are Genesis 5,21-24 on Enoch, four verses which have given rise to an enormous corpus of Enoch-literature, and Genesis 6,1-4 on the sons of God and the giants, also four verses which have turned out to become a fountainhead of haggadic developments. In this paper we want to focus upon the haggada evoked by some lines on 'a mighty hunter before the Lord', Nimrod, in Genesis 10.8-12.

The Biblical data are scarce. The text runs as follows: "(8) Cush became the father of Nimrod; he was the first on earth to be a mighty man. (9) He was a mighty hunter before the Lord; therefore it is said: 'Like Nimrod a mighty hunter before the Lord'. (10) The beginning of his kingdom was Babel, Erech, and Accad, all of them in the land of Shinar. (11) From that land he went into Assyria and built Nineveh, Rehoboth-Ir, Calah, (12) and Resen between Nineveh and Calah; that is the great city" (RSV). Further Nimrod is only mentioned in passing in 1 Chronicles 1,10, where Gen. 10:9 is quoted, and in Micah 5,5, where Assyria is called the land of Nimrod.

We do not know exactly when post-biblical speculation about our enigmatic hunter began to develop, for, unfortunately enough, the first piece of haggadic evidence we have is rather uncertain since Nimrod's name is not mentioned in it, and whether or not he is implied there, is very controversial. In one of the fragments of Pseudo-Eupolemus, in fact an *adespoton*,[1] we read the following: "Abraham traced his family to the giants. While these giants were living in Babylonia, they were destroyed by the gods because of their wickedness. One of them, Belus, escaped death and came to dwell in Babylon. There he built a tower and lived in it. It was named Belus, after Belus who built it" (quoted from Alexander Polyhistor by Eusebius, *Praeparatio Evangelica* IX 18, 2).[2] It is clear that we have here a medley of allusions to Genesis 6 (both the motive of the giants and that of the flood) and Genesis 11 (the building of the tower of Babel). As we shall presently see, in other instances of linking Gen 6 to Gen 11, the intermediate chain is Nimrod from Gen 10. The problem in this case, however, is that if Belus, who is one of the giants that built the tower, is identical with Nimrod, he also is

---

[1] See on this matter C.R. Holladay, *Fragments from Hellenistic Jewish Authors I: Historians* (Chico: Scholars Press, 1983) 158-9.

[2] Translation by Holladay, *Fragments* 177.

said to have escaped the flood, which would imply an identification of Noah
and Nimrod! And indeed, Martin Hengel speaks of "this identification of
Noah and Nimrod = Bel-Kronos, which necessarily follows from the text".[3]
Odd as this identification may seem at first sight, Hengel rightly points out
that no less peculiar identifications can be found elsewhere in early Jewish
literature, for instance of Shem and Melchizedek, of Pinehas and Elijah, and
more instances could be mentioned. And it should be borne in mind that
there are clear traces of a positive image of Nimrod in other passages still to
be discussed. Moreover, there existed indeed speculations in early Jewish
haggadic circles about whether or not Noah might be descended from the
giants of Genesis 6.[4] So an identification of Noah and Nimrod should be regarded as a distinct haggadic possibility. Nevertheless, we cannot attain
certainty in this question. First, Eusebius quotes Alexander Polyhistor as
saying that he found these data 'in some anonymous writings', which may
imply that he drew here upon several authors; second, the plural 'gods' may
even imply that one of these authors was not a Jew at all; third, these observations suggest that what we have in this fragment is "a potpourri of traditions, most probably thrown together by Alexander Polyhistor out of dispa-
rate elements".[5] Hence we should be careful in drawing too firm conclusions from this passage.

The earliest Jewish writer mentioning Nimrod explicitly, as far as I know, is
Philo of Alexandria. In his writings one finds a clear creation of a negative
image of our hunter. Of course, in a typically Philonic way, Nimrod is alle-
gorized. In his *Quaestiones in Genesim* II 81-82 Philo first remarks that
Ham, Nimrod's grandfather, stands for evil and that Ham's son Cush stands
for 'the sparse nature of earth' and is a symbol of unfruitfulness and barren-
ness. Nimrod is Cush's son because spiritual unproductiveness can only

---

3   *Judaism and Hellenism* (Philadelphia: Fortress, 1981) II 60 n. 244 There Hengel po-
    lemicizes with B.Z. Wacholder, Pseudo-Eupolemos' Two Greek Fragments on the Life
    of Abraham, *HUCA* 34 (1963) 94 (83-113). J. Freudenthal, *Hellenistische Studien,
    I+II: Alexander Polyhistor und die von ihm erhaltenen Reste judaeischer und samari-
    tanischer Geschichtswerke* (Breslau: Skutsch, 1875) 94, quotes a remark from the
    'History of Armenia' by the early mediaeval Armenian Christian scholar Moses of
    Chorene to the effect that Belus and Nimrod are to be identified. Hengel is followed by
    Holladay, Fragments 187 n. 46, and by P. W. van der Horst, The Interpretation of the
    Bible by the Minor Hellenistic Jewish Authors, in M. J. Mulder (ed.), *Mikra. Text,
    Translation, Reading and Interpretation of the Hebrew Bible in Ancient Judaism and
    Early Christianity* (CRINT II 1) (Assen-Philadelphia: Van Gorcum-Fortress,1988)
    541.

4   See *1QGenAp II 16* and *1 Enoch* 106:8, and cf. J. P. Lewis, *A Study of the Interpreta-
    tion of Noah and the Flood in Jewish and Christian Literature*, Leiden: Brill, 1968, 14;
    see also the pertinent remarks in E. Schürer, *The History of the Jewish People in the
    Age of Jesus Christ* III 1, rev, ed. by G, Vermes, F. Millar, M. Goodman (Edinburgh:
    Clark, 1986) 332-333.

5   Thus R. Doran in J. H. Charlesworth (ed.), *The Old Testament Pseudepigrapha* II
    (Garden City: Doubleday, 1985) 878.

produce giants, i.e., people who honour earthly things more than heavenly.
"For in truth he who is zealous for earthly and corruptible things always
fights against and makes war on heavenly things and praiseworthy and
wonderful natures, and builds walls and towers on earth against heaven. But
those things which are (down) here are against those things which are (up)
there. For this reason it is not ineptly said, 'a giant before (enantion) God',
which clearly is opposition to the Deity. For the impious man is none other
than the enemy and foe who stands against[6] God." Philo then adds that
Nimrod should be translated as 'Ethiopian', i.e. the black one, because he
has no participation in light. In *De gigantibus* 65-66 Philo remarks on Gen
6,4 that the sons of the earth surrender to the nature of the flesh instead of to
reason. "It was Nimrod who began this desertion (...), his name means
'desertion' (*automolesis*)". In these two very brief passages from the first
half of the first century C.E. we have in a nutshell a number of haggadic
elements that will return time and again in later haggadic developments. Let
us look briefly at these elements.[7]

The first thing to be noted is the connection of Nimrod with the story of the
giants in Genesis 6 on the one hand and with the story of the tower of Babel
in Genesis 11 on the other. There are several reasons for this connection.
The offspring of the sons of God are called *gibborim* (LXX *gigantes*) in Gen
6,4, and Nimrod is called a *gibbor* (LXX *gigas*) in Gen 10,8-9. This suggested to the early haggadists that Nimrod may have been one of the giants of
Genesis 6. In Gen 10,10 the beginning of Nimrod's kingdom is said to have
been Babel in the land of Shinar, and in Gen 11,1-10. the people who settled
in the land of Shinar are said to have built a city there which was called Babel (v.9). If that city was the beginning of Nimrod's kingdom, he cannot but
have been one of its builders. So Nimrod who was one of the giants of Genesis 6, was also the one who had Babel built. All this is implied in these
two short passages of Philo. Second, Philo etymologizes Nimrod's name:
his name means 'desertion'. This element too will recur in other writings
where the name Nimrod is repeatedly explained from the Hebrew word *marad*, 'to rebel' (against God, that is), which comes very close to Philo's notion of desertion from God, if it is not identical to it.[8] Third, because Nimrod is a son of Cush, Philo calls him an Ethiopian, a black man. This element helped to blacken Nimrod in the development of the tradition, whereas
the Biblical text itself does not do anything of the sort.[9] Finally, Philo ex-

---

[6]   The Greek text probably also had *enantion*, but the Armenian version, which is our
      only textual witness here, has a different word than the one used in the phrase 'a giant
      before God'.

[7]   See also the useful comments in D. Winston and J. Dillon, *Two treatises of Philo of
      Alexandria. A Commentary on De Gigantibus and Quod Deus Sit Immutabilis* (Chico:
      Scholars Press, 1983) 69-71 and . 272.

[8]   See L. L. Grabbe, *Etymology in Early Jewish Interpretation. The Hebrew Names in
      Philo* (Atlanta: Scholars Press, 1988) 191.

[9]   On the evaluation of blacks in antiquity see F. M. Snowden, *Blacks in Antiquity*.

ploits the fact that the LXX version of Gen 10,9 calls him a mighty hunter *enantion* the Lord. This word, used by the LXX translators as equivalent of *liphne*, could also have the meaning of 'against'; so Nimrod's activities must have been directed against the Lord. This element will recur in the targumim and elsewhere, but most explicitly in St. Augustine, when he says about the phrase that Nimrod was a great hunter before the Lord:

"Some interpreters have misunderstood this phrase, being deceived by an ambiguity in the Greek, and consequently translating it as 'before the Lord' instead of 'against the Lord'. It is true that the Greek *enantion* means 'before' as well as 'against'. (...) It is in the latter sense that we must take it in the description of Nimrod; that giant was 'a hunter against the Lord'. For the word 'hunter' can only suggest a deceiver, oppressor and destroyer of earth-born creatures. Thus he, with his subject peoples, began to erect a tower against the Lord, which symbolizes his impious pride" (*De Civitate Dei* XVI 4).

When we now turn to Pseudo-Philo, an author about whom we know nothing but who lived probably in the second half of the first century C.E., we find a full-blown Nimrod haggada.[10] In his *Liber Antiquitatum Biblicarum* the following elements are worth mentioning. In *LAB* 4:7, Gen 10,9 is quoted as 'he began to be arrogant (*superbus*) before the Lord'. In 5:1 the sons of Ham make Nimrod their leader and in 5:5 Nimrod has all the sons of Ham pass in review. Finally in ch. 6 we find for the first time the story that will have such a rich future, namely the direct confrontation of Nimrod with Abraham. We are told that the leaders of the three tribes of Shem, Ham, and Japheth planned to build the great tower in Babel but that 12 men, including Abraham, refused to join the project because they were worshippers of the Lord. Joktan, who is the chief of the leaders, puts these men in jail although he does not do so wholeheartedly being a secret worshipper of the Lord himself. He offers them a possibility to escape and only Abraham declines this offer. Nimrod, however, wants the men to be punished severely. When he finds out that only Abraham is left in jail, he demands that he be thrown alive into a fiery furnace. This happens but God sees to it that Abraham does not suffer the least injury in the flames. Whereas 83,500 others are burnt by the fire that leaps forth out of the furnace, Abraham escapes unscathed.

What is the background of the development of such a motif that is so evidently modelled upon the story of the three young men in the fiery furnace in Daniel 3?[11] We know from later sources (e.g. *Genesis Rabbah*, see be-

---

Ethiopians in the Greco-Roman Experience,(Cambridge (Mass.)-London: Belknap, 1970).

10   I used the edition by D. J. Harrington et al., *Pseudo-Philon, Les antiquités bibliques,* 2 vols, (Paris: Cerf, 1976), and Harrington's translation in Charlesworth, *OTP* II (see n.5).

11   On the role of Daniel 3 in this story see also G. Vermes, The Life of Abraham, in his *Scripture and Tradition in Judaism* (Leiden: Brill, 1973) 88 (67-126). and already B.

low) that the words *Ur Kasdim* in Gen 15,7 ('I am the Lord who brought you out of Ur Kasdim') were taken to mean 'the fire of the Chaldaeans' since Ur was read as *'or, "*flame, fire'.[12] If God himself said that he had rescued Abraham from the fire of the Chaldaeans, if Babel was the centre of the Chaldaeans, if Nimrod was the king of Babel, and if Nimrod was the archrebel against God, then inevitably there must have been a confrontation between these two men, the more so since a conflict over idolatry was suggested by the fact that Joshua 24,2 said: "Your fathers lived of old beyond the Euphrates, Terah, the father of Abraham and of Nahor; and they served other gods". A conflict between Abraham and Terah over the idols in the city of Nimrod is one of the stock elements in most of the haggada on these persons. Nevertheless, we can clearly see that the motive of confrontation between Nimrod and Abraham is here still in its infancy. They are not the only characters on stage and the plot is relatively simple. We cannot be sure whether Pseudo-Philo is the originator of the motif. Two centuries earlier, in *Jubilees* 12, we already find the connection of Ur of the Chaldaeans with the motif of fire, but Nimrod does not figure there[13]. Neither is there a confrontation between Abraham and Nimrod in Pseudo-Philo's contemporary Josephus, as we shall presently see. This suggests that the motif may not yet have been widespread in this early period.

Josephus relates in his *Antiquitates* I 113-114 about the people in the plain of Shinar that they suspected that God was plotting against them in urging them to emigrate, in order that, being divided, they might be more open to attack:

"They were incited to this insolent contempt of God by Nimrod [lit. Nebrodes], grandson of Ham the son of Noah, an audacious man of doughty vigour. He persuaded them to attribute their prosperity not to God but to their own valour, and little by little transformed the state of affairs into a tyranny, holding that the only way to detach men from the fear of God was by making them continuously dependent upon his own power. He threatened to have his revenge on God if He wished to inundate the earth again, for he would build a tower higher than the water could reach and avenge the destruction of their forefathers".

Beer, Zur Jüdischen Sagesgeschichte, *MGWJ* 4 (1855) 59-65.

[12] See e.g. H. L. Strack - P. Billerbeck, *Kommentar zum Neuen Testament aus Talmud und Midrasch* IV 1 (Munchen: Beck, 1928) 454 n.4, and J. Bowker, *The Targums and Rabbinic Literature* (Cambridge: CUP, 1969) 187f.

[13] Also in the second century B.C.E. we find Philo Epicus stating that Abraham "left the splendid enclosure of the giants" (fragm. 1, 4-5). This seems to imply that Babel was built by the giants, but the poet does not name Nimrod as one of them. Nevertheless it is clear that the haggadic process was fully on its way already in the middle of the second century B.C.E. (which can also be seen in Judith 5:5-8). For a full and well-balanced discussion of the difficult lines 4-5 of Philo Epicus' first fragment see now C. R. Holladay, *Fragments from Hellenistic Jewish Authors: Poets* (Atlanta: Scholars Press, 1989) 254-256.*l*

As we already remarked, there is no conflict with Abraham here. But there are some other new elements. For besides the by now familiar components of Nimrod's building the tower and his rebelling attitude towards God, we find here Nimrod as the instigator of the people of Shinar's suspicion that God was plotting against them by urging a migration which would divide them and so expose them to attack, and of their consequent refusal to colonize. Building the tower now becomes partly a measure taken to counteract God's command to migrate and colonize, partly also a measure to prove that God would not be able to bring a new flood over the earth. We can observe here how the various ingredients from Genesis 6, 10 and 11 get more and more interwoven.[14]

It is time to turn to the rabbinic evidence. The targumim yield some interesting insights. Let us look at some of their renderings of Gen. 10 and begin with an exceptional piece of evidence, viz. Pseudo-Jonathan's rendition of Gen 10,11. Whereas in 10,9 the translator had said that Nimrod was "a mighty rebel before the Lord, wherefore it is said that from the day on which the world was created there has not been any like Nimrod a mighty hunter and a rebel (*mrwdh*) before the Lord", in 10,11 Nimrod is unexpectedly "immortalized as the outstandingly righteous individual of his generation"[15] by the following words: "Out of that land (sc. Shinar) Nimrod went forth and ruled in Asshur because he had not wished to associate with the project of the generation of the divisions [cf. Gen 10,25]. And he left those four cities, and the Lord settled him elsewhere instead, and he built other towns, Nineveh, etc." Several comments are in order here. Firstly, the fact that Nimrod is here said to have left Babel is a consequence of the fact that in the Hebrew text the words *min ha' arets hahi' yatsa' 'ashur* were taken to mean 'he left that country for Asshur' instead of 'Asshur left that country'. Once Nimrod was made the grammatical subject of *yatsa'*, a reason had to be found for his leaving the country of Babel. Apparently because he left before chapter 11, he must have been opposed to the building of the tower. There are other traces of such or similar traditions. To be sure, they are found in Christian writings, but there is little doubt that their authors drew upon Jewish sources, as was so often the case with these Syrian writers, namely Ephraem and Ishodad.[16] In his commentary on Gen 10,9, Ephraem Syrus remarks: "Nimrod was a strong giant before the Lord becau-

---

14 On Nimrod's role in Josephus' rendering of Genesis see the extensive and excellent discussion by Th. W. Franxman, *Genesis and the "Jewish Antiquities" of Flavius Josephus,* (Rome: Biblical Institute Press, 1979) 93-121, esp. 96-98.

15 E. Levine, *The Aramaic Version of the Bible* (Berlin: W. de Gruyter, 1988) 35. Levine cites this instance as one of the many cases where in the very same targum one finds midrashic elements that are mutually contradictory. "This reflects the eclectic use of sources, the variant purposes to which midrash was put, and the latitudinarian approach to targum itself" (*ibid.*).

16 A. Levene, *The Early Syrian Fathers on Genesis* (London: Taylor's Foreign Press, 1951) esp. 123ff.

se in accordance with God's will he waged war upon the peoples in order to spread them out to the areas that God had allotted them. Therefore, if someone wants to bless a leader or king, he says: May you become like Nimrod, a strong giant before the Lord, triumphant in the wars of the Lord".[17] And Ishodad of Merv remarks in his comments on the same verse that the wish 'may you become like Nimrod, a brave hunter before the Lord, was in earlier times a common way of greeting a leader, and that Nimrod became so famous by God's will because he had combatted the builders of the tower of Babel and driven them away from the city; he had left there only Peleg, who still spoke Hebrew, the primaeval language, which was thus preserved under Nimrod's rule.[18] These passages make it fairly certain that there must have been a probably fairly extensive positive Nimrod haggada, which has all but disappeared from early Jewish literature, even though the Bible itself nowhere specifically states that Nimrod had an evil character. Pseudo-Eupolemus and Pseudo-Jonathan have preserved some traces of this positive approach.[19]

When we now look at Pseudo-Jonathan on Gen 11,28, we again meet a new motif:

"And it came to pass, when Nimrod cast Abram into the fiery furnace because he would not worship his idol and there was no power for the fire to burn him, that Haran's [Abraham's brother] heart became doubtful, and he said: 'If Nimrod prevails, I will be on his side, but if Abram prevails, I will be on his side'. And when all the people who were there saw that the fire had no power over Abram, they said in their hearts: 'Is not Haran, the bro-

---

17   See the translation in R.-M. Tonneau, *Sancti Ephraem Syri in Genesim et in Exodum commentarii* (CSCO 153) (Louvain: Durbecq, 1955) 52-3.

18   See the translation in C. van den Eynde, *Commentaire d'Isodad de Merv sur l'Ancien Testament, I: Genèse,* (CSCO 156) (Louvain: Durbecq, 1955) 143-146. On the matter of Hebrew in the Nimrod-haggada see also L. Ginzberg, Die Haggada bei den Kirchenvätern und in der apokryphischen Litteratur, *MGWJ* 43 (1899) 468-470.485. The following two works do not yield anything for our subject: R. Devreesse, *Les anciens commentateurs grecs de l'Octateuque et des Rois,* (Vatican City: Bibliotheca Apostolica, 1959), and F. Petit, *Catenae graecae in Genesim et Exodum,* vol. I (Turnhout: Brepols, 1977).

19   Levene, *Early Syrian Fathers* (n. 16) 85, quotes from a Syriac ms. on the Pentateuch in the Mingana collection the following section: "Of Nimrod, Scripture says, 'He was a mighty hunter before the Lord'. It was according to the will of God that he should be renowned; and he made war on those who built the tower and he first captured Babylon. Therefore it is said, 'Be like unto Nimrod', as when one blesses his neighbour with any kind of blessing". At pp. 201-2, Levene makes the interesting observation that Ibn Ezra in his commentary discards the unfavourable traditions regarding Nimrod and does not deduce any 'rebelliousness' from the name Nimrod, but explains that Nimrod was the first man to show the prowess of man over beast and that he built altars on which he offered burnt offerings to God. Ibn Ezra was censured for that by Nachmanides.

ther of Abram, full of divining and charms, and has he not uttered a spell over the fire to stop it burning his brother?' At once fire fell from the heavens and consumed him [Haran], and *Haran died in the presence of his father* (Gen 11,28), even as he was burnt in the land of his birth in the fiery furnace which the Kasdai had made for Abram his brother."[20]

The biblical text of Gen 11,28 runs: "Haran died before his father Terah in the land of his birth, in Ur of the Chaldaeans". Again, probably, the text was taken to mean that Haran died in the fire (*'ur*) of the Chaldaeans, so that Nimrod now becomes guilty of the death of Abraham's brother.

Another new element found in Pseudo-Jonathan is the identification of Nimrod with Amraphel, one of the kings mentioned in Genesis 14. On Gen 14,1 this targum remarks that Amraphel was the same as Nimrod who had said that Abraham should be thrown into the fire, obviously with an etymological play on *'amar* and *hippil* (or *pil*). The real reason behind this identification, however, may have been the fact that Amraphel is said in the biblical text to have been 'king of Shinar' in the days of Abraham. But of course the king of Shinar in Abraham's time was known to have been Nimrod. And then one could find corroborative evidence for this identification in the folk-etymological analysis of the name Amraphel: *'amar pil,* 'he said: throw!'. This etymological derivation is discussed explicitly in the Talmud (see below). Targum Onkelos does not yield much of relevance for our purpose apart from the fact that Nimrod is here called 'a powerful potentate' (*gibbar taqiph*), perhaps because the translator associated the Hebrew *tsayid* with *metsudah,* 'stronghold, fortress'.[21] Targum Neofiti on Gen 10,9 calls Nimrod "a hero in sin before the Lord". And the Fragment Targum *ad loc.* has: "He was very mighty at the hunt and mighty in sin before the Lord. He would trap men by their tongues (i.e. words) and say to them: Depart from the laws of Shem and cling to the laws of Nimrod".[22] Here we see that 'hunter' is understood metaphorically as one who knows how to ensnare people; that is why he is called 'mighty in sin' or 'a hero in sin'. This expression recurs in the targum on 1 Chron 1,10; and the same targum on 28,3 says that God saved Abraham from the fiery furnace into which Nimrod had thrown him because he would not worship his idol.[23] Let me quote finally from the targum to Qoh 4,13:

---

[20] Translation and discussion of this passage in Bowker, *Targums* (n. 12) 183, 187f.

[21] Thus B. Grossfeld, *The Targum Onqelos to Genesis* (Edinburgh: Clark, 1988) 61. Cf. also M. Aberbach - B. Grossfeld, *Targum Onkelos to Genesis* (New York: Ktav, 1982) 69f.

[22] See M. L. Klein, *The Fragment-Targums of the Pentateuch,* 2 vols. (Rome: Biblical Institute Press, 1980) I 49 and II 11. R. le Déaut, *Targum du Pentateuque* I (Paris: Cerf, 1978) 136-9. M. L. Klein's *Genizah Manuscripts of Palestinian Targum to the Pentateuch,* 2 vols. (Cincinnati: HUC Press, 1986) has no material on Nimrod.

[23] R. le Déaut - J. Robert, *Targum des Chroniques,* 2 vols. (Rome: Biblical Institute Press, 1971) I 40 and 156, II 9 and 142.

"Better like Abraham, the poor youth in whom was the spirit of prophecy from the Lord and to whom the Lord was known when he was three years old, and he would not worship an idol, than the wicked Nimrod, who was an old and foolish king. And because Abraham would not worship an idol, he threw him into the burning furnace, and a miracle was performed for him from the Lord of the world, and he delivered him from it. Even after this, Nimrod had no sense to be admonished not to worship the idol which he worshipped before. For Abraham went out from the family of idolaters and reigned over the land of Canaan, and during Abraham's reign Nimrod became destitute in the world".[24]

Some more targumic passages could be added, but these may suffice to show in a nutshell the growth of a tradition in the period from the second to the seventh centuries of our era.

When we now turn to Talmud and Midrashim, we do find some new details added to the picture, but basically the story remains the same. Let us look at some passages at random.[25] In b.*Eruvin* 53a we read: "'And it came to pass in the days of Amraphel' (Gen 14,1). Rav and Samuel are at variance. One holds that his name was Nimrod; and why was he called Amraphel? Because he ordered our father Abraham to be cast into a burning furnace (*she'amar wehippil le'Abraham 'abinu betokh kibshan ha'esh*). But the other holds that his name was Amraphel; and why was he called Nimrod? Because in his reign he led all the world in rebellion against himself [=God] (*shehimrid 'et kol ha'olam kullo 'alav bemalkhuto*)." We see here two more instances of the etymologies already known to us. The motif that Nimrod led the whole world to rebellion against God is also found in b.*Pesahim* 94b and b.*Hagiga* 13a, where Nebuchadnezzar is called a 'grandson of Nimrod', i.e. Nimrod's spiritual descendant because of his rebellion against God and his attempt to force other people into the same attitude.[26] In b.*Avoda Zara*

---

24 E. Levine, *The Aramaic Version of Qohelet* (New York: Sepher Hermon Press, 1978) 34. Cf. Levine's *Aramaic Version of the Bible* (n. 15) 184f. n. 13.

25 Older surveys can be found in B. Beer, *Leben Abraham's nach Auffassung der jüdischen Sage*, (Leipzig: Leiner, 1859) 7-19 with notes on pp. 105-116. M. Seligmann, Nimrod, *Jewish Encyclopedia* 9 (1905) 309. M.J. bin Gorion, *Die Sagen der Juden* II (Frankfurt: Ritter und Loening, 1914) 17-25, 56-59, 73-74, 103-124, 160-161. L. Ginzberg, *The Legends of the Jews* I (Philadelphia: Jewish Publication Society, 1909) 174-217 with notes in vol V (1925) 198-218. A. S. Rappoport, *Ancient Israel: Myths and Legends* I (London: Mystic Press, 1987 (repr.)) 226-253. See also the short notice by the editor in the *Encyclopaedia Judaica* XII (1972) 1167.

26 The etymological play with *mrd* is also found in connection with 1 Chron 4,18, 'the daughter of Pharaoh, whom Mered took', about which it is remarked in b.*Megillah* 13a: "Was Mered his name? Was not Caleb his name [cf. 1 Chron 4,15]? The Holy One, blessed be He, said: 'Let Caleb, who rebelled (*marad*) against the plan of the spies, come and take the daughter of Pharaoh, who rebelled against the idols of her father's house'." There can be little doubt that Jerome goes back to Jewish etymological speculations when in his *Liber interpretationis hebraicorum nominum* he quotes as mea-

3a we read: "The Holy One, blessed be He, will say: 'Some of yourselves shall testify that Israel has observed the entire Torah. Let Nimrod come and testify that Abraham did not worship idols'." (In *Av. Zar.* 53b the tower of Babel is called 'the house/temple of Nimrod' and regarded as an idol which its worshippers abandoned). A nice haggadic trait is found in b.*Pesahim* 118a, where it is said: "When the wicked Nimrod cast our father Abraham into the fiery furnace, Gabriel said to the Holy One, blessed be He: 'Sovereign of the universe, let me go down, cool [it], and deliver that righteous man from the fiery furnace'. The Holy One, blessed be He, said to him: 'I am unique in my world and he is unique in his world; it is fitting for Him who is unique to deliver him who is unique'. But because the Holy One, blessed be He, does not withhold the [merited] reward of any creature, He said to him: 'Thou shalt be privileged to deliver three of his descendants' [sc. Hananiah, Mishael, and Azaryah]". To conclude our little Talmudic anthology, in b.*Hullin* 89a God says: "I bestowed greatness upon Nimrod, but he said: 'Come, let us build a city' (Gen 11,4)". Here we see a final trace of an image of Nimrod as a man initially bestowed with favours by God but later corrupted by his lust for power. On the whole we can say that the Talmud does not add really new elements to the Nimrod-haggada.

Some new elements, however, can be found in the haggadic midrashim, especially in *Bereshit Rabba*, as was to be expected. In *Ber. R.* 23:7 (on 4,26) it is said that the word 'begin' or 'beginning' is used four times in the text of Genesis (4,26; 6,1; 10,8; 11,6) in the sense of rebelling. Two of these passages are about Nimrod, also 11,6, on the basis of which text it is said that God smote Nimrod's head, exclaiming: 'It is he who has incited them to rebel'. (The same tradition in *Ber. R.* 26:4, on 6,1). This application of the hermeneutic rule of analogy is a new element supporting the growing tradition of Nimrod as the arch-rebel against God. In this midrash we also find a parallel drawn between Esau and Nimrod in *Ber. R.* 37:2-3 and 63:13. Of course, this is due to the fact that in Gen 25,27 it is said that "Esau was a skilful hunter". This suggested a rivalry between the two. In the latter passage it is said that "Nimrod was seeking to slay him [Esau] on account of the garment which had belonged to Adam [and which Esau now possessed], for whenever he put it on and went into the field, all the beasts and birds in the world would come and flock around him." Elsewhere (e.g. *Pirqe de Rabbi Eliezer* 24) we find the reverse situation, namely that Nimrod had received via his forefathers the garments of skin that God had made for Adam (Gen 3,21), from Ham who had stolen them out of the ark of Noah, and that when Esau saw them, he became jealous because Nimrod's success in hunting was due to the fact that he wore these coats of skin which made the animals prostrate before him. Hence he slew Nimrod.[27] In *Ber. R.* 38:13 (on

---

nings of the name Nimrod: ty*rannus, profugus, transgressor, apostata* (P. de Lagarde, *Onomastica Sacra* (Goettingen: Vandenhoeck, 1870) 9 and 52; also pp. 69 and 124 in the CCSL ed., vol. 72 (Turnhout: Brepols, 1959)).

[27] The elaboration of this theme can best be studied in the extensive Nimrod-haggada in

11,28) we find the motif that Nimrod proposes to Abraham: 'Let us worship the fire'. This is followed by a long discussion between the two resulting in Abraham's being thrown into the fire and being saved, whereas Haran dies in the same fire. Interesting is the motif of fire-worship, since we know from other sources that Nimrod was sometimes identified with Zoroaster who was regarded as the one who introduced the worship of fire. In these same sources we also see that Nimrod-Zoroaster is viewed as the originator of astrology and magic[28] Although testimonies about Nimrod as the originator of fire worship and star worship are found in Christian sources, esp. the Pseudo-Clementine *Homiliae* IX 4-5 (cf. the *Recognitiones* I 30) and the so-called *Cave of the Treasures* 27[29], there can be little doubt that the identification of Nimrod and Zoroaster had a Jewish origin. Bousset has aptly remarked:

"Auch den Juden des babylonischen Tieflandes musz [Zoroaster] von einer bestimmten Zeit an als der Urheber der in ihrer Umgebung herrschenden heidnischen Religion, als der bekannteste und hervorragendste Religionsstifter des Heidentums erschienen sein. So wurde auch für sie Zoroaster Babylonier, Schöpfer der babylonischer Weisheit und Haupt der Chaldäer. Von dort war dann nur ein Schritt zur Identifikation Zoroaster-Nimrod. Die Gestalt des in der jüdischen Sage viel behandelten Tyrannen Nimrod und die des persischen Religionsstifters, dessen Religion auch im babylonischen Tieflande die herrschende geworden war, fliessen nunmehr zusammen, und so haben wir in dieser Identifikation Nimrod-Zoroaster, die auf den ersten Blick wie die Phantasie eines müszigen Kopfes ansieht, einen letzten deutli-

---

the *Sefer ha-Yashar*, which we leave out of account here since we want to restrict the paper to ancient sources. For the late date of Sefer ha-Yashar see H. L. Strack - G. Stemberger, *Einleitung in Talmud und Midrasch* (München: Beck, 1982) 300.

28 See W. Bousset, *Hauptprobleme der Gnosis*, (Göttingen: Vandenhoeck & Ruprecht, 1907 (repr. 1973)) 144ff., esp. 369-378. J. Bidez - F. Cumont, *Les mages hellénisés. Zoroastre, Ostanès et Hystaspe d'après la tradition grecque*, 2 vols. (Paris: Les Belles Lettres, 1938) I 42-44, II 50-55, 60-61, 120-125. K. Preisendanz, Nimrod (1), Pauly-Wissowa's *Realencyclopädie* XVII (1936) 624-627. H. J. Schoeps, *Aus frühchristlicher Zeit*, (Tübingen: Mohr, 1950) 19-24. On the early mediaeval traditions about Nimrod as astrologer see C. H. Haskins, *Studies in the History of Mediaeval Science*, (Cambridge (Mass.): Harvard University Press, 1924) 336-345. Bidez-Cumont II 60f. and Preisendanz 625 also discuss the identification of Nimrod with Orion, a giant and hunter (!) from Greek mythology, in some late sources; I leave this out of account for reasons of space and because this identification probably does not have a Jewish origin.

29 Cf. also the following remark by Epiphanius, *Panarion* I 3, 2-3: "Nimrod, the son of Cush the Ethiopian, the father of Asshur, ruled as a king. (...) The Greeks say that he is Zoroaster and that he went on further east and became the pioneer settler of Bactria. (3) Every transgression in the world was disseminated at this time, for Nimrod was an originator of wrong teaching, astrology and magic, which is what some say of Zoroaster. But in actual fact this was the time of Nimrod the giant; the two, Nimrod and Zoroaster, are far apart in time" (transl. by F. Williams, *The Panarion of Epiphanius of Salamis*, Book I (Leiden: Brill,1987)16-17).

chen Nachklang eines ungemein wichtigen religionsgeschichtlichen Vor-
ganges, nämlich des Vorwärtsdringens der persischen Religion in das baby-
lonische Tiefland."[30]

Much more could and should be said about this fascinating identification,
but space forbids. Anyway, it is clear that the image of Nimrod as the arch-
rebel against God lent itself easily for identification with a person who in a
certain religio-historical constellation could be regarded as the founder of
paganism *par excellence*, in this case the influential Zoroaster.

Back to the midrashim. In *Qohelet Rabba* II 14, 1, where the biblical text
has "The wise man, his eyes are in his head, but the fool walks in darkness",
it is interpreted as alluding to Abraham and Nimrod. The element of darkness is reminiscent of Philo's description of Nimrod as the black one who
does not participate in the light (and cf. also *Gen. R.* 42:4 where Nimrod is
called a Cushite, i.e. Ethiopian, because his father was Cush). In *Devarim
Rabba* II 27 the ministering angels declare before God, "Lo, he [Abraham]
is standing before Amraphel, lo, his sentence is being pronounced, lo, he is
about to be burned". God replied: "I will protect him". When he was cast
into the fiery furnace, God came down and delivered him. Whence this? For
it is said: "I am the Lord that brought you out of Ur of the Chaldees" (Gen
15,7)'. In other haggadic midrashim we have passages dealing with Abraham's being persecuted or sentenced to death or thrown into the fire by
Nimrod, about Nimrod (= Amraphel) being defeated by Abraham, etc. etc.,
but they do not add to our knowledge of the haggada we have already seen
(see *Shir ha-Shirim Rabba* 8, 8, 2: *Vayyiqra Rabba* 27:5, 28:4, 36:4;
Midrash Tehillim 24:8; *Pesiqta Rabbati* 18:3, 33:4; *Pesiqta de Rav Kahana*
8:2; *Tanhuma, Lekh lekha* 2; etc.)[31].

The development does not stop at the end of antiquity. A look at *Pirqe de
Rabbi Eliezer* and especially at *Sepher ha-Yashar* reveals that our hunter
continued to quicken the imagination. And this development went on not
only in Jewish but also in Christian and especially in Islamic circles.[32] Several of the minor midrashim in Jellinek's collection even stand under the
suspicion of being influenced by Islamic Nimrod legends.[33] Be that as it

---

[30] Bousset, *Hauptprobleme* (n.28) 377. Cf. Schoeps' careful remark, "Die Identifikation
Nimrod-Zoroaster könnte bereits rabbinisch sein", in his *Aus frühchristlicher Zeit*
(n.28) 32.

[31] More passages on Nimrod in the haggadic midrashim can be found in the Index Volume to the Soncino translation of the Midrash Rabba.

[32] See besides the surveys mentioned in n. 25, esp. the dissertation by H. Schützinger,
Ursprung und Entwicklung der arabischen Abraham-Nimrod-Legende, diss. Bonn
1962 (unpublished).

[33] See A. Jellinek, *Beth ha-Midrasch*, I 25-34 (*Ma'aseh 'Avraham 'avinu* = A. Wünsche,
Aus Israels Lehrhallen I 14-34), II 118-119 (*Ma'aseh 'Avraham* = Wünsche I 42-45), V
40-41 (*Midrash de 'Avraham 'avinu* = Wünsche I 46-47). References to other mediaeval sources can be found in M. Gaster, *The Exempla of the Rabbis* (New York: Ktav,

may, we have surveyed enough material to draw some provisional conclusions about the developments of the Nimrod haggada and the reasons behind that process.

We have seen that haggada in which Nimrod is mentioned explicitly is found for the first time in the first century C.E. But since we know from Jubilees, from Pseudo-Eupolemus, and from Philo the Epic poet, that already in the second century B.C.E. there was Abraham-haggada in which there had been made a connection between Abraham and the giants, between the tower of Babel and the giants, and between the tower of Babel and Abraham, it is hardly thinkable that the Nimrod-connection was made only two centuries later. Presumably it is accidental and due only to the vicissitudes of fortune that no texts with Nimrod haggada prior to the turn of the era have been preserved. The fact, however, that, once such haggada turns up in the first century C.E., Nimrod is not yet *the* but only one of the antagonists of Abraham, seems to indicate that the growth of Nimrod into the archrebel against God was a gradual process; and the absence of Nimrod in the writings from Qumran seems to point in the same direction.

In this process there were various factors at work. Most probably the earliest factor was the circumstance that the biblical text called Nimrod a *gibbor/gigas*, using the same word as in Gen 6,4 for the offspring of the rebelling sons of God. Additional to that was the fact that Nimrod's kingdom was in Babel in the land of Shinar according to Gen 10, where also the tower was built according to Gen 11, which seemed to leave no other possibility than that Nimrod built the tower. Once Babel and Ur Kasdim were identified and *'ur kasdim* was taken to mean 'the fiery furnace of the Chaldaeans', Abraham must of course have met his famous contemporary and compatriot, and this meeting could only have been an inimical confrontation, resulting in Abraham's miraculous delivery from the fire (on the basis of Gen 15,7). That there must have been such a confrontation was confirmed by the biblical text of Gen 14 which mentions a war between Abraham and several kings among whom the king of Shinar whose name, Amraphel, indicated that he had said to throw Abraham into the furnace. This same king was of course also responsible for the death of Abraham's brother, Haran, who did die in Ur Kasdim (Gen 11,28). Finally, Nimrod's bad character was made clear by his own name which indicated beyond any doubt that he was a rebel (*mrd*) against the Lord and by the word 'hunter' that was also used for his competitor Esau; and for Greek-speaking Jews also by the expression 'a hunter before = *enantion* = against the Lord.

So we see that in the post-biblical exposition of these few biblical verses a wide gamut of haggadic potential is brought to fruition.

1968, repr. of the 1924 ed.), 185. For a discussion of mediaeval manuscript illustrations to Nimrod haggada see K. Appel, Abraham als dreijähriger Knabe im Feuerofen des Nimrod, *Kairos* 25 (1983) 36-40.

14. SEVEN MONTHS' CHILDREN IN JEWISH AND CHRISTIAN LITERATURE FROM ANTIQUITY

In several Jewish and Christian texts from the first five or six centuries of the Christian era we find the curious notion that some of the important figures of Biblical times were seven months' children[1]. The persons referred to are Isaac, Moses, Samuel, Mary and Jesus. In this article these texts will be presented and an attempt will be made to explain what the background is of this idea, an idea which has no basis in the text of the Bible.

In Pseudo-Philo, *Liber Antiquitatum Biblicarum*, XXIII, 8, God speaks as follows: *Et dedi ei [= Abraham] Ysaac et plasmavi eum in metra eius que [= quae] eum genuit, et precepi ei ut cicius restituens redderet eum mihi in mense septimo. Et propterea omnis mulier que [= quae] pepererit septimo mense vivet filius eius, quoniam super eum vocavi gloriam meam*[2].
Another text in which Isaac is presented as a seven months' child, and as well as Isaac the prophet Samuel, is in the Babylonian Talmud, *Rosh Hashanah* 11a: "Whence do we know that Isaac was born on Passover? Because it is written, *On the [next] festival I will return unto thee [Gen., 18, 14].* Now when was [the angel] speaking? Shall I say [he was speaking] on Passover and referring to Pentecost? Could she bear in fifty days? Shall I say then that [he was speaking on] Pentecost and was referring to Tishri? Even in five months could she bear? I must suppose then that he was speaking on Tabernacles and referring to Passover. Even so, could she bear in six months? It has been taught that that year was a leap year. All the same, if the Master deducts the days of uncleanness, the time is too short? Mar Zutra replied: Even those who hold that when a woman bears at nine months she does not give birth

* The author wishes to thank his colleagues Dr. R. van den Broek and Dr. A. van der Kooy for some valuable references, and Dr. James Pankhurst for the correction of the English.

1. The *Shorter Oxford English Dictionary* describes a child born at the seventh month as "a seven months' child".
2. "And I gave him Isaac and formed him in the womb of her that bore him and commanded it that it should restore him quickly and render him unto me in the seventh month. And for this cause every woman that bringeth forth in the seventh month, her child shall live, because upon him did I call my glory" (translation by M.R. JAMES, *The Biblical Antiquities of Philo*, London, 1917 [repr. New York 1971], 142-3). For the Latin text I have used the edition by G. KISCH, *Pseudo-Philo's Liber Antiquitatum Biblicarum*, Notre Dame, 1949.

before the month is complete, admit that if she bears at seven months she can give birth before the month is complete, as it says, *And it came to pass after the cycle of days* [*I Sam.*, 1, 20]; the minimum of cycles is two and the minimum of days is two»[3]. Each cycle (*tekufah*) consists of three months (the year being divided into four cycles) and two cycles consist, therefore, of six months. As the text speaks of Hannah's conception of Samuel, the Talmud takes it as proof that Samuel too was born after six months and two days. Very much the same text is found in *Niddah* 38b and *Jebamoth* 42a.

The tradition is well attested that Moses was born after six or seven months. The texts that testify to this tradition range from the Tannaitic period to the end of the Middle Ages[4]. I only quote some important instances. In *Targum Pseudo-Jonathan* on *Exod.*, 2, 2 we read : «And the woman [= Jochebed] conceived and bore a son [= Moses] at the end of six months; and she saw him to be a child of steadfastness (or, of steadfast life) and hid him three months, which made the number nine»[5]. In *Mekhilta de Rabbi Shimon ben Jochai* p. 6, 17 Epstein-Melamed[6] we read : «The Egyptians counted nine months for her, but she bore in six months». This is said, of course, to explain why in *Ex.*, 2, 2 it could be written that Jochebed hid Moses for three months. This was only possible because the Egyptians expected the birth of the child three months later than it was actually born. In some texts (e.g. *Shemoth Rabbah* I 19) the curious detail is added that Jochebed was 130 years old when she bore Moses[7].

It is interesting to see that in a later stage of development this tradition is explained away. *Shemoth Rabbah* I 20 clearly rationalizes when it comments on the words «and she [= Jochebed] hid him three months» (*Ex.*, 2, 2) with : «[This was possible] because the Egyptians counted from the time he took her back, when she was already three months pregnant with him». The tradition that Moses

3. The translation is by M. Simon in the Soncino edition, London 1938, 41. The Soncino-translations of the Talmud and Midrash will be used throughout this article.

4. See L. GINZBERG, *The Legends of the Jews*, V (1925), 397 n. 44. E. B. LEVINE, *Parallels to Exodus of Pseudo-Jonathan and Neophyti I*, in A. DiEZ MACHO (ed.), *Neophyti I*, vol. III, Madrid-Barcelona, 1971, 424. A large number of haggadic traditions about Moses' birth are collected by R. BLOCH, *Moïse dans la tradition rabbinique*, in H. CAZELLES (and others), *Moïse, l'homme de l'alliance*, Paris, 1955, 102-118. Surprisingly and disappointingly Bloch wholly omits the data about the length of his gestation.

5. Translation by J. W. ETHERIDGE, *The Targums of Onkelos and Jonathan ben Uzziel on the Pentateuch with the Fragments of the Jerusalem Targum*, I (1862), 446.

6. J. N. EPSTEIN-E. Z. MELAMED (edd.), *Mekhilta d'Rabbi Shim'on ben Jochai*, Jerusalem, 1955.

7. On the midrashic chronology implied here see J. HEINEMANN, *210 Years of Egyptian Exile*, in *Journal of Jewish Studies*, 22 (1971), 19-30.

was born after six months is taken to mean : six months after Jochebed's remarriage with Amram, who (in *Sh. R.* I 13) is said to have divorced his wife, who was already three months pregnant, after Pharaoh's decree but to have immediately remarried her after Miriam reproved him strongly for his action. David Daube's comments are worth quoting[8] : «One or two orthodox solutions [sc. to the problem that Moses was born whereas the Israelites had no sexual intercourse in Egypt at that time] are still extant. For example, when Pharaoh promulgated his decree and Amram, because of his threat to any male offspring, divorced Jochebed, she was already in the third month of pregnancy. But the relative lateness of this explanation is obvious. First the narrative of the separation of Amram and Jochebed is preserved in two sources; yet only one of these [sc. *Shemoth Rabbah* I 13 and I 20] contains the notice that she was already with child. Secondly, if she was already with child, how could her husband hope to thwart Pharaoh's plan by divorcing her? Clearly, in the original version of the narrative she was not pregnant»[9].

Of New Testament persons[10] it is said of Mary and of Jesus that they were born at seven months. In the *Protevangelium Jacobi*, V, 2 we read about Anna, the mother of Mary : καὶ ἐπληρώθησαν οἱ μῆνες αὐτῆς ὡς εἶπεν ἕξ, τῷ δὲ ἑβδόμῳ μηνὶ ἐγέννησεν ˝Αννα. True, the majority of manuscripts omits the number "six" and reads "in the ninth month". But since Testuz published the Bodmer Papyrus of this text[11] in 1958, which is the oldest and best extant manuscript of this treatise, there is no more doubt that «the seventh month» was in the

8. *The New Testament and Rabbinic Judaism*, London, 1956, 7.

9. For later texts on Moses' early birth see GINZBERG, *Legends*, V, 397, n. 44, though some of his references are faulty. To mention only one example : *Midrash Haggadol* on *Ex.* II 2 says that in the night that Jochebed became pregnant Pharaoh had a dream. "Then the Egyptians counted nine months for they did not know that all prophets are born in only seven months, and Moses is the father of the prophets". (The Hebrew text is in M. MARGULIES (ed.), *Midrash Haggadol on the Pentateuch. Exodus*, Jerusalem, 1956, 24). See also Rashi's commentary on *Ex.*, 2, 2. Cf. M. ABRAHAM, *Légendes juives apocryphes sur la vie de Moïse*, Paris, 1925, 49.

10. A fourth Old Testament instance mentioned by GINZBERG, *Legends*, VI, 217, does not belong here. It is Ichabod, the son of Phineas, who is born after seven months according to Josephus, *Antiquitates*, V, 361. The reason that he is born is that the mother dies from fright when she hears of Phineas' death. In *Seder Olam (Rabbah)*, II, 10f. (p. 9 in the edition of B. Ratner (1897, repr. 1966), p. 5 in the edition of A. Marx (1903)) we find the very short remark that the sons of Jacob were born in seven months. This theme recurs in *Pirqe de Rabbi Eliezer* 36 ("Lea bore her sons after seven months"). In the light of the following discussion it would seem to me that we find here an expansion of the motif towards the famous patriarchs whereas the original background has been lost. That is also the case with the expansion to the prophets in *Midrash Haggadol*, quoted above.

11. M. TESTUZ (ed.), *Papyrus Bodmer V. Nativité de Marie*, Geneva, 1958.

original text [12]. And this is confirmed by the fact that one of the three Armenian versions also has : «in the seventh month» [13].

As to Jesus : there is a dubious fragment of the Gospel according to the Hebrews [14], quoted by Pseudo-Cyrillus of Jerusalem in his *Discourse on Mary Theotokos* (which is preserved only in Coptic), where Jesus is said to have been born after seven months [15] : «It is written in the [Gospel] to the Hebrews that when Christ wished to come upon the earth to men the Good Father called a mighty 'power' in the heavens which was called 'Michael', and committed Christ to the care thereof. And the 'power' came down into the world, and it was called Mary, and [Christ] was in her womb for seven months (*afšope hñ teskalahè ñsašf ñebot*). Afterwards she gave birth to Him, and He increased in stature, and He chose the apostles, who preached him in every place». Here again, just as in *Protev. Jac.*, V, 2, there are witnesses that read "nine months" [16], but the secondary character of such a reading is obvious. That such traditions about Jesus did exist, is confirmed by Epiphanius, *Panarion*, LI, 29, 3, where, in a discussion of speculation on Jesus' birth-date, he speaks of τὴν ὑπόνοιαν τῶν τινῶν λεγόντων ἐν παραδόσει, ὡς ὅτι διὰ ἑπτὰ μηνῶν ἐγεννήθη [17].

How to explain this feature in the passages quoted? Both L. H. Feldmann [18] and S. Liebermann [19] refer to the ancient Greek theory that seven months' children are viable whereas eight months' children are

---

12. See TESTUZ, *op. cit.*, 48-50. It is adopted by E. DE STRYCKER, *La forme la plus ancienne du Protévangile de Jacques* (Subsidia Hagiographica, 33), Brussel, 1961, 86ff. See also O. CULLMANN, "Kindheitsevangelien", in E. HENNECKE-W. SCHNEEMELCHER, *Neutestamentliche Apokryphen*, I, Tübingen, 1959, 282 (contrast M. R. JAMES, *The Apocryphal New Testament*, Oxford, 1924, 41).

13. DE STRYCKER, *op. cit.* 462. It is nice to see how both Testuz and de Strycker try to explain this "seventh month". Testuz 51 n. 1 remarks : "Il faut supposer que l'ange avait annoncé la naissance de Marie au second mois de la grossesse". And de Strycker, 87, n. 6 : "Nous ne pensons pas que l'auteur ait eu en vue une naissance miraculeusement anticipée. Les "six mois" et le "septième" sont comptés à partir du retour de Joachim, retour qui suit de plus d'un mois la conception miraculeuse". These evasions are comparable to the way that *Shemoth Rabbah* I 20, for example, deals with the tradition of Moses' birth at seven months.

14. PH. VIELHAUER, *Judenchristliche Evangelien*, in HENNECKE-SCHNEEMELCHER, *op. cit.*, I, 88, strongly doubts whether it actually belongs to that Gospel. Nevertheless he prints it as fragment nr. 1 on p. 107. Cf. JAMES, *Apocryphal N.T.*, 8. This uncertainty, however, does not affect our discussion.

15. In E. A. W. BUDGE, *Miscellaneous Coptic Texts in the Dialect of Upper Egypt*, London, 1915, 60 (Coptic text) and 637 (English translation).

16. E.g. Cod. 583 of the Pierpont Morgan Library; see H. HYVERNAT (ed.), *Bibliothecae Pierpont Morgan Codices Coptici photographice expressi*, vol. 41, Rome 1922, 294.

17. *Ibid.*, LI, 29, 6 he says : τινὲς δέ φασιν, ὡς δέκα μῆνας ἐνεκυμονήθη.

18. In the Prolegomena of the reprint of James' translation of Pseudo-Philo, New York, 1971, CX.

19. *Hellenism in Jewish Palestine*, New York, 1950, 76f.

not. This was indeed a widespread theory in antiquity, based on popular beliefs concerning the number seven. As early as in Herodotus, it is reported as a well-known fact : in *Hist. VI*, 69 the mother of Demaratus, king of Sparta, tells him that he has been begotten by the hero Astrabacus and was born after seven months. But Ariston, his putative father, ὅτε αὐτῷ σὺ ἠγγέλθης γεγενημένος, πολλῶν ἀκουόντων οὐ φήσειέ σε ἑωυτοῦ εἶναι (τὸν χρόνον γάρ, τοὺς δέκα μῆνας, οὐδέκω ἐξήκειν), ἀιδρείῃ τῶν τοιούτων κεῖνος τοῦτο ἀπέρριψε τὸ ἔπος. τίκτουσι γὰρ γυναῖκες καὶ ἐννεάμηνα καὶ ἑπτάμηνα, καὶ οὐ πᾶσαι δέκα μῆνας ἐκτελέσασαι. ἐγὼ δὲ σὲ ὦ παῖ ἑπτάμηνον ἔτεκον. But though in origin a popular theory[20], it was developed firstly by Greek philosophers, foremost among them Pythagoras or his school, and secondly by Greek physicians, especially Hippocrates[21]. Some texts will suffice to illustrate this. Alexander of Aphrodisias, *Problemata Physica*, II, 47 : διὰ τί τὰ ἑπτάμηνα βρέφη ζώσιμα, τὰ δ' ὀκτωμηνιαῖα οὐκέτι; ὅτι ὁ ἑπτὰ ἀριθμὸς τέλειός ἐστι τῇ φύσει, ὡς μαρτυρεῖ Πυθαγόρας καὶ οἱ ἀριθμητικοὶ καὶ οἱ μουσικοί· ὁ δ' ὀκτὼ ἀτελής[22]. Galen, *Defin. medic.*, 450 : διὰ ποίαν αἰτίαν τῶν ἑπταμήνων γονίμων ὄντων τὰ ὀκτάμηνα ἄγονά ἐστιν; λέγεται οὕτως· ὅτι ὁ ὀκτὼ ἀριθμὸς ἄρτιός ἐστι καὶ συνεζευγμένος μὴ κρίσιμος ὤν· ὁ δὲ ἑπτὰ ἀριθμὸς περιττὸς καὶ οὐδὲ συνεζευγμένος καὶ διὰ τοῦτο κρίσιμος[23]. Very important in this respect is Galen's *Phil. hist.*, 34 (XIX pp. 331-334 Kühn) : διὰ τί ἑπτάμηνα γόνιμα, a chapter in which he presents the views of the important philosophers and physicians (Empedocles, Timaeus, Polybus, Diocles, Hippocrates, Aristotle) on this matter. Galen himself also wrote a treatise Περὶ ἑπταμήνων, which was until 45 years ago only known in an Arabic translation, but now the Greek

---

20. See P. DIEPGEN, *Die Frauenheilkunde der alten Welt*, München, 1937, 160f. W. H. ROSCHER, *Die enneadischen und hebdomadischen Fristen und Wochen der ältesten Griechen. Ein Beitrag zur vergleichenden Chronologie und Zahlenmystik* (Abhandlungen der königlichen Sächsischen Gesellschaft der Wissenschaften, Philologisch-historische Klasse, XXI, 4), Leipzig, 1903, 51f. 67.

21. W.H. ROSCHER, *Die Hebdomadenlehren der griechischen Philosophen und Ärzte* (Abhandlungen der königlichen Sächsischen Gesellschaft der Wissenschaften, Philologisch-historische Klasse, XXIV, 6), Leipzig, 1906, esp. 33ff. Cf. also his earlier study *Die Sieben- und Neunzahl im Kultus und Mythus der Griechen* (ibid., XXIV 1), Leipzig, 1904, 23. On hebdomadic speculations in Greek embryology see also J. MANSFELD, *The Pseudo-Hippocratic Tract Περὶ Ἑβδομάδων Ch. 1-11 and Greek Philosophy*, Assen, 1971, 164ff.

22. In I.L. IDELER, *Physici et medici Graeci minores*, Amsterdam, 1963 (= one volume reprint of the 2 volumes edition of 1841), I, p. 65. Already this text illustrates that this theory has more to do with arithmetic speculations than with empiricism. Cf. the remark of the Pythagorean Hippo of Metapontum in Censorinus, *De die natali*, VII, 2 : *septimo* [*sc. mense*] *partum iam esse maturum eo quod in omnibus numerus septenarius plurimum possit*. See ROSCHER, *Hebdomadenlehren*, 36f.

23. In *Medici Graeci*, XIX, p. 454 Kühn (Leipzig, 1830).

text has been partially discovered[24]. His great forerunner Hippocrates wrote a treatise Περὶ ὀκταμήνων (*Oct.*) and under Hippocrates' name there also circulated a Περὶ ἑπταμήνου (*Sept.*) which contested several views of Περὶ ὀκταμήνων[25]! (In particular, the view that an eight months' child was not viable was a debated issue in antiquity[26]). From these and many other writings one might quote at random to illustrate this current opinion about seven months' children[27]. That this theory also penetrated into Judaism is illustrated by Philo and the Rabbis. E.g. Philo, *Opif. mundi*, 124 : καὶ τὰ κατὰ γαστρὸς βρέφη μησὶν ἑπτὰ τελειογονεῖσθαι πέφυκεν, ὡς παραδοξότατόν τι συμβαίνειν. γίνεται γὰρ τὰ ἑπτάμηνα γόνιμα, τῶν ὀκτωμηνιαίων ὡς ἐπίπαν ζῳο- γονεῖσθαι μὴ δυναμένων. — *Leg. alleg.*, I, 9 : τίς γὰρ οὐκ οἶδεν ὅτι τῶν βρεφῶν τὰ μὲν ἑπτάμηνα γόνιμα, τὰ δὲ πλείω χρόνον προσλα- βόντα, ὡς ὀκτὼ μῆνας ἐνδιαιτηθῆναι γαστρί, κατὰ τὸ πλεῖστον ἄγονα[28]; From the Mishnah, *Jebamoth* 4, 2 : «If it is in doubt whether what is born is a nine-months' child of the former [husband] or a seven-months' child of the latter [husband], he must put her away» (cf. 11, 6)[29]. The Gemara on this passage in the Babylonian Talmud, *Jebamoth* 37a : «Most women bear at nine months and a minority at seven» (cf. 80b; *Niddah* 8b, 24b, 27a). *Shabbath* 135a : « It was taught by our Rabbis : For a seven-months' infant one may desecrate the Sabbath, but for an eight-months' infant one may not desecrate the Sabbath. For one in doubt whether he is a seven-months' or an eight-months' infant, one may not desecrate the Sabbath. An eight-months' infant is like a stone and may not be handled» (cf. 136a). From

24. See R. WALZER, *Galens Schrift über die Siebenmonatskinder*, in *Rivista degli Studi Orientali*, 15 (1935), 323-357. This article contains, besides an Introduction, the Arabic text, the Greek text and a German translation.

25. Both treatises are now easily accessible in the new edition (with translation and commentary) by H. GRENSEMANN (ed.), *Hippokrates. Über Achtmonatskinder. Über das Siebenmonatskind* (Corpus Medicorum Graecorum, I, 2, 1), Berlin, 1968.

26. See GRENSEMANN's Introduction, *passim*; and DIEPGEN, *Frauenheilkunde* 162f.

27. See besides the references in the works of Diepgen and Roscher, the numerous passages quoted by J.H. WASZINK in his commentary on Tertullianus, *De Anima*, 37, 4 (p. 428; Amsterdam, 1947), and especially by B.H. STRICKER, *De geboorte van Horus*, III, Leiden, 1975, 338f. See e.g. PS-ARIST., *Hist. anim.*, VII, 4, 584a36ff.; PLUTARCH, *Plac. philos.*, V, 18, 907F-908C; MACROBIUS, *Comm. in Somn. Scip.*, I, 6, 14-16; JOH. LYDUS, *De mensibus*, II, 12; PS-HIPPOCRATES, *Nutr.*, 42. One might add some texts that prove that the facts did not always fit in with the theory : CICERO, *Ep. ad Att.*, X, 18, 1 : *Tullia mea peperit ... puerum* ἑπταμηνιαῖον. *Quod* εὐτόκησεν *gaudeo. Quod quidem est natum perimbecillum est.* Cf. also THEOPHANES CONFESSOR, *Chronographia*, 45 (MG, 108, 169A).

28. The long passage *Opif.*, 89-128, as well as *Leg. Alleg.*, I, 8-16, is devoted to a discussion of the heptadic structure of reality; cf. *Leg. Alleg.*, I, 8 : χαίρει δὲ ἡ φύσις ἑβδομάδι. Cf. *Pesikta de Rab Kahana* 23, 10. On Jewish hebdomadic interests see N. WALTER, *Der Thoraausleger Aristobulos*, Berlin, 1964, 67-81 and 166-171.

29. H. DANBY, *The Mishnah*, Oxford 1933, 223.

the Midrashim, *Bereshith Rabbah* XIV 2 : «There is a viable birth at nine [months] and a viable birth at seven [months]. R. Huna said : When the foetus is so formed as to be born at seven months, and it is born either at seven or at nine months, it is viable; if born at eight months, it cannot live. When it is formed so as to be born at nine but yet it is born at seven months, it cannot live, and all the more so if it is born at eight months. R. Abbahu was asked : 'How do we know that when the foetus is fully developed at seven months it is viable?' 'From your own [language] I will prove it to you', replied he : 'Live, seven; go, eight'".[30] Here too one might go on quoting[31].

But it is more useful now to adduce only some texts that will make clear why in *Rosh Hashanah* 11a, in Targum *Pseudo-Jonathan* on *Exod.*, 2, 2, in *Mekhilta R.S.* p. 6 and in *Protev. Jacobi*, V, 2 it is said of Isaac, Samuel, Moses and Mary that they were born after *six* months, whereas elsewhere or even in the same texts they are called *seven* months' children. Very illuminating in this respect is a text in Hippocrates, *Oct.*, 4, 8-10 (pp. 88, 17-90, 2 Grensemann), which I will quote in Grensemann's translation for the sake of clarity : "Die Siebenmonatsgeburten treten nach 182 Tagen und einem Bruchteil ein, der hinzukommt. Denn wenn man auf den ersten Monat 15 Tage rechnet, auf die fünf Monate aber 147,5 Tage — denn in ungefähr 59 Tage vollenden sich zwei Monate — so bleiben unter dieser Voraussetzung für den siebten Monat, d.h. bis zur Hälfte des Jahres, (etwas) mehr als 20 Tage, da ein Bruchteil des Tages zu dem Bruchteil hinzukommt"[32]. In his commentary (on p. 111) Grensemann remarks : "Bei dieser Rechnung ist darauf zu achten, dasz unter Monaten Mondmonate zu verstehen sind (2 Mondmonate sind 59 Tage, ein Mondmonat etwa 29,5 Tag) — unter dem Jahr aber ein Sonnenjahr (über 365 Tage) und

---

30. In his translation, *Midrash Rabbah* I, London 1939, 112 n. 1 FREEDMAN notes : «ζῆτα, the Greek letter *Zeta*, whose numerical value is seven, is phonetically like ζήτω, let it live!, while ἦτα (the letter η), whose numerical value is eight, sounds like ἴτω, let it go! (i.e. die)". But LIEBERMANN, *Hellenism in Jewish Palestine*, 77 says : «Since ζ equals 7 and η 8 the cryptogram has to be deciphered as : ζῇ τὰ ἑπτὰ ⟨μᾶλλον⟩ ἢ τὰ ὀκτώ, i.e. "Infants of seven months are more likely to survive than those of eight"». This solution was first proposed by L. COHN in *Monatsschrift für Geschichte und Wissenschaft des Judentums*, 44 (1910), 568f. (in a review of S. KRAUSS, *Griech. u. lat. Lehnwörter im Talmud, Midrasch und Targum*, 2 vols., 1898-9).

31. Cf. *Ber. Rabbah* 20, 6; *Bamidbar Rabbah* 4, 3. For more passages see again STRICKER, *De geboorte van Horus*, III, 339. n. 3039 and J. PREUSS, *Biblisch-talmudische Medizin* (1911), 456f., who discusses these texts.

32. Οἱ δὲ ἑπτάμηνοι γίνονται ἐκ τῶν ἑκατὸν ἡμερέων καὶ ὀγδοήκοντα καὶ δύο καὶ προσεόντος μορίου. ἢν γὰρ τοῦ πρώτου λογίσῃ μηνὸς πεντεκαίδεκα ἡμέρας, τῶν δὲ πέντε μηνῶν ἑκατὸν καὶ τεσσαράκοντα καὶ ἑπτὰ καὶ ἥμισυ ἡμέρης — ἐν γὰρ ἑξήκοντα μιῆς δεούσῃσιν ἡμερῇσιν ἐγγύτατα δύο μῆνες ἐκτελεῦνται —, οὕτως οὖν τούτων ἐόντων ἐς τὸν ἕβδομον μῆνα περιγίνονται ἡμέραι πλεῖον ἢ εἴκοσιν ἥμισει τοῦ ἐνιαυτοῦ τῆς ἡμέρης τοῦ μέρεος τῷ μέρει προσγινομένου.

dasz ferner das halbe Jahr als halbes Sonnenjahr gerechnet wird, nicht als das Sechsfache eines Mondmonates». So the word "month" is used in two ways in our sources. And those who use it in the sense of lunar month, as does Hippocrates, say that a seven-months' child is born after exactly a half year, that is : six months in the other sense. Moreover, of the first month only the second half is counted, *i.e.* from the supposed moment of conception onwards. Cf. Polybus[33] in Clemens Alexandrinus, *Strom.*, VI, 16, 6 : ἡ ἀπὸ τροπῶν ἐπὶ τροπὰς κίνησις τοῦ ἡλίου ἐν ἓξ συντελεῖται μησίν ... φασὶ δὲ καὶ τὸ ἔμβρυον ἀπαρτίζεσθαι πρὸς ἀκρίβειαν μηνὶ τῷ ἕκτῳ, τουτέστιν ἑκατὸν ἡμέραις καὶ ὀγδοήκοντα πρὸς ταῖς δύο καὶ ἡμίσει, ὡς ἱστορεῖ Πόλυβος ὁ ἰατρὸς ἐν τῷ περὶ ὀκταμήνων. Cf. Aetius, *Placita* V 18, 5 : Πόλυβος ἑκατὸν ὀγδοήκοντα δύο καὶ ἥμισυ ἡμέρας γίνεσθαι εἰς τὰ γόνιμα. εἶναι γὰρ ἑξάμηνα, ὅτι καὶ τὸν ἥλιον ἀπὸ τροπῶν ⟨ἐπὶ τροπὰς⟩ ἐν τοσούτῳ χρόνῳ παραγίνεσθαι, λέγεσθαι δὲ ἑπτάμηνα, ὅτι τὰς ἐλλειπούσας ἡμέρας τοῦ πρώτου μηνὸς ἐν τῷ ἑβδόμῳ προσλαμβάνεσθαι[34]. Of course, there were other ways of reckoning; see only Varro in Censorinus, *De die natali* 11, 2, who speaks of *septemmestrem, qui decimo et ducentesimo die* [= on the 210th day] *post conceptionem exeat ab utero.* And Galen says that practically all seven-months' children are born between 184 and 204 days after the conception[35]. That Hippocrates' and Polybus' way of reckoning was also known in Jewish circles is again proved by Philo and the Rabbis. E.g. in his long passage on the *hebdomas* in *Opif.* he says in 116 : ὅ τε μέγας ἡγεμὼν ἡμέρας ἥλιος διττὰς καθ' ἕκαστον ἐνιαυτὸν ἀποτελῶν ἰσημερίας, ἔαρι καὶ μετωπώρῳ, ... ἐνεργεστάτην παρέχεται πίστιν τοῦ περὶ τὴν ἑβδόμην θεοπρεποῦς. ἑκατέρα γὰρ τῶν ἰσημεριῶν ἑβδόμῳ γίνεται μηνί. The same reasoning is found in *Decal.*, 161, *Spec. leg.*, I, 182 and II, 150. For Rabbinic material we may refer to the texts mentioned above in connection with Samuel's birth (*Rosh Hashanah* 11a; *Niddah* 38b; *Jebamoth* 42a).

As, however, all this material does not provide us with a solution to the problem why such an early birth is ascribed to these five Biblical persons, we need other materials for further clarification. We have to ask : are there texts in Greek and Latin literature where concrete instances (be it mythical or historal) of seven months' children are mentioned? Yes, there are, but these instances are as rare as in Jewish and Christian literature, amounting to only six or seven cases. First of all, Apollo, about which case there are only some late testimonies.

---

33. Polybus was a pupil of Hippocrates.
34. See on these two texts of Polybus Grensemann, *op. cit.*, 55ff. See also Galen's comments on Hippocrates' way of reckoning, *Sept.* 49ff. (Walzer's translation in *Rivista degli Study Orientali*, 15 [1935], 351).
35. *Sept.* 8f. (Walzer's translation, *ibid.* 349).

A scholion on Callimachus, *Hymn.*, IV, 251 : ἑπταμηναῖος ... ἐτέχθη ὁ Ἀπόλλων. Further the *Hypothesis* to Pindarus, *Pyth.* : ἑπτάφθογγον δὲ αὐτὴν [sc. the lyre] ἐποίησεν [sc. Apollo]. ... τάχα ἑπτὰ φθόγγοις αὐτὴν ἐκέρασε διὰ τὸ αὐτὸν ἑπταμηναῖον γεγενῆσθαι[36].

There are more texts on Dionysus[37] as ἑπταμηναῖος, but the traditions are in conflict here. One tradition says that he was born after six or seven months as a full-grown baby out of Semele, another that after his premature birth at seven months he still had to mature for some months in Zeus' thigh, yet another that he was born as a full-grown seven months' child out of Zeus' thigh! Diodorus Siculus I, 23, 4 says of Semele : ταύτην δὲ ὑφ᾽ ὅτου δήποτε φθαρεῖσαν ἔγκυον γενέσθαι, καὶ τεκεῖν ἑπτὰ μηνῶν διελθόντων βρέφος τὴν ὄψιν οἷόνπερ οἱ κατ᾽ Αἴγυπτον τὸν Ὄσιριν γεγονέναι νομίζουσι. This was actually Osiris[38], but Orpheus later on made the Greeks believe that it was Dionysus, says Diodorus[39]. An anonymous author in Westermann's *Mythographi*[40], p. 385 gives the following full and amusing account of Dionysis' birth : Σεμέλη δὲ Κάδμου ἦν θυγάτηρ. ταύτης ἠράσθη ὁ Ζεὺς καὶ συγγίνεται αὐτῇ, ἡ δὲ συλλαβοῦσα εἶχεν ἐξ αὐτοῦ τὸν Διόνυσον. ἡ δε Ἥρα ζηλοτύπως φερομένη σχηματίζεται πρόσωπον τροφοῦ ἐγνωσμένης τῇ Σεμέλῃ, καὶ συμβουλεύει αὐτῇ τῇ Σεμέλῃ ἐγκύῳ οὔσῃ ὅτι "αἴτησαι τὸν Δία συγγενέσθαι σοι ὥσπερ συγγίνεται τῇ Ἥρᾳ". συνεγίνετο δὲ ὁ Ζεὺς τῇ Ἥρᾳ μετὰ βροντῶν καὶ κεραυνῶν. ταῦτα δὲ συνεβούλευεν ἡ Ἥρα τῇ Σεμέλῃ, ἵνα ἐρχομένου τοῦ Διὸς μετὰ κεραυνῶν πρὸς αὐτὴν ὡς θνητὴ καταφλεχθήσεται, καὶ μηκέτι ἔχοι τὴν ἀντίζηλον. ὃ δὴ καὶ γέγονε. τοῦ γὰρ Διὸς ἐλθόντος πάλιν πρὸς τὴν Σεμέλην ἤτησεν ἡ Σεμέλη οὕτως αὐτη συγγενέσθαι ὡς τῇ Ἥρᾳ· καὶ ὡς συνεγένετο αὐτῇ, κεραυνοῦται καὶ ἀπόλλυται ἡ Σεμέλη. καὶ τότε λαβὼν ὁ Ζεὺς τὸν Διόνυσον ἔμβρυον ὄντα ἔρραψεν ἐν τῇ ἑαυτοῦ μηρῷ· καὶ ὕστερον ἐν τῷ ἑβδόμῳ μηνὶ ἐλθὼν ὁ Ἑρμῆς ἀναπτύσσει τὸν μηρὸν τοῦ Διὸς καὶ γεννᾶται, ὥς φασιν, ὁ Διόνυσος.

Very different as to the time of Dionysus' birth are the following accounts : Apollodorus, *Bibl.*, III, 4, 3 : Ζεὺς δὲ ... παραγίνεται εἰς τὸν θάλαμον αὐτῆς (= Σεμέλης) ἐφ᾽ ἄρματος ἀστραπαῖς ὁμοῦ καὶ βρονταῖς, καὶ κεραυνὸν ἵησιν. Σεμέλης δὲ διὰ τὸν φόβον ἐκλιπούσης,

36. Quoted from A. BOECKH, *Pindari Opera*, II, Leipzig, 1819, 297.

37. PROCLUS, *Comm. in Timaeum*, III, 200 C (II p. 197 Diehl), says of Apollo and Dionysus : ὁ ἀριθμὸς κοινός ἐστιν ἀμφοτέροις ἡ ἑβδομάς. ROSCHER, *Hebdomadenlehren*, 210, n. 292, thinks that ARNOBIUS, *Adv. Nat.*, III, 10 (*deas ... praepropero partu septimanas edere aliquando foeturas*) refers to Apollo and Dionysus. This is doubtful, the more so if one realizes that Semele, Dionysus' mother, was not a goddess (see H. J. ROSE, *A Handbook of Greek Mythology*[6], London, 1958, 149).

38. For an Egyptian text (*Osiris Mystery*, 97-98) on Osiris as a seven months' child see STRICKER, *De geboorte van Horus*, III, 246f.

39. Cf. PLUTARCH, *Is. et Os.*, 35, 364 E ὁ αὐτός ἐστι [sc. Osiris] Διονύσῳ.

40. A. WESTERMANN (ed.), ΜΥΘΟΓΡΑΦΟΙ, Brunswick, 1843.

ἐξαμηνιαῖον τὸ βρέφος ἐξαμβλωθὲν (!) ἐκ τοῦ πυρὸς ἁρπάσας ἐνέρραψε τῷ μηρῷ. ... κατὰ δὲ τὸν χρόνον τὸν καθήκοντα Διόνυσον γεννᾷ Ζεὺς λύσας τὰ ῥάμματα. Exactly the same account is found in a scholion on Homer, *Ilias* XIV 325, and also Lucian, *Dial. deor.*, IX (12), 2, 228 says that, when Semele was burnt, Hermes cut open her womb and brought to Zeus the half-formed seven-months' child (ἀτελὲς ... τὸ ἔμβρυον ἑπτάμηνον), that had to finish its growth in Zeus' thigh for two months. The same tradition must lie behind Philo's statement, *Omnis probus liber*, 130, that Zeus pulled out the fruit of her womb in a premature stage of existence (τὴν τοῦ κατὰ γαστρὸς φύσιν ἠλιτό-μηνον[41]). A spurious line in Cornutus, *Nat. deor.*, 2 (p. 10 Osann; not in Lang's edition), says : (Ζεὺς) ἔτεκε δὲ καὶ τὸν Διόνυσον ἐκ τοῦ ἰδίου μηροῦ ἐπταμηνιαῖον παρὰ τῆς Σεμέλης. This too points in the same direction. All these texts do not admit of a decision as to which tradition was the older one, though the one that Dionysus as a seven months' child was not viable looks more primitive. Be that as it may, to speak of Dionysus as a classical and famous example of a seven months' child, as Roscher and Stricker do[42], needs some qualification[43].

Another more or less dubious case is Heracles, which has to be dealt with together with Eurystheus, Heracles' great antagonist, which is most unanimously attested as a seven months' child. Already in Homer, *Ilias*, XIX, 115-118, Eurystheus is said to have been born in the seventh month by a trick of Hera, who delayed the birth of Heracles : ἡ δ᾽ ἐκύει φίλον υἱόν [sc. Eurystheus], ὁ δ᾽ ἕβδομος ἑστήκει μείς [= μήν]. ἐκ δ᾽ ἄγαγε πρὸ φόωσδε καὶ ἠλιτόμηνον ἐόντα, ᾽Αλκμήνης [= Heracles' mother] δ᾽ ἀπέπαυσε τόκον. (See for the whole story *Il.*, XIX, 95ff.). All later texts draw the correct conclusion that Eurystheus was a seven-months' child, as for example a scholion on *Il.*, XIX, 118f. : ῞Ηρα δὲ ζηλοτύπως διατεθεῖσα τὰς μὲν ᾽Αλκμήνης ὠδῖνας ἐπέσχεν, ᾽Αντιβίαν δέ, ... τὴν Σθενέλου γυναῖκα, κυοφοροῦσαν Εὐρυσθέα ἑπτάμηνον τεκεῖν ἐποίησεν· ὅθεν καὶ τὰ ἑπτάμηνα γεννώμενα ζωῆς μοῖραν εἴληχε (see also Apollodorus, *Bibl.*, II, 4, 5). As to Heracles however, two testimonies say that he was a ten months' child, whereas others say he was a seven months' child. *Hypothesis IV* to Hesiod's *Scutum*[44] says : (αὕτη μὲν ἐγέννησε τὸν Εὐρυσθέα ἑπτάμηνον ...) ᾽Αλκμήνη δὲ ἐγέννησε τὸν ῾Ηρακλέα δεκάμηνον. That

---

41. ἠλιτόμηνος means : missing the right month.

42. ROSCHER, *Die Sieben- und Neunzahl* ..., 27; STRICKER, *De geboorte van Horus*, 283.

43. In this connection it is interesting to point out that until the twentieth century there was a carnival celebration in Thracia with all kinds of Dionysian elements, among which a seven months' child was an important one. See J.G. FRAZER, *The Golden Bough, VII : Spirits of the Corn and of the Wild I*, London, 1912, 26.

44. In A. RZACH's edition of Hesiod, Leipzig, 1902, 270.

this tradition is old is proved by Plautus, *Amphitryo* 479-483 : *nunc de Alcumena dudum quo dixi minus, hodie illa pariet filios geminos duos: alter decumo post mense nascetur puer quam seminatust, alter mense septumo; eorum Amphitruonis alter est, alter Iovis.* However, a scholion on Homer, *Ilias*, XIV, 323, says : ἐρασθεὶς αὐτῆς [sc. ᾽Αλκμήνης] ὁ Ζεὺς καὶ εἰκασθεὶς ᾽Αμφιτρύωνι ἐμίγη καὶ υἱὸν ἐποίησεν. ὁμοίως δὲ καὶ ᾽Αμφιτρύων τῇ αὐτῇ νυκτί. ἤδη δ' ἐκείνης τὸν ἑπταμηνιαῖον χρόνον τῆς μίξεως ἐχούσης, γεννᾶται Ἡρακλῆς μὲν ἐκ Διός, Ἰφικλῆς δὲ ἐξ ᾽Αμφιτρύωνος. ... ἡ ἱστορία παρὰ Φερεκύδει[45]. And in Iamblichus, *Vita Pyth.* 152, we read : Ἡρακλεῖ δὲ δεῖν θυσιάζειν ὀγδόῃ τοῦ μηνὸς ἱσταμένου σκοποῦντας τὴν ἑπτάμηνον γένεσιν[46]. So there have been two contradictory traditions about the birth of Heracles.

To sum up the results concerning the mythical figures : there are only two late texts on Apollo; conflicting traditions on both Dionysus and Heracles; only Eurystheus is unanimously attested as seven months' child from Homer onwards.

As to non-mythical persons, I know only two texts that mention instances. Firstly there is a passage in Pliny, *Nat. Hist.*, VII, 38-39, which also reflects an interesting piece of discussion (possibly going back to Ps-Aristotle, *Hist. anim.* VII 4, 584a36ff.) : *homo toto anno et incerto gignitur spatio, alius septimo mense, alius octavo et usque ad initium undecimi; ante septimum mensem haut umquam vitalis est, septimo non nisi pridie posterove pleniluni die aut interlunio concepti nascuntur. (39) tralaticium in Aegypto est et octavo gigni, iam quidem et in Italia tales partus esse vitales contra priscorum opiniones. variant haec pluribus modis : Vistilia Gliti ac postea Pomponi atque Orfiti clarissimorum civium coniunx ex his quattuor partus enixa, septimo semper mense, genuit Suillium Rufum undecimo, Corbulonem septimo, utremque consulem, postea Caesoniam Gai principis coniugem octavo.* Another more important instance is found in Lydus, *De mensibus*, IV, 105 (p. 105 Wünsch) : οἱ πολλοὶ τῶν ἱστορικῶν φασι τὸν Καίσαρα [= Julius Caesar] ἑπτάμηνον τεχθῆναι, καὶ διὰ τοῦτο τὸν ἕβδομον μῆνα [sc. July] τοῦ ἱερατικοῦ ἐνιαυτοῦ εἰς τὴν οἰκείαν μεταβαλεῖν προσηγορίαν. Also the text in Herodotus, VI, 69 on the Spartan king Demaratus, quoted

---

45. Whether the scholiast correctly refers to Pherecydes we cannot judge. There was a Pherecydes who wrote in the sixth century B.C. and one who wrote in the fifth century B.C. (But see *Fr. Gr. Hist.*, I A, 79 Jacoby).

46. Though this tradition cannot be reconciled to the one of Heracles as δεκάμηνος, ROSCHER goes too far when he says : «Wenn es bei Iamblich v. Pyth. 152 (...) heiszt : Ηρακλεῖ [?] δὲ δεῖν θυσιάζειν ὀγδόη [?] τοῦ μηνὸς ἱσταμένου, σκοποῦντας τὴν ἑπτάμηνον αὐτοῦ γένεσιν, so liegt hier entweder eine arge Verwechselung des Apollon und Herakles seitens des Iamblichos oder eine schwere Verderbnis der überlieferten Worte vor. Mann sollte unbedingt erwarten : ᾽Απόλλωνι δὲ δεῖν θυσιάζειν ἑβδόμη [ζ' nicht η'] τοῦ μηνὸς κτλ." (*Die Hebdomadenlehre ...*, 210).

above, belongs to this category. Summing up : there were traditions concerning the birth after six or seven months of two gods (Apollo, Dionysus), a hero (Heracles), a mythical king (Eurystheus), a historical king (Demaratus), a great dictator (Julius Caesar) and a consul (Corbulo). Thus these are not ordinary figures, but all of them outstanding personages.

Now it is significant that of these seven persons the majority have a superhuman origin : Apollo, Dionysus and Heracles were begotten by Zeus, Eurystheus was a great-grandson of Zeus (his father Sthenelos being a son of the hero Perseus), Demaratus was begotten by the hero Astrabacus. Concerning Julius Caesar there are no sources that relate his supernatural conception, but, as Weinstock says, in his study of traditions about Caesar's birth : "the circumstances of Caesar's birth must have been miraculous, to indicate his great destiny. With his early youth they were no doubt described in the lost chapters of Suetonius and Plutarch"[47]. At least, Apollo and Venus were his far ancestors (Weinstock, op. cit. 12-18). And in view of the materials collected in the present article it is not rash to assume that Julius Caesar too was said to have had a more than human origin.

This may give us one of the clues to our problem. For with respect to the five Biblical personages there are also traditions concerning their more than human origin. For Jesus we need only refer to Matthew, 1, 18 and Luke, 1, 35. For Mary the *Protevangelium Jacobi* itself indicates clearly that she was not begotten by her human father. When in IV, 2 the angel says to Joakim : ἐπήκουσεν κύριος ὁ θεὸς τῆς δεήσεώς σου. κατάβηθι ἐντεῦθεν. ἰδοὺ ἡ γυνή σου Ἄννα ἐν γαστρὶ εἴληφεν, the whole context leaves no doubt whatsoever that Joakim no share in the begetting of Mary[48]. As to the Old Testament persons : for Isaac

---

47. S. WEINSTOCK, *Divus Julius*, Oxford, 1971, 19. How much historiography about Caesar must have been lost is clear from Lydus' remark (οἱ πολλοὶ τῶν ἱστορικῶν κτλ, see above), a text which, surprisingly, is not mentioned by Weinstock.

48. E. DE STRYCKER, *op. cit.* 81, n. 3 says on εἴληφα : "La plupart des mss. et une partie des versions ont ici le futur *concevra*. Mais le papyrus [sc. Bodmer 5], en confirmant la leçon de [... follows a number of mss.], montre que le parfait *a conçu* est authentique. L'auteur a donc certainement eu en vue une conception miraculeuse. Mais bientôt s'élevèrent contre cette idée des objections d'ordre dogmatique (...), et saint Épiphane s'efforce d'expliquer que ce parfait signifie un futur, sans pourtant se risquer déjà à changer le texte, comme firent des reviseurs postérieurs. (...) Le P. Peretto pense que le parfait εἴληφα se rapporte à une conception de Marie selon les vois normales, et donc antérieur au départ de Joachim pour le désert. Mais ceci n'est guère compatible avec le texte du *Protévangile*. C'est *après* le départ de son mari qu'Anne se met à prier pour obtenir une descendance. Ensuite, l'ange lui apparait et lui dit : 'Anne, Anne, le Seigneur Dieu a exaucée ta prière. Tu concevras et tu enfenteras, et on parlera de ta postérité dans le monde entier' [IV 1]". See also the convincing discussion of this problem by O. PERLER, *Das Protevangelium des Jakobus nach dem Papyrus Bodmer V*, in *Freiburger Zeitschr. für Philos. und Theol.*, 6 (1959), 23 ff.

we may refer to Philo who says that God begot Isaac (*Leg. all.*, III, 219 : Ἰσαὰκ ἐγέννησεν ὁ κύριος, cf. *Mut. nom.*, 130-132.137) and that in spite of Abraham's co-operation one may most rightly call God Isaac's father (*Det. pot. insid.*, 124 ὁ θεὸς ... τοῦ Ἰσαὰκ ὀρθότατα λέγοιτ' ἂν εἶναι πατήρ, cf. *Cher.*, 45)[49]. Still more clearly it is said in Rabbinic literature that Isaac was miraculously conceived, e.g. *Bereshith Rabbah* 47,2 where a Rabbi says : «[Sarah] lacked an ovary, but the Lord fashioned an ovary for her» (cf. 53, 5)[50]. Targum *Pseudo-Jonathan* on *Gen.*, 21, 1 also says in this connection : «The Lord wrought a miracle for Sarah»[51]. And in *Gal.*, 4, 21-31 Paul stresses the miraculous nature of Isaac's birth and practically denies that Abraham was his father. Dibelius asserts «dasz Philo wie Paulus auf eine gemeinsame Interpretation zurückgehen, nach der Isaak ohne Zutun Abrahams erzeugt wurde»[52]. Concerning Samuel there is no clear tradition that he had a superhuman father, for in *1 Sam.*, 1, 19 it is said that Elkana begot him by Hanna, but in a sense this case is comparable to Isaac, for in both cases the mother was barren and hence the conception was miraculous and wrought with the aid of God. That also Jochebed and Hanna were felt to be parallel cases is proved by the fact that Hanna too, like Jochebed, is said to have been 130 years of age when she conceived Samuel[53]. Moreover, Samuel's birth has clearly been a model for the miraculous birth of Mary in the *Protevangelium Jacobi*[54].

The same applies to Moses : Jochebed, his mother, is said to be 130 years old when she conceived Moses (e.g. *Shemoth Rabbah* I 19) and *Pseudo-Jonathan* on *Ex.*, 2, 1 explicitly says that a miracle was worked in her. David Daube[55] concludes from a survey of the materials about Moses' conception that there was an old Midrash that the mother of Moses conceived from God himself[56].

49. Also Pseudo-Philo, *Ant. Bibl.*, XXIII 8 (see above) says : "I (= God) gave him (= Abraham) Isaac and formed him in the womb of her that bore him". In *Cher.*, 47 Philo says of Rebecca and Zippora that they conceived without a mortal man.

50. See P. Billerbeck, *Kommentar zum Neuen Testament aus Talmud und Midrasch I*, München, 1926, 49f.

51. Etheridge, *op. cit.*, I 220.

52. M. Dibelius, *Jungfrauensohn und Krippenkind. Untersuchungen zur Geburtsgeschichte Jesu im Lukasevangelium*, in *Botschaft und Geschichte*, I, Tübingen, 1953, 31 ; cf. *ibid.*, 33 "Sie ist ein Theologumenon des hellenistischen Judentums, dasz die ausschliessliche Urheberschaft Gottes bei gewissen Geburten durch fromme Frauen behauptet".

53. See Ginzberg, *Legends*, IV, 59.

54. See Perler, *art. cit.*, 25.

55. *The New Testament and Rabbinic Judaism*, London 1956, 5-9.

56. Daube also makes the important observation that "the notion of a supernatural or virgin birth was not absolutely alien to the Jewish mind" (p. 8). Cf. W. D. Davies, *The Setting of the Sermon on the Mount*, Cambridge 1964, 81f. For criticism of Daube see Ch. Perrot, *Les récits d'enfance dans la haggada antérieure au IIᵉ siècle de notre ère*, in *Recherches de science religieuse* 55 (1967), 502 n. 55 (481-518).

Thus we may safely conclude that in antiquity a birth after six or seven months is practically only attributed to persons that were begotten by divine beings or whose conception had been miraculous in one way or another.

That there is a close causal link between the short pregnancy and the manner of begetting or conceiving is confirmed by a remark in Pseudo-Hippocrates, *Sept.*, 6-9 : ὁρῶμεν κατὰ τὸ περιέχον καὶ κατὰ τὴν γῆν προώρους καρποὺς ῥυσμοῦσθαι, ὅκωσπερ ἐν Αἰγύπτῳ πάντα πρόωρα γίνεται, πολλά τε καὶ διὰ παντὸς ὥρου διὰ πολυφιλίαν τῆς γῆς καὶ τὴν θέρμην τῆς περιοκωχήσιος. ὡσαύτως οὖν καὶ περὶ τὰ σκήνεα φιλέει γίνεσθαι τὰ ἑπτάμηνα. καὶ ὅταν ἡ ἔχουσα ἐς κύησιν εὖ ἥκη εἰς ὑποδοχὴν τὴν ὑπὸ τοῦ ἄρρενος καὶ τὸ ἄρρεν ὠργημένον ἢ καλῶς πρὸς τὸ καταβάλλειν γένεσιν ῥυθμοῦ, τότε δὴ σκῆνος συγκρίνεται καὶ τελεόμενον γίνεται. συμφορὴ γὰρ ἀνάγκῃ κρατερῇ μὴν κατέχεται τελεωθῆναι ὥσπερ τὸ τελεόμενον κατὰ τὸν ῥυθμόν, ἄλλως τε οὐκ ἄνυστον (p. 122, 12-20 Gr.)[57]. In his commentary on this passage Grensemann says : "der Verfasser ... stellt die Geburt mit sieben Monaten als Frühgeburt in Parallele zur Frühreife von Früchten, unter Hinweis auf die besonderen Naturbedingungen des Wunderlandes Ägypten, das durch die Güte des Bodens und das Klima als besonders fruchtbar gilt. Beim Siebenmonatskind entsprechen den besonders günstigen Bedingungen, die in Ägypten zur schnellen Reifung der Früchte beitragen, besonders günstige Bedingungen während der Zeugung. ... deutlich wird, warum es Ausnahmen von dieser normalen Zeitspanne [scil. 9 or 10 months] gibt : dadurch nämlich, dasz sich die Eltern physisch und psychisch in einem besonders günstigen Zustand befinden" (p. 128-9). Well, one can hardly imagine a more favourable condition, both physical and psychical, than when one of the parents is a god or a hero or the Holy Spirit and the other is a beloved one of that divine being. I might add a quotation from the physician Vindicianus, 12 : *Hic de septemmensium causa nascendi conicit compendiosam foetus perfectionem fieri, quotiens summo temperamento (!) primordiorum confectum semen in matricem venerit*[58]. There is no doubt : when a child is born after six or seven months and is viable, its conception

57. In GRENSEMANN's translation (p. 123) : "... der Beobachtung, dasz gemäsz dem Klima und der Bodenbeschaffenheit Früchte vor der Zeit reif werden, wie z.B. in Ägypten wegen der Güte des Bodens und der Wärme der Atmosphäre alles eher, in groszer Zahl und während des ganzen Jahres reif wird. Ebenso pflegen nun auch, was die Entwicklung der Körper betrifft, die Siebenmonatskinder zu entstehen. Und wenn die zukünftige Mutter in guter Verfassung von dem Manne empfangt und der Mann voller Begierde ist, ein gestaltetes Wesen zu zeugen, da formt sich dann ein Körper und entsteht, indem er sich voll entwickelt. Denn das Ereignis (?) wird von einem starken Zwang gehalten, sich zu vollenden wie das, was sich nach dem rechten Zeitmasz vollendet. Anders ist es nicht möglich".

58. I quote from GRENSEMANN, *op. cit.* 63. Vindicianus lived in North-Africa in the fourth century A.D.

must have been under very favourable circumstances. No better circumstances than when the father is divine.

There is still another motif which may have played a part in the development of the traditions concerned, though not a great part because of its pagan character, *viz.* the favourable position of the planets (and hence their good influence) at the birth of seven months' children[58a]. See for instance Galen, *Phil. hist.* 34, p. 333f. Kühn:

οἱ δὲ μαθηματικοὶ τοὺς ὀκτὼ μῆνας ἀσυνδέτους φασὶν εἶναι καὶ διὰ τοῦτο ἐστερῆσθαι πάσης γενέσεως, τοὺς δὲ ἑπτὰ συνδετικούς. τὰ δὲ ἀσύνδετα ζῷα ἔχειν τοὺς οἰκοδεσποτοῦντας φαύλους τῶν ἀστέρων. ἂν γάρ τις τούτων τὴν ζωὴν καὶ τὸν βίον κληρώσῃ, δυστυχῆ ἔσεσθαι καὶ ἄχρονον σημαίνει. ἀσύνδετα δέ ἐστι ζῴδια ὀκτὼ ἀριθμούμενα οἷον κριὸς πρὸς σκορπίον ἀσύνδετος, ταῦρος πρὸς τοξότην ἀσύνδετος, δίδυμοι πρὸς αἰγόκερον, καρκίνος πρὸς ὑδροχόον, λέων πρὸς ἰχθύας, παρθένος πρὸς κριόν. διὰ τοῦτο καὶ τὰ ἑπτάμηνα καὶ δεκάμηνα γόνιμα εἶναι, τὰ δὲ ὀκτάμηνα διὰ τὸ ἀσύνδετον τοῦ κόσμου φθείρεσθαι. Cf. also Censorinus, *De die natali* 8, 10 : *a loco sexto conspectus omni caret efficientia : eius enim linea nullius polygoni efficit latus. At a septimo zodio, quod est contrarium, plenissimus potentissimusque conspectus quosdam iam maturos infantes educit, qui septemmestres appellantur, quia septimo mense nascuntur.* It was this motif that survived till late in the Middle Ages[59]. But since the influence of the stars as they stood at one's birth was a rather un-Jewish and un-Christian tenet it is not reflected in the early Jewish and Christian sources. It will have played no great part, perhaps no part at all.

By way of conclusion we may say that although the motif of the special giftedness of seven months' children also occurs outside the Greek sphere of influence[60], we have in the present case an example of Greek influence on Judaism and Christianity. The motif has probably gone by way of Hellenistic Judaism into Christianity and Rabbinic Judaism[61]. It is one of the many examples of the coming-into-being of legends about Biblical persons under external influence[62].

58a. In H.G. EVELYN WHITE's Loeb edition of Ausonius (London, 1919) one can find a diagram illustrating this, facing p. 180.

59. See H. PLOSS-M. BARTELS, *Das Weib in der Natur- und Völkerkunde. Anthropologische Studien*, I, Leipzig 1908[11], 943f. P. DIEPGEN, *Frau und Frauenheilkunde in der Kultur des Mittelalters*, Stuttgart, 1963, 229.

60. See F. VON ANDRIAN, *Die Siebenzahl im Geistesleben der Völker*, in *Mitteilungen der anthropologischen Gesellschaft in Wien*, 31 (1901), 225-274, esp. 252, and ROSCHER, *Die Enneadischen und Hebdomadischen Fristen und Wochen* (1903), 67, n. 197.

61. It is a clear case of "Hellenistisches in der rabbinischen Anthropologie", to quote the title of R. MEYER's work of 1937.

62. One would expect to find similar traditions about two other Biblical persons, *scil.* Simson and John the Baptist, but I could find nothing of the sort.

SELECT INDEXES

Names and subjects

Biblical passages

Non-biblical passages

(Only passages that are dealt with at some length have been included in this index, except those from writings which are mentioned in the titles of the articles e.g. Ps-Phoc., Ezek., Test. Job, LAB)

A. Jewish

This book contains a collection of 14 essays on various aspects of ancient Jewish religion and literature and their relevance for the study of early Christianity. There are contributions on Jewish Greek authors (Pseudo-Phocylides, Ezekiel the dramatist, minor historians and epic writers), on the situation of Jews and Samaritans in the diaspora in the light of recent discoveries, on images of women in some of the pseudepigrapha (Testament of Job, Pseudo-Philo's LAB), on some elements in Jewish mysticism of late antiquity, on the development of Nimrod haggada in the Hellenistic and Roman period, and on some problems of biblical interpretation in the light of ancient anthropological theories. Several less well-known aspects of early Judaism are brought to the fore in these essays.

ISBN 3-7278-0683-4 (Universitätsverlag)
ISBN 3-525-53915-0 (Vandenhoeck & Ruprecht)

NOVUM TESTAMENTUM ET ORBIS ANTIQUUS (NTOA)

Bd. 1   MAX KÜCHLER, *Schweigen, Schmuck und Schleier.* Drei neutestamentliche Vorschriften zur Verdrängung der Frauen auf dem Hintergrund einer frauenfeindlichen Exegese des Alten Testaments im antiken Judentum.
XXII–542 Seiten. 1986.

Bd. 2   MOSHE WEINFELD, *The Organizational Pattern and the Penal Code of the Qumran Sect.* A Comparison with Guilds and Religious Associations of the Hellenistic-Roman Period.
104 Seiten. 1986.

Bd. 3   ROBERT WENNING, *Die Nabatäer – Denkmäler und Geschichte.* Eine Bestandesaufnahme des archäologischen Befundes.
Ca. 264 Seiten und 19 Karten. 1986.

Bd. 4   RITA EGGER, *Josephus Flavius und die Samaritaner.* Eine terminologische Untersuchung zur Identitätsklärung der Samaritaner.
412 Seiten. 1986.

Bd. 5   EUGEN RUCKSTUHL, *Die literarische Einheit des Johannesevangeliums.* Der gegenwärtige Stand der einschlägigen Forschungen. Mit einem Vorwort von Martin Hengel.
344 Seiten. 1987.

Bd. 6   MAX KÜCHLER/CHRISTOPH UEHLINGER (Hrsg.), *Jerusalem, Texte – Bilder – Steine.*
238 Seiten. 1987.

Bd. 7   DIETER ZELLER (Hrsg.), *Menschwerdung Gottes – Vergöttlichung von Menschen.*
236 Seiten. 1988.

Bd. 8   GERD THEISSEN, *Lokalkolorit und Zeitgeschichte in den Evangelien.* Ein Beitrag zur Geschichte der synoptischen Tradition.
348 Seiten. 1989.

Bd. 9   TAKASHI ONUKI, *Gnosis und Stoa.* Eine Untersuchung zum Apokryphen des Johannes.
208 Seiten. 1989.

Bd. 10   DAVID TROBISCH, *Die Entstehung der Paulusbriefsammlung.* Studien zu den Anfängen christlicher Publizistik.
176 Seiten. 1989.

Bd. 11   HELMUT SCHWIER, *Tempel und Tempelzerstörung.* Untersuchungen zu den theologischen und ideologischen Faktoren im ersten jüdisch-römischen Krieg (66–74 n. Chr.).
444 Seiten. 1989.

Bd. 12   DANIEL KOSCH, *Die eschatologische Tora des Menschensohnes.* Untersuchungen zur Rezeption der Stellung Jesu zur Tora in Q.
516 Seiten. 1989.

Bd. 13   JEROME MURPHY-O'CONNOR, O.P., *The École Biblique and the New Testament: A Century of Scholarship (1890-1990).* With a Contribution by Justin Taylor, S.M.
208 Seiten. 1990.

Bd. 14   PIETER W. VAN DER HORST, *Essays on the Jewish World of Early Christianity.*
260 Seiten. 1990.

DATE DUE

HIGHSMITH   # 45220